Women's Movement Media: A Source Guide

Women's Movement Media: A Source Guide

by
Cynthia Ellen Harrison

R. R. BOWKER COMPANY
A Xerox Education Company
New York & London, 1975

Published by R. R. Bowker Company (a Xerox Education Company)
1180 Avenue of the Americas, New York, N.Y. 10036

Library of Congress Cataloging in Publication Data

Harrison, Cynthia.
    Women's movement media.

    Includes indexes.
    1. Feminism—United States—Bibliography. 2. Feminism—Information services—United States. 3. Library resources on women—United States. 4. Women's periodicals—Bibliography. 5. Women—Societies and clubs—Directories. I. Title.
Z7964.U49H37   016.30141′2′0973   75-2484
ISBN 0-8352-0711-0

For Richie,
and for my parents,
Herbert and Jean Hacken Harrison

Contents

Preface . . . . *ix*

How to Use This Book . . . . *xi*

I PUBLISHERS, DISTRIBUTORS, NEWS SERVICES, AND
   PRODUCTS *1*

   Movement Publishers *3*
   Periodicals *14*
   Nonprint Media. *31*
   News Services, Book Stores, and Specialized Book Distributors . . *43*
   Products by Feminists for Feminists. *46*

II WOMEN'S RESEARCH CENTERS AND LIBRARY
    RESEARCH COLLECTIONS *51*

III WOMEN'S ORGANIZATIONS AND CENTERS *59*

    U.S. National *61*
    U.S. Local. *82*
    Canadian National *98*
    Canadian Local *99*

IV GOVERNMENTAL AND QUASI-GOVERNMENTAL
    ORGANIZATIONS AND AGENCIES *103*

    International. *105*
    U.S. Federal *106*
    U.S. Local. *111*
    Canadian National. *133*
    Canadian Local *134*

V SPECIAL INTERESTS *137*

   Art and Communications *139*
   Civil Rights and Legal Services *145*
   Education *149*
      General *149*
      Children's Education and Welfare. *151*
      Continuing Education *155*
      Women's Studies *157*
   Employment. *165*
      Consultants *165*
      Counseling and Training. *167*
      Labor Rights *177*

Ethnic and Religious Groups. *180*
Health, Physical, and Social Welfare Rights. *186*
  Abortion, Birth Control, Health. *186*
  Prison Groups *194*
  Self-defense and Anti-Rape *195*
  Lesbian Interests. *197*
  Political Action. *199*
  Professions *204*
  Miscellaneous *216*

Geographic Index. *219*
Media Title Index. *243*
Name Index of Groups. *255*
Subject Index of Groups *265*

Preface

There is no doubt that the need for information and materials on women and feminism has been felt in every sector of society—from individuals and community groups to educational and governmental institutions. Although scholarly material has been made more or less accessible by the conventional indexing services, the material generated by Movement members for each other has been much more difficult to obtain. This is particularly unfortunate in that it is precisely this material that is the key to the Women's Movement and is in many cases the most interesting.

This inaccessibility is due to the nature of the organization of the Women's Movement. Small women's groups, funded by individual contributors (or with no money at all), collect data, write pamphlets, produce films or filmstrips, institute courses of all kinds, manufacture goods, and have no money to advertise their work. The feminist community is alerted via Movement periodicals which publicize at no charge or for a small fee, but this kind of listing is not easily retrievable, certainly not by librarians or researchers who do not subscribe to every feminist periodical.

The very proliferation of these relatively small and unaffiliated groups (for there is no organized hierarchy in the Women's Movement, which is truly a grass-roots movement) makes them extremely difficult to track down, and this presents a problem in the compilation of a guide of this kind. The groups included herein were located by the use of a number of Movement periodicals, a couple of dated lists of groups, and some published material. Approximately 2,000 questionnaires were sent out, many of which were not returned due to the demise of the group or an address which could not be located. Very few groups who responded were not included, although some whose thrust did not, after all, concern women were eliminated. A handful of organizations who did not return questionnaires are listed.

This is a compendium of *sources* of information, rather than just a bibliography, for the output of the Women's Movement grows daily, and those interested in keeping abreast of the latest efforts will want to be placed on mailing lists or to know which group would be most likely to provide current information on the topic of their interest. The annotations, therefore, are designed to let the user know the kinds of materials available in general, so that catalogs can be obtained for the most recent information. (Prices will, of course, be out of date, and are supplied as an indicator of the general cost level.)

The *Source Guide* includes approximately 550 descriptions of organizations, arranged by function, type or main interest of the group, which supply books, periodicals, films, tapes, records, services, and information on and for women. Since the Women's Movement is a vital one, many groups are in a state of flux and some may no longer exist. New groups, however, will have sprung up in their places. In view of this, unavoidably, some organizations which are no longer active may be listed.

The description of each group depended almost entirely on the response to the questionnaire and on the materials sent to me. Where prices, frequency of publication, or other information is not given, it may be generally assumed that the group did not supply that information. All material in quotation marks is taken x *Preface*

directly from written or printed notices sent by the organization. Even where quotation marks are not used, the group's remarks are closely paraphrased. The listing of a publication, film, record, etc., available from a group does not constitute a judgment of its value, but merely makes known its existence. Because the information supplied in catalogs and brochures is not uniform, data in the annotations varies. However, letters inquiring for more information may elicit free samples of a group's work.

Movement periodicals will be especially helpful in keeping up with new groups or publications. KNOW (see entry 13) is always publishing new articles; *The Canadian Newsletter of Research on Women* (entry 45) will be useful for locating new research projects; and *Women Studies Abstracts* (entry 89) will include new published material. Newspapers keep track of local groups and State Commissions on Women often keep directories of women's groups in the state. In addition, NOW chapters (see entry 163) and women's centers are frequently good sources of local activities.

It is hoped that this guide will aid the many people who are interested in finding out what feminists are doing—from the woman working on an anti-rape project who wants to see what others have already done, to the social studies teacher looking for audiovisual materials for her or his class, to the librarian building a women's collection in response to community demand. My aim has been to make this task easier by collecting in one volume what could only be found by checking hundreds of ephemeral listings and writing to as many places. I hope I've helped to spread the word.

I have a great many people to thank who gave generously of their time and skills to help with this endeavor. I would like to start with Patricia Glass Schuman who was the moving spirit behind it all; she has been constantly encouraging. Especial thanks are also due to the many sisters who took so much time in filling out the questionnaires (occasionally more than once) which made this book possible. In return, I hope this guide proves useful to them all. Credit and gratitude go to Shirley Glass, Margaret Boyle, and Joan Marshall, for compiling, respectively, the Media Title Index, the Geographic Index, and the Subject Index. I am also grateful to Madeline Miele, Deirdre Boyle, Jan Vreeland, Kyle Ahrold, Eleanor Herridge-Cariaga, Shelia Sivil Pepper, Taryn Fisher, Tom Chiappa, Edward Pulver, Betty Pulver, Ruth Lenusky, David Lenusky, Kathy-Ann Lenusky and Michael Lenusky for their assistance. Constance Gilbert Neiss, Susan Vreeland-Chiappa, Joan Vitale and my sister Wendy Peppin Pulver all deserve an extra measure of appreciation for their tremendous contribution usually under pressure of time. Finally, I have to express my deep gratitude and love to my friend and help-mate, Richard Joseph Peppin, who believes in me.

Cynthia Ellen Harrison

Verona, N.J.
September 1974

How to Use This Book

This multimedia resource guide is a classified listing of more than 550 groups serving women's interests. These organizations are described in one of five main sections.

Part I is composed of organizations whose major purpose is to produce or handle one or more forms of media, or other product of interest to feminists. Groups are arranged by major activity and are then listed alphabetically.

Part II comprises organizations which collect and offer resource materials for research. These groups are arranged alphabetically.

Part III includes organizations which have a wide range of activities and which may produce various kinds of media, in addition to offering services to women and participating in various projects. For convenience, these groups are arranged geographically by country, state or province.

Part IV is a list of governmental agencies, arranged geographically as in Part III.

Part V lists groups which have one primary focus (e.g., abortion, rape, women in the arts). Ten specific areas of interest are considered, and groups are listed alphabetically by the name of the parent organization within these areas of interest.

Each entry generally includes an entry number, the organization's title, address, phone number, contact person, a brief annotation stating the group's purpose, and a listing of available items. Some organizations and their services fall into several different categories and there are many cross-references to help the reader locate such entries.

In addition, there are four indexes: a geographic index of groups; a title index of available media, broken down by type of media; an index of groups by name; and a subject index of groups. These indexes will be useful for ascertaining what groups are active in a given state, locating a particular filmstrip or radio tape, finding the address of a certain group, or searching for all groups working on a particular subject. The Media Title Index should be helpful to the librarian who is building a collection on women's issues or involved in locating difficult-to-find titles for patrons, or for the programs chairperson of a social group, who wants to develop a program on feminism. Community organizers will be able to consult the Geographic Index to find out who is working locally, statewide, or nationally on various projects.

While the resource guide is arranged by general subject, there are many specific subject areas which are not identified in the general structure. The researcher seeking materials on sexism in language or nonsexist education can turn directly to the Subject Index to find them. Readers should note that the numbers found in these indexes refer to the entry number, not the page number, of the appropriate organization.

Entries reflect information available before this book went to print. Readers are urged to consult groups for current prices and availability of materials.

I. Publishers, Distributors, News Services, and Products

Movement Publishers

1   BOSTON WOMEN'S COLLECTIVE, INC.   490 Beacon St., Boston, Mass.
    02115. (617) 251-1561. Elizabeth Curtis, 76 Wenham St., Jamaica Plains,
    Mass. 02130.

Publishes *The Women's Yellow Pages* (2nd ed., 1973), to help put women
"in contact with people, organizations, and agencies who can help them meet their
needs, both in crisis and in daily living." Other projects are the New England
Women's Resource Center, a data bank for women's information, and a photography exhibition. The collective was formerly "The Digging Stick."

2   BOSTON WOMEN'S HEALTH BOOK COLLECTIVE.   Box 192, West
    Somerville, Mass. 02144. Founded 1969.

A women's collective which has developed a laywoman's course on health,
women, and their bodies. Originally published by the New England Free Press,
Our Bodies, Our Selves is currently distributed by Simon & Schuster in a new edition for $2.95. Topics include anatomy and physiology, sexuality, myths about
women, venereal disease, birth control, abortion, pregnancy, childbirth, medical
institutions, and women, medicine, and capitalism. There are many illustrations,
diagrams, and photographs.

3   CANADIAN WOMEN'S EDUCATIONAL PRESS.   280 Bloor St., W., Suite
    305, Toronto, Ont., Can. Founded February 1972. 18 members.

A collective "established to synthesize and print material emerging out of the
Canadian women's movement." Some examples are the current *Women Unite!*
($7; paper $3) and *The Day Care Book* ($1.50). Forthcoming publications include
two nonsexist children's books, songs by Rita MacNeil, and *Marxism and Feminism*.

4   LUCINDA CISLER.   Box 240, New York, N.Y. 10024.

Publishes *Women: A Bibliography* (July–October 1970; 50¢). The 36-page
pamphlet, one of the earliest bibliographies of material relevant to the second wave
of feminism, covers books, government documents, periodicals, and journal articles.
Books available in paperback are noted, as well as items "worthy of special attention." Some entries have one-line annotations. The publications are listed under
subject headings: general works, historical studies, economics, work and child care,
law and politics, sociology and social commentary, anthropology, psychology and
psychiatry, sex and sexuality, reproduction, clothes, biography, literature, socialism, the women's movement. Updated editions are planned.

3

5   DAUGHTERS, INC. Plainfield, Vt. 05667. (802) 454-7141. Founded December 1972. Parke Bowman, June Arnold.

Publishers of books by women emphasizing profits for authors rather than the publisher. Five novels have been published to date: Selma Lagerloff's *The Treasure*, Blanche Boyd's *Nerves*, The Carpenter's *The Cook and the Carpenter*, Rita Mae Brown's *Rubyfruit Jungle*, and *Early Losses* by Pat Burch. All five for $16 or $3.35 each.

THE DIGGING STICK. See 1.

6   ELIZABETH CADY STANTON PUBLISHING CO. 5857 Marbury Rd., Bethesda, Md. 20034. (301) 229-7067. Nancy Gager, founder and publisher.

Publishes the *Women's Rights Almanac 1974* ($4.95), a 624-page reference guide containing a state-by-state directory of essential facts and statistics about women; biographies of all U.S. Congresswomen; essays on women's issues, like credit, lesbianism, marriage and divorce, and abortion; a month-by month breakdown of events of 1973; a list of women's organizations and periodicals; and a bibliography. "The first book-length almanac in the world to focus on women and women's issues," the editors plan to update the almanac annually.

7   THE FEMINIST PRESS. Box 334, Old Westbury, N.Y. 11568. (516) 876-3086. Founded 1970. Verne Moberg. 20–30 members.

A nonprofit, tax-exempt, educational and publishing corporation, designed to change the nature of women's education and to challenge sex-role stereotypes in books, schools, and libraries. Listed here are some of their publications, with prices; asterisks denote children's books.

Danish, B. *The Dragon and the Doctor* $1.00
Davis, R. H. *Life in the Iron Mills* (1861) $1.95
Ehrenreich, B. and English, D. *Complaints and Disorders* $1.25
Ehrenreich, B. and English, D. *Witches, Midwives and Nurses* $1.25
Freeman, M. W. *Collected Stories* $2.00
Gilman, C. P. *The Yellow Wallpaper* (1892) $1.25
Heyn, L. L. *Challenge to Become a Doctor: The Story of Elizabeth Blackwell* $1.50
Hochschild, A. R. *Coleen the Question Girl* $2.00
Katz, B. *Nothing but a Dog* $1.50
Kearns, M. *Kaethe Kollwitz* $2.00
Lucido, C. *Community Workshops on Children's Books* $1.50
Lupton, M. J. *Elizabeth Barrett Browning* $1.50
Mangi, J. *The ABC Workbook* $1.00
Mason, B. A. *The Girl Sleuth: A Feminist Guide to Nancy Drew and Her Sisters* $2.00
Maury, I. *My Mother the Mail Carrier* $1.50
Moberg, V. *Consciousness Razors* 50¢
Moberg, V. *A Child's Right to Equal Reading* 35¢
Oakley, M. A. *Elizabeth Cady Stanton* $1.50
Rich, G. *Firegirl* $1.95
Rose, M. B. *The Life and Times of My Mother and Me* $2.00
Smedley, A. *Daughter of Earth* (1929) $2.50 paper; $8.00 cloth
Terry, M. *Approaching Simone*, A play based on the life of Simone Weil $1.50

Van Voris, J. *Constance de Markievicz* (an Irish freedomfighter) $1.50
Widerberg, S. **I'm like Me* (poems) $1.50; **Amelia Earhart Storypack* #1
$1.00

Feminist Press has also produced the first packet in a photo-poster series of
women important in our past. The first packet ($5) includes photo-posters of
Elizabeth Cady Stanton, Charlotte Perkins Gilman, and Kaethe Kollwitz. In addition, the press conducts Community Workshops on Children's Books and inservice
courses for teachers.

The Clearinghouse on Women's Studies (CWS), an educational project of the
Feminist Press, was established to "maintain information about women's studies in
higher education, secondary and elementary education." CWS publishes *Women's
Studies Newsletter* (q., $5/yr., $10, institutions) which details new courses, curricular materials, grants, new publications, and employment opportunities; *Guide
to Current Female Studies*, I, II, and III ($1 plus 25¢ postage each); *Female Studies
VI & VII*, syllabi and course descriptions (VI, $3.50; VII, $4 plus 50¢ postage);
Feminist Resources for Schools and Colleges: A Guide to Curricular Materials ($1
plus 25¢ postage); *High School Feminist Studies* ($2.50 plus 25¢ postage); *Non-
sexist Curricular Materials for Elementary Schools* ($5 plus 40¢ postage); and *Who's
Who and Where in Women's Studies* ($3). See also Women's Studies section.

8   FEMINIST WRITER'S WORKSHOP. 1260 Verde Vista Rd., Santa Barbara,
Calif. 93105. (805) 969-2938. Founded June 1972. Linda Malotch. 6
members.

"To encourage women to write feminist materials and to publish their work."
Surprise for Everyone, a nonsexist children's book about Christmas in a commune,
sells for $1.25. An anthology of feminist poetry is in press.

9   FORD ASSOCIATES, INC. 701 S. Federal Ave., Butler, Ind. 46721.
(219) 868-5133.

Publishes *Directory of Women Attorneys in the United States*, $10, with over
6,000 names and addresses of qualified women attorneys. Resumes are kept on
file and are made available to prospective clients. Profits are to be used in the pro-
motion of women's rights. Also publishes the *Women's Legal Handbook Series on
Job and Sex Discrimination*, (7 volumes, $10 each): Vol. 1, Civil Rights Act; Vol. 2,
At Federal Level; Vol. 3, Title VII and Cases; Vol. 4, Equal Pay; Vol. 5, Equal
Rights Amendment; Vol. 6, State Commission on Women; and Vol. 7, Government
Administration Agencies.

10   ANN FORFREEDOM. Box 25514, Los Angeles, Calif. 90025.

Publishes *Women Out of History; A Herstory Anthology* (1972, $3.50),
which includes an annotated Herstory Bibliography, pictures, poems, research
papers, theory papers, and a herstory quiz. The book aims to make people aware of
how little women's history is known and to give historians a survey upon which to
build future research. Order single copies from above; bulk copies from Midnite
Special Bookstore, 1335½ W. Washington Blvd., Venice, Calif. 90291.

11   MARIJA MATICH HUGHES. Box 702; 2116 F St., N.W., Washington, D.C.
20037.

Publishes a bibliography, *The Sexual Barrier* ($5; Supp. I, 1971, $3; Supp. II,
1972, $3) covering laws and conditions governing the employment of women. Ma-

terials include books, pamphlets, and government documents in English "designed to help lawyers, legislators, women and the general public in researching women's rights." Revised edition is in progress.

12   JOYFUL WORLD PRESS. 468 Belvedere St., San Francisco, Calif. 94117. (415) 566-2787. Founded June 1971. Shirley Boccaccio. 5 staff members.

Publishers of nonsexist children's books and feminist posters. Some books available are *Penelope and the Mussels, Penelope and the Earth,* and *Penelope Goes to the Farmer's Market* ($2 each plus 25¢ postage and handling). Posters include "Fuck Housework" and "A Woman's Poem" ($2 each; $12 for 12 copies).

13   KNOW, INC. Box 86031, Pittsburgh, Pa. 15221. (412) 241-4844. Founded 1969. Anne Pride, 214 Dewey St., Pittsburgh, Pa. 15221.

A nonprofit tax-exempt feminist publishing and distribution collective corporation with three objectives: to disseminate women's movement literature inexpensively, to construct an information network for social change, and to succeed enough to pay women for their work in the movement. Originally published only inexpensive reprints of articles, but now publishes original articles, paperback books, and one hardback, *I'm Running Away from Home but I'm Not Allowed to Cross the Street* by Gabrielle Burton.

Also distributes reprints of numerous articles by and about women (5¢–45¢), *Female Studies I–V* (see also Feminist Press, entry 7), *Women and the Law: A collection of Reading Lists* (75¢), and numerous other reports, nonsexist children's books, biographies, records, posters, packets, and pamphlets. Write for complete literature list.

KNOW NEWS, issued approximately ten times a year, contains announcements of conferences and demonstrations, job openings, legislation, and ads for feminist products. Aims to share ". . . the information we receive from all over the country." Each issue usually concentrates on a specific topic or event of current importance to feminists and is free with a tax deductible contribution of $4 or more from individuals ($6, Canada; $8, institutions and foreign).

14   LAVENDER WOMAN. Box 60206. 1723 W. Devon St., Chicago, Ill. 60660. Founded September 1971. Susan Edwards. $3/yr.; $6, institutions.

A collective publishing the lesbian/feminist newspaper *Lavender Woman,* as well as films, anthologies of essays, poetry, and articles of interest to lesbians, such as *Thunder from the Earth* (a poetry anthology, $1.95) and *Lavender* (a film, $15 rental fee).

15   LANLYRE LIGGERA. 66 Teel St., Arlington, Mass. (617) 646-0499.

Publishes *Woman Is My Name* (50¢), a songbook with 12 songs: "Dying in Childhood," "Shadows in a Mirror," "Old Woman," "Latchkey Children," "Annie, Come Down," "Silver Jet," "Woman in White," "When I Was Five," "Ericka's Dream," "Woman Is My Name," "Soujourner Truth," and "Calypso Hefner."

16   LOLLIPOP POWER, INC. Box 1171, Chapel Hill, N.C. 27514. (919) 967-5085. Founded 1970.

"A woman's liberation collective that writes, illustrates, and publishes books for the liberation of young children from sex stereotyped behavior and role models. . . . Lollipop Power is publishing books which emphasize a wide variety of choices upon which young children may build their images of themselves and their world. . . . Both girls and boys may be adventurous and independent, emotional and expressive. Adults of both sexes may work to support a family, and share responsibilities in the home. Children may find love and joy, as well as problems to solve, within a variety of social settings and family lifestyles." Books available are paperback picture books which sell for $1.50 each.

Chapman, Kim Westsmith. *The Magic Hat* (ages 5-9).
de Poix, Carol. *Jo, Flo and Yolanda* (ages 3-7).
Eichler, Margrit. *Martin's Father* (ages 2-6).
Goldsmid, Paula. *Did You Ever?* (ages 2-5).
Goodyear, Carmen. *The Sheep Book* (ages 2-7).
Hazen, Nancy. *Grownups Cry Too* (all ages).
Lenthall, Patricia Riley. *Carlotta and the Scientist* (ages 5-9).
Phillips, Lynn. *Exactly Like Me* (ages 4-8).
Surowiecki, Sandra Lucas. *Joshua's Day* (ages 3-6).

17 MAMA'S PRESS. 2500 Market St., Oakland, Calif. (415) 653-5033. Founded March 1972. Shoshana, 692 B Fairview, Oakland, Calif. 94609.

A feminist press, publishing drawings and literature to and from women and children. Titles include *Monster Coloring Book* (50¢), *Let Them Be Said* by Susan Griffin (poetry, $1), *True Story* by Alta (short stories, 85¢), and *Feeding Ourselves* by the Berkeley Women's Health Collective (nutrition, 35¢).

18 MATRIX: FOR SHE OF THE NEW AEON. Box 4218, North Hollywood, Calif. 91607.

A three-volume anthology of poetry, prose, and illustrations ($2/vol.; 3 vols., $5; 40 percent discount for bulk orders).

19 MONTREAL HEALTH PRESS, INC. (Les Presses de la Santé de Montréal, Inc.). Box 1000, Station G, Montreal 130, Que., Can. (514) 844-5838. Founded 1967. Shirley Gardiner, 3724 Coloniale, Apt. B, Montreal, Que., Can.

"A nonprofit group, who research, edit, write, photograph, illustrate medical literature for mass cheap distribution." Distributes two useful publications, *The Birth Control Handbook* and the *VD Handbook*, available also in Spanish and French editions. Individual copies are free (25¢ for the first copy plus 10¢ for each additional copy up to 20 for postage and handling). For larger orders, write for price lists.

20 NANNY GOAT PRODUCTIONS. Box 645, Laguna Beach, Calif. 92652. (714) 494-3092. Founded March 1972. Joyce Sutton.

Writes, draws, and publishes underground comic books and health manuals in comic book form "to destroy taboos that are destructive to women and do away with any mythology that holds us back from full development as people." Two books are available: *Tits & Clits*, #1 (50¢) and *Abortion Eve* (50¢), which depicts, in comic book style, the experience of a group of women who decide to have abortions.

21 NEW ENGLAND FREE PRESS. 60 University Sq., Somerville, Mass. 02143. (617) 628-2450. Founded 1968.

A cooperative printshop and publishing house, owned by the three men and three women who work there and who share all tasks. The press is committed to disseminating the whole spectrum of radical ideas through the publication of pamphlets. Following are pamphlets of interest to women, arranged by topic.

Women's Liberation—How and Why

Asimov, I. *Uncertain, Coy and Hard to Please The Myth of Femininity* 10¢

Benston, M. *The Political Economy of Women's Liberation* 10¢

Bernick, K. *Marxism: a Syllabus Design for a Women's Course* 5¢

Black Panther Sisters Talk about Women's Liberation 5¢

Dunbar, R. *Female Liberation as the Basis for Social Revolution* 10¢

Hopper, P. and Soldz, S. *I Don't Want to Change My Lifestyle—I Want to Change My Life* 5¢

Jones, B. and Brown, J. *Towards a Female Liberation Movement* 20¢

Kaufer, K. and Christoffel, T. *The Political Economy of Male Chauvinism* 10¢

Limpus, L. *Liberation of Women: Sexual Repression and the Family* 5¢

McAfee, K. and Wood, M. *What Is the Revolutionary Potential of Women's Liberation?* 15¢

Mitchell, J. *Women: The Longest Revolution* 15¢

Radicalesbians. *Woman Identified Woman, and a Letter From Mary* 5¢

Tax, M. *Woman and Her Mind: The Assaults of Daily Life: Female Schizophrenia, Consumerism, a Marxist Analysis* 25¢

Uphaste Bookstore. *Books by Women (and Some Men) Relevant to Women's Liberation.* bibliography 30¢

Weisstein, N. *Psychology Constructs the Female; or, The Fantasy Life of the Male Psychologist* 15¢

Women in History

Atkins, M. *The Early Feminist Movement in the U.S.* 20¢

Belden, J. *Gold Flower's Story: Women's Liberation in Revolutionary China* 30¢

DuBois, E. *Struggling into Existence: the Feminism of Sarah and Angelina Grimke* 10¢

Engels, F. *The Early Development of the Family* 30¢

Greene, F. *A Divorce Trial in China* 10¢

Reed, E. *The Myth of Women's Inferiority: Women's Role in Prehistoric Societal Development* 15¢

Rubenstein, D. R. *How the Russian Revolution Failed Women* 20¢

Wells, L. *American Women: Their Use and Abuse* 10¢

Women in Their Places

Breibart, V. *Day Care, Who Cares?: Government and Day Care Plans* 10¢

Densmore, D. *Sex Roles and Female Oppression* 10¢

deRivera, A. *Jumping the Track: High School Student* 5¢

Gordon, L. *Families* 25¢

Gross, L. and MacEwan, P. *On Day Care* 5¢

Langer, E. *Women of the Telephone Company* 20¢

Mainardi, P. *The Politics of Housework* 5¢

Mull, B. *Our Struggle against Levi-Strauss* 10¢

On the Job Oppression of Working Women: A Collection of Articles; Secretary, Housewife, Switchboard Operator, Nurse, Cocktail Waitress 20¢

Poor Black Women 5¢

Shell, L. *The Lonely Girl in the Big City* 20¢

Vogel, L. *Women Workers: Some Basic Statistics* 10¢

Warrior, B. *Women and Welfare* 5¢

Welfare: The Big Lie 5¢

Winkler, I. *Women Workers: The Forgotten Third of the Working Class* (*Statistics*) 20¢

Women and Socialism: Women in the Liberation Struggle—an Overview; Ma Bell Has Fleas—and a Lot of Angry Workers 20¢

Women Control Their Bodies

Birth Control Handbook 5¢, single orders only

Koedt, A. *The Myth of the Vaginal Orgasm* (a seminal article) 5¢

Poster of a *Pregnant Man* (11 X 17) 5¢

Women's Liberation Stickers (8½ X 11 sheet of 12 stickers) 5¢

22 NEW HOGTOWN PRESS. 12 Hart House Circle, University of Toronto, Toronto 5, Ontario, Can. (416) 928-4909. Founded 1972. 9 members.

Originally the literature distribution service of the Canadian Union of Students, which was continued by the University of Toronto Students' Administrative Council, and which now operates independently. Distributes literature centering on the working class and writings from the Canadian Left in general. Aims "to promote a comprehensive selection of literature dealing with critical issues in Canadian society from a socialist perspective." Listed here are some of their titles.

Aberle, K. *The Origin of the Family* 15¢

Aberle, K. *Women in Evolution* 20¢

Atkins, M. and Hynes, M. *The Hidden History of the Female/A History of the Rise of Women's Consciousness in Canada and Quebec* 45¢

Benston, M. *The Political Economy of Women's Liberation* 25¢

Ehrenreich, B. and English, D. *Nurses: A History of Women Healers* $1.25

Goldfield, E. *A Woman Is a Sometime Thing* 30¢

Halifax Women's Bureau. *Women at Work in Nova Scotia* $1.25

Lexchin, J. *The Exclusion of Women from Canadian Medical Schools* n.p.

Limpus, L. *Sexual Repression and the Family* 10¢

Willis, E. *Consumerism and Women* 15¢

Working Women's Association. *Women's Work: A Collection of Articles by Working Women* 25¢

23 NEW SEED PRESS. Box 3016, Stanford, Calif. 94305. Becky Stickgod.

"A nonprofit publisher of feminist and radical children's books." Seeks manuscripts and illustrations "free from racial, class and sex role stereotyping, history books about women and minorities, fables and fairy tales about change and how things could be." Currently scheduled books include a series called *Children and Their Families*, which will portray individual children in various nontraditional families; a fairy tale *Some Things You Just Can't Do by Yourself*, in which Laura, and Fanshen, the magic bear, redistribute the land in their kingdom; and *And So They Helped Each Other Out*, two small cartoon fables about cooperation.

24 THE NEW WOMAN'S SURVIVAL CATALOG: A WOMAN-MADE BOOK. Box 90, Planetarium Station, New York, N.Y. 10024. Kirsten Grimstad, Susan Rennie, Eds. $5.

A large paperbound catalog, "conceived, researched, written, photographed, designed, typeset, [and] pasted-up by six women. . . . This book catalogues and documents activities which, unlike women's businesses and enterprises that have existed all along, are aimed explicitly at the development of an alternative woman's culture. . . . It is meant, above all, to be a self-help tool for ALL women to take control of their lives." The book lists women's movement groups, with illustrations and photographs, and a description of their activities and the products or services they offer. Sections focus on Communications, Art, Self-health, Children, Learning, Self-defense, Work and Money, Getting Justice, and Building the Movement. A minimum of 20 percent of the royalties of the book are to be returned to the women's movement. A second edition is planned.

25   OUR CATALOGUE COMPANY. Box 3, 6504 Pardall Rd., Isla Vista, Calif. 93017. (805) 968-5774. Founded July 1973. Peg McGinnis, Miki Chavez, Coors.

A feminist publishing company, planning to provide "a constantly updated reference source of women's movement activities" and an "effective tool for communication between sisters." *Our Catalogue* is published triannually.

26   PATHFINDER PRESS, INC. 410 West St., New York, N.Y. 10014. (212) 741-0690. Founded 1969. Louise Armstrong, Promotion Dir.

A radical publishing house with special emphasis on current topics. Books of interest to women are: Jenners, L., *Feminism and Socialism* ($5.95, paper $1.95); Lamb, Myrna, *Mod Donna and Scyklon Z* ($5.95, paper $2.25); and Reed, E., *Problems of Women's Liberation* ($3.95, paper $1.45).

Following is a list of pamphlets of interest to women.

Castro, F. and Jenness, L. *Women and the Cuban Revolution* 35¢
Cowley, J., *Pioneers of Women's Liberation* 25¢
Dawson, K. et al., *Kate Millett's Sexual Politics—A Marxist Appreciation* 60¢
Jenness, L. et al., *Abortion: A Woman's Right* 35¢
Miller, R. et al., *In Defense of the Women's Movement* 25¢
Reed, E., *Is Biology Woman's Destiny?* 50¢
Stone, B., *Sisterhood is Powerful* 35¢
Vidal, M., *Chicanos Speak Out* 35¢
Waters, M., *Feminism and the Marxist Movement* 60¢
Woodroofe, D., *Sisters in Struggle 1848–1920* 60¢

27   PRAXIS PRESS. Box 903, Park Ave. Sta., Tallahassee, Fla. 32302. (904) 222-7080. Bob Broedel, 308 S. Macomb St., Tallahassee, Fla. 32301.

A very small publishing house, specializing in movement materials, now oriented towards the People's Science Movement. Has published *PM 3: The Women's Movement, Where It's At* (1971), a seven-page listing of women's movement periodicals, media efforts, research/resource aids, newsletters, packets, pamphlets, etc. "A valuable document in its day," it is now out-of-date, and available free on request.

28   RAINBOW INSTITUTE. Box 13907, Univ. of Calif., Santa Barbara, Calif. 93107. Founded 1972. Peter K. Suczek.

Promotes children's and adult's nonsexist materials and sex education materials. Available is a children's nonsexist coloring book ($1.25; 75¢ each for ten copies or more, 65¢ for 50 copies or more).

29   SAPPHO '71. 60 Steven Court, Fairfax, Calif. 94930. (415) 454-6535. Founded May 1971. Harriette Frances.

A collection of lesbian/feminist poetry and drawings by Harriette Frances (San Francisco: Donahue/Arlington Publishing Co., 1971, 41 pp., $2.50). Poems include "Forest Fire," "Paradox," "Bride of Christ," "Dawn and Dusk," "S.O.S.," and "Not Who I Am," among others.

30 SHAMELESS HUSSY PRESS. Box 424, San Lorenzo, Calif. 94580. Founded 1969.

A one-woman publishing house. Publishes books, posters, and the *Shameless Hussy Review*, an annual anthology of poetry and pictures (75¢, $1 to institutions). Posters are 60¢ each: Union House, Love Poem, The Vow. Books include: Alta, *Letters to Women* (poetry; 60¢, $1 to institutions); Mackay, M., *Immersion* (fiction; 75¢, $1 to institutions); Mariah, P., *Personae Non Gratae* (poetry; 60¢, $1 to institutions).

31 SOJOURNER TRUTH PRESS. Box 7684, Atlanta, Ga. 30309.

A publishing company, now only distributing *Sleeping Beauty*, a lesbian fairy tale, with drawings and hand calligraphy, 25 pp., 50¢ plus 20¢ postage and handling per copy (55¢ for airmail; 80¢ overseas). Make checks payable to Vicki Garbriner.

32 TIMES CHANGE PRESS. Penwell Rd., Washington, N.J. 07882. (201) 689-6659. Founded 1970.

"A small not-for-profit alternative press publishing material on personal/ political liberation; primarily feminist material, but also works on men's consciousness raising, gay liberation, alternative lifestyles. . . ." Discounts available to discussion groups, bookstores, women's centers, etc. Following is a selected list of publications of interest to women.

Allen, Pamela, *Free Space: A Perspective on the Small Group in Women's Liberation* $1.35
Alta, *Burn This and Memorize Yourself: Poems for Women* $.50
Goldman, Emma, *The Traffic in Women and Other Essays on Feminism* $1.35
Negrin, Su, *A Graphic Notebook on Feminism* $1.25
Rizzi Salo, Marcia, *Some Pictures from My Life: A Diary* $1.35
Taylor, Kathryn, *Generations of Denial: 75 Short Biographies of Women in History* $1.35
Woodhull and Claflin's Weekly: The Lives and Writings of Notorious Victoria Woodhull and Her Sister Tennessee Claflin $1.25

Posters are also available; write for catalog. Orders to TCP, Monthly Review Press, 116 W. 14 St., New York, N.Y. 10011.

33 TODAY PUBLICATIONS AND NEWS SERVICE. National Press Bldg., Washington, D.C. 20004. (202) 628-6663. Founded 1970. Myra E. Barrer.

Provides assistance "to various women's organizations in both publishing and nonpublishing capacities," and publishes *Women Today*, "the only biweekly national newsletter accredited by the White House, Congress and all major Government organizations in Washington, D.C., both as a news service and as reporters." (Looseleaf, $15.) Also publishes *Women's Organizations and Leaders*, edited by Myra E. Barrer ($25). The 1973 directory "is a current and comprehensive directory and guide to more than 8000 women's organizations and their leaders. Individual women, active in the women's movement, through their actions or writings are also listed. The directory lists in alphabetical order each organization . . . and leaders along with a description of the activities and goals of the organization as stated by the organization." There are alphabetical, geographic, and subject indexes. Periodic updates are planned.

34   UNDERWATER WOMEN OF THE 20TH CENTURY RENAISSANCE.
Box 377, Piermont, N.Y. 10968. (914) 359-2017. Founded April 1973.
Loris Bangs, 264 Piermont Ave., Piermont, N.Y. 10968. 5 members.

Although presently formulating new goals, the group was established for the
purpose of publishing *To Oedipus, From Mother* by Jocasta Gyne (paper, $1.95),
"a statement from a type of women who has not yet been heard with the woman
movement. . . . She is an older woman, of the type and generation who responded to
the 'womanly' role (expectation by expectation) without ever formulating any articulate protest. She is a housewife. . . . She has found her role both deeply re-
warding and deeply frustrating, but has had no gauge by which to measure *herself*.
Her book . . . is an attempt to describe the rewards and frustrations of her experience and their cause and effect in relation to the main stream. . . .

"Our group relates to this woman more directly than we relate to the
brilliant, articulate young women with practical goals who are currently running the
woman's movement. (We bless them. We admire them. They are giving us courage
to speak, but we urge them to listen. They are our daughters.). . . The book was
written by an individual woman who—like the rest of us—is nobody in her own
right. The name "Jocasta Gyne" (the mother of Oedipus) is a sort of species name,
meant to represent all of us . . ."

35   UNITED FRONT PRESS. Box 40099, San Francisco, Calif. 94140.
Founded January 1973. Kathleen Drolet.

Publishers of pamphlets about working people, their history, and current
struggles. Following is a list of pamphlets of interest to women.

Beal, F., *Double Jeopardy: To Be Black and Female* 20¢
Greene, F., *A Divorce Trial in Canada* 10¢
McAfee, K. and Wood, M. *Bread and Roses* 10¢
Mitchell, J., *Women: The Longest Revolution* 15¢
The Political Economy of Women's Liberation 15¢
Pollard, V. and Keck, D. *They Almost Seized the Time* 15¢
Women and Socialism 20¢
Wood, M., *We May Not Have Much, but There's a Lot of Us* 25¢

36   VIOLET PRESS. Box 398, New York, N.Y. 10009.

A lesbian/feminist press publishing literature by and about lesbians for all
women. Will also provide, for 10¢, a list of anthologies, newspapers, and magazines
that want lesbian poetry and presses that will print lesbian work. Works currently
available are: Winant, Fran, *Looking at Women* (poems, $1); *We Are All Lesbians*
(a poetry anthology, $2); *Lesbians and the Health Care System* (personal testimony
of N.Y. Radicalesbians, 75¢); and *A Lesbian Record* (songs and music by Flash and
Fran). Discounts for bulk orders.

37   THE WHOLE WOMAN CATALOG. Box 1171, Portsmouth, N.H. 03801.

Unable to find funding to publish a second edition, WWC currently plans to
operate as a clearinghouse of information on the women's movement, supplying
information on request concerning women's groups, projects, etc. in various areas.
Wishes to receive current information on women's groups and money to cover
postage and supplies.

38   WOLLSTONECRAFT INC. 6399 Wilshire Blvd., Suite 507–508, Los Angeles, Calif. 90048. (213) 653-1745. Founded January 1973. Annette Welles, Pres.

This publishing company specializes in "books that are relevant." Subjects include legal hangups (Alexander, *Women under the Law*), how-to-do-it books (Billings, *The Womansbook*, $6.95), consciousness raising (Nichols, *On the Verge*, $6.95), assault (Norman, *Rape*, $6.95), and humor (Wittels, *Ms. ERY*, $3 paper). Bulk rates are available.

39   ZIZI PRESS. 610 W. 110 St., New York, N.Y. 10025.

Publishes *The Little Prick* ($1.25 plus 20¢ postage): "a feminist views and exposes the prick and his attitudes." More feminist products are in the works: children's books, silk screen cards, and calendars.

Periodicals

ACTION. See 234.

ACTION FOR CHILDREN (newsletter). See 394.

ADVOCATES FOR WOMEN BULLETIN. See 430.

40 AIN'T I A WOMAN. Box 1169, Iowa City, Iowa. 52240. Founded June 1970. Every three weeks. $5, individuals; $13, foreign; $20, institutions.

Gay, feminist tabloid concerned with political analysis and theory. Articles cover such topics as rape, health care, Vietnam, relationship of class to feminism, reformism, motherhood, day care, and lesbianism, as well as poetry, letters to the editor, and advertisements.

41 ALERT, THE CONNECTICUT LEGISLATIVE REVIEW FOR WOMEN. Box 437, Middletown, Conn. 06457. (203) 342-1462. Founded November 1972. Harriette Behringer, Ed. 12/yr.; $4, individual; $15, corporate.

"A nonprofit, nonpartisan newsletter that informs Connecticut women of events that concern them in the State legislature, covering such topics as women and power, marriage and divorce, the E.R.A., women and money, work and education, and a legislative wrap-up." *Alert* also sells posters and maintains a speakers' bureau.

ALVERNO RESEARCH CENTER ON WOMEN NEWSLETTER. See 143.

42 AMAZON QUARTERLY. 554 Valle Vista, Oakland, Calif. 94610. (415) 832-4239. Founded September 1972. Gina Roberson and Laurel Akers, Eds. q. $4/yr.; $5 foreign.

A nationwide lesbian feminist arts journal. "Each issue contains 72 pages of the best in fiction, visual art, essays, reviews, poetry and biographies of little known women artists and writers." Contributions are invited; include a stamped self-addressed envelope if material is to be returned.

AMERICAN ECONOMICS ASSOCIATION, COMMITTEE ON THE STATUS OF WOMEN IN THE ECONOMICS PROFESSION NEWSLETTER. See 520.

AMERICAN LIBRARY ASSOCIATION SRRT TASK FORCE ON WOMEN NEWSLETTER. See 524.

AMERICAN PHILOGICAL ASSOCIATION, CAUCUS NEWSLETTER. See 527.

AMERICAN STATISTICAL ASSOCIATION, CAUCUS FOR WOMEN IN STATISTICS. NEWSLETTER. See 533

43 APHRA. Box 893, Ansonia Sta., New York, N.Y. 10023. (212) 595-0622. Founded September 1969. Elizabeth Fisher, and others, Eds. q. $4.50/yr.; $1.50/issue.

A feminist literary magazine, "named for Aphra Behn (1640-89), first woman to earn her living by writing." Includes fiction, drama, poetry, artwork, criticism, and nonfiction. Each issue is devoted to a theme; some previous topics have been matriarchy, aging, marriage, "the whore issue." Contributions should be sent with a stamped self-addressed envelope for return of manuscripts.

ASSOCIATION FOR THE STUDY OF ABORTION NEWSLETTER. See 463.

ASSOCIATION FOR WOMEN IN MATHEMATICS NEWSLETTER. See 536.

ASSOCIATION FOR WOMEN IN PSYCHOLOGY NEWSLETTER. See 537.

ASSOCIATION OF WOMEN IN SCIENCE NEWSLETTER. See 539.

44 AURORA. 24 De Baun Ave., Suffern, N.Y. 10901. Lynne Farrow, Ed. Irreg. 4 issues for $4.

Provides information on specific ways women can change their lifestyles in theory and practice. Emphasis is on selfhelp, but fiction, poetry, and artwork are included. Entire production is done by *Aurora* volunteer staff. Financial contributions are welcome. A recent issue included the following articles: "Poor Country Women," "A Feminist Look at Children's Books," "Sisters in the Skin Trade," "The Day Care Question," "Sororicide, or How Some Sisters Are Real Killers," and "Female Liberation as the Basis for Social Revolution."

BRAINCHILD. See 357.

BREAKTHROUGH. See 249.

CFUW NEWS. See 228.

CSW NEWS. See 325.

CWSS NEWSLETTER. See 172.

CALIFORNIA COMMISSION ON THE STATUS OF WOMEN. NEWSLETTER. See 261.

45   CANADIAN NEWSLETTER OF RESEARCH ON WOMEN. Dept. of Sociology, Univ. of Waterloo, Waterloo, Ontario, Can. (519) 885-1211. Founded Spring 1972. Dr. Margrit Eicher. 3/yr. $4, individuals; $9, institutions.

Aims to "establish and/or improve communication among people in Canada who are doing research on women; to list on-going research on Canadian women in particular; to list selected relevant research on the international scene; and to provide for an exchange of ideas on courses about sex roles or women."

CATALYST. QUARTERLY REPORT. See 434.

THE CATHOLIC CITIZEN. See 453.

46   CHANGE: A WORKING WOMAN'S NEWSPAPER. 968 Valencia St., San Francisco, Calif. 94117. (415) 626-1056. Founded January 1971. Kathy Frederick, 1666 Page St. San Francisco, Calif. 94117. bi-m. $2/yr.; $5, institutions.

Subscriptions and sales cover about 10 percent of costs of publishing the 4,000 copies of the paper, most of them distributed in downtown San Francisco. Articles are usually written jointly, and jobs are rotated on the paper. In one issue there were articles on day care, striking workers at Shell Oil Co., the Vietnamese war, and the nature of temporary employment. Work has been temporarily suspended on *Change*, and the collective is now preparing a booklet about working women, with articles on unions, sexuality, the nuclear family, racism, and sexism as it affects women in their workplace.

THE CHRONICLE. See 228.

CONNECTIONS. See 500.

COORDINATING COMMITTEE ON WOMEN IN THE HISTORICAL PROFESSION NEWSLETTER. See 542.

DAY CARE NEWSLETTER. See 404.

DELAWARE GOVERNOR'S COUNCIL FOR WOMEN ANNUAL REPORT. See 265.

DO IT NOW. See 163.

47   EARTH'S DAUGHTERS. 944 Kensington Ave., Buffalo, N.Y. 14215. (716) 838-6346. Founded February 1971. Judith B. Kerman. irreg. $2.50 for 6 issues.

A feminist arts periodical, founded to publish the best possible writing and artwork by women.

EQUAL OPPORTUNITIES. See 307.

48   EVERYWOMAN. 10438 W. Washington Blvd., Venice, Calif. 90291. 1970. Every 3 weeks. $5.

A movement newspaper containing news and news analyses, articles ranging from women's history to lesbians, the New Left, pornography, and other relevant issues. A "Manglish" column dissects the English language for examples of sexism. Also includes poetry and book reviews.

EVERYWOMAN'S CENTER NEWSLETTER. See **189**.

49 THE EXECUTIVE WOMAN. 747 3rd Ave., 29th floor, New York, N.Y. 10017. Founded 1973. m. except June and July. $20/yr.

A newsletter created especially for women entrepreneurs. One issue included articles on "Executive Power," "The Executive Suite and How to Get There," and profiles of some of today's successful businesswomen. Each issue includes a special feature column on a specific field such as women in education or women in advertising, reports on current business trends, publications, courses and management training workshops, psychological studies and career tips, and commentaries like "Bank Credit for Women," "Personal Investments," "How to Finance Your Own Business."

50 FEMINIST ART JOURNAL. 41 Montgomery Pl., Brooklyn, N.Y. 11215. Founded January 1972. Candy Newser, Ed. q. $2/4 issues.

An outgrowth of the women artists movement, dealing with women in the arts, past and present. "We publish scholarly articles, interviews and profiles about distinguished women artists, plus spirited accounts of the current activities of the women artists movement. We also feature pieces dealing with art world issues in such key areas as criticism, museumology, art education, etc." One of its editors is a painter; the other is a critic. Contributors include painters, sculptors, film makers, poets, photographers, craftswomen, and art historians.

51 THE FEMINIST BULLETIN. Box 262, Scarborough, N.Y. 10510. (914) 762-2541. Founded April 1972. Jody Israel. m. $4/yr.; $3, students.

A newsletter for those involved in or interested in the women's movement in Westchester County and the surrounding area, published by the Westchester Women's Liberation Coalition. Disseminates information, provides a means of communication among groups and individuals, and promotes the aims of the women's movement. Replaces *On Our Way* newsletter.

FEW'S NEWS AND VIEWS. See **543**.

FEMALE LIBERATION NEWSLETTER. See **190**.

FEMINIST. See **219**.

FEMINIST REVOLUTION. See **200**.

FEMINIST THERAPY REFERRAL COLLECTIVE NEWSLETTER. See **470**.

52 THE FIFTH ESTATE. 4403 Second Ave., Detroit, Mich. 48201. (313) 831-6800. Founded November 1965. L. Schaefer. bi-w. $9, individuals; $20, institutions.

An independent newspaper, published collectively, covering news of all people's struggles: women, Blacks, workers, etc. One issue included articles on consumerism, the Detroit Women's Resource Center, and a book review on *Witches, Midwives and Nurses.*

53   51%: A PAPER OF JOYFUL NOISE FOR THE MAJORITY SEX. Box 371, Lomita, Calif. 90717. Founded June 1972. Norma Wilson. m. $4/yr.

A broadside containing poetry, graphics, letters, and articles on motherhood, power, psychology and aging, among other topics.

54   FOCUS: A JOURNAL FOR GAY WOMEN. Boston Daughters of Bilitis, Rm. 323, 419 Boulston St., Boston, Mass. 02116. Founded 1972. m. $5/yr.

Mimeographed newsletter aimed toward the acceptance of lesbianism and other female alternatives. Includes letters, addresses, "happenings," full-length features, poetry, recent legislation, and a calendar of events sponsored by the Boston Daughters of Bilitis.

FOCUS ON WOMEN. See **196**.

FOR WOMEN ONLY. See **186**.

FRONT PAGE. See **187**.

55 . GAY LIBERATOR. Box 631-A, Detroit, Mich. 48232. (313) 833-1920. Founded April 1970. m. $3/12 issues.

Gay Liberation paper published by a six-member collective. One issue included articles on psychosurgery, job harrassment, entrapment, self-defense, gays in China, book reviews, and a calendar.

56   GAY SUNSHINE: A JOURNAL OF GAY LIBERATION. Box 40397, San Francisco, Calif. 94140. (415) 824-3184. Winston Leyland, Ed. bi-m. $5/yr. Free to prisoners.

"An open forum for the publication of consciousness-raising articles, graphics, poetry and other material by gay people." Sponsors Gay Liberation Book Service, which distributes books and poetry by gay men and women.

57   GOLD FLOWER: A TWIN CITIES NEWSPAPER FOR WOMEN. Box 8341. Lake St. Sta., Minneapolis, Minn. 55408. (612) 827-2345. Founded November 1971. Susan Cushman. m. $3/yr.

A community newspaper to put women in touch with each other. Issues have included pieces on songwriter Malvina Reynolds, lesbianism, venereal disease, a book review, and advertisements.

THE HAND. See **217**.

HEALTH PAC BULLETIN. See **473**.

58   HER-SELF, COMMUNITY WOMEN'S NEWSPAPER. 225 E. Liberty St., Suite 200, Ann Arbor, Mich. 48108. (313) 663-1285. Founded May 23, 1972. Belita H. Cowan. m. $4, individuals; $10, institutions.

A feminist newspaper to "promote awareness and recognition of women's projects, activities, contributions and achievements and to train women in journalism and newspaper production skills." Some articles are: "Sterilization Butchery," "Choose Your Poison: The 'Mini Pill' Hits the Market," "Comic Book Cuties: Another Sexist Fantasy," and "Fanny: Womanrock." Film reviews and news briefs are also included.

HUMAN RIGHTS FOR WOMEN NEWSLETTER. See 380.

HYPATIA. See 174.

ILLINOIS CITIZENS FOR THE MEDICAL CONTROL OF ABORTION NEWSLETTER. See 474.

IN TOUCH. See 308.

IOWANS FOR THE MEDICAL CONTROL OF ABORTION NEWSLETTER. See 475.

IOWOMAN. See 284.

JOURNAL OF NAWDAC. See 546.

JOURNAL OF THE AMERICAN MEDICAL WOMEN'S ASSOCIATION. See 525.

KNOW NEWS. See 13.

59 THE LADDER. Box 5025, Washington Sta., Reno, Nev. 89503. (816) 333-8705. Founded October 1956. Gene Damon, Ed. bi-m. $7.50/yr.

One of the oldest feminist magazines. Originally published by Daughters of Bilitis for lesbian women, since 1970 it has directed itself to all women seeking human dignity. Articles explicitly relate the oppression of lesbians to the oppression of heterosexual women, covering such subjects as women authors, lesbians and the Church, sex roles, and other philosophical and literary topics. Includes some poetry and book reviews. *Index to the Ladder* and *The Lesbian in Literature*, a bibliography, by Gene Damon and Lee Stuart, both $4.25, are also available.

LAVENDER WOMAN. See 14.

LAZETTE. See 506.

60 LESBIAN TIDE. 373 N. Western St. #202, Los Angeles, Calif. 90004. (213) 467-3931. Founded August 1971. Barbara McLean. m. $7.50/yr.

An independent, feminist lesbian magazine published by a collective of gay women, including news articles, poetry, and interviews. Some past articles have been "Put a Women's Revolution First," "Custody Fight Continues," "Gay Civil Rights—Top Priority," and "An Army of Lovers." Regular features include "Where It's At" (a national directory), a bar guide, and calendar of events for the Los Angeles area.

THE LIBERATED GRAPEVINE. See 210.

61 THE LIBERATOR. 1404 Grand Ave., Fort Worth, Tex. 76106. (817) 624-2486. Founded August 1972. Martha Lindsey, Pub. 8/yr. $3/ 12 issues.

"An independent journal of commentary on feminist issues. Dedicated to the premise that everybody ought to be free, whether they want to be or not, or failing that, should at least have the right to choose their own prison." Deals particularly with issues pertinent to the feminist movement in Texas. Some articles have been: "Legislature's Stance on Abortion Raises Church-State Question," "Supreme Court Strikes Down Texas Abortion Law," "Texas Women Win Equality," and "Leviticus and St. Paul on Women."

LILITH. See 209.

62   MAJORITY REPORT. 74 Grove St., New York, N.Y. 10014. (212) 929-9862. Founded May 1971. Nancy Borman. m. $3/yr.; $5, libraries.

"First published as a mimeographed newsletter on May 10, 1971, *MR* has grown to a 20-page tabloid newspaper with a circulation of over 11,500. The staff consists of 12 women, all equally owners, and all sharing the work of the paper. Editorial decisions are made democratically. Through *Majority Report*, women have learned skills and functions traditionally alloted to men: typesetting, design, photography, advertising sales, distribution management, news reporting.

"*Majority Report* provides an alternative to the existing media . . . newspapers, where women are still relegated to the 'Women's Page' . . . TV news where women's liberation is treated as the joke of the day . . . news magazines that seem to feel that printing the facts is 'going too far' . . . and strives to offer fair and thorough coverage of women's issues in the New York area, and to summarize national and international events of interest to women."

Recent features have included: "Five Reasons Not to Eat Meat at All"; "What Happened to a Women Who Tried to Get Off Welfare by Giving Her Husband Custody of the Children"; "Ti-Grace Atkinson's Reply to 'Up from the Kitchen Floor'"; and "A 98% Effective Birth Control Method that Works by Astrology."

Majority Report carries advertising at low rates for all business and products of interest to feminist readers, and is sold at news stands and bookstores in the New York City metropolitan area. Back issues are available. The editors are also compiling an international directory of the women's movement.

63   MARIN WOMEN'S NEWS JOURNAL. Box 1412, San Rafael, Calif. 94960. (416) 454-5560. Founded May 1972. Bev Terwoman. m. $4/yr.

Published by a feminist collective as a source of expression for women and a medium of stimulation and communication. The journal encourages written contributions from women and men, and provides "education, news, public announcements and an open forum for women writers and artists." Bumper strips are also available: "Uppity Woman," "The Revolution Begins at Home," and "Sister."

MEDIA REPORT TO WOMEN. See 374.

MISSOURI COMMISSION ON THE STATUS OF WOMEN NEWSLETTER. See 300.

MOMMA: THE NEWSPAPER/MAGAZINE FOR SINGLE MOTHERS. See 564.

THE MONTHLY EXTRACT, AN IRREGULAR PERIODICAL. See 481.

64 MOTHER LODE. 334 Winfield St., San Francisco, Calif. 94110. (415) 285-7087. Founded January 1971. Sandy Boucher, Jeri Robertson. irreg. $1.50/6 issues.

A broadsheet newspaper published by a collective to communicate feminist ideas. Each issue has been devoted to a specific subject, such as feminism, women in prison, families, Medicare, lesbian mothers, posters, and poetry. Back issues sell for 25¢ to 50¢ each.

65 MOVING OUT MAGAZINE. Box 26, U.C.B., Wayne State Univ., Detroit, Mich. 48202. (313) 577-3409. Founded 1970. bi-a. $1/yr.

A feminist literary magazine edited by a cooperative of about 20 women "who recognize the need for a medium through which women can share their experiences and ideas." Contributions of artwork, short stories, essays, poetry, and photographs are welcome.

66 MS. 370 Lexington Ave., New York, N.Y. 10017. Founded Spring 1972, Gloria Steinem, Pres. m. $9/yr.

"A full-fledged national magazine . . . created and controlled by women" to generate income and give women "serious . . . honest coverage." The price of the magazine permits freedom from pressure by advertisers, but group deductions are available for women's groups, and some free issues are available to women who cannot pay at all. The editors state "We want a world in which no one is born into a subordinate role because of visible difference, whether that difference is of race or of sex." The staff is run communally, not heirarchically.

Features include Forum, "a place to be more theoretical; to discuss the future implications of this revolt against the caste systems of sex and race; to suggest new tactics and ideas; and to criticize tactics and ideas that aren't working"; *Ms.* Gazette, "a news section that [reports] on local events and Women's Movement news [as well as] short items that are of national interest"; and The Family of Women, "a series of photographic essays." *Ms.* also includes monthly letters to the editor, Ms. on the Arts, Stories for Free Children (nonsexist children's stories), Notes From Abroad, a classified section, poetry, and fiction: Some articles have been "Lesbian Mothers," "Helen Gahagan Douglas," "Men: Vasectomy—My Right to Choose," "Toys for Free Children," and "What about POW Wives?" *Ms.* has also published a children's record "Free to Be . . . You and Me" ($6.50).

The Ms. Foundation for Women is sponsored by *Ms.* "to give grants to deserving women's projects that are not yet being funded by traditional sources." The foundation will be the recipient of some of the profits from the magazine. An anthology, *The First Ms. Reader*, was published by Warner Paperback ($1.50).

Ms. requests nonfiction writers to send clippings of past work, plus a letter describing "the specific way" the subject is to be approached, before submitting a completed manuscript. Every manuscript sent is read.

NABW JOURNAL. See 547.

NASHVILLE WOMEN'S CENTER NEWSLETTER. See 224.

NATIONAL ACTION COMMITTEE ON THE STATUS OF WOMEN IN CANADA NEWSLETTER. See 229.

NATIONAL ASSOCIATION FOR REPEAL OF ABORTION LAWS NEWS-LETTER. See 480.

NATIONAL ASSOCIATION OF COLLEGE WOMEN BULLETIN. See 161.

NATIONAL ASSOCIATION OF COLLEGE WOMEN JOURNAL. See 161.

NATIONAL ASSOCIATION OF WOMEN LAWYERS. PRESIDENT'S NEWSLETTER. See 548.

NATIONAL BUSINESS WOMAN. See 162.

NATIONAL COALITION OF AMERICAN NUNS NEWSLETTER. See 451.

NATIONAL COUNCIL OF WOMEN OF CANADA NEWSLETTER. See 230.

NATIONAL ORGANIZATION FOR NON-PARENTS NEWSLETTER. See 565.

NATIONAL WOMAN'S PARTY BULLETIN. See 511.

67   NEW DIRECTIONS FOR WOMEN IN NEW JERSEY. Box 27, Dover, N.J. 07801. (201) 366-6036. Founded July 1971. Paula S. Kassell, Ed. q. $3/4 issues.

Statewide news quarterly to inform women in New Jersey about equal rights in legislation, employment, abortion, advertising, education, the arts, family, and religion. Gives extensive coverage of books by, for, and about feminists and non-sexist children's books. Special issues have covered education and books, employment and child care, and the women's movement in New Jersey.

68   THE NEW FEMINIST. New Feminists. Box 597, Sta. A, Toronto, Ont., Can. M5W 1E4. Founded November 1969. Val Perkins. q. $3/yr.

Radical feminist mimeographed newsletter including articles and news of particular interest to women in Canada, as well as general news and features on consciousness, chauvinism, and the movement.

N.J. STATE COMMISSION ON WOMEN ANNUAL REPORT. See 308.

NEW YORK RADICAL FEMINISTS NEWSLETTER. See 199.

NEW YORK STATE WOMEN'S UNIT NEWS. See 311.

NEWFOUNDLAND STATUS OF WOMEN COUNCIL NEWSLETTER. See 236.

NEWS AND LETTERS. See 194.

69   NINE TO FIVE: NEWSLETTER FOR BOSTON AREA OFFICE WORKERS. 2 Brookline St., Cambridge, Mass. 02139. Founded September, 1972: bi-m.; contrib.

Written by and for Boston area office workers and hopes to help unionize them. A sample issue included letters from readers, an article on the Harvard Office Workers Group, and exercises to prevent backaches for typists. Welcomes comments, letters, articles, drawings, and photographs.

NO MORE FUN AND GAMES; A JOURNAL OF FEMALE LIBERATION. See 188.

NOW ACTS. See 163.

70 OFF OUR BACKS: A WOMEN'S NEWS JOURNAL. 1724 20 St., N.W., Washington, D.C. 20009. (202) 234-8072. Founded May 1970. m. $5/yr., $6, Canada; $15, institutions and libraries.

A national women's news journal which publishes news, fiction, features, poetry, book and movie reviews, and graphics. Features frequent thematic issues. Some articles have been "Court Abortion Ruling," "Women's Studies," "Vietnamese Women," "Women's Music," and "Lesbian Feminist Politics." Includes advertising. Bulk rates available.

OHIO WOMAN. See 321.

OMAHA MAYOR'S COMMISSION ON THE STATUS OF WOMEN ANNUAL REPORT (Omaha, Nebr.). See 302.

ON CAMPUS WITH WOMEN. See 389.

ON OUR WAY. See 51.

ON THE WAY. See 168.

ONTARIO COMMITTEE ON THE STATUS OF WOMEN NEWSLETTER. See 238.

OREGON COUNCIL FOR WOMEN'S EQUALITY NEWSLETTER. See 215.

OTTAWA WOMEN'S CENTRE NEWSLETTER. See 239.

71 OUR GENERATION. 3934 rue St. Urbain, Montreal, 131, Quebec, Can. Founded Fall 1961. Lucia Kawaluk. q. 4 issues/$5, individuals; $10, institutions; 8 issues/$9.50, individuals; $19, institutions.

"Founded in the Fall of 1961, *Our Generation* has evolved a radical analysis relevant to our industrial/technological society. Beginning with the relations between nation-states in the age of the super-bomb, to the dimensions and nature of social revolution, the journal attempts from a libertarian socialist perspective to be of service to people who want to pursue an interrelated range of social questions. The Montreal and Toronto editorial collectives of *Our Generation* seek to encourage research and social analysis in the areas of critical social theory, the development of the respective social and national liberation movements in Quebec and Canada, and a radical analysis of industrial societies in general."

Other items, besides the periodical, are available from the literature department. A women's liberation kit may be ordered for $5.50 (a $6.10 value).

Following is a list of titles in the kit.

Burn This and Memorize Yourself: Poems for Women by Alta, 50¢
Female Liberation as a Basis for Social Revolution by Roxanne Dunbar, 20¢
Free Space: A Perspective on the Small Group in Women's Liberation by Pamela Allen, $1
Generations of Denial: 75 Short Biographies of Women in History by Kathryn Taylor, $1
A Graphic Notebook on Feminism by Su Negrin, $1
Liberation of Women: Sexual Repression and the Family by Laurel Limpus, 20¢
The Myth of the Vaginal Orgasm by Ann Koedt, and a response, *Fucked-Up in America* by Nancy Mann, 20¢
The Political Economy of Women's Liberation by Margaret Benston, 20¢
Psychology Constructs the Female by Naomi Weisstein, 20¢
Sex Roles and Female Oppression by Dana Densmore, 20¢
Toward a Female Liberation Movement by B. Jones and J. Brown, 20¢
The Traffic in Women and Other Essays by Emma Goldman, $1.44.
Women: The Longest Revolution by Juliet Mitchell, 20¢

There is also a kit of new Canadian women's liberation materials: *Women Unite!* from the Canadian Women's Educational Press (see entry 3), $3; *The Day Care Book* (on cooperative day care) also from the Canadian Women's Educational Press, $1.50; *Women's Work* by the Working Women's Association of Vancouver, 25¢; *Working in Hospitals* by the Working Women's Association of Vancouver, 25¢; *Mother Was Not a Person*, edited by Margaret Andersen, $3.95. Kit price is $4.50 (a $5 value).

Other women's liberation materials available are: *The Political Economy of Women* by Union for Radical Economics (also containing several bibliographies), $1; *Witches, Midwives and Nurses, A History of Women Healers* by B. Ehrenreich and D. English, $1; and *A Divorce Trial in China* by Felix Greene, 10¢. Include 50¢ postage and handling for each kit ordered. On individual item orders of $1 or less add 25¢ postage and handling; $1.01 to $5, add 50¢ postage and handling; $5.01 to $10, add $1 postage and handling; and over $10, use your judgment regarding postage and handling. A discount of 15% will be given to bookstores and distributors on bulk orders for resale.

72 PANDORA. Box 94, Seattle, Wash. 98105. (206) 633-2440. Founded October 1970. Sharon Haywood. bi-w. $5/yr.

An independent Seattle women's newspaper which tries "to maintain communication and sisterhood among various groups; and to give fair and accurate coverage to [local] events and projects which concern women's struggle for equality." Some articles have been "Sports at U.W.: Equal but Separate," "Group Urges End to Sex-Role Stereotyping in Schools," "Gay Women's Resource Center Denied Funds by United Way," and "Opinion: Friedan Unresponsive to Movement."

PEDESTAL. See **233.**

PENNSYLVANIANS FOR WOMEN'S RIGHTS NEWSLETTER. See **218.**

POPULATION ASSOCIATION OF AMERICA. WOMEN'S CAUCUS NEWSLETTER. See **550.**

73 PRIME TIME: FOR THE LIBERATION OF WOMEN IN THE PRIME OF
LIFE. 232 E. 6 St., Apt. 5C, New York, N.Y. 10003. (212) 260-2874.
Founded September 1971. Marjory Callins. m. $5/12 issues; $3.50 if
unemployed or on social security.

An independent monthly which reports on the national older women's liberation movement to combat ageism, sexism, and racism. It contains articles, poems,
and news, and runs a Speakers Bureau and an Information Service for readers.
Issues have included articles on male chauvinism, the international feminist conference, women and money, and returning to school, as well as letters to the editor,
classified ads, and notices for and from older women's liberation groups.

74 PRO SE: THE NATIONAL LAW WOMEN'S NEWSLETTER. 79
Dartmouth St., No. 2, Boston, Mass. 02116. (617) 262-6720. Founded
October 1971. Karen Porter. m. $5, individuals; $3, law students; $25,
libraries (for 5 copies of each issue).

An independent, monthly newsletter to maintain communication and sisterhood among women at law schools around the country and to cover events and
projects which concern law women's struggles for equality and humanity. Deadline
for copy is the fifteenth of each month. Signed articles, letters to the editor, and
artwork from all women law students are welcome. One issue included articles on
women in law school, women's law collectives, prostitution, abortion, book reviews, and national conference notes.

RAPE CRISIS CENTER NEWSLETTER (University City, Mo.). See **502**.

RIGHT ON SISTER. See **174**.

SACRAMENTO COMMUNITY COMMISSION FOR WOMEN
NEWSLETTER. See **263**.

ST. JOAN'S BULLETIN. See **453**.

SASKATCHEWAN ACTION COMMITTEE NEWSLETTER. See **244**.

SASKATOON WOMEN'S LIBERATION NEWSLETTER. See **245**.

THE SECOND WAVE. See **190**.

SHAMELESS HUSSY REVIEW. See **30**.

SIREN FEMINISTS NEWSLETTER. See **513**.

SISTER. See **175**.

SISTER: NEW HAVEN WOMEN'S LIBERATION NEWSLETTER. See **179**.

SISTERHOOD (Boston Theological Institute). See **444**.

75 SISTERS. San Francisco Daughters of Bilitis, 1005 Market St., Suite 402,
San Francisco, Calif. 94103. 1972. m. $5.

Contains articles relating to the lesbian/feminist community, short stories,
poems, cartoons, graphics, an occasional book review, and a calendar of events for
the bay area.

76 SKIRTING THE CAPITOL: A NEWSLETTER ABOUT LEGISLATION AND WOMEN. Box 4569, Sacramento, Calif. 95825. (916) 481-2417. Founded July 1967. Marian Ash, Ed. $15/yr.

A nonpartisan newsletter "to keep women informed about legislative issues [in California] affecting them, and to promote more intelligent participation by women in the legislative process." According to the publisher, this is the first newsletter of its kind in the nation.

SOCIETY FOR WOMEN IN PHILOSOPHY NEWSLETTER. See 554.

SOCIETY OF WOMEN ENGINEERS NEWSLETTER. See 556.

SOCIOLOGISTS FOR WOMEN IN SOCIETY NEWSLETTER. See 557.

SOJOURNER. See 375.

77 SPEAKOUT, A FEMINIST JOURNAL. 184 Washington Ave., Albany, N.Y. 12210. (518) 462-5083. Founded January 1972. m. 25¢/copy; $3/yr. (12 issues); $5, institutions.

"*Speakout* is a feminist newsjournal dedicated to the women's movement. We attempt to give any women who desires to contribute (or speak out) the opportunity to do so. . . . We hope that more women will join us and help us grow." Issues have included articles on women's conferences, lesbianism, sterilization, poverty, women's art, abortion, women's law firms, black feminism, and the international women's movement, as well as poetry, selections from the feminist press, letters to the editor, employment opportunities, and announcements.

78 THE SPOKESWOMAN. 5464 S. Shore Dr., Chicago, Ill. 60615. (312) 363-2580. Founded June 1970. Karen Wellisch, Ed. m. $7/yr; $12, institutions.

An independent, monthly newsletter of women's news which covers " . . . the latest developments in employment, education, child care, abortion, legislation, legal action, welfare, politics, media and women's organizations. We review new publications, articles, reports, surveys, documents and conferences. . . . The *Spokeswoman* also introduces you to groups of women who have organized to fight discrimination whenever and wherever they find it. . . . Side-by-side with our news runs our monthly help wanted section featuring jobs never before advertised to women."

79 THE SPORTSWOMAN MAGAZINE. Box 7771, Long Beach, Calif. 90807. Founded March 1973. Marlene Johnson, Ed. 6/yr., $4.50.

Devoted to promoting women in sports. Features are planned on women athletes, discrimination against women in sports, and sports in which women participate. "Billie Jean King—Tennis Wonder Woman," "Sports Scholarships for Women," "Miss Softball America," "Judy Lilly—Champion Drag Racer," "Denise Long—Basketball's No. 1 Woman," and "Althea Gibson" have been some articles. Local and national tournaments and events are noted.

STEWARDESSES FOR WOMEN'S RIGHTS NEWSLETTER. See 558.

TELL-A-WOMAN. See 220.

TEXAS CITIZENS FOR ABORTION EDUCATION NEWSLETTER. See 488.

80 THE TEXAS WOMAN. 1208 Baylor, Austin, Tex. 78703. (512) 474-1798. Founded April 1973. Carol Stalcup. m. $6/12 issues.

"To circulate information among and about Texas feminists, to be a showplace for women's culture, to keep Texas women apprised of activities of interest to them." One issue included articles on women's history, women artists, sexism in education and sports, as well as poetry, book reviews, photographs, conference reports, and advertisements.

81 13TH MOON. 101–16 120 St., Richmond Hill, N.Y. 11419. (212) 849-2565. Founded Spring 1973. Kathleen Chodor, Ed. s-a. $1/issue.

Journal of the Writing Organization for Women at the City College of New York, which provides a forum for the creative writing of women. Desires "to help create and define a women's mythology in the field of art, especially poetry." Also organizes women's poetry readings.

TRANSITION. See 226.

TRIPLE JEOPARDY. See 454.

UNION WAGE. See 441.

UNITED NATIONS NEWSLETTER ON THE STATUS OF WOMEN. See 247.

UNITED STATES CITIZEN'S ADVISORY COUNCIL ON THE STATUS OF WOMEN ANNUAL REPORT. See 250.

82 UP FROM UNDER: A NEW MAGAZINE BY, FOR AND ABOUT WOMEN. 339 Lafayette St., New York, N.Y. 10012. (212) 260-1040. Founded September 1969. Grace Ann Dunphy. q. 5 issues, $3, individuals; $5, institutions. Prepaid bulk rates (25 copies or more, 50¢/copy).

Attempts to respond to the needs of working class women. Includes survival and "how to" articles and case histories, such as: "The Complex Inferiority Problem," "Caution: Health Care May Be Hazardous to Your Health," "Drowning in the Steno Pool," "Getting Together: The Small Group in Women's Liberation," "Planned Obsolescence: The Middle Aged Woman," "Giving Birth to Dignity," "The Liberation of Children," "To My White Working Class Sisters," as well as poetry, book reviews, and a history column.

83 US MAGAZINE. 4213 W. Bay Ave., Tampa, Fla. 33616. (813) 839-2892. Founded March 1973. Ginger Daire-Reber. m. $7/yr.

A news and literary feminist publication whose purpose is to bring feminist news to all areas of Florida.

VALLEY WOMEN'S CENTER NEWSLETTER. See 191.

VANCOUVER STATUS OF WOMEN NEWSLETTER. See 232.

VOICE FOR CHILDREN. See 399.

WASHINGTON AREA WOMEN'S CENTER NEWSLETTER. See 182.

WEAL NEWSLETTER. See 386.

84   WHOLE WOMAN NEWSPAPER. Women's Center, 836 E. Johnson St., Madison, Wis. 53703. (608) 244-0773. Founded September 1972. $3.50/yr; $10, institutions.

A feminist newspaper. One issue included articles on women in the East, lesbianism, and Joan of Arc, as well as poetry, notes on recent events, letters to the editor, and advertisements.

WIA: WOMEN IN THE ARTS NEWSLETTER. See 371.

THE WINDSOR WOMAN. See 241.

85   THE WOMAN ACTIVIST. 2310 Barbour Rd., Falls Church, Va. 22043. (703) 573-8716. Founded January 1971. Flora Crater, Ed. m. $5/yr., individual; $10, institutions.

"A monthly action bulletin for women's rights to provide current information and calls to act 'from the Courthouse to the White House'." Gives status of bills in Congress of interest to women, prints relevant excerpts from the *Congressional Record*, and recommends actions for women to take each month; i.e., letter-writing and lobbying.

86   WOMAN BECOMING. 1318 Singer Pl., Apt. 2, Wilkinsburg, Pa. 15221. Founded December 1972. Cassandra George. s-a. $1/issue, Pittsburgh; $1.50/issue, out-of-town.

A feminist literary magazine, which includes political polemics, fiction, poetry, and drawings.

WOMANKIND. See 184.

WOMANPOWER, A MONTHLY REPORT ON FAIR EMPLOYMENT FOR WOMEN. See 428.

A WOMAN'S PLACE NEWSLETTER. See 235.

WOMAN'S WORLD. See 200.

WOMANSPACE JOURNAL. See 370.

87   WOMEN: A JOURNAL OF LIBERATION. 3028 Greenmount Ave., Baltimore, Md. 21218. (301) 235-5245. Founded Fall 1969. Margaret Blanchard. irreg. $4/vol. (4 issues); $10, institutions.

"Encouraged by the growth and spirit of the women's movement, *Women: A Journal of Liberation* goes into its third volume of publication. Since the Journal was started . . . it has served as an expression of the ideas and creativity of a developing women's consciousness. We feel our magazine fills two purposes: to introduce women to our movement, and to further dialogue among women who are working for revolutionary change in our society. Our thematic format allows for an in-depth exploration of various problems and issues facing us." Thematic issues, available for $1 ($2.50 to institutions) include: Women in History, Women in the

Arts, Women in Revolution, Women as Workers under Capitalism, Sexuality, Aging, Children, Health Care, and Women Locked Up. Artwork, photography, articles, fiction, and poetry related to the themes of the issues are welcomed; articles should be limited to 5,000 words.

WOMEN FOR CHANGE NEWSLETTER. See 225.

WOMEN IN CELL BIOLOGY NEWSLETTER. See 553.

WOMEN IN COMMUNICATIONS, INC. MATRIX. See 559.

WOMEN IN COMMUNICATION, INC. NEWSLETTER. See 559.

88 WOMEN IN STRUGGLE. Box 325, Winneconne, Wis. 54986. Founded August 1970. J. C. Taylor, Ed. bi-m.

Newsletter on women's issues for Wisconsin. Recent writings included: "Jeanette Rankin—1880-1973," "Abortion Hearings," "Sports Notes," "Wisconsin Notes," and "Political Notes."

WOMEN LAWYERS JOURNAL. See 548.

89 WOMEN STUDIES ABSTRACTS. Box 1, Rush, N.Y. 14543. (716) 533-1376. Founded 1971. Sara Stauffer Whaley, Ed. q. $8.50, individuals; $7, students; $12, libraries and institutions.

Abstracts "articles, chapters of books, monographs, on the education and socialization of women; sex roles and characteristics; employment; sexuality; family; mental and physical health; family planning, childbirth, and abortion; history, literature, and art; the media; interpersonal relations; and the Women's Liberation Movement." Also includes an index to book reviews, and contains occasional bibliographical essays.

WOMEN TODAY. See 33.

WOMEN'S CAUCUS FOR POLITICAL SCIENCE NEWSLETTER. See 560.

WOMEN'S CENTER NEWSLETTER (Cambridge, Mass.). See 192.

WOMEN'S CENTER NEWSLETTER. (Poughkeepsie, N.Y.). See 207.

WOMEN'S INFORMATION CENTER NEWSLETTER. (Toronto, Can.). See 240.

WOMEN'S INTERART CENTER NEWSLETTER. See 375.

WOMEN'S LIBERATION CENTER NEWSLETTER. (Norwalk, Conn.). See 180.

WOMEN'S LIBERATION UNION NEWSLETTER. (Kansas City, Mo.). See 195.

WOMEN'S LOBBY QUARTERLY. See 514.

90   WOMEN'S PRESS. Box 562, Eugene, Oreg. 97401. (503) 344-4455. 1970. Kathy Mallea. m $3/yr.; 20¢/copy.

A women's newspaper collective reporting on the women's movement and raising feminist consiousness.

91   WOMEN'S RIGHTS LAW REPORTER. 180 University Ave., Newark, N.J. 07102. Founded July 1971. bi-a. $15/6 issues; $28, libraries; $3/single issue.

Published by law students at Rutgers School of Law, "to keep lawyers informed on recent developments in areas of law that effect women" and to aid feminist litigation. Covers education, health care, employment, abortion, marriage and divorce, etc.

92   WOMEN'S STUDIES: AN INTERDISCIPLINARY JOURNAL. Dept. of English, Queens College, Flushing, N.Y. 11367. (212) 445-7500. Founded 1972. Wendy Martin, Ed. 3/yr. $10, individuals; $29, libraries and institutions.

"Provides a forum for the presentation of scholarship and criticism about women in the field of literature, history, art, sociology, psychology, law, political science, economics, anthropology and the sciences. It also publishes poetry, short fiction, film and book reviews." Typescripts must be original work and should be submitted in triplicate to the Editor. Subscription orders should be sent to Gordon & Breach Science Publishers, 1 Park Ave. S., New York, N.Y. 10016.

WOMEN'S STUDIES NEWSLETTER. See 7.

93   WOMEN'S TRACK & FIELD WORLD. Box 371, Claremont, Calif. 91711. Founded June 1967. Vince Reel, Ed. m $5/yr.; 50¢/issue.

"The only publication in the world devoted exclusively to women's track and field." Also rents instructional films and publishes *WTFW Yearbook* ($5).

WOMEN'S VOICE OF GREATER HARTFORD. See 181.

94   WOMENSPORTS. 1660 S. Amphlett Blvd., Suite 266, San Mateo, Calif. 94402. (415) 574-4622. Founded 1974. Rosalie Muller Wright, Ed. m. $1/issue; $7.95/yr.

A new women's sports magazine copublished by Billy Jean and Larry W. King, which offers comprehensive coverage of women and sports. One issue included articles on swimming, basketball, sprinting, team sports, equipment, the psychology of women in sports, and relevant legislation.

WONAAC NEWSLETTER. See 495.

WYOMING COMMISSION ON THE STATUS OF WOMEN ANNUAL REPORT. See 348.

YWCA MAGAZINE. See 167.

YWCA WOMEN'S CENTER NEWSLETTER (Providence, R. I.). **See 223.**

ZERO POPULATION GROWTH. NATIONAL REPORTER. See 498.

Nonprint Media

(See also Art and Communications.)

95 ALLEND'OR PRODUCTIONS. 4321 Woodman Ave., Sherman Oaks, Calif. 91403. (213) 968-4622.

A film company which produces the following films of interest to women.

Planned Families (20 min., color, purchase $200, 16mm). Designed to teach the clinic patient the "how" of all modern, medically approved birth control methods. Spanish version available.

Freedom from Pregnancy (11 min., color, purchase $125, 16mm; 8mm; Super 8). Continues *Planned Families.* Designed to inform the clinic patient about the modern, medically approved tubal ligation and vasectomy operations. Spanish version available.

Unwanted Pregnancy (9 min., color, purchase $125, 16mm; 8mm; Super 8). Explores choices open to a pregnant woman: keeping the baby, adoption, or abortion. Emphasizes family planning methods.

ALVERNO COLLEGE RESEARCH CENTER ON WOMEN. See 143.

AMERICAN ASSOCIATION OF UNIVERSITY WOMEN. See 158.

AMERICAN MEDICAL WOMEN'S ASSOCIATION. See 525.

96 ANARYGOS FILM LIBRARY. 1815 Fairburn Ave., Los Angeles, Calif. 90025. (213) 474-9960. Founded June 1964. A. H. Cominos, Dir.

Distributor of Super-8 film loops on historical subjects, compiled from authentic newsreel sources, with film notes and bibliography; e.g., *Women Win Voting Rights.* Each cartridge runs approximately four minutes and costs $15.95.

ASSOCIATION FOR THE STUDY OF ABORTION. See 463.

ASSOCIATION OF AMERICAN LAW SCHOOLS COMMITTEE ON WOMEN IN LEGAL EDUCATION. see 538.

ATHENA ASSOCIATES. See 127.

BOYLE/KIRKMAN ASSOCIATES, INC. See 424.

CAMBRIDGE-GODDARD GRADUATE SCHOOL. See 416.

CELL 16. See 188.

CHANGE FOR CHILDREN. See 395.

CHICO WOMEN'S CENTER. See 173.

CHILDREN'S LIBERATION WORKSHOP. See 397.

CHINA BOOKS AND PERIODICALS. See 119.

97   CHURCHILL FILMS. 662 N. Robertson Blvd., Los Angeles, Calif. 90060. (213) 657-5710. Priscilla Forance.

A producer/distributor of 16mm educational films with a few available in 8mm. Films may be bought, rented, or leased and come with study guides. These three films will be of interest to women:

Campaign (20 min., color, purchase $230) Grass roots campaign of woman running for state senator.

Other Women, Other Work (20 min., color, purchase $230) Primarily for junior/senior high school girls seeking alternatives for careers other than the current stereotype.

Sylvia, Fran and Joy (25 min., b/w, purchase $150) How three young women feel about the roles of housekeeper, wife, and mother.

CINEMA FEMINA. See 365.

CLEARINGHOUSE FOR FEMINIST MEDIA. See 358.

98   CREATIVE FILM SOCIETY. 7237 Canby Ave., Reseda, Calif. 91335. (213) 881-3887. Founded 1957. Robert Pike, Exec. Dir.

Following is a list of films by women, a strong point of this company.

Charlie Company By Nancy Edell (9 min., color, rental $10).

Circles by Doris Chase (7 min., color, rental $15, purchase $135).

Color Rhapsodie by Mary Ellen Bute (7 min., color, rental $10, purchase $135).

Cycles by Linda Jassim (11 min., color, rental $15, purchase $135).

Enigma by Lillian Schwartz and Ken Knowlton (5 min., color, rental $22.50, purchase $135).

A Painter's Journal by Renata Druks and featuring Anais Nin (10 min., color, rental $10).

Phyllis and Terry by Eugene and Carol Marner (36 min., b/w, rental $20).

Polka Graph by Mary Ellen Bute (6 min., color, rental $4, purchase $120).

Rama by "Sugar" Cain (16 min., color, rental $15).

Spook Sport by Mary Ellen Bute (9 min., color, rental $10, purchase $135).

EMMA WILLARD TASK FORCE ON EDUCATION. See 401.

FEMINIST HISTORY RESEARCH PROJECT. See 149.

FEMINIST RESOURCES FOR EQUAL EDUCATION. See 402.

FEMINIST WOMEN'S HEALTH CENTER SELF-HELP CLINIC. See 471.

FORT WORTH EDUCATIONAL TASK FORCE. See 403.

GEORGE WASHINGTON UNIVERSITY, CONTINUING EDUCATION
FOR WOMEN CENTER. See 410.

HERSTORY. See 156.

99 HERSTORY FILMS, INC. 137 E. 13 St., New York, N.Y. 10003. (212)
260-0324. Founded 1974. Marian Hunter, Dir.

"Herstory Films is a women's 16mm production company making films to
document the important actions and events in the lives of women otherwise distorted or ignored by the established media." Two films are available for rental or
purchase: *Roll Over* (10 min., color, rental $20, purchase $200) which is about
women working in typical and atypical situations; and *Do You Take This Woman?*
(b/w) about the myth and reality of marriage, and including speakers from the
N.Y. Radical Feminists' Conference on Marriage.

100 IMPACT FILMS. 144 Bleeker St., New York, N.Y. 10012. (212) 674-3375.
Founded 1966. Fred Deutsch.

Film distributor of documentary, experimental, and feature films covering
feminist concerns and consumerism.
Behind the Veil (50 min., color, rental $95, purchase $600).
Black Woman (52 min., b/w, rental $45).
The Ceiling (40 min., b/w, rental $40).
Goodbye in the Mirror (80 min., b/w, rental $50).
Growing Up Female (60 min., b/w, rental $70, purchase $375).
Roberta Flack (30 min., color, rental $40).
Something Different (80 min., b/w, rental $50).
Three Lives, produced by Kate Millet (70 min., color, rental, $75, purchase
$750).
Women Talking (80 min., b/w, rental $50, purchase $650).
Women Who Have Had an Abortion (29 min., color, rental $40, purchase
$325).
You Don't Have to Buy War, Mrs. Smith with Bess Myerson (30 min., b/w,
rental $25, purchase $200).

INDIANAPOLIS MAYOR'S TASK FORCE ON WOMEN. See 283.

INFORMATION CENTER ON THE MATURE WOMAN. See 150.

INTERSTATE ASSOCIATION OF COMMISSIONS ON THE STATUS OF
WOMEN. See 249.

JACQUELINE CEBALLOS PRODUCTIONS. See 425.

JOHNS, NORRIS ASSOCIATES. See 429.

LANLYRE LIGGERA. See 15.

LAVENDER WOMAN. See 14.

101 McGRAW-HILL CONTEMPORARY FILMS. 1221 Ave. of the Americas, New York, N.Y. 10020. (212) 997-6613. Eileen G. Roth.

A film and audiovisual production and distribution organization which publishes a catalog on multiethnic materials which includes materials on women.

Films

Aretha Franklin, Soul Singer (25 min., color, rental $25, purchase $325).

Cleo from 5 to 7 (90 min., b/w, classroom rental $50, admission charged $75).

A Doll (10 min., color, rental $14.50, sale $145).

Donna and Gail: A Study in Friendship (49 min., b/w, rental $25, sale $350).

Fear Women (29 min., color, rental $11, sale $275).

Gertrude Stein: When This You See, Remember Me (90 min., 3 parts, color, classroom rental $50, admission charged $75, sale $850).

Harriet Tubman and the Underground Railroad (54 min., b/w, rental $29, sale $350).

Helen Keller and Her Teacher (27 min., color, rental $29, sale $350).

I Am Somebody (18 min., color, rental $30, sale $360).

Laurette (20 min., b/w, rental $12).

Margaret Sanger (15 min., b/w, rental $12, sale $90).

Mariana (29 min., color, rental $11, sale $260).

Phoebe: Story of a Premarital Pregnancy (28 min., b/w, rental $14, sale $200).

The Women Get the Vote (27 min., b/w, rental $10, sale $150).

Women on the March: The Struggle for Equal Rights (60 min., 2 parts, b/w, rental $28, sale $410).

Women up in Arms (19 min., b/w, rental $8, sale $130).

Filmstrips

Jane Addams. Susan B. Anthony (part of the American Leaders Series; each one $7.50).

Patricia Harris (part of Black Americans in Government Series; $20 with record and guide, $22 with cassette and guide).

Shirley Chisholm (part of Black Americans in Government Series; $20 with record and guide, $22 with cassette and guide).

102 MACMILLAN AUDIO BRANDON. 34 MacQuesten Pkwy S., Mt. Vernon, N.Y. 10550. (914) 664-5051. Robert Edelson, Promotion Dept.

A nontheatrical 16mm film distributor with many feature films of interest to women. A price list for the following films will be sent upon request.

Bed and Sofa (U.S.S.R.) "one of the earliest films depicting women's liberation."

The Country Doctor (U.S.S.R.) "female doctor must overcome mistrust."

The Nun (France) "Diderot story of 18th century woman who becomes a nun against her wishes."

The Pumpkin Eater (Great Britain) "psychological study of neurotic married woman."

Salt of the Earth (U.S.) "role of women in Mexican-American zinc-miners' strike."

Schmeerguntz (U.S.) "experimental study of married woman."

She and He (Japan) "wife examines her role in marriage."

Window Water Baby Moving (U.S.) "experimental film showing natural childbirth."

Woman (U.S.) "1918 film of woman's degraded status from Garden of Eden to World War I."

103 MEDIA PLUS, INC. 60 Riverside Dr., New York, N.Y. 10024. (212) 873-5343. Founded 1968. Ann Grifalconi, Pres.

Produces and distributes educational film strip programs, posters and stickers. One program is *The Silenced Majority: A Women's Liberation Multimedia Kit* containing five color filmstrips with five records or cassettes: *Liberation Now*; *Women, Jobs and the Law*; *Women and Education*; *This Ad Insults Women*; and *Rapping with the Feminists.* Narrated by Arlene Francis and designed for high school, college, or adult audiences the cost is $75 for records and $85 for tapes. Other programs are also available.

MS. See **66**.

NATIONAL ASSOCIATION FOR REPEAL OF ABORTION LAWS. See **480**.

NATIONAL FEDERATION OF BUSINESS AND PROFESSIONAL WOMEN'S CLUBS, INC. See **162**.

NEW FEMINIST TALENT, INC. See **365**.

104 NATIONAL FILM BOARD OF CANADA. 150 Kent St., Ottawa, Ont., Can. (613) 992-4166. 3155 Cote de Liesse Rd., Montreal 379, Quebec, Can. 1251 Ave. of the Americas, New York, N.Y. 10020. (212) 586-2400, ext. 277. Founded May 1939.

The official filmmaker and distributor of Canada, which produces films in French and English. Its films "relate to the common interests of Canadians and the interests they share with other people around the world." Also produces filmstrips, slide sets, overhead projectuals, multimedia kits, and photo stories. Productions are available for use by schools, universities, television stations, theaters, and commercial outlets. Distribution is international. Following is a list of films of interest to women. Write for catalog for distributor and price information.

A Matter of Life (65 min., b/w). A young Montreal matron, abandoned by her husband, works in a clothing factory to support her three children.
Mrs. Case (14 min., b/w). A single parent attempts to bring up her children in an impoverished area of a big city.
Three Women Stories: Caroline, Fabienne, Francoise (each part 29 min., b/w). Three films portraying the change in the life of women in French Canada.
Women on the March: The Struggle for Equal Rights (2 parts, 29 min. each, b/w). A film record of the tempestuous struggle for equal rights that characterized the suffragist movement.

105 NEW DAY FILMS. Box 315, Franklin Lakes, N.J. 07417. (201) 891-8240. Founded 1971. Liane Brandon. 6 members.

A group of independent filmmakers who have formed a distributive cooperative concerned with women's experience, ideas, feelings, and situations that relate to the changing consciousness of women today. Some films for women are listed below.

Anything You Want to Be (8 min., rental $15, purchase $100).
Betty Tells Her Story (20 min., rental $25, purchase $200).
Growing Up Female (60 min., rental $60, purchase $375).
It Happens to Us (30 min., rental $30, purchase $325).

Joyce at 34 (28 min., rental $35, purchase $350).
Sometimes I Wonder Who I Am (5 min., rental $12, purchase $85).
Woo Who? May Wilson (33 min., rental $35, purchase $375).

N.J. WOMEN'S INFORMATION AND REFERRAL SERVICE. See 152.

106 NEW LINE CINEMA. 121 University Pl., New York, N.Y. 10024. (212) 674-7460. Founded 1967. Elaine Sperber, Spec. Events Coor.

A film distribution company whose "philosophy has been to make available whatever is unique and exciting in film." Following are some films of special interest to women: *The Girls* (*Flickorna*) by Mai Zetterling (100 min., b/w., $250); *The Best of the New York Festival of Women's Films*, a group of short films made entirely by women: *Crocus* by Suzan Pitt Kraning, *Cycles* by Linda Jassim, *Opening/ Closing* by Kathleen Laughlin, *The Gibbous Moon* by Nancy Ellen Dowd, and *Commuters* by Claudia Weill ($300); and *Tales* by Cassandra Gerstein (70 min., b/w, $125).

Prices represent average rental, and cost is contingent on exhibition context, admission charged, and particular needs. "No New Line film has ever been prevented from showing because of unreasonable price."

107 NEWSREEL. 26 W. 20 St., New York, N.Y. 10011. (212) 243-2310. Founded October 1967.

"In Newsreel films it is the people who speak out, and they speak out strongly against economic exploitation, racism, sexism, and U.S. military aggression in Southeast Asia. Newsreel's goal is to place the power of the film media into the hands of the poor and working people, to serve their interests and needs. The various Newsreel groups have made over sixty documentaries. All the films are made in conjunction with grass-roots organizers—in the community and on the job." Following is a list of feminist productions.

Childcare: Peoples Liberation (20 min., rental $20).
Day of Plane Hunting (20 min., rental $20).
Growing Up Female (60 min., rental $70).
Herstory (9 min., rental $10).
Jeannette Rankin Brigade (8 min., rental $10).
Make Out (5 min., rental $10).
My Country Occupied (30 min., rental $35).
She's Beautiful When She's Angry (17 min., rental $20).
The Woman's Film (40 min., rental $50).
Women of Telecommunications Station #6 (20 min., rental $35).

Contact the nearest Newsreel office for rental; discounts are available to high schools.

Ann Arbor Newsreel, Box 321, Ann Arbor, Mich. 48107. (313) 769-7353.
Boston Newsreel, 595 Massachusetts Ave., Cambridge, Mass. 02139. (617) 864-2600.
Detroit Newsreel, 3576 Piquette, Detroit, Mich. 48211. (313) 925-8975.
Lawrence Newsreel, 815 Vermont St., Lawrence, Kans. 66044. (913) 842-9142.
Milwaukee Newsreel, 1618 W. Wells, Milwaukee, Wis. 53233. (414) 342-4020.
San Francisco Newsreel, 1232 Market St., San Francisco, Calif. 94102. (415) 621-6195.

Yellow Springs Newsreel, Antioch Union, Antioch College, Yellow Springs, Ohio 45387. (513) 767-8001.

108 PACIFICA PROGRAM SERVICE/PACIFICA TAPE LIBRARY. 5316 Venida Blvd., Los Angeles, Calif. 90019. (213) 913-1625. Founded 1947. Lucy Robins.

Pacifica Foundation is a broadcasting institution with four stations: KPFA (Northern California), KPFK (Southern California), WBAI (New York), and KPFT (Houston) and 60 affiliate stations, "mostly educational noncommercial stations." Its aim is "to explore the causes of strife between individuals and nation . . ." Pacifica Tape Library provides audio tapes and cassettes of Pacifica programs for schools, colleges and libraries; Pacifica Program Service is a broadcast distribution service to non-profit/educational radio stations located principally on school, college and university campuses throughout the U.S. and Canada. Both carry many tape programs of interest to women. Pacifica states: "Many currents of social change have converged to make the New Feminism an idea whose time has come. Better education has broadened women's views beyond the home, heightened their awareness of the possibilities—and their sense of frustration when those possibilities are not realized. Just who is the American woman and where is she going? The following programs represent a variety of perspectives, past and present, on this question." These include:

Abortion: Beyond Legalization (54 min.)
Adrienne Rich Reading Her Poems (19 min.)
The Affair of Gabrielle Russier (58 min.)
All Issues are Women's Issues (39 min.)
American Women in History (65 min.)
An Evening with Anais Nin (91 min.)
An Interview with Anais Nin (24 min.)
An Interview with Juliette Mitchell (43 min.)
Bard At Large (44 min.)
The Changing Lives of Women Around the Globe (70 min.)
The Contemporary Lesbian: Beyond Stereotypes (87 min.)
Courageous Sisters (60 min.)
Do Women Dare? (60 min.)
Dream Power (43 min.)
Education and the Weaker Sex (15 min.)
Feminist Art Movement (38 min.)
Feminist Forum: The Equal Rights Amendment (27 min.)
Feminist Forum: Selling Women Short (28 min.)
Feminist Forum: Women's National Abortion Action Coalition (27 min.)
Germine Greer Meets the National Press Club (58 min.)
Growing Up Female in the 50's (78 min.)
Here She Is!: The Making of Miss America (55 min.)
Kathleen Cleaver on Black Panther Politics & The Feminist Movement (34 min.)
A Lady Doesn't Take Karate (55 min.)
The Lawrence Strike (35 min.)
The Lesbians (50 min.)
Me Jane, You Tarzan (35 min.)
Menstrual Blood (46 min.)
Mothers and Daughters (38 min.)
Off We Go ("Air Wacs") (52 min.)

On Sylvia Plath (89 min.)
The Plight of Women in Broadcasting (70 min.)
Poems for Uppity Women (22 min.)
Promise Her Anything (71 min.)
Pro-Life: The Movement in California Against Abortion (61 min.)
Psychology of Abortion & Birth Control (55 min.)
The Psychology of Inferiority (15 min.)
Reaction to "Three Women" (32 min.)
Robin Morgan Reads Her Poems (37 min.)
Sappho Was A Right On Woman (59 min.)
Sexual Liberation and Women's Liberation (75 min.)
She Also Ran . . . (31 min.)
Sherry Finkhine on Abortion (26 min.)
Shirley Chisholm at Mills College: Women in Politics—Why Not? (66 min.)
Socialization: The Pink Blanket Routine (17 min.)
Three Women by Sylvia Plath (26 min.)
Training Woman to Know Her Place (60 min.)
True Story (60 min.)
Womankind: Everyone Was Brave (15 min.)
Womankind: Radical Feminists (30 min.)
Woman's Abortion Coalition (58 min.)
A Woman's Cry (58 min.)
Women as Health Consumers (65 min.)
Women in Art (62 min.)
Women in Media (60 min.)
Women in the Arts: In The Beginning (34 min.)
Women in the Universities (15 min.)
Women is Losers (63 min.)
Women of the Press: Harriet Van Horne (21 min.)
Women's Center Feminist Theatre (60 min.)
Women's Liberation and the Arts (65 min.)
Women's Liberation in Mexico (25 min.)
The Women's School: Woman's Liberation and Black Civil Rights (72 min.)

Pre-paid prices to schools, colleges, libraries and educational organizations are $8.50 for 30 minutes or less, $10.00 for 31 to 60 minutes, $12.00 for 61 to 90 minutes, $14.00 for 91 to 120 minutes, and $16.00 for 121 to 150 minutes. Specify cassette or 7″ reel 3¾ ips, title and price of each program. PTL tapes or cassettes cannot be used for broadcast. Radio stations contact Pacifica Program Service.

PLANNED PARENTHOOD FEDERATION OF AMERICA, INC. See 482.

PROJECT HEAR. See 398.

RADICAL WOMEN (Seattle, Wash.). See 227.

109   RADIO FREE PEOPLE. 133 Mercer St., New York, N.Y. 10012. (212) 966-6729. Founded 1967. Jeriann Hilderley.

"Radio Free People is a collective of volunteers which provides a radical perspective on the daily struggles of people to free themselves from oppressive institutions. We not only support this struggle, we are proud of it. Our contribution is in the production and distribution of audiotaped programs. We make available tapes of talks, songs, poetry, documentaries, collages and drama having to do with revolutionary social change. Many of these are produced by us; others are sent to us by movement groups and artists for distribution. These programs are used by over 100 radio stations, as well as many community groups, classes and individuals." Following is a list of tapes of interest to women (see end of list for explanation of price codes).

Beverly Grant: Chain Reaction (50 min., $6 for 2 track, $10 for 1 track). Songs.

Cock Rock (13 min., price code B). A second look at rock music.

Diane di Prima Reads (29 min., price code D).

Diane Di Prima: The Revolutionary Letters (29 min., price code D). A reading.

Free Our Sisters, Free Ourselves (29 min., price code D). A documentary of Nov. 22, 1969 Black Panther rally in New Haven, Conn.

Gettin' On Woman (18 min., price code B). Songs, sung by Beverly Grant.

I Wish I Knew How It Would Feel to Be Free (31 min., price code D). A rap session.

I'm a Woman (36 min., price code D). Poetry, music, raps.

I'm Female, I'm Proud (29 min., price code D). Deals with business, advertising, and women.

Interview with Angela Davis (25 min., price code C).

Laying Down the Tower (36 min., price code E). Poems by Marge Piercy.

Marge Piercy: Poems (30 min., price code D).

My Body Is Mine to Control (31 min., price code D). Songs, sung by Beverly Grant.

Ruthie Gorton: Last Days of Rome (60 min., $6 for 2 track, $10 for 1 track).

Ruthie Gorton: This Bird Is Learning How to Fly (60 min., $6 for 2 track, $10 for 1 track). Songs by Ruthie Gorton.

This Tape Is about Abortion (10 min., price code A).

Up Against the Mattress: Down in the Valley (10 min., price code A). A consciousness-raiser.

Women in Prison (10 min., price code A).

Price Code	7½ ips		3¾ ips	
	1st class	*4th class*	*1st class*	*4th class*
A	$2.60	$2.10	$1.85	$1.55
B	3.60	2.85	2.50	2.20
C	4.50	3.75	3.20	2.85
D	5.70	4.50	3.85	3.40
E	8.00	6.60	5.55	4.85

Institutional Rate: All tapes $10, A–D; $20, E.

110 RADIO FREE WOMEN OF WASHINGTON, D.C. 1725 17 St., N.W., No. 115, Washington, D.C. 20009. (202) 332-8032. Founded February 1972. Shirl Smith.

Feminist radio productions producing 30-and 60-minute radio tapes. Sixty-minute tapes include interviews with Margaret Sloan and Gloria Steinem; women from the Washington area Women's Center (how it got started and what it hopes to be); Carol Burris (Women's Lobby, Inc.); Myrna Lamb (playwright); and The Furies (a lesbian separatist collective). Available on 30-minute tapes are interviews with Robin Morgan; Jill Johnson; the DC Rape Crisis Center and the politics of rape; the Washington area Feminist theatre; Anna Marie Troger on the women's movement in Germany; Cris Williamson, singer/writer; Washington area Women's Center; Women's Institute for Freedom of the press; Sydney Abbott; National Committee on Household Employment; and Maria Roas della Costa on the women's movement in Italy and Selma James on the women's movement in England.

There are issue-oriented programs on leadership: a discussion with Bev Fischer and Charlotte Bunch, two local leaders with the women's movement; separatism, i.e., lesbian, and class, and race separatism; a discussion with waitresses on their work; Lily's Open House (a social place for lesbians); classism in the women's movement; women and cable television; and technology and poetry by lesbians Rita Mae Brown and Lee Lally.

Price Information (per show); $5, 7½ ips stereo reel to reel; $4.50, 3¾ ips stereo reel to reel; $4.50, stereo cassette tapes. For 30-minute shows, shows on the flip side of the tape cost an additional $2.50.

111   ROUNDER RECORDS. 65 Park St., Somerville, Mass. 02143.

"An antiprofit collective that produces records and concerts and distributes other very small record labels." Dedicated to making available noncommercial music of American culture: bluegrass, black country blues, and protest music. Available records are: "Mountain Moving Day" by the New Haven and Chicago Women's Liberation Rock bands, $3.50, and "Aunt Molly Jackson" protest songs, $3.50.

112   SECOND MOON MUSIC 12347 17 Ave., N.E., Seattle, Wash. 08125. (206) 364-9936. Founded January 1972. Jody Aliesan.

Items currently available are: "You'll Be Hearing More from Me," LP album of feminist songs, written and sung by Jody Aliesan, $4.25; $3.32 bulk and *To Set Free*, poems by Jody Aliesan, $1.50; 85¢ bulk.

SOPHIA SMITH COLLECTION. See 154.

U.S. EQUAL EMPLOYMENT OPPORTUNITY COMMISSION. See 256.

VALLEY WOMEN'S CENTER FILM CO-OP. (Northampton, Mass.). See 191.

113   WOMEN MAKE MOVIES, INC. 107 W. 26 St., New York, N.Y. 10001. (212) 929-6477. Founded 1969. Ariel Doughtery, Sheila Parge, Co-Dirs.

A nonprofit, educational, tax-exempt corporation which administers Chelsea Picture Station, a neighborhood media workshop. Teaches professional film, video, and radio skills to those who would not ordinarily receive such training. Aims to present a wide national audience with a new image about the real lives of women, through films like those listed below.

Domestic Tranquility (7 min., b/w, rental $12.25, purchase $70).
Fear (7 min., b/w, rental $12.25, purchase $70).
For Better or Worse (7 min., rental $12.25, purchase $70).
Girl, You Need a Change of Mind (8 min., b/w, rental $14, purchase $80).
It's a Miracle (5 min., b/w, rental $8.75, purchase $50).
Just Looking (6 min., b/w, rental $10.50, purchase $60).
Katie Kelly (5 min., b/w, rental $8.75, purchase $50).
Paranoia Blues (5 min., b/w, rental $8.75, purchase $50).

Sweet Bananas (30 min., color, rental $30, purchase $300).
Testing, Testing, How Do You Do? (4 min., color, rental $8, purchase $40).
The Trials of Alice Crimmins (6 min., b/w, rental $10.50, pruchase $60).
The Women's Happy Time Commune (50 min., color, rental $50, purchase
$500).

WOMEN ON WORDS AND IMAGES. See 407.

WOMEN'S CENTER (Cambridge, Mass.). See 192.

WOMEN'S CENTRE, YWCA (Montreal, Can.). See 243.

114 WOMEN'S FILM COOP. 200 Main St., Northampton, Mass. 01060. (413)
586-2011. Founded 1970.

A collective which rents and maintains a library of feminist films. WFC plans
to establish a resource center including facilities for filmmaking, videotaping, radio
productions and "other media arts from which women have traditionally been ex-
cluded." A catalog is available with film annotations, reviews of commerical films,
and a list of film distributors ($1.50, individuals, $2, institutions). The catalog fits
a loose-leaf binder. Following is a list of films available from WFC.

Abortion (30 min., b/w, $20).
Breakfast Dance (6 min., b/w, $10).
Do Blonds Have More Fun (1½ min., color, $5).
Happy Mother's Day (30 min., b/w, $50).
Home Movie (10 min., b/w $15).
Make Out (10 min., b/w, $10).
Sisters (21 min., color, $25).
Sometimes I Wonder Who I Am (10 min., b/w, $10).
Windy Day (20 min., color, $25).
Women in Viet Nam (slides, $10).
Women's Film (50 min., b/w, $50).
Women's Images in Advertising (slides, $10).

WOMEN'S HEALTH CLINIC. See 493.

WOMEN'S INTERART CENTER. See 375.

115 WOMEN'S INVOLVEMENT PROGRAM. 341 Bloor St., W., Suite 309,
Toronto, 181, Ontario, Can. (416) 921-6591. Founded January 1972.

A woman's video production crew desiring to use media for the documenta-
tion of women's struggles and exchange of information and experiences.

All programs are available for a $10 weekly rental charge (plus $20 deposit) to
individuals and groups, and $20 weekly rental to institutions.

Following is a list of programs available on one-half inch video tape.

Abortion: history of abortion practices, attitudes and the law.
Anatomy and Birth Control: study of the female reproductive system and
birth control methods.
Another Generation: discussion among women over 30.
Free Mum, Free Dad, Free Daycare: discussion of daycare.
History I: women in Canadian history from 1608 to 1867.
History II: women in Canada from 1867 to the 1950s.

Rape, Justice and Karate: a discussion of rape.
Rita MacNeil: half-hour performance by Canadian feminist composer and
   singer.
Socialization: how socialization begins and continues to influence children.
Women at Work: interviews with women workers, paid and unpaid.

WOMEN'S LIBERATION CENTER OF PHILADELPHIA. Media Workshop.
See **220.**

WOMEN'S LIBERATION UNION (Kansas City, Mo.).   See **195.**

WOMEN'S MEDIA EXCHANGE. See **376.**

WOMEN'S RESOURCE CENTER, UNIVERSITY OF UTAH. See **226.**

WOMEN'S TRACK AND FIELD WORLD. See **93.**

YOUNG WOMEN'S CHRISTIAN ASSOCIATION OF THE U.S.A. See **167.**

News Services, Bookstores, and Specialized Book Distributors

News Services

THE CSW REPORT. See 325.

FEMINIST PARTY. See 510.

116 LIBERATION NEWS SERVICE. 160 Claremont Ave., New York, N.Y. 10027. (212) 749-2200. Founded August 1967.

Provides news from a radical perspective to underground, college, and community papers, radio stations, and radical organizations here and abroad. Semiweekly packets of news copy and graphic material are sent out Tuesdays and Fridays to approximately 600 subscribers. A wide variety of subjects are covered, including the women's movement. Rates are on a sliding scale from $20 a month for underground newspapers to approximately $40 a month for commercial organizations.

117 WOMEN'S NEWS SERVICE. 8881 W. Pico St., Los Angeles, Calif. 90035. (213) 837-1977. Founded March 1973. Lindsey Lambert, Exec. Dir.

Produces a daily 50-minute package of women's news for radio syndication.

Bookstores and Book Distributors

118 AMAZON BOOKSTORE. 808 W. Lake St., Minneapolis, Minn. 55408. (612) 824-5407. Founded 1971.

A feminist bookstore run by a working collective of women, to provide women in the area with books, periodicals, pamphlets, and posters, by, for, and about women as cheaply as possible (10 percent below cover price) or through a lending library. Write for catalog.

119 CHINA BOOKS AND PERIODICALS. 2929 24 St., San Francisco, Calif. 94110. (415) 282-6945. Also 125 Fifth Ave., New York, N.Y. 10003. (212) 677-2650. Also 900 W. Armitage, Chicago, Ill. 60614. (312) 549-3236.

National U.S. distributor and importer of publications from China and Vietnam, with many titles of interest to women. Children's books include *The Little Doctor* (35¢) and *Stories from Liu Hu-lan's Childhood* (35¢). Among other books and pamphlets are *New Women in New China* (1973, 80 pp, 50¢); *Red Detachment of Women* (1973, 169 pp., $2.50); *Chinese Women Liberated* by Russell Maud (50¢); and *A Daughter of Han* by Lao T'ai-t'ai, as told to Ida Pruit (254 pp., $2.95). Also available are a postcard set, *Red Detachment of Women* (50¢), and two records, "The White Haired Girl" (33⅓ LP, $8.95) and "Red Detachment of Women," #6165-67 (33⅓ LP, $8.95).

120   Q. M. DABNEY & CO., INC. Box 31061, Washington, D.C. 20031. (301) 423-9077. Founded 1968. Donna L. Mason.

Booksellers specializing in old and out-of-print books on women. A catalog is available for 25¢.

121   FEMINIST BOOK MART. 162-11 9th Ave., Whitestone, N.Y. 11357. (212) 767-0633. Founded March 1971. Donna Loercher, Pres.

"A national book service distributing women's literature and nonsexist children's books to individuals, schools, libraries, groups, etc." Run and staffed by feminists, the Feminist Book Mart has an extensive, 20-page catalog with recommended books on women's health, sexuality, marriage, biography, women and the arts, fiction, children's books, and paperbacks. Bulk rates are available.

122   FIRST THINGS FIRST—BOOKS FOR WOMEN—A FE-MAIL ORDER HOUSE AND MOBILE UNIT. 23 7 St., S.E., Washington, D.C. 20003. (202) 546-4951. Founded January 1973. Susan Sojourner.

"A nonprofit educational corporation to disseminate books, posters, articles, jewelry, etc. on women's liberation, feminist, the problems of the sexist society, nonsexist children's materials and books by and about women authors, poetc, etc." Provides a basic list of juvenile and adult books for libraries.

GAY LIBERATION BOOK SERVICE. See 56.

KNOW INC. See 13.

123   LABYRIS BOOKS. 33 Barrow St., New York, N.Y. 10014. (212) 741-3460.

Feminist bookstore, carrying books of interest to women by movement and commercial publishers, including books for young readers.

MIDNITE SPECIAL BOOKSTORE. See 10.

NEW HOGTOWN PRESS. See 22.

OUR GENERATION. See 71.

124   SISTERHOOD BOOKSTORE. 1357 Westwood Blvd., Los Angeles, Calif. 90024. (213) 477-7300. Founded November 1, 1972. Adele Wallace, Simone Gold, Gahan Phillips, partners.

Has a large selection of feminist books (biographies, poetry, novels by and about women), journals, posters, jewelry, bumper stickers, pottery, and nonsexist children's books.

VANCOUVER WOMEN'S BOOKSTORE. See 233.

125 THE WOMAN'S VOICE BOOKSTORE. 673 S. Pearl St., Denver, Colo. 80209. (303) 733-1178. Founded December 1972. Lea Kell, 2499 Pierce St., Denver, Colo. 80214.

Stocks materials on women's liberation, health care, psychology and sociology of women, autobiography and biography of women, drama and poetry of interest to women, fiction, and nonsexist children's literature. This feminist enterprise also sells posters, jewelry, records, pins, stationary, T-shirts, newspapers, journals, and pamphlets. Write for literature list.

WOMEN'S INFORMATION CENTRE (Toronto, Can.) See 240.

Products by Feminists for Feminists

ALERT, THE CONNECTICUT LEGISLATIVE REVIEW FOR WOMEN.
See 41.

126 AMANI. 2720 Keynier Ave., Los Angeles, Calif. 90034. (213) 836-6155.

Jewelry for the women's movement, available for use as fund-raisers: pendants, rings and pins, in antiqued gold plate or rhodium plate. Send for brochure.

127 ATHENA ASSOCIATES, INC. 1400 N. Uhle St., Arlington, Va. 22201. (703) 527-5144. Founded January 1973. Sandra M. Hill, Treas. 605 N. Florida St., Arlington, Va. 22203.

A feminist corporation which designs, manufactures, distributes and sells products relating to the women's movement; and also provides consulting services to the women's movement. Available now is a 45 rpm stereo record of original feminist songs written by Mary E. Lord and Georgia W. Fuller and sung by Mary E. Lord. The record has three songs: "She Made the Hurricane," "Love Is Life," and "Remeeting Tomorrow." Single record is $1.25; three records, $3.25. Rates for more copies are available on request.

128 BEAHIVE ENTERPRISES. Box 87, Williamsbridge Sta., Bronx, N.Y. 10467. (212) 655-7843. Founded August 1970. Bea Baron, Pres.

A mail-order feminist business selling movement fund-raisers, such as buttons, jewelry, bumper stickers, posters, T-shirts, stationery, etc. to feminist groups and to individuals. Bulk rates are available. Also sells movement literature. A catalog costs 25¢.

CELL 16. See 188.

CHICAGO WOMEN'S GRAPHICS COLLECTION. See 184.

CHINA BOOKS AND PERIODICALS. See 119.

CLITARTISTS. See 359.

129 COLLAGE AND ROAD CRAFTS. 246 Sparks St., Ottawa, Can. Founded July 1971. Alma Norman, 207 Charlotte St., No. 4, Ottawa, Ontario, Can.

A shop providing encouragement and an outlet for craftswomen, especially those just starting.

130   BARBARA B. COOPER HANDWEAVING AND JEWELRY. Franconia College, Franconia, N.H. 03580. (609) 443-5973.

Feminist pendants available in brass, copper, or silver, and handwoven shoulder bags. Write for brochure.

131   THE EQUATION COLLECTIVE INC. Box 4307, Sunnyside, N.Y. 11104. (212) 392-8374. Founded October 1972. Lorraine M. Allen, Pres.

A toiletries company planning "to become an alternative to the unanimously sexist toiletries companies which now exist, and to open up employment opportunities for women who have been denied advancement in this field." Presently available is ginger ale-scented equality gift soap-on-a-rope, $3.

132   ERA ENTERPRISES. Box 1301, Capital Hill Sta., Seattle, Wash. 98112. (206) 325-0793. Founded 1973. Shirlie Kaplan, 1508 10th Ave., E., Seattle, Wash. 98102.

A wholesale and retail mail-order firm selling feminist products, established to design and make consciousness-raising items for the women's movement. Products include the ERA tote bag ($3 plus 39¢ postage), stationery, posters, bumper stickers, patches, greeting cards, jewelry, book plates, address labels, and labels with feminist slogans. Write for brochure.

THE FEMINISTS. See 198.

FIRST THINGS FIRST—Books for Women—**A Fe-Mail Order House and Mobile Unit.** See 122.

133   ALICA FOSTER'S PATCHWORK FASHIONS AND CRAFTS. 1643 Beaver St., Santa Rosa, Calif. 95404. (707) 528-1326. Founded June 1973. Alica Foster.

A one-woman, feminist, mail-order fashions and crafts business which sells patchwork, calico, gingham clothes, pillows, and accessories. Write for catalog.

134   GREYFALCON HOUSE. 60 Riverside Dr., New York, N.Y. 10024. (212) 873-5543. Founded 1970. Ann Grifalconi, Pres.
See also Media Plus, Inc., entry 103.

Produces posters and stationery with a woman's liberation theme. Graphics include ". . . God Created Women . . ." (b/w, 20″ X 28,″ $2 each) and ". . . Ain't I a Woman . . ." (2-color, 23″ X 34,″ $3 each).

JOYFUL WORLD PRESS. See 12.

KNOW, INC. See 13.

135   LIBERATION ENTERPRISES. 131 Joralemon St., Brooklyn, N.Y. 11201. (212) 852-0033. Founded February 1972. Stephanie Marcus.

Products include jewelry in brass and silver, stationery, rubber stamps, aprons, sweatshirts and posters designed and/or produced by feminists.

136 MÅNA WORKSHOP. Box 11618, Fort Worth, Tex. 76109. (817) 923-2498. Founded 1972. Shirley Hillard, Pres. 3800 Trailwood La., Fort Worth, Tex. 76109.

Produces original designs in bumper stickers, recycled paper stationery products, and educational teaching aids. Bumper stickers of interest to feminists include "She Is Risen," "Trust in God—She'll Provide," "Women Belong in the House—and in the Senate" (50¢ each or $3/dozen, direct mail; wholesale prices available for retail outlets.

MARIN WOMEN'S NEWS JOURNAL. See **63.**

MEDIA PLUS, INC. See **103.**

NEW ENGLAND FREE PRESS. See **21.**

137 JOYCE NIELSEN, FEMINIST JEWELRY. 638 S. Mansfield Ave., Los Angeles, Calif. 90036. (213) 933-2876 or 938-0353.

Offers a selection of rings, pendants, and buckles in gold plate and sterling silver in various feminist designs. Write for brochures and prices.

NOW FEMINIST PRODUCTS CATALOG. See **163.**

SHAMELESS HUSSY PRESS. See **30.**

SISTERHOOD BOOKSTORE. See **124.**

138 SOUL SURVIVOR. 143 Woodland Ave., New Rochelle, N.Y. 10805. (914) 632-8252. Founded July 1973. Pat McLean.

A mail-order business owned and operated by women, "to offer women high quality, handmade merchandise for low prices." All merchandise is designed by women and made to order. Clothing, handbags, jewelry, and belts are available. Write for catalog.

139 THOSE UPPITY WOMEN. 873 North A-1-A, Indialantic By-the-Sea, Fla. 32903. (305) 724-2580. Founded April, 1973. Patricia B. Windle.

Jewelers who operate a feminist boutique called "Patrician Gems." Ten percent of all profits are donated to feminist causes. Pendants, earrings, and rings are available, and will also make up designs on request and purchase feminist designs created by others. Write for brochure.

TIMES CHANGE PRESS. See **32.**

140 FERNE WILLIAMS. 35 Beverly Rd., West Orange, N.Y. 07052. (201) 731-0967.

Manufactures feminist jewelry (rings, pendants, pins, earrings, and keychains) in brass, silver, and gold. Also makes bumper stickers: "A Woman's Place Is Everyplace," "Support Your Local Feminist," and "Trust in God, She'll Provide," 50¢ each. Canvas bags with the word "Ms." on them are also available. Write for price information.

WOMAN'S VOICE BOOKSTORE. See **125.**

141 WOMEN ENTERPRISES, INC. 242 E. 50 St., New York, N.Y. 10022. (212) 593-1484. Founded June 1972. Mildred Margiotta.

A mail-order business for feminist products including jewelry, books, clothing, cosmetics, posters, and stationery. Write for catalog.

WOMEN'S EQUITY ACTION LEAGUE. See 386.

142 WOMEN'S HERITAGE SERIES, INC. 1167 HiPoint St., Los Angeles, Calif. 90035. (213) 935-3379. Founded April 1970. Virginia A. Bratfisch.

"The first all-woman corporation in HERstory dedicated exclusively to the production of materials by women for the feminist movement. It began its work as a spontaneous 'collective' in January 1969, when a group of five women, . . . committed to the new feminist movement, pooled their skills to research and produce the *Women's Heritage Calendar and Almanac* and eight additional women also all active in the movement, joined them to . . . pay for its printing. Legally incorporated now, the goals of Woman's Heritage are primarily to help build the movement, to educate, to raise consciousness and, above all, to effect change."

Available publications include: *Women's Heritage Calendar and Almanac*, first edition $2, Index 25¢; *Alice Paul*, booklet $1; *Elizabeth Cady Stanton*, booklet $1; and *Lucy Stone*, booklet $1.

Posters include: Womanpower, $1; The Woman Who Dared, $1; Confrontation, serigraph $5, poster $1; and On Target, $1. Other items are The Brassy, pendant $6; Power of Personhood, stationery $1.25; The Woman's Column, set of 4 facsimiles $1; and Woman & Man, game $7.95.

ZIZI PRESS. See 39.

II. Women's Research Centers and Library Research Collections

Centers and Collections

ALUMNAE ADVISORY CENTER, See 431.

143 ALVERNO COLLEGE, RESEARCH CENTER ON WOMEN. 3401 S. 39 St., Milwaukee, Wis. 53215. (614) 671-5400. Founded April 1970. Kathleen Casey Gigl, Coor.

"Aims to contribute empirical and historical data, innovative research, and imaginative implementation which will provide a framework for the study, the discussion, and finally, the resolution of the problem of women's self-identity, women's status, women's role in today's and tomorrow's world. Files contain a wealth of material, . . . including information regarding sex stereotyping, discrimination, the image of women and men past, present, and for a positive future; sexism in schools, books, toys, advertising and other media; numerous bibliographies and seminar reports. All reports from the Labor Department and the Women's Bureau are on file back to 1966."

A series of videotape interviews with Wisconsin suffragists and other women, as well as slide film presentations, were developed with the intention of making them available to schools and other groups. *Sex Stereotyping in Children's Books,* filmed by WTMJ, points out in five three-minute segments how children's books fail to create a good model for young girls. A videotape copy and the original films are available. The biweekly *Alverno Research Center on Women Newsletter* carries news of accessions to the library, significant events concerning women, and a listing of local feminist organizations' activities. Reports from four RCW seminars can be bought by mail order: *Women in Public Life in Wisconsin* ($1), *Conference on Women Theologians* ($1), *Midwest Conference on Women's Studies* ($1), and *The Education of Women* (25¢). Audiovisual aids in the form of tapes, slides, videotapes, games, and kits may be rented, and RCW operates a Speakers' Bureau for local and out-of-town groups.

144 BENTLEY HISTORICAL LIBRARY, MICHIGAN HISTORICAL COLLECTIONS. Beal and Bonisteel Sts., Ann Arbor, Mich. 48104. Founded 1935. Robert M. Warren, Dir.

Repository for manuscripts, photographs, and books relating to the state of Michigan, which includes a good collection of women's history materials. *Preliminary Bibliography of Resources for Women's History at the Michigan Historical Collections, 1971* is available.

BUSINESS AND PROFESSIONAL WOMEN'S FOUNDATION. See 162.

CENTER FOR WOMEN IN MEDICINE. See 540.

145   CENTER FOR WOMEN POLICY STUDIES. 2000 P St., N.W., Suite 508, Washington, D.C. 20036. (202) 872-1770. Founded March 1972. Jane Chapman, Margaret Gates, Co-Dirs.

The center provides an interdisciplinary approach to the identification, analysis, and solution of problems related to the status of women in society. This nonprofit, tax-exempt organization works with women's and professional organizations, public interest law firms, and governmental commissions.

146   CONNECTICUT COLLEGE LIBRARY, AMERICAN WOMAN'S COLLECTION. New London, Conn. 06320. (201) 442-1630. Founded 1944. Mary McKenzie.

"Miscellaneous papers, letters, clippings, and books relating to Alice Hamilton, Belle Moskowitz, Frances Perkins, Prudence Crandall Philleo, and Lydia H. Sigourney. Most of manuscript material uncatalogued and not easily accessible."

147   COUNCIL ON ECONOMIC PRIORITIES. 456 Greenwich St., New York, N.Y. 10013. (212) 431-4770. Founded November 1969. Sherry Koehler, Admin. Dir.

Nonprofit corporation researching, compiling, and disseminating information on the extent big businesses exercise social responsibility regarding fair employment practices, environmental preservation, production of war materials, overseas investment, and political influence. Issues reports like *Shortchanged*, a bank-by-bank analysis of employment opportunities for minority groups and women at 18 commerical banks in six cities (Dunellen Press, $12.50; paper $5.95).

148   EAGLETON INSTITUTE, CENTER FOR THE AMERICAN WOMAN AND POLITICS. Rutgers University, New Brunswick, N.J. 08901. (201) 828-2210. Founded July 1971. Ruth B. Mandel and Ida F. S. Schmertz.

A research and educational center committed to increasing knowledge about American women's participation in government and politics. "Center activities include: planning and testing model educational programs, generating and sponsoring research, convening conferences and symposia, publishing and disseminating information." Maintains a special collection of materials on women and politics. Some publications are *Women State Legislators: Report from a Conference* ($1); Kirkpatrick, J., *Political Woman*, Basic Books, 1974 ($10); and a case study of the Democratic Party in Connecticut by A. Beck.

EVERYWOMAN'S CENTER (Amherst, Mass.). See 189.

149   FEMINIST HISTORY RESEARCH PROJECT. 218 S. Venice Blvd., Venice, Calif. 90291. (213) 823-4774. Founded November 1972. Sherna Gluck, Ann Forfreedom.

Aims to find primary historical material about women in the early twentieth century, in a feminist context; to prepare materials for schools, groups, or individuals; and to direct research on women in ancient and modern history. The group is presently collecting taped oral interviews with women who were active suffragists and who organized other women during the period 1910–1930. Plans to establish a clearinghouse for women's research and to digest material which will eventually become a full-fledged journal. Tax-deductible contributions are requested. A 20-minute slide/tape show about women in the suffrage and trade union movements is available to be shown in California for $75 plus transportation fee; videotape version for rental is planned.

150 INFORMATION CENTER ON THE MATURE WOMAN. 3 W. 57 St., New York, N.Y. 10019. (212) 757-6802. Founded November 25, 1968. Sondra K. Gorney, Dir.

Works to change public and private attitudes about the important and useful roles the mature woman can play. Acts as clearinghouse for information on all phases of the life of American women over 40—economics, education, health and medicine, sociology, psychology, physiology, and leisure and cultural activities. The center provides news and features to publications and for radio programs, conducts a speakers' bureau, and maintains a resource library.

151 LIBRARY OF CONGRESS. 10 First St., S.E., Washington, D.C. 20540. (202) 426-5000. Mary C. Lethbridge, Info. Off.

The national library of the U.S. which has a "continuing interest in the collection of personal papers of important women, as well as the papers of organizations. There are many published and unpublished materials by and about women in the Library's collections." The Manuscript Division includes the papers of a number of organizations of particular interest to women; among them are the National Consumers League, the League of Women Voters, The National American Woman's Suffrage Association, and the National Women's Trade Union League of America. Other sources of particular interest to women are the papers of Margaret Sanger, Clara Barton, Clare Boothe Luce, Edna St. Vincent Millay, and Helen Rogers Reid. Two registers of papers of women have been published by the Library: Florence Jaffray Harriman, Ambassador to Norway (1937–1941), and Minnie Maddern Fiske, American actress. For a full list of the division's holdings, one should consult the following:

> Garrison, C. W. *List of Manuscript Collections in the Library of Congress to July 1931* (1932)
> Hamer, Philip M., ed. *Guide to Archives and Manuscripts in the United States* (1961)
> Library of Congress, *Handbook of Manuscripts* (1918)
> Library of Congress, *National Union Catalog of Manuscript Collections* (1959)
> Library of Congress, *Quarterly Journal* (1943 to date)
> Librarian of Congress, *Annual Reports* (1897 to date)
> Powell, C. Percy. *List of Manuscript Collections in the Library of Congress July 1931 to July 1938* (1939)

MONTGOMERY COUNTY COMMISSION FOR WOMEN. See **292.**

NATIONAL WOMAN'S PARTY. FLORENCY BAYARD HILLES LIBRARY. See **511.**

152 N.J. WOMEN'S INFORMATION AND REFERRAL SERVICE. Montclair Public Library. 50 S. Fullerton Ave., Montclair, N.J. 07042. (201) 744-0500. Founded 1973.

"Established by a grant from the state of New Jersey, the purpose of the service is twofold: to learn the interests and needs of women in the state; and to provide imporved sources for information on subjects relevant to those interests and needs." The service was begun originally as a pilot program in five New Jersey libraries: Montclair, Madison Township, Union City, Ocean County, and Rutherford. Statewide implementation is in the discussion stage. Each library maintains a list of referral agencies and a large collection of books, films, filmstrips, and pamphlets on subjects of interest to women. Questions are answered on subjects such as child care, counseling, legal aid, family planning, and educational and career opportunities. Inquiries are received in person or by telephone, and individuals are either given the necessary information or referred to appropriate experts or agencies.

ONTARIO MINISTRY OF LABOR, WOMEN'S BUREAU. See 353.

153   RADCLIFFE COLLEGE, THE ARTHUR AND ELIZABETH SCHLES-
      INGER LIBRARY ON THE HISTORY OF WOMEN IN AMERICA.
      3 James St., Cambridge, Mass. 02138. (617) 495-8647. Founded 1943.
      Patricia Miller King, Dir.

The Schlesinger Library has one of the largest collections in the world of source material on the history of American women from 1800 to the present. Its holdings include 210 major collections of papers on individual women, 35 archives of important women's organizations, 13,000 volumes, as well as journals, newsletters, and microfilm reels. Some of the subjects covered by the library's holdings are: woman suffrage, medicine, education, law, family service, labor, and the women's liberation movement. The library's inventories and card catalog were published by G. K. Hall (1973).

154   SMITH COLLEGE, THE SOPHIA SMITH COLLECTION. Northampton,
      Mass. 01060. (413) 584-2700, ext. 622. Founded 1942. Mary-Elizabeth
      Murdock, Dir.

"A major research facility containing thousands of books, manuscripts, pamphlets, miscellanea and periodicals that relate to womens' social and intellectual history. A fifty-five page illustrated catalog, *Catalog of the Sophia Smith Collection* (1971, $1.00), presents selected primary and secondary sources in some detail as an aid to scholars doing research in women's history." The *Picture Catalog,* (128 pp., 1972, $6), "compiled from the extensive research files of the Sophia Smith Collections enables you to order rare prints of hundreds of notable people, places and events. Available subjects include Susan B. Anthony, Carrie Chapman Catt, Emmeline Pankhurst, Anna Howard Shaw, Lucy Stone, suffrage parades and cartoons . . . Sojourner Truth, Lucretia Mott . . . and the Y.W.C.A." among other subjects. The price of individual photographs depends on the intended use of each print; publication price of individual photographs is $21.50.

155   UNIVERSITY OF NORTH CAROLINA AT GREENSBORO,, WALTER
      CLINTON JACKSON LIBRARY. Greensboro, North Carolina 27412.
      (919) 379-5284. Founded 1891. Emilie W. Mills, Spec. Col. Libn.

Maintains a special collection on women from the sixteenth century to 1900, including: the Homan collection of books on the history of physical education for women; works from the library of Anthony Ludovici, covering subjects in anthropology, sociology, and the history of women of all ages; and many works about early suffrage movements. Also published Minnie Hussey, *The Women's Collection: A Bibliography* . . . for the years 1937-1943, 1944-1949, and 1950-1956 supplements ($1 each). Lists mostly works published after 1900.

WASHINGTON AREA WOMEN'S CENTER. LIBRARY PROJECT. See 182.

WOMAN'S PLACE NEWSLETTER (St. John's, Newfoundland). See 237.

WOMEN IN COMMUNICATIONS, INC. NATIONAL RESOURCE CENTER. See 559.

THE WOMEN'S CENTER (Barnard College). See 202.

WOMEN'S CENTRE, YWCA (Montreal, Can.). See 243.

156 WOMEN'S HISTORY RESEARCH CENTER, INC. 2325 Oak St., Berkeley, Calif. 94708. (415) 524-7772. Founded 1968. Laura X, Dir.

A small tax-exempt foundation maintaining the International Women's History Archive about the current women's movement and a Topical Research Library of 2,000 files which documents the position of women past and present, in all walks of life, in many countries and ethnic groups, in history, in women's organizations, in events, and in roles. The archive and library have been created by hundreds of women since the Center was founded.

All inquiries must include $1 and a stamped self-addressed envelope. The Center is open to all women, by appointment only. Following is a list of works published by the Center.

Bibliographies on Women, Indexed by Topic $2.00
The Catalog $16.00 to women; $10 to institutions
Directory of Films by and/or about Women $3.00 to women; $5.00 to institutions
Directory of Women's Periodicals $3.00 to women; $10.00 to institutions
Female Artists Past and Present $4.00
NOW Newsletter Directory $3.00
Synopsis of Women in World History $1.20 to women; $2.00 to institutions
Women's Songbook $3.00
Women's Studies Courses, Indexed by Topic $5.00

The library has also arranged with Bell & Howell, Micro Photo Division (Old Mansfield Rd., Wooster, Ohio 44691) to publish *Herstory*, microfilmed editions of nearly 300 women's journals, newspapers and newsletters from the 1960s and 70s. *Herstory* ($550) is on 35 mm microfilm; it includes a title index which gives inclusive dates and reel locations. *Herstory 1 Update* is now available and covers the period October 1, 1971 to June 30, 1973. *Herstory 2* is a microfilm set of periodicals begun after October 1, 1971, and goes to June 30, 1973. *Herstory 1 Update* and *Herstory 2* can be ordered directly from the Women's History Research Center.

WOMEN'S INFORMATION CENTRE. (Toronto, Can.). See 240.

WOMEN'S LAW CENTER. See 387.

WOMEN'S LIBERATION UNION (Kansas City, Mo.). See 195.

WOMEN'S RESOURCE CENTER, (University of Utah.) See 226.

157   ZION RESEARCH LIBRARY. Boston University, 771 Commonwealth Ave., Boston, Mass. 02215. (617) 353-3724. Founded 1920. Wilma Corcoran, Libn.

A nonsectarian Protestant library for the study of the Bible and the history of the Christian Church. Zion maintains a special collection on the church and woman. Pamphlets and books (mostly rare) on the status and work of women in churches are for use only at the library.

III. Women's Organizations and Centers

U.S. National (including local listings for NOW chapters)

158 AMERICAN ASSOCIATION OF UNIVERSITY WOMEN. 2401 Virginia Ave. N.W., Washington, D.C. 20037. (202) 785-7700. Alice L. Beeman, Gen. Dir. 175,000 members. Dues: $6.50.

Organization of women college graduates, working for the recognition of women as responsible citizens and for the elimination of discrimination on the basis of sex. The AAUW maintains a national roster of qualified women, awards about 100 graduate fellowships to women annually through the AAUW Educational Foundation, conducts The College Faculty Program to assist mature women to prepare to teach college, maintains a Research Information Service on women's education and employment, and sponsors conferences. The association has 1,700 local branches. Many publications are available, including *Woman's Place?* a panel discussion (16mm sound film, b/w, $3 rental fee to AAUW members; $15, outside groups). Write for publications list.

AMERICAN CIVIL LIBERTIES UNION WOMEN'S RIGHTS PROJECT. See. 377.

CATALYST. See 434.

159 LEAGUE OF WOMEN VOTERS OF THE UNITED STATES. 1720 M St., N.W., Washington, D.C. 20036. (202) 296-1770. Julia Wolfe Kirn, Pub. Rel. Dir. 153,000 members.

An outgrowth of the original woman suffrage movement, the League now aims "to promote political responsibility through informed and active participation of citizens in government; to render such other services in the interest of education in citizenship as may be possible." Nonpartisan, the league works on local, state, and national levels; it is open to all women citizens 18 years or older. "Support of equal rights for all, regardless of race or sex makes explicit the League's support for equal rights for women. By motion, the 1972 convention authorized action at the state and local level in opposition to discriminatory practices against women and support of the Equal Rights Amendment." *The ERA: What It Means to Men and Women* is a campaign flyer answering some of the questions raised about the effect of the ERA (100 for $3).

160 THE LUCY STONE LEAGUE, INC. 133 E. 58 St., New York, N.Y. 10022. (212) 688-6380. Marjorie May, Dir. of Pub. Dues: $10/yr.

A center for research and information on the status of women, which opposes injustice and discrimination against women in legal, economic, educational and social relationships. It sponsors scholarships, organizes and supports memorial libraries, and maintains archives for women. Membership is open to both men and women interested in achieving the goal of both sexes as complete partners in our society.

NATIONAL ASSOCIATION FOR REPEAL OF ABORTION LAWS. See 480.

161   **NATIONAL ASSOCIATION OF COLLEGE WOMEN.** 1501 11 St., N.W., Washington, D.C. 20001. Founded 1923. Odessa W. Farrell, Pres. 3,000 members. Dues: $10.

Acts as a "link between women college graduates and the fulfillment of . . . creativity, responsibility and involvement. The Association provides a nationwide organizational structure to stimulate and coordinate the concerns and activities of local groups of college women for constructive work in education, public and civic affairs and human relations; encourages the extension of the professional acumen and disciplines of college women to a leadership role on local, national and international levels; promotes a closer union and fellowship among college women." The association grants annual graduate fellowships for doctoral studies and publishes a quarterly *Bulletin* and an annual *Journal*.

NATIONAL ASSOCIATION OF WOMEN ARTISTS. See 364.

162   **NATIONAL FEDERATION OF BUSINESS AND PROFESSIONAL WOMEN'S CLUBS, INC.** 2012 Massachusetts Ave., N.W., Washington, D.C. 20036. (202) 293-1100. Founded July 1919. Lucille H. Shriver, Exec. Dir. 170,000 members. Dues: $6.

A women's organization working to elevate the standards for, and to promote the interests of, women in business and the professions; to bring about a spirit of cooperation among business and professional women in the U.S.; and to extend opportunities to these women through education by industrial, scientific, and vocational activities. NFBPW sponsors National Business Woman's Week, Young Career Women Program, and a contributory fund for ratifications of the Equal Rights Amendment and conferences. The Business and Professional Women's Foundation, the tax-exempt educational and research foundation of the NFBPW, administers a library and research center, scholarships, fellowships, management training seminars, and a career awareness project.

NFBPW maintains a talent bank, and publishes *National Business Woman* magazine plus a variety of other items:
> *The Dual Profession Family; Research Summary* (1971, 25¢); *International Women,* an excerpt tape recording from the Oral History Collection (10 min., reel $3.50, cassette $4); *Sex Discrimination in the Academic World; Research Summary* (1970, free); and *Women Executives; Annotated Bibliography* (1970, 50¢).

163   **NATIONAL ORGANIZATION FOR WOMEN.** 1957 E. 73 St., Chicago, Ill. 60649. (312) 922-4536. Founded 1966. Karen De Crow, Pres.
See also NOW Legal Defense and Education Fund, 383.

"The purpose of NOW is to take action to bring women into full participation in the mainstream of American society now, exercising all the priveleges and responsibilities thereof in truly equal partnership with men." NOW will "initiate or support action, nationally, or in any part of this nation, by individuals or organizations, to break through . . . prejudice and discrimination against women in government, industry, the professions, the churches, the political parties, the judiciary, the labor unions, in education, science, medicine, law, religion and every other field of importance in American society."

Goals are: ratification of the ERA; the end of discrimination in employment; revision of state "protective" laws for women; equal opportunity in education; elimination of sexism in curricula; freely available high-quality child care; paid maternity leave; revision of income tax and social security laws; abortion law repeal and wide availability of birth control information; revision of marriage, divorce, and family laws; equal representation of women in government; prohibition of sex discrimination in public facilities; reform of portrayal of women in the media; ordination of women clergy in all faiths; liberation of men from the masculine mystique; reform of volunteer practices; and social justice for all oppressed groups.

NOW works through committees, task forces, and over 500 local chapters. Almost every chapter publishes a newsletter; several publish many other items of interest, some of which are listed below.

Available from NOW National Office

> *The Beginnings of a Long and REAL Revolution,* a slide documentary by Toni Carabillo, consisting of 200 slides, a prerecorded tape with narration, and a 25-page script. (Rental: $15 to NOW chapters, $25 to non-NOW groups; purchase: $100; all plus shipping and handling charges.)
>
> *Do It Now* (m., free to members).
>
> *The First Five Years—1966-1971* (free).
>
> *Moynihan, Poverty Programs, and Women—A Female Viewpoint,* by Merilee Dolan.
>
> *NOW Acts* (q., free to members; $5 to non-members).

Available from NOW Chapters (write to address given)

> Abortion slide tape show (20 min., $20). Shirley Glowski, 38155 N. Bonkay St., Mt. Clemens, Mich. 48043.
>
> *Are Women Equal under the Law?* (50¢). Gene Boyer, 318 Front St., Beaver Dam, Wis. 53916.
>
> *Dick and Jane as Victims: Sex Stereotyping in Children's Readers* ($1.50). Central New Jersey NOW, Box 2163, Princeton, N.J. 08540.
>
> *How We (Finally) Got the* Stockton Record *to Desegregate Its Help Wanted Ads* (free with stamped envelope). San Joaquin NOW, Box 5073, Stockton, Calif. 95204.
>
> Library kit ($2). Cleveland NOW, Box 7147, Cleveland, Ohio 44128.
>
> *New Jersey Teenagers and Contraception* (50¢). Anne Yohn, NOW, Box 823, Red Bank, N.J. 07001.
>
> *Probable Cause for Alarm* ($2). Central New Jersey NOW, Box 2163, Princeton, N.J. 08540.
>
> *Sex Bias in the Public Schools* ($2.25). New York NOW, 28 E. 56 St., New York, N.Y. 10022.
>
> *Sex Discrimination in Employment: What to Know About It, What to Do About It* (75¢). NOW, 45 Newbury St., Boston, Mass. 02116.
>
> *Sister, Can You Spare a Dime?* by Gene Boyer (contribution requested for fundraising). Gene Boyer, 218 Front St., Beaver Dam, Wis. 53916.

In Addition, "a *Directory of Feminist Services* will soon be published. It will be circulated to NOW members initially, with plans to expand it later." It will enable feminists to utilize the services of other feminists. It will also include a Professional Roster (attorneys, engineers, psychologists, physicians, CPAs, investment counselors, etc.) Services will be listed alphabetically and geographically. Write for rates to Nikki Beare, Ed., *Directory of Feminist Services*, 7220 S. W. 61 Ct., S., Miami, Fla. 33143. (305) 665-7611. Feminist products are listed in the *NOW Feminist Products Catalog*, available to subscribers for $1/yr. Write for further information to Judith Meuli, Ed., 1126 Hi Point St., Los Angeles, Calif. 90035.

The following list is an address guide to local and state NOW groups.

ALABAMA
Alexander City NOW, Kathleen Imhoff, Pres., Rt. 1, Box 62, Dadeville 36853

Huntsville NOW, Box 2204, Main Station, Huntsville 35804

Montgomery NOW, Sarah Jane Stewart, Pres., 454 S. Goldwaite St., Montgomery 36104

ALASKA
Fairbanks, Alaska NOW, Judy Dial, Conv., 306 10th, Fairbanks 99701

ARIZONA
Phoenix NOW, Edythe Jensen, Pres., 737 W. Colter, No. 169, Phoenix 85013

State of Ariz. NOW, Shirley Fahey, State Coor., 6802 Opatas, Tucson 85715

Tucson, Ariz. NOW, M. K. O'Brien Staley, Pres., 2143 N. Northway, Tucson 85716

ARKANSAS
Little Rock NOW, Pat Johnson, Conv., 8205 Louanda Dr., Little Rock 72205

CALIFORNIA
Bakersfield NOW, Box 3195, Bakersfield 93305

Bakersfield NOW, Diane Andrews, Pres., 2801 S. H St., No. 30, Bakersfield 93304

Berkeley NOW, Box 7112, Berkeley 93307.

Berkeley NOW, Jean Pedersen, Co-Pres., 1168 Cragmont Ave., Berkeley 94708

Blythe, Calif. NOW, Helaine Blythe, Conv., 310 N. Sola, Blythe 92225

California NOW, Eve Norman, State Coor., 1157 S. Spaulding, Los Angeles 90019

California NOW, Helen Damouth, Asst. State Coor., 935 Peninsula Way, Menlo Park 94025

Conejo Valley NOW, Nicola Kester, Conv., 4134 Santa Rosa Dr., Moorpark 93021

Contra Costa County NOW, Box 4794, Walnut Creek 94596

Contra Costa County NOW, Carol Reich, Coor., 1076 Carol Lane, No. 37, Lafayette 94549

Corona, Calif. NOW, Betty Leonti, Conv., 1068 Linerona, Corona 91720

Davis NOW, Bonnie Schoenborne, Conv., 619 Pole Line Rd., Apt. 264, Davis 95616

Fresno NOW, Donna McKittrick, Pres., 5786 E. Kings Canyon, Apt. A, Fresno 93727

Harbor-South Bay, Calif. NOW, Colleen Wilson, Pres., 1806 Vallecito Dr., San Pedro 90732

Hermosa, Calif. NOW, Lee Dula, Conv., 330 Cochise Ave., Hermosa Beach 90254.

Hollywood, Calif. NOW, Judith Meuli, Conv., 1126 Hi Point, Los Angeles 90035

Humboldt County NOW, Yvonne Fairbairn, Conv., Star Rt., Box 3, Hydesville 95547.

Imperial, Calif. NOW, Mark J. Shahan, Conv., Imperial Valley College, 380 E. Aten Rd., Imperial 92251

Laguna Beach NOW, Dolores Ferrell, Pres., 1900 Rimrock Canyon Rd., Laguna Beach 93651

La Puente, Calif. NOW, Eileen Pfeffer, Conv., 1401 S. Harbor, No. 6W, La Habra 90631

Long Beach NOW, Box 15306, Long Beach 90815

Long Beach, Calif. NOW, Elizabeth Pomeroy, Pres., 2144 Shipway Ave., Long Beach 90815

Los Angeles NOW, 8864 W. Pico Blvd., Los Angeles 90035

Los Angeles NOW, Jean Stapleton, Pres., 1169 S. Hi Point, Los Angeles 90035

Los Gatos NOW, Patricia E. Kowitz, Conv., 2700 Sand Hill Rd., Suite 21, Menlo Park 94025

Marin County Chapter NOW, Box 2924, San Rafael 90702

Marin County NOW, Lee Hunt, Pres., 71 Monte vista, Novato 94947

Menlo Park NOW, Patricia E. Kowitz, Conv., 2700 Sand Hill Rd, Suite 21, Menlo Park 94025

Merced, Calif. NOW, Penelope Woods, Conv., 356 E. 21 St., Merced 94340

Monterey NOW, Box 1661, Monterey 93940

Monterey NOW, Lynne Yates-Carter, Pres., 1140 Monarch La., No. 107, Pacific Grove 93950

North San Diego County NOW, Box 1727, Oceanside 92054

North San Diego County NOW, Sharon Lafragiola, Conv., 435 E. Washington, No. 307, Escondido 92025

Norwalk NOW, Barbara Landis, Conv., 12708 Halcourt Ave., Norwalk 90650

Orange County NOW, Box 15228, Santa Ana 92705

Orange County NOW, Helen Lotos, Pres., 1674 Marguerite, Corona Del Mar 92625

Pacific Palisades, Calif. NOW, Lee Walker, Conv., 1511 Amalfi Dr. Pacific Palisades 90272

Palo Alto NOW, Enid A. Davis, Pres., 1050 Newell Rd., Palo Alto 94303

Palos Verdes Peninsula NOW, Box 1084, Palos Verdes Estates 90274

Palos Verdes Peninsula NOW, Dee Compton, Pres., 8 Blackwater Canyon, Rolling Hills 90274

Pomona Valley, Calif. NOW, Joan Richardson, Pres., 333 Sycamore Ave., Claremont 91711

Redding NOW, Mary Ellen Meader, Conv., 5781 Old 44th Dr., Redding 96001

Ridgecrest NOW, Maria Morris, Conv., Rte. 1, Box 3504, Ridgecrest 93555

Riverside-San Bernardino, Calif. NOW, Box 1112, Riverside 92502

Riverside-San Bernardino NOW, Barbara Parker, Pres., 3509 Brockton, Riverside 92501

Sacramento NOW, Box 13176, Sacramento 95813

Sacramento (New) NOW, Maria Del Drago, Conv., 2665 Portola Way, Sacramento 95818

San Diego NOW, Box 22264 San Diego 92122

San Fernando Valley, Calif. NOW, Eileen Bergesch, Pres., 23100 Cohasset St., Canoga Park 91301

San Francisco NOW, Box 1267, San Francisco 94101

San Francisco NOW, Lorraine Lahr, Pres., 635 34 Ave. San Francisco 94121

San Gabriel Valley NOW, Cheryl S. Miller, Pres., 838 San Pascual, Los Angeles 90042

San Joaquin NOW, Box 4073, Stockton 95204

San Joaquin NOW, Carol Benson, Pres., 8510 McDuff Ct., Stockton 94207

San Jose NOW, Box 2-G, San Jose 95109

San Jose NOW, Janet Camagna, Conv., 3200 Payne Ave. No. 415, San Jose 95117

San Mateo County NOW, Marilyn Previn, Pres., Box 1663 Burlingame 94010

Santa Barbara County NOW, Box 931, Goleta 93017

Santa Barbara NOW, Elin Scheff, Pres., 6155 Coloma Dr., Goleta 93017

Santa Cruz County NOW, Box 665, Soquel 95073

Santa Cruz County NOW, Jessica Wick, Pres., Box 20, Boulder Creek 95006

Santa Maria NOW, Lianne Hutton, Conv., 3943 Hillview, Santa Maria 93454

Solano NOW, Deborah Miller, Conv., 2701 Mankas Blvd., Fairfield 94533

Sonoma County, Calif. NOW, Karen Orcutt, Conv., 15467 Marty St., Glen Ellen 95442

South Bay NOW, Christine Klemmer, Pres., 3498 Shafer, Santa Clara 95051

Southeast Los Angeles NOW, Fern Palmer, Pres., 7716 Westman Ave., Whittier 90606

Stanislaus County NOW, Yvonne Allen, Pres., 912 Hackberry, Modesto 95350

Taipei NOW, Anne W. Cheatham, Conv., HSA, Box 28, Taipei American School, APO San Francisco 96263

Ventura, Calif. NOW, Susan Magnone, Pres., Box 2101, Ventura 93001

Visalia NOW, Vivien Cienfuegos, Conv., 2725 E. Westcott, Visalia 93277

COLORADO

Boulder, Colo. NOW, Sara Mayer, Pres., 918 Juniper, Boulder 80302

Colorado NOW, Diana Berghausen, State Coor., 1501 Village La., Fort Collins 80521

Denver NOW, Susan Allen, Pres., 2337 Dexter St., Denver 80207

Durango NOW, Box 1617, Durango 81301

Durango NOW, Margaret Lang, Pres., Box 3362, Durango 81301

El Paso County NOW, Nancy Black, Pres., Box 1387, Colorado Springs 80901

Ft. Collins, Colo. NOW, Diana Berghausen, Pres., 1501 Village La., Ft. Collins 80521

Grand Junction NOW, Henrietta Hay, Pres., 2576 Galley La., Grand Junction 81501

Greeley NOW, Kathy Shannon, Conv., 836 30 Ave. Court, Greeley 80631

Gunnison NOW, Dr. Betty Spehor, Conv., Western State College, Gunnison 80230

Longmont NOW, Rita Nofsinger, Conv., 824 Collyer, Longmont 80501

Mesa NOW, Henrietta Hay, Conv., 2576 Galley La., Grand Junction 81501

Metropolitan Denver NOW, 2560 S. Everett, No. 7, Lakewood 80227

Pueblo NOW, Kay Whitlock, Conv., 2417 Grand Ave., Pueblo 81003

CONNECTICUT

Central Conn. NOW, Ann Bandazian, Pres., 21 Dogwood Rd., Weathersfield 06109

Connecticut NOW, Judy Pickering, State Coor., 28 Lincoln Ave., Norwich 06360

Essex County, Conn. NOW, Edie Baldoni, Contact, Comstock St., Ivoryton 06442

Fairfield NOW, Rita Childs, Conv., 211 Lloyd Dr., Fairfield 06430

Greater Bridgeport, Conn. NOW, Vera Stecker, Pres., 715-32 Frenchtown Rd., Bridgeport 06606

Greenwich Conn. NOW, Barbara Martin, Pres., 20 Brookside Dr., Greenwich 06830

New Haven, Conn. NOW, Margaret Fine, Pres., 130 High Top Cr., Hamden 06514

North Eastern Conn. NOW, Claire Connelly, Conv., RFD 1, Coventry 06238

Southeastern Conn. NOW, Joan Witmer, Pres., 50 Old Norwich Rd., Quaker Hill 06375

Stamford, Conn. NOW, Ms. Kelly Curts, Chairperson, 93 Givens Ave., Stamford 06902

Stratford, Conn. NOW, Carole Liberman, Conv., 220 Pilgrim La., Stratford 06497

Western Conn. NOW, Barbara Levine, Pres., 204 Ridgeview Ave., Fairfield 06430

Westport NOW, Priscilla Brennan, Conv., 146 N. Kings Hwy., Westport 06880

DELAWARE

Delaware NOW, Jean Conger, Pres., 2917 Jaffe Rd., Arundel, Wilmington 19808

Kent County NOW, Laureen Warwick, Conv., 64 South Fairfield Dr., Dover 19901

Newark, Del. NOW, Muriel Durham, Conv., 151 Thorne La., Apt. 7, Newark 19711

FLORIDA

Brevard County NOW, Nancy Curtis, Conv., 31 Barton Ave., Rockledge 32955

Broward County, Fla. NOW, Carole Freidman, Pres., 5531 S.W. 2 St., Plantation 33314

Dade County NOW, Box 265, Coconut Grove 33133

Daytona-Ormond Beach NOW, Martha Bennett, Conv., Box 185, Ormond Beach 32074

Deland NOW, Andrea Westmoreland, Conv., 238 N. Florida Ave., No. 13, Deland 32720

Florida NOW, Karen Coolman, State Coor., 1911 Bayview Dr., Ft. Lauderdale 33305

Fort Myers NOW, Mary Baldauf, Conv., 823 Entrada Ave., Fort Myers 33901

Gainesville NOW, Edna Saffy, Conv., 608 S.E. Second Pl., Gainesville 32601

Jacksonville NOW, Glenna Goad, Pres., Box 8590, Jacksonville 32211

North Palm Beach County NOW, Angela Ford, Pres., Box 1128, Lake Worth 33460

Orland NOW, Barbara Baker, Pres., 105 Springwood Pl., Maitland 32751

Pensacola, Fla. NOW, Karen Bieger, Contact Person, 433 Edison Dr., Pensacola 32501

Polk County NOW, Joanna Wragg, Pres., Box 3469, Lakeland 33802

St. Johns County NOW, Peggy Jo Caraway, Conv., 42 Magnolia Dr., St. Augustine 32084

St. Petersburg, Fla. NOW, Bonnie L. Lamp, Pres., 201 38 Ave. S.E., St. Petersburg 33705

Sarasota NOW, Jo Ferrazzi, Conv., 3350 S. Osprey Ave., Apt. 210A, Sarasota 33579

South Dade County NOW, Ruth A. Householder, DVM Pres., 8875 S.W. 152 St., Miami 33158.

South Palm Beach NOW, Margaret Barovich, Pres., 8 Burning Tree La., Boca Raton 33432

Talahassee NOW, Dr. Margaret Y. Menzel, Pres., 1605 Kolopakin, Tallahassee 32301

Tampa, Fla. NOW, Von Kerik, Pres., 7208 9 Ave., Tampa 33619

GEORGIA

Albany NOW, Jean Duffy, Conv., 2304 W. Gordon Rd., No. 122, Albany 31705

Athens NOW, Mary Atkeson Trawick, Conv., 1439 S. Milledge, Athens 30601

Atlanta NOW, Box 54045, Civic Center, Atlanta 30308

Atlanta, Ga. NOW, Peg Nugent, Pres., 2250 Cheshire Bridge Rd. N.E., Atlanta 30324

Columbus, Ga. NOW, Betty Hart, Conv., Columbus College, Columbus 30907

CSRA NOW, Teresa N. Nasif, Pres., 1046 Alexander Dr., Augusta 30904

Dekalb County NOW, Tex Ann Reid, Conv., 2839 Greenrock Trail, Doralville 30340

Douglas County NOW, Pat Weir, Conv., 7139 Linda Dr., Lithia Springs 30057

Georgia NOW, Martha W. Gaines, State Coor., 2444 E. Adina Dr., Atlanta 30324

Macon NOW, Brenda O'Reilly, Conv., 6550 Perkins Dr., Macon 31206

Rome NOW, Judy Tabor, Conv., Box 1182, Rome 30162

St. Simon's Island NOW, Carolyn Porter, Conv., 1909 First Ave., St. Simon's Island 31522

Savannah NOW, Beth Kinstler, Conv., 8 Stillwood Ct. N., Savannah 31406

South Central Georgia NOW, Lorena & Elizabeth Weeks, Co-Convs., Box 52, Wadley 30477

South Metro. Atlanta, Ga. NOW, Diane McCuiston, Pres., 2001 Sylvan Rd. S.W., No. 3D, Atlanta 30310

HAWAII

Hilo, Hawaii NOW, Jo Ann TeSelle, Conv., 184 Puueo St., Hilo 96720

Honolulu NOW, Dr. Vivian Walker, Pres., 1948 Puowaina Dr., Honolulu 06813

IDAHO

Idaho Falls NOW, Anne Burdick, Pres., 2161 Aegean Ave., Idaho Falls 83401

ILLINOIS

Aurora NOW, Jane West, Conv., 369 South Ave., Aurora 60505

Champaign NOW, Suzanne Guy, Pres., 406 N. James, Champaign 61820

Chicago NOW, 2830 N. Burling, N.E., Chicago 60657

Chicago NOW, Mary Ann Lupa, Pres., 1648 West Sherwin, Chicago 60626

Decatur, Ill. NOW, Marlene E. Mason, Conv., 886 West Wood, Apt. 4, Decatur 62522

DuPage County NOW, Box 623, Glen Ellyn 60137

Du Page County NOW, Joan Oliva, Pres., 818 Valley View Dr., Glen Ellyn 60137

Edwardsville NOW, Beatrice Stegeman, Conv., 410 West Union, Edwardsville 62025

Fox Valley-Elgin, Ill. NOW, Marline Valla Rennels, Pres., 1023 N. Spring, Elgin 60120

Greater Champaign NOW, McKinley Foundation, 809 S. 5 St., Champaign 61820

Illinois NOW, Irene Bennett, State Coor., 7620 78 St., Rock Island 61201

Lake County NOW, Jane Paxton, Pres., 2706 Elizabeth Ave., Zion 60099

McHenry, Ill. NOW, Judy Longmeyer, Conv., 705 W. Peter St., McHenry 60050

North Suburban Chicago NOW, Terri Tepper, Pres., 261 Kimberley Dr., Barrington 60010

Quad Cities, Ill. NOW, Joan Eastlund, Pres., 2401 30 St., Rock Island 61201

Rockford, Ill. NOW, Loretta Norris, Pres., 910 N. Church St., Rockford 61103

Southern Ill. NOW, Carolyn C. Weiss, Pres., 400 N. Oakland Ave., Apt. 24, Carbondale, 62901

Southwest Cook County NOW, Julia Maciewicz, Conv., 9701 Ravinia Lane, No. 3, Orland Park 60462

Springfield, Ill. NOW, Carol Dornan, Acting Pres., 814 W. Edwards, Springfield 62704

INDIANA

Anderson NOW, Paula Cole, Conv., 812 W. 7 St., Anderson 46012

Bloomington, Ind. NOW, Rachel Wampler, Pres., 800 N. Smith Rd., 1Z, Bloomington 47401

Elkhart, Ind. NOW, Maraland Williams, Conv., Box 475, Bristol 46507

Franklin, Ind. NOW, Cheryl Burnham Denk, Conv., Box 35B, RR5, Franklin 46131

Indiana NOW, Pat Gillespie, State Coor., 2616 Eastgate Lane, Apt. 16A, Bloomington 47401

Indianapolis, Ind. NOW, Norma Card, Pres., 834 N. Emerson, Indianapolis 46219

Lake County NOW, Barbara Bogert, Pres., 6328 Ohio Ave., Hammond 46323

Muncie NOW, Wynola Richards, Pres., 21 South Dr., Delaware Acres Mobile Muncie 47302

South Bend NOW, Ruth W. Lee, Conv., 518 E. Haney Ave., South Bend 46613

Terre Haute NOW, Sharon Hogan, Conv., 630 Ash St., Apt. 30E, Terre Haute 47804

Tippecanoe County NOW, Rona Ginsberg, Pres., 112 Knox Dr., West Lafayette 47906

Tri-State NOW, Lynne Schrum, Pres., Box 731, RR2, Newburgh 47630

Valparaiso NOW, Jacqueline Beutler, Conv., 1059 Avondale Ave., Valparaiso, 46383

IOWA

Ames, Iowa NOW, Trudy Peterson, Pres., 2304 Ferndale, Ames 50010

Cedar Rapids NOW, Box 45, Cedar Rapids 52406

Cedar Rapids Women's Caucus, Rae Visnapuu, Pres., 890 31 St., Marion 52302

Clinton, Iowa NOW, La Vonne Hicks Maresca, Conv., 209 S. 4 St., Clinton 52732

Des Moines NOW, Kay R. Plymat, Pres., 2002 Motley, Des Moines 50315

Dubuque, Iowa NOW, Susan Gorrell, Pres., 1125 Highland Pl., Dubuque 52001

Iowa NOW, Irene Talbott, State Coor., 2002 Motley, Des Moines 50315

Mount Pleasant, Iowa NOW, Yvonne Shafer, Conv., 308 Plantation Apt., W. Monroe St., Mount Pleasant 52641

Pocahontas, Iowa NOW, Carol J. Davis-Olson, Rte. 1, Pocahontas 50574

U. of Northern Iowa NOW, Marie Kloss, Conv., Dept. of Psychology, U. of Northern Iowa, Cedar Falls 50613

KANSAS

Kansas NOW, Dr. Bonnie R. Patton, Pres., Box 58, Rte. 1, Lawrence 66044

Manhattan NOW, Anne Liedtke, Pres., 1415 Normandy, No. 219, Manhattan 66502

Ottawa NOW, Quincalee Striegel, Pres., 1010 S. Hickory, Ottawa 66067

Topeka NOW, Mildred Burleigh, Conv., 8790 Park South Court, E., Apt. 102, Topeka 66609

Wichita, Kans. NOW, Marjorie C. Miville, Pres., 3906 E. Central, Wichita 67208

KENTUCKY

Bowling Green NOW, Judy Kane, Conv., 901 Jackson, Apt. D9, Bowling Green 42101

Kentucky NOW, Carolyn Weeks, State Coor., 2380 Valley Vista, Louisville 40205

Louisville NOW, Leila Cushman, Co-chairperson, 2158 Sherwood, Louisville 40205

LOUISIANA

Baton Rouge, La. NOW, Elizabeth Normand, Pres., 621 Park Blvd., Baton Rouge 70806

Hammond NOW, Nadine Henneman, Conv., Box 23A, Rte. 1, Hammond 70401

Louisiana NOW, Margaret P. Stanley, State Coor., 9508 Wild Valley Rd., Baton Rouge 70810

Monroe-Quachita Parish, La. NOW, Box 874, Monroe 71201

Monroe-Quachita Parish, La. NOW, Jenny Coon, Pres., 1133 S. Grand, Apt. 1, Monroe 71201

New Orleans NOW, Box 13604, New Orleans 70125

New Orleans NOW, Annabelle Walker, Pres., Box 13604, New Orleans 70125

Shreveport-Bossier, La. NOW, Linda Martin, Pres., 380 Albany, Shreveport 71105

MAINE

Heart of Maine NOW, JoAnn M. Fritsche, Pres., MRB 128, Bangor 04401

Kennebunk NOW, Mary Iyer, Pres., 17 Stacy St., Saco 04072

State of Maine NOW, Lois Reckitt, State Coor., 38 Myrtle St., South Portland 04106

MARYLAND

Anne Arundel NOW, Naomi Mestanas, Pres., 727 Rosedale St., Annapolis 21401

Baltimore City, Md. NOW, Carolyn Fertitta and Carolyn Sheehan, Coconvenors, 4805 Melbourne Rd., Baltimore 21229

Baltimore County NOW, Sherry Rudman, Pres., 6216 Green Meadow Pkway., Baltimore 21209

Carroll County NOW, Karen Shein, Pres., 519 E. Main St., Westminster 21740

Frederick County NOW, Olivia Reusing, Conv., 1400 Haven Rd., B32 Hagerstown 21740

Hagerstown, Md. NOW, Olivia F. Reusing, Pres., 1400 Haven Rd., B32 Hagerstown 21740

Howard County NOW, Allenna Leonard, Conv., 10534 Faulkner Ridge Circle, Columbia 21044

Maryland NOW, Casey Hughes, State Coor., 1400 Bayside Dr., Edgewater 21037

Montgomery County NOW, Box 2301, Rockville 20852

Montgomery County NOW, Judy Waxman, Pres., 19036 Canadian Ct., Gaithersburg 20760

National Capital Area NOW, Mary B. Bailey, Pres., Box 189, Garrett Park 20766

Northern Prince George's NOW, Suzanne Batra, Pres., 2Q Plateau Pl., Greenbelt 20770

South Prince George's County NOW, Marjorie C. Clingan, Pres., 9301 Temple Hill Rd., Clinton 20735

MASSACHUSETTS

Eastern Mass. NOW, Marilyn S. Freifeld, Pres., 46 Hull St., Boston 02113

Lexington NOW, Carol Waldron, Pres., 464 Concord Ave., Lexington 02173

Massachusetts NOW, Patricia T. Desmond, State Coor., 18 Kilby St., Quincy 02169

Newton, Mass. NOW, Ruth Baden, Conv., 18 Cedar St., Newton Centre 02159

Norfolk NOW, Joann Anthony, Conv., 28 Bradford, Sharon 02067

North Shore, Mass. NOW, Carol Annis, 25 Baker Rd., Nahant 01908

Pittsfield NOW, Cecilia Rosenthal, Conv., Colonial Village, Williamstown 02167

Plymouth NOW, Marlene K. Goldstein, Pres., 14 Winthrop Rd., Hingham 02043

South Middlesex, Mass. NOW, Joyce Furia, Pres., 87 Higgins Rd., Framingham 01701

U. of Mass. NOW, Sally Stewart, Conv., 24 Riverview Ave., Haverhill 01830

Worcester NOW, Stephanie Riopel, Conv., 36 Scandinavia Ave., Worcester 01603

MICHIGAN

Ann Arbor NOW, Vivian Shaner, Pres., 2 Buckingham Ct., Ann Arbor 48104

Benton Harbor-St. Joe NOW, Glenis Harrel, Conv., 1816 S. Lakeshore Dr., St. Joseph 49085

Big Rapids NOW, Edith A. Donahue, Box 261, RR 1, Big Rapids 49307

Detroit NOW, Joan Israel, Pres., 17554 Birchcrest, Detroit 48221

Flint, Mich. NOW, Karen Quay Stiehler, Pres., 1718 W. Pierson Rd., Bldg. D, 20, Flint 48504

Houghton, Mich. NOW, Joan Monberg, Conv., 214 Mason, Hancock 49930

Kalamazoo NOW, Joanne Betz, Conv., Box 301, Comstock 49041

Lansing, Mich. NOW, Martha W. Eger, Pres., 1214 N. Genesee Dr., Lansing 48915

Macomb County NOW, Shirley Glowski, Conv., 16500 Hall Rd., Rm. B107, Mount Clemens 48043

Michigan NOW, Lee Lavalli, State Coor., 1750 Culver, Dearborn 48124

Midland NOW, Mary Ettinger, Conv., 4400 Berkshire, Midland 48640

Muskegon-Ottawa, Mich. NOW, Portia M. Mummert, Pres., 73 W. Dale Ave., Muskegon 49441

Oakland County NOW, Sandra Carpenter, Conv., 564 Overhill Rd., Birmingham 48010

Port Huron, Mich. NOW, Nancy Maywar, Conv., 1221 13 St., Port Huron 48060

Schoolcraft NOW, Sylvia Vukmirovich, Pres., 14481 Nola, Livonia 48154

Taylor NOW, Kendra Anderson, Conv., 14312 Cornell, Taylor 48180

Traverse City NOW, Connie Kopp, Box 167, Kewadin 49648

Western Michigan NOW, Lois Heyboer, Pres., 1013 Don Hertog, S.W. Grand Rapids 49502

MINNESOTA

Little Falls NOW, Karen Nelson Foltmer, Conv., RFD No. 5, Little Falls 56345

Minnesota NOW, Roberta I. Pettit, State Coor., 1767 Blair Ave., St. Paul 55104

Rochester NOW, Mary Kay Bouise, Pres., 3007 N.W. 51, Rochester 55901

St. Croix Valley NOW, Diane Chartier, Conv., 822 S. Third St., Stillwater 55082

St. Paul, Minn. NOW, Susan Shaw, Conv., 1517 Grand Ave., St. Paul 55105

Southern Minnesota NOW, Esther B. Holley, Pres., 604 4 St., S.W., Austin 55912

Twin Cities, Minn. NOW, Virginia Watkins, Pres., Box 1348, Minnetonka 55343

Wayzata NOW, Marceline Donaldson, Conv., 2540 Old Beach Rd., Wayzata 55391

MISSISSIPPI

Jackson NOW, Box 9673, Northside Sta., Jackson 39206

Jackson NOW, Dr. Madge Pfaffman, Pres., 4068 Redwing Ave., Jackson 39216

Meridian NOW, Florence Sinclaire, Conv., 2319 34 Ave., Meridian 39301

Mississippi NOW, Ted. R. Williams, State Coor., 199 Treehaven Dr., Jackson 39212

Pascakoula, Miss. NOW, Mary Ann Campbell, Conv., Box 1144, Pascakoula 39567

U.S.M. Hattiesburg NOW, Darlene Carra, Conv., U.S.M. Box 910, Southern Sta., Hattiesburg 39401

MISSOURI

Cape Girardeau, Mo. NOW, Pam Hearn, Conv., 1837 Stoddard St., Cape Girardeau 63701

Chillicothe NOW, Janet Van Walraven, Conv., Box 625, Chillicothe 64601

Columbia NOW, Rachel Davis, Pres., 1653 Highridge Circle, Columbia 65201

Greater Kansas City NOW, Sandra L. Byrd, Pres., 3201 N.E. 59 Terr. No. 5 Kansas City 64119

Jefferson City NOW, Alice Fischer, Conv., 559 C Senate Ct., Jefferson City 65101

Kirksville NOW, Rebecca Gallo, Conv., 20 Scott St. Terr., Kirksville 63501

Missouri NOW, Mary Anne Sedav, State Coor., 3716 A Fairview, St. Louis 63113

St. Charles, Mo. NOW, Sharon St. Moritz, Pres., 3202 Southwick, St. Charles 63301

St. Louis NOW, Box 16132, Clayton 63119

St. Louis, Mo. NOW, Christine Guerrero, Pres., 6021 Pershing, St. Louis 63112

MONTANA

Butte NOW, Geraldine Cooney, Acting Pres., 1447 Dewey, Butte 59701

Great Falls NOW, Valerie Anne Littlefield, Pres., 36 Birch St., Great Falls 59405

Missoula Mont. NOW, Billie Bohanan, Conv., 1840 S. Higgins, Missoula 59801

State of Utah NOW, Carolyn Stoehr, State Coor., 1816 3 Ave., Great Falls 59401

NEBRASKA

Grand Island Nebr. NOW, Judy Stueven, Conv., Box 307, Rte. 3, Grand Island 68801

Kearney, Nebr. NOW, Mary Harder, Conv., 415 W. 22, Kearney 68807

Lincoln NOW, Shirley Linderholm, Pres., 2330 N. 74 St., Lincoln 68507

Nebraska NOW, Ellie Shore, State Coor., 3225 Holdrege, Lincoln 68503

Omaha NOW, 2718 N. 97 St., Omaha 68134

Omaha NOW, Cherie Kipple, Pres., 130 N. 34 St., Omaha 68131

NEVADA

Southern Nevada NOW, Elaine Mills, Pres., 1235 S. 9 St., Las Vegas 89104

State of Nevada NOW, Ethel Barina, State Coor., 3861 Royal Crest St., No. 6, Las Vegas 89109

NEW HAMPSHIRE

Hanover NOW, Kate Tuckerman, Conv., 5 Conant Rd., Hanover 03755

Merrimack N.H. NOW, Eleanor Marshall, Conv., 16 Hilton Dr., Merrimack 03054

NEW JERSEY

Central New Jersey NOW, Box 2163, Princeton 08540

Central New Jersey NOW, Joan C. Errickson, Coor., Box 183A, R.R. 1, Blackwell Rd., Pennington 08534

Edison NOW, Terri E. Patterson, Conv., 136 L Marina Dr., Edison 08817

Essex County NOW, Connie Gilbert Neiss, Pres., 50 Montclair Ave., Montclair 07042

Lakeland Area, N.J. NOW, Renee Wallace, Pres., 69 Omaha Ave., Rockaway 07866

Middlesex County NOW, Box 94, Iselin 08830

Middlesex County NOW, Susan Presby, Pres., 24 Dayton Dr., Apt. 157A, Edison 08817

Monmouth County NOW, Anne Yohn, Pres., 11 Aberdeen Terrace, New Monmouth 07748

Morristown NOW, Jean Merrit, Conv., RD 1, Boonton 07005

New Jersey NOW, Debbie Hart, State Coor., 15 Roosevelt Pl., Montclair 07042

Northern New Jersey NOW, Box 353, Ho Ho Kus 07423

Northern New Jersey NOW, Laureen Helen, Pres., 343 W. Clinton Ave., Tenafly 07670

Ocean County NOW, Pearl Richmond, Pres., 110 Whittier Rd., Brick Town 08723

Passaic County Chapter NOW, Box 552, Clifton 07012

Passaic County NOW, Dorothy M. Forte, Pres., Box 1051, Valley Sta., Wayne 07470

Somerset County NOW, Box 186, Martinsville 08836

Somerset County NOW, Judy Weiss, Conv., 801 Stangle Rd., Martinsville 08836

South Jersey NOW, Judy Holzer, Pres., 70 N. Main St., Mullica Hill 08062

Summit Area NOW, Barbara Scaiff, Conv., Box 102, Murray Hill 07974

Union County NOW, Debra Matrick, Pres., 47 Wabeno Ave., Springfield 07081

Westfield NJ NOW, Sally Leranger, Conv., 823 Nancy Way, Westfield 07090

NEW MEXICO

Albuquerque NOW, Marcy Levine, Pres., Box 26262, Albuquerque 87126

Deming NOW, Pat Bonneau, Contact, 1220 E. Orange, Deming 88030

Los Alamos NOW, Ruth Theobald, Pres., 1063 48 St., Los Alamos 87544

Roosevelt County NOW, Carol Mast & Susan Edwards, Co-Pres., 605 S. Dallas, Portales 88130

Sante Fe NOW, Clara Hawkes, Pres., 1550 6 St., No. 53, Santa Fe 87501

NEW YORK

Albany NOW, Liz Craiglow, Pres., Emma Willard School, Troy 12180

Alfred, NY NOW, Shirley Wurz, Conv., Vice Pres. for Student Affairs, State University College, 811 Court St., Utica 13502

Auburn NOW, Elizabeth Cirillo, Conv., 7 Jefferson St., Auburn 13021

Batavia NOW, Rebecca McKinney, Conv., Box 34, Attica 14011

Binghamton Area, NY NOW, Peggy Holehouse, Co-Pres., 94 Grand Blvd., Binghamton 13905

Binghamton Area, NY NOW, Frances Pipp, Co-Pres., 909 Arbor Dr., Endicott 13760

Bronx NOW, Katherine Todd, Pres., 5532 Netherland Ave., Bronx 10471

Brooklyn NOW, Miriam Klein, Pres., 35 Paerdegat-13 St., Brooklyn 11236

Buffalo, NY NOW, Diane K. Bettencourt, Pres., 305 15 St., Buffalo 14213

Central New York NOW, Geri Kenyon, Pres., 509 S. Beech St., No. 3, Syracuse 13210

Dunkirk-Fredonia NOW, Rose Sebouhian, Conv., 103 Steuben, Fredonia 14063

Elmira NOW, Alicia Fedelman, Conv., 608 W. 4 St., Elmira 14901

Genesee Valley, NY NOW, Ellie Holm, Pres., 1224 Genesee St., Rochester 14611

Geneseo, NY NOW, Susan F. Bailey, Pres., 40 Oak St., Geneseo 14454

Hamilton, NY NOW, Barbara Loveless, Conv., 40 Lebanon St., Hamilton 13346

Ithaca NOW, Ingrid Olsen-Tjensvold, Pres., 202 Winston Dr., Ithaca 14850

Jamestown NOW, Marsula G. Guarino, Conv., 612 Lafayette St., Jamestown 14701

Jefferson County NOW, Marcia Feldman, Pres., 5457 Plank Rd., Burrville Falls, Watertown 13601

Kirkland College NOW, Pennylynn Kornacker, Conv., Kirkland College, Clinton 13323

Long Island NOW, Linda Lamel, Pres., Box 158, Old Village Station, Great Neck 11023

Lower Westchester NOW, Sioux Taylor, Conv., 185 Hillcrest Rd., Mt. Vernon 10552

Middletown NY NOW, Cynthia Harris-Pagano, Conv., 40 Highland Ave., Otisville 10963

New Paltz NOW, Roberta M. Ottaviari, Conv., 46 N. Chestnut St., New Paltz 12561

New York NOW, Judy Wenning, Pres., 47 E. 19 St., New York 10003

New York NOW, Nola Clair, State Coor., 1804 Jefferson Tower Bldg., Presidential Plaza, Syracuse 13202

Niagara Falls, NY NOW, Kathy Nevins, Co-Pres., 507 2 St., Youngstown 14174

NOWestchester, Box 81, North Salem 10560

Oakdale, NY NOW, Rita Boehn, Conv., Dowling College, Oakdale 11769

Orleans NOW, Marta Goodale, Conv., 326 E. State St., Albion 14411

Plattsburgh NOW, Mildred Cominy, Contact, State Univ. of Arts & Sciences, Plattsburgh 12901

Post College NOW, Dr. Alice Scourby, Conv., C. W. Post College, Greenville 11548

Potsdam NOW, Dorothy Codkin, Pres., 7 Wellings Dr., Potsdam 13676

Queens NOW, Donna Loercher, Pres., 162-11 9 Ave., Whitestone 11357

Remsen, NY NOW, Clara Watson, Conv., RD #1, Remsen 13438

Rockland County NOW, Lois Weinstein, Conv., 11 Buckman Pl., Muncie 10952

Schenectady NOW, Shari Michele, Contact, 198 Kingsley Rd., Burnt Hills 12027

Skidmore College, NY NOW, Carol Brady, Conv., Skidmore College, Saratoga Springs 12866

South Shore, NY NOW, Irene Wolf, Pres., 183 Cedar La., Babylon 11702

So. Suffolk NOW, Vivian Lenox Viemeister, Conv., 14 Baywood La., Bayport 11705

Staten Island NOW, Janet Long, Pres., 90 Benedict Ave., Staten Island 10314

Suffolk County NOW, Dana Van Buskirk, Conv., 13 Huyler Rd., Setauket 11785

Syracuse NOW, Geri Kenyon, Pres., 509 S. Beech St., No. 3, Syracuse 13210

Utica NOW, Ellen Rockefeller, Pres., Dawes Ave., Clinton 13323

Wappinger Falls NOW, Alice Moskus, Contact, 17 Wendy Rd., Wappinger Falls 12590

West Bronx, NY NOW, Irma Diamond, Conv., 640 W. 231 St., Riverdale 10463

Westchester County NOW, Miriam Eldridge, Pres., 2360 Bunney Ct., Yorktown Heights 10598

Western Suffolk Co. NOW, Dorothy Pierce, Conv., 27 Dryden Ray, Commack 11725

NORTH CAROLINA

Buncombe Co., NC NOW, Magen Curtis, Pres., 15 Busbee Rd., Asheville 28803

Chapel Hill-Durham NOW, Miriam K. Slifkin, Pres., 313 Burlage Circle, Chapel Hill 27514

Charlotte NOW, Karen Olsen Edwards, Pres., 300 A. Wakefield Dr., Charlotte 28209

Durham NOW, Nancy Z. Gabis-Levine, Pres., 200 Seven Oaks Rd., Apt. 15-E, Durham 27704

Fayetteville NOW, Vonna Vigilione, Pres., Box 856, Rte. 8, Fayetteville 28304

Goldsboro NOW, Peggy Dube Rundell, Conv., 27-21 Billy Francis Dr., Goldsboro 27530

Greensboro NOW, Jane Patterson, Conv., 1702 Liberty Dr., Greensboro 27408

Greenville NOW, Stephanie Carstarphen, Conv., 2115 Southview Dr., Greenville 27834

Havelock NOW, Pat Shehi, Conv., Box 197-C-1, Rte. 2, Havelock 28532

Jacksonville NOW, Sandy Chernicky, Conv., Box 472, Rte. 3, Jacksonville 28540

North Carolina NOW, Rebecca Patterson, State Coor., 1155 C Salem Dr., Charlotte 28209

Raleigh NOW, Jo Perry, Conv., 3216 Ruffin St., Raleigh 27607

Statesville NOW, Marty Lance, 236-C Kelly St., Statesville 28677

Wilmington, NC NOW, Jan Fisher & Barbara Jones, Co-Conv., 720 Montclair Dr., Wilmington 28401

Winston-Salem NOW, Nancy Drum, Pres., Rte. 1, Lassater Rd., Clemons 27102

NORTH DAKOTA

Dickinson NOW, Cathryn Hintze, Conv., 346 8 Ave. W, Dickinson 58601

Fargo, ND–Moorhead, Minn. NOW, Liz Mattern, Conv., 126 Oak Manor Ct., Fargo 58102

Grand Forks NOW, Anita Wasik, Conv., 570 Carleton Ct., Grand Forks 58201

State of North Dakota, Anita Wasik, State Coor., 570 Carleton Ct., Grand Forks 58201

OHIO

Akron NOW, Kay Greenleaf, Pres., 167 Beck Ave., Akron 44302

Avon Lake, Ohio NOW, Trudy Cassellman Verser, Conv., 33393 Electric Blvd., E-2, Avon Lake 44012

Cincinnati NOW, Marcia Maclin, Information Coor., 2624 Bremont Ave., Cincinnati 45237

Cleveland NOW, Box 7147, Cleveland 44128

Cleveland, Ohio NOW, Susan Mallula Johnson, Pres., 3340 Milverton Rd., Shaker Hts. 44120

Columbus, Ohio NOW, Mary Malis, Pres., 5254 Karl Rd., Columbus 43229

Dayton NOW, June Judy, Conv., 38 Sparks St., Trotwood 45426

Delaware, Ohio NOW, Nellice Woltemade, Conv., 74 W. Central, Delaware 43015

Erie County, Ohio NOW, Pat Arnold, Conv., 401 Tecumseh Pl., Huron 44839

Fairborn, Ohio NOW, Anne Breyfogle, Conv., 1225 Peidmont, Fairborn 45324

Greater Toledo Area NOW, Kae Fox, Pres., 2006 Evansdale Ave., Toledo 43607

Kent NOW, Susan Whitney, Conv., 1737 Holly Dr., Kent 44240

Knox County NOW, Box 1686, Gambier 43022

Knox County NOW, Mary Crise, Co-Pres., Drawer A, Danville 43014

Know County NOW, Glenda Enderle, Co-Pres., Box 593, Gambier 43022

Mansfield, Ohio NOW, Mary Porter, Conv., 2500 W. Main St., Mansfield 45840

Ohio NOW, Jan Burnside, State Coor., 67 E. Kossuth, Apt. D, Columbus 43206

Steubenville NOW, Marianne Purkey, Pres., Box 3, Richmond 43944

Wooster, Ohio NOW, Marilyn J. Wilkins, Pres., 661 N. Buckeye, Wooster 44691

Youngstown NOW, Lyla L. Pilorusso, Pres., 4999 Greenbrier Dr., Girard 44420

OKLAHOMA

Norman, Oklahoma NOW, Lynn Persing, Box 5723, 1607 Cross, Norman 73069

Oklahoma City NOW, Astrid Clark, Conv., 318 N.W. 20th Oklahoma City 73103

Shawnee NOW, Wanda Peltier, Pres., Rte. 1, Macomb 74852

Tulsa NOW, Marianne Ballard, Pres., 10710 S. Oswego, Tulsa 74135

OREGON

Klamath Falls NOW, Cindy Barrett and Salley F. Fronsman-Walker, Co-Convs., 219 S. 11 St., No. 306, Klamath Falls 97601

Lane County NOW, Linda Gould McClure, Conv., 925 W. Broadway, Eugene 97402

Portland NOW, Box 843, Portland 97207

Portland NOW, Ruby C. Sanborn, Co-Coor., Rte. 3, Box 1095, Troutdale 97060

Roseburg, Oregon NOW, Nell Dalros, Conv., 374 W. Bardine, Roseburg 97470

Williamette Valley NOW, Carolyn Hutton, Pres., 920 Tamarak, N.E., Salem 97303

PENNSYLVANIA

Altoona, Pa. NOW, Patricia West, Conv., 1610 Bell Ave., Altoona 16602

Beaver County, Pa. NOW, Mary Frances Young, Pres., Sunrise Hills, Industry 15052

Berks County, Pa. NOW, Hannah E. Salvatore, Conv., RD I, Box 38, Womelsdorf 19567

Centre County NOW, Roberta Ferens Ames, Conv., 105 East Curtin St., Bellefonte 16823

East Hills NOW, Margalo Bennett, Conv., 270 Cascade Rd., Pittsburgh 15221

Erie, Pa. NOW, Barbara Starrett, Conv., 709 Nevada Dr., Erie 16506

Greater Greensburg, Pa. NOW, Mary Lois Bartolomucci, Pres., 300 Beaver Rd., Jeannette 15644

Harrisburg, Pa. NOW, 603 Brandt Ave., New Cumberland 17070

Hershey NOW, Beverly Jones, Conv., 457 Leearden Rd., Hershey 17033

Johnstown, Pa. NOW, Gretchen Walker, Pres., Box 1011, Johnstown 15907

Lafayette College NOW, April Cordts and Shelly Marcelli, Conv., Box 830, Gates 204, Easton 18042

Lehigh Valley, Pa. NOW, Carol Bloch, Co-Pres., 2821 Fernor St., Allentown 18103

Lehigh Valley, Pa. NOW, Janet Leander, Co-Pres., 672 Alma Dr., Allentown 18103

McKeesport NOW, Dr. Jean Merriman, Conv., 1403 Cornell St., McKeesport 15123

Ohio Valley North Hills NOW, Barbara Kowalski, Pres., 417 Tierra Pl., Pittsburgh 15237

Northeast-Lower Bucks Co. NOW, Rosemary Capirchio, Pres., Box 163, Penndel 19047

Oakland, Pa. NOW, Charlene Ehler, Conv., 7711 Stanton Ave., Pittsburgh 15218

Pennsylvania NOW, Eleanor Small, State Coor., 132 Sunridge Dr., Pittsburgh 15234

Philadelphia, Pa. NOW, Jan Welch, Pres., 311 Armat St., Philadelphia 19144

Pittsburgh NOW, Phyllis Wetherby, Pres., 116 Avenue L, Pittsburgh 15221

Pocono, Pa. NOW, Nat Lutfy, Conv., Summit Rd., Swiftwater 18370

Pottstown NOW, Elizabeth McCaslin, Pres., 642 High St., Pottstown 19464

South Hills NOW, Eleanor Smeal, Pres., 132 Sunridge Dr., Pittsburgh 15234

Swarthmore NOW, Ruth Hamilton, Conv., 630 N. Chester Rd., Swarthmore 19081

University Park, Pa. NOW, Helen R. Baer, Conv., Human Relation Lab, Pennsylvania State Univ., Hazel Union Bldg., University Park 16802

Washington County, Pa. NOW, Susan Olson, Conv., Box 732, Washington 15301

RHODE ISLAND

Rhode Island NOW, Miriam Kapsinow, State Coor., 18 Whitin Ave., Warwick 02888

Rhode Island NOW, Jean Boyd, Co-Pres., 15 Bluff Ave., Barrington 02806

Rhode Island NOW, Miriam Kapsinow, Co-Pres., 18 Whitin Ave., Warwick 02888

SOUTH CAROLINA

Aiken County NOW, Isabel Vandervelde, Conv., 240 Newberry St., N.W., Aiken 29801

Charleston NOW, Box 3233, Charleston 29407

Columbia NOW, Box 3005, Columbia 29230

Columbia NOW, Eunice Holland, Pres., 711 Sunset Dr., Columbia 29203

Greenville NOW, Bonnie Tapp, Pres., 514 Watts Ave., Greenville 29601

Hilton Head NOW, Diane Light and Mary Fraser, Co-Convs., Sea Pines Plantation, Hilton Head 29928

Piedmont NOW, Barbara R. Strack, Pres., 7-L Mills Rd., Clemson 29631

Spartanburg NOW, Marjorie C. Keller, Pres., 561 Woodland St., Spartanburg 29302

State of South Carolina NOW, Pat Collair, State Coor., 6-15 Prince Hall Apts., Spartanburg 29301

SOUTH DAKOTA

Brookings NOW, Sue Sandness, Pres., 1815 Dakota St., Brookings 57006

Madison NOW, Norine M. Oppold, Conv., Dakota State College, Madison 57042

Sioux Falls NOW, Lona Crandall, Pres., Lincoln Hills, RR 3, Sioux Falls 57101

South Dakota NOW, Mary Lynn Myers, State Coor., 1312 E. Church, Pierre 57501

Vermillion NOW, Sandra Block, Pres., 908 E. Lewis, Vermillion 57069

TENNESSEE

Chattanooga NOW, Box 87, Chattanooga 37401

Chattanooga Area NOW, Helen Burns, Pres., 2704 McCallie Ave., Apt. 4, Chattanooga 37304

Cookeville NOW, Dr. Jettie McWilliams, Conv., College of Education, Tenn. Technological Univ., Cookeville 38501

Huntingdon NOW, Martha H. Edwards, Conv., Rte. 1, Huntingdon 38344

Johnson City NOW, Patricia G. Smyth, Conv., 1300 Peterson Pl., Johnson City 37601

Knoxville NOW, Mary Hendrix, Contact, 1611 Laurel Ave., No. 418, Knoxville 37916

Memphis NOW, Marian K. MacInnes, Pres., Box 12224, Memphis 38112

Nashville NOW, Jo H. Railsback, Pres., 2003 19 Ave. South, Nashville 37212

Oak Ridge NOW, Vivian S. Hiatt, Conv., 201 Waddell Circle, Oak Ridge 37830

Tennessee NOW, Pat Welch, State Coor., 502 Linwood Blvd., Nashville 37205

UTM NOW, Deborah Swanner, Pres., UTM Clement, 441-L, Martin 38237

TEXAS

Arlington NOW, Jennifer J. Hurn, Pres., 806 W. Mitchell, Apt. 316, Arlington 76013

Austin NOW, Sue Ricket, Pres., 1208 Baylor, Austin 78701

Bay Area NOW, Rosemary Mendenhall, Conv., 18100 Nassau Bay Dr., No. 50, Houston 77058

Dallas County NOW, Martha Savage, Pres., 13709 Preston, No. 114, Dallas 75234

Denton NOW, Jean M. Coyle, Conv., 306 S. Locust St., Denton 76201

Fort Worth NOW, Ms. Peg Knapp, Pres., 2200 Winton Terrace East, Ft. Worth 76109

Hidalgo County NOW, Paula Shockley, Conv., 1019 W. Samano, Edinburg 78539

Houston NOW, 3602 Milam, Houston 77006

Huntsville NOW, Pat Altenburg, Conv., Rte. 5, Box 28, Huntsville 77340

San Antonio NOW, Suzanne De Satrustequi, Pres., 515 Ogden St., San Antonio 78212

Texarkana NOW, Mary R. Lewis, Conv., Box 5095, Texarkana 75501

Val Verde County NOW, Pam Smith, Conv., 9093-A Lawhorn, Laughlen AFB, Del Rio 78840

Waco NOW, Yveta Phillips, Pres., 6509 Landmark, Waco 76710

UTAH

Provo NOW, Millie Bushman, Conv., 523 North 100 West, No. 9, Provo 84601

Salt Lake City NOW, Carolyn Young, Pres., 1632 South Wasatch Dr., Salt Lake City 84108

Salt Lake City NOW, Box 8361, Foothill Sta., Salt Lake City 84108

State of Utah, Carol Toomey, State Coor., 473 First Ave., No. 3, Salt Lake City 84103

VERMONT

Bennington College NOW, Barbara H. Smith, Conv., Bennington 05201

South Londonderry NOW, Joyce Caliaro, Conv., South Londonderry 05155

Vermont NOW, Susan Paris, State Coor., Box 187, Shelburne 05482

VIRGINIA

Blacksburg NOW, Larry Sink, Conv., 508 E. Main, Apt. 4, Christianberg 24073

Charlottesville NOW, Cathy Klarfeld, Conv., 116 Howard Dr., Charlottesville 22903

Danville NOW, Joyce H. Weiblen, Pres., 105 B Sedgefield Ct., Danville 24541

Harrisonburg NOW, L. Leotus Morrison, Conv., Madison College, Harrisonburg 22801

Lynchburg NOW, Jean Gilpatrick, 3 N. Princeton Circle, Lynchburg 24503

Martinsville NOW, Pat Dunlavy, Conv., 701 Corn Tassel Trail, No. 23, Martinsville 24112

Newport News NOW, Laura B. Farris, Conv., 610 Randolph Rd., Newport News 23605

Northern Virginia NOW, Bonnie Helen Armstrong, Pres., 7833 Enola St., McLean 22101

Peninsula NOW, Gerlinde Quartero, Pres., 201 Mistletoe Dr., Newport News 23606

Petersburg NOW, Mary A. James, Conv., 129 S. Sycamore St., Petersburg 23803

Richmond NOW, Zelda K. Nordlinger, Conv., 6824 Shawnee Rd., Richmond 23225

Roanoke NOW, Elise B. Heinz, Conv., 1400 N. Uhle St., Arlington 22201

State of Virginia NOW, Barbara Leerskov, State Coor., 39 Nash St., Herndon 22070

Tidewater NOW, Margaret Debolt, Pres., 724 Abbey Arch, Virginia Beach 23455

Virginia Beach NOW, Betsy L. Bretz, Pres., 4325 Cambria Circle, Virginia Beach 23455

Williamsburg NOW, Joanne F. Carroll, 222B Waller Mill Rd., Williamsburg 23185

Wise NOW, Donna Hurley, Conv., Box 478, Wise 24293

WASHINGTON

Bellevue-Eastside NOW, Sharon Anderson, Pres., 13027 S.E. 76 St., Renton 98055

Bellingham-Whatcom NOW, Marsha Trew, Pres., 1200 Lincoln, No. 183, Bellingham 98225

Federal Way-Auburn NOW, Jean Smith, Pres., 2401 S.W. 316 St., Federal Way 98002

Highline NOW, Geraldine Emery, Pres., 23612 100 Ave. S.E., No. 85, Kent 98031

Kitsap County NOW, Dolores Doninger, Pres., Box 762, Bremerton 98310

Longview NOW, Sylvia Marstero, Conv., 1619 24 St., Longview 98632

Olympia NOW, Carroll B. Dick, Pres., 406 Stillwell, Olympia 98506

Pullman-Moscow, ID NOW, Celia Banks, Conv., S.E. 120 Derby St., Pullman 99163

Renton NOW, Peggy Bardarson, Pres., 320 Renton Ave. South, Renton 98055

Seattle-King County NOW, Jean Withers, Co-Pres., 2317 Franklin E., Seattle 98102

Seattle-King County NOW, Susan Lane, Co-Pres., 3702 E. Union, Seattle 98122

Snohomish County NOW, Julie Ballard, Co-Pres., 208-6301 St. Albion Way, Mountlake Terrace 98043

Snohomish County NOW, Terri Walsh, Co-Pres., 129 S. Ferry, Monroe 98272

Spokane NOW, Box 432, Spokane 99210

Spokane NOW, Patricia E. Marx, Pres., E. 504 19 St., Spokane 99203

Tacoma NOW, Janice Stonestreet, Pres., 5903 Lagoon La. N.W., Gig Harbor 98335

Tri City NOW, Anne P. Wallace, Contact, 89 Waldron Pl., Richland 99352

Vancouver NOW, Shirley Crase, Co-Conv., 2308 E. Reserve, Vancouver 98661

Vancouver NOW, Sharon Versteeg, Co-Conv., 602 W. Evergreen Blvd., Vancouver 98660

Washington NOW, Jan Swanson, State Coor., 20015 43 St., S.E., Bothell 98011

Yakima NOW, Karen D. Norton, Pres., 4623½ Kenward Way, Yakima 98901

WEST VIRGINIA

Charleston NOW, Karen Kuhns, Conv., 1591 E. Washington St., Charleston 25305

Mor-Fair NOW, Letty Stewart, Pres., Rte. 4, Box 266, Morgantown 26505

WISCONSIN

Alverno College, Women's Research Center, 3401 S. 39 St., Milwaukee 53215

Beaver Dam NOW, Doris Ingres, Conv., 1009 West St., Beaver Dam 53916

Central Wisconsin NOW, Carol Leonard, Pres., Rte. 4, Box 101, Stevens Point 54481

Eau Claire NOW, Margo V. House, Pres., 432 W. Grand Ave., Eau Claire 54701

Fox Cities NOW, Agnes K. Van Eperen, Pres., 1510 Palisades Dr., Appleton 54911

Green Bay NOW, Sally Bender, Pres., 1626 Farlin Ave., Green Bay 54302

Kenosha NOW, Bonnie Stelnicki, Pres., 4316 Taft Rd., Kenosha 53140

La Crosse NOW, Vivian Munson, Conv., 371 S. 21 St., La Crosse 54601

Madison NOW, Nadine A. Goff, Pres., 116 E. Gilman St., D2, Madison 53703

Marshfield Area NOW, Eileen Kelz, Pres., 1407 N. Peach, No. 13, Marshfield 54449

Milwaukee NOW, Box 174, Milwaukee 53201

Milwaukee NOW, Carolyn Mueller, Pres., 721 E. Carlisle Ave., Milwaukee 53217

Ripon NOW, Bonnie Brody, Pres., 648 Watson St., Ripon 54971

Rock County NOW, Judith Hansen Adler, Co-Conv., 320 Oakland Ave., Janesville 53545

Rock County NOW, Chris Correra, Co-Conv., 2128 Staborn Dr., Beloit 53511

Sheboygan County NOW, Darlene J. Navis, Pres., RR 1, Oostburg 53070

Sturgeon Bay NOW, Marion Stern, Conv., 4191 Bayshore Rd., Sturgeon Bay 54235

Two Rivers–Manitowoc NOW, Joan Leannah, Conv., 1416 25 St., Two Rivers 54241

Waukesha NOW, Christina Mueller, Conv., 1563 Racine Ave., Waukesha 53186

Winnebago NOW, Phyllis Roney, Pres., 111 Zarling Ave., Oshkosh 54901

Wisconsin NOW, Margo V. House, State Coor., 432 W. Grand Ave., Eau Claire 54701

WYOMING

Casper NOW, Carole Aspinwall, Pres., 3003 Nob Hill Dr., Caper 82601

Cheyenne NOW, Janet J. Felker, Pres., 504 Bent Ave., Cheyenne 82001

Laramie NOW, Julia Hewgley, Conv., 1726 Downey St., Laramie 82070

University of Wyoming NOW, Pat Hays, Pres., 601 Downey Hall, Laramie 82070

CANADA

Vancouver NOW, Lisa Hobbs, Conv., 2250 Granville St., Vancouver 9

PUERTO RICO

Condado NOW, Trudi Feldman, Conv., Edgewater House, Apt. D1-E, Condado 00907

FOREIGN

Paris NOW, Nikki Econonos, Conv., c/o Anderson, 326 Rue St. Jacques, Paris, France 75005

164 NATIONAL WELFARE RIGHTS ORGANIZATION. 1424 16 St., N.W., Washington, D.C. 20036. (202) 483-1531. Founded June 1967. Johnnie Tillmon, Exec. Dir. Dues: $1, welfare recipients; $5 Friends of Welfare Rights.

Although not limited exclusively to women, this group deals with welfare rights, an issue of critical importance to many women. It was founded to inform welfare recipients of their rights; to fight for less repressive legislation; and to give legal assistance in the welfare field. There are 800 local groups. A publications list is available, which includes the following items concerning women: *The Woman from Welfare Rights* (25¢) and *Welfare Is a Woman's Issue* (25¢).

NATIONAL WOMEN'S POLITICAL CAUCUS. See 512 for national and local listings.

PLANNED PARENTHOOD FEDERATION OF AMERICA. See 482.

165   WOMEN'S ACTION ALLIANCE. 370 Lexington Ave., New York, N.Y. 10017. (212) 685-0800. Founded January 1972. Grace Helen McCabe, Exec. Dir. No fees.

This nonprofit, tax-exempt organization was formed as a central information and resource agency for activists in the women's movement. It provides information and technical help to women who want to start local action projects, and it links women who are working on similar projects in different areas of the country. WAA guides women to helpful materials or may create the materials for them. The alliance refers women to organizations and to sympathetic professionals: lawyers, psychologists, and doctors. Model projects created by the alliance involve continuing education at Brooklyn College and in Boston, an investigation of sex discrimination in public employment in Boston, and a welfare education project in Baltimore. WAA information packets cost $1.25.

166   Women's Coalition for the Third Century. 45 Frances Ave., Cambridge, Mass. 02138. (617) 495-4536. Founded September 1973. Patricia Budd Kepler.

A coalition of women's organizations and individuals "to unite women around the Bicentennial year and to affect America's Third Century, by recovering women's history, celebrating women's present and creating America's future." Aims to attract national attention to women's potential and contributions to this nation, via symposia, films, television programs, and other nationally coordinated activities.

WOMEN'S EQUITY ACTION LEAGUE. See 386.

WOMEN'S NATIONAL ABORTION ACTION COALITION. See 495.

167   YOUNG WOMEN'S CHRISTIAN ASSOCIATION OF THE U.S.A. 600 Lexington Ave., New York, N.Y. 10022. (212) 753-4700. Founded 1858. Ida Sloan Snyder, Dir. of Communications. 2,400,000 members.

"The Association draws together into responsible membership women and girls of diverse experiences and faiths that their lives may be open to new understanding and deeper relationships and that together they may join in the struggle for peace and justice, freedom and dignity for all people." In the United States, programs are underway in 8,197 different locations in 49 states. Local "Ys" often maintain referral services for women and, in some cases, women's centers, as well as collections of printed material of interest to women. The YWCA publishes *The YWCA Magazine* (9/yr; $3.50) and many other publications, including those listed below.

> *Exploring Human Space*, guidelines for volunteers wishing to work with economically deprived adolescent girls ($2.75).
> *Feminine Figures*, annual leaflet of selected facts about American women and girls (sold only in pkgs. of 5, 1-4 pkgs. 80¢ each).
> *Ferment of Freedom*, a study/discussion guide for groups of women who seek to relate their role as women to their Christian faith and to participate in social change, by Dr. Letty M. Russell (1-24 copies, $1.25 each).

Racism and Sexism, a careful look at their similarities and differences, plus a bibliography (sold only in pkgs. of 10, $1.50 each).

Sex Education—Let's Get Going, multimedia material—records, color slides, and reading materials—to help groups consider what sex education is, whose job it is, the role of the schools and community, and attitudes of youth and adults, by Helen F. Southard ($5.00).

U.S. Local

(See also U.S. National, National Organization for Women.)

Alaska

168 ANCHORAGE WOMEN'S LIBERATION MOVEMENT GROUP. Box 1721 A SRA, Anchorage, Alaska 99507. (907) 344-3083. Founded December 1970. Sylvia A. Munsey. 300 members.

Aims to "promote equality of both women and men in all areas of our society." Projects include borough-wide assessment of women's needs, weekly rap sessions, changes in Human Rights Commission statutes, speakers bureau, women's center, rape relief clinic, and aid for teen-age girls. Publishes a monthly newsletter *On the Way* ($3.50/yr.).

Arizona

169 WOMEN'S CENTER. 1414 S. McAllister St., Tempe, Ariz. 85281. (603) 968-0743. Founded January 1973. Judy Bates, 107 E. 7 St., Tempe, Ariz. 85281.

A referral and information service concerning birth control, employment, welfare, health, the women's movement, pregnancy services, roommates, gynecology, and therapy. Organizes consciousness-raising groups; maintains a small library.

California

170 BERKELEY WOMEN'S AFFIRMATIVE ACTION UNION. Box 840, Berkeley, Calif. 94701. Founded 1973. Jean Miller, 2713 Ellsworth, No. 1, Berkeley, Calif. 94704.

A feminist group working toward enforcement of local, state, and federal laws prohibiting sex discrimination in employment and city services. Special projects involve support of the Special Women's Project in the Berkeley Public Library and equal treatment in the Berkeley Parks and Recreation Department.

171 BERKELEY WOMEN'S CENTER. 2134 Allston Way, Berkeley, Calif. 95704. (415) 548-4343. Founded January 1973. Peggy Fulder.

Offers information, provides drop-in facilities for women, and makes referrals for jobs, physical and mental health, and housing. Helps to organize other women's groups and to sponsor programs to raise women's consciousness.

172 CENTER FOR WOMEN'S STUDIES AND SERVICES. 908 F. St., San Diego, Calif. 92101. (714) 239-8355. Founded 1970. Carol Rowell.

Dedicated to identifying and meeting the needs of women and fighting the oppression and exploitation of women. CWSS operates The Women's Storefront which provides the following services: vocational counseling; job referral; one-to-one and group counseling concerning pregnancy, abortion, alcoholism, crisis intervention, and drug addiction; referrals to other organizations; information regarding educational programs and financial assistance; and the Bonnie Bergquist Memorial Scholarship Fund. The center works with the California Institute for Women and the California Rehabilitation Center for Women, and offers parole plan assistance for early release as well as a referral service for emergency temporary housing. The CWSS operates a feminist library and reading room, and publishes the following publications:

CWSS Newsletter; *International Bibliography of Women Writers*; *The Oppression of Women in the Hard Drug Culture*; *Rainbow Snake* (an anthology of women poets); and *Women of the Convicted Class*.

173 CHICO WOMEN'S CENTER. 730 W. 2 St., California State University, Chico, Calif. 95926. (916) 345-6561. Founded Spring 1971. Fran Wigstaff, 1502 Bidwell Dr., Chico, Calif.

Aims "to increase the awareness of women of their unique position in society and to service women's special needs by serving as a clearing house for many diverse women's activities." Operates a women's health cooperative and community outreach seminars; supports women's studies on campus; and compiles data on women's resources in the local area. Offers information on women's studies, tapes of the center's 1971 conference, and a slide show called *To Be Free* (arrangements can be made for viewing).

174 ISLA VISTA WOMEN'S CENTER. 6504 Pardall Rd., Isla Vista, Calif. 93017. (805) 968-8809. Founded March 1970.

Housed in an apartment, the center has a library and reference room, and can provide a place to stay for the night. The center offers a women's reading group; and sponsors the Women's Radio Collective, which produces a program from 7 to 7:30 p.m. on KCSB radio Monday nights, a health collective, auto mechanics classes, self-awareness groups, rape prevention, and self-defense. The center publishes *Hypatia*, a quarterly feminist magazine, and *Right-on, Sister*, a monthly newsletter ($1/yr.).

175 WESTSIDE WOMEN'S CENTER. 218 S. Venice Blvd., Venice, Calif. 90291. (213) 823-4774. Founded March 1972. Mary Crane.

"An open center for any woman." Organizes consciousness-raising groups, Liberation Workshops, radical therapy, divorce and abortion counseling, and a referral service. Publishes *Sister* newsletter (m., $3/yr.) on various themes of concern to women.

176   WOMEN'S RESOURCE CENTER AT UNIVERSITY OF CALIFORNIA,
        LOS ANGELES. 90 Powell Library, 405 Hilgard St., Los Angeles, Calif.
        90024. (213) 825-3945. Founded May 1972. Susan Dunn, Coor.

   Provides information, referrals, and programs covering the whole spectrum of
women's concerns. Offers programs on women as consumers, financial development, consciousness-raising, radical therapy, and development of groups.

Colorado

177   VIRGINIA NEAL BLUE RESOURCE CENTERS FOR COLORADO
        WOMEN. Colorado Women's College, 1800 Pontiac St., Denver, Colo. 80220.
        (303) 399-8303. Founded February 1972. Pauline A. Parish, Dir.
        See also Colorado Commission on the Status of Women, 264.

   Established by the Colorado Commission on the Status of Women, the centers are concerned with women in the areas of employment, counseling, education
and training, and the home and family. Their functions are: to develop and implement programs for women; to serve as a clearinghouse of information and resources
for women and women's organizations; and to coordinate their work with other
agencies and groups within the local areas whose services are relevant to women.
Branches are located at El Paso Community College, Colorado Springs, Colo.
80904; Southern Colorado State College, Pueblo, Colo. 80010; and Adams State
College, Alamosa, Colo. 81101. The branches carry out the following services:
workshops for mature women aimed at expanding life-style options; business/in-
dustry/labor consultations which seek to decrease job discrimination; training programs to upgrade existing skills, or to teach new ones; workshops on consumer economics; career and employment counseling for women; referral services to existing
agencies within the community; and collection of local statistics. Publications available are those published by the Colorado Commission on the Status of Women, and
Opportunities Part Time: A Guide to Work and Further Training for Women, Sally
Allen, ed. (1972, $2.50).

178   WOMEN'S LIBERATION COALITION. Rm. 181, U.M.C., University of
        Colorado, Boulder, Colo. 80302. (303) 443-2211. Founded 1966. Mary
        Ann Thomas. 40 members.

   Aims "to educate women about sexual oppression so that they may effect
radical social change." The coalition plans women's studies courses, and sponsors
speakers and films.

Connecticut

179   NEW HAVEN WOMEN'S LIBERATION. 3438 Yale Sta., New Haven, Conn.
        06520. (203) 436-0272. Founded 1970.

   A resource and support center for women and a coalition of semiautonomous
smaller groups. Operates a women's liberation center, an abortion referral service, a
personal counseling service, and divorce counseling; and sponsors various women's
cultural events—art, band, and theater. Publishes *Sister: New Haven Women's Lib-*

eration Newsletter ($2, individuals; free to women on welfare and in prison). One issue included poetry, photographs, book reviews, news items, letters, and articles on abortion and the meat boycott.

180 WOMEN'S LIBERATION CENTER. 11 N. Main St., South Norwalk, Conn. 06856. (203) 853-2162. Founded April 1972. 300 members.

Aims "to promote liberation for all," and publishes a monthly newsletter ($2.50/yr.).

181 WOMEN'S LIBERATION CENTER OF GREATER HARTFORD. 11 Amity St., Hartford, Conn. 06106. (203) 523-8949. Founded December 1972. Pat Cook, Laurie Green, 118 Babcock St., Hartford, Conn. 06106.

A multipurpose drop-in center where women can meet with one another. Offers courses in self-defense, a referral service, peer counseling, consciousness-raising groups, pregnancy and abortion counseling, a lesbian drop-in center, a loan fund, special programs, and lectures. Publishes the newsletter, *Women's Voice of Greater Hartford* (m, $2.50/yr.).

District of Columbia

182 WASHINGTON AREA WOMEN'S CENTER. 1736 R St., N.W., Washington, D.C. 20009. (202) 232-5045. Founded August 1972. Gerri Traina. 1000 members. Hours: 10 a.m.–10 p.m., every day.

Nonprofit educational and service organization serving women in the Washington area. The center houses the following activities: Woman's Legal Defense Fund, (202) 232-5293; Rape Crisis Center, (202) 333-RAPE; Women's Health and Abortion Project, Abortion Counseling, (202) 483-4632; Domestic Relations Project; Feminist Counseling Collective; Employment Discrimination Counseling Project; Credit Counseling Project; Sojourner Truth School for Women; courses in mechanics, self-defense, women's history, and public speaking; Library Project; Child Care Collective; and the Women's Center Coffeehouse, known as "Sophie's Parlor," and its monthly newsletter.

Georgia

183 WOMEN'S INFORMATION CENTER. Atlanta Y.W.C.A. 45 11 St., N.E., Atlanta, Ga. 30309. (404) 892-3476. Founded February 1971. Maxine Robinson, Dir.

An information and referral center for the community. Maintains a feminist library, and is developing a project on women and crime.

Illinois

184 CHICAGO WOMEN'S LIBERATION UNION. 852 W. Belmont St., Chicago, Ill. 60657. (312) 348-4300. Founded Fall 1969. 350 members. Dues: $15/yr., if possible. Hours: 10 a.m.–4 p.m., Mon.–Sat.

A city-wide radical women's organization, with approximately 20 chapters and work groups which meet in various parts of the city and on several college campuses to struggle "for the liberation of women and against sexism in all sections of society. Included in this struggle is the struggle for the rights of sexual self-determination for all people and for the liberation of all homosexuals, expecially lesbians." Work groups deal with services, education, and direct action around issues of health care, labor, child-care, education, etc. Direct Action for Rights in Employment (DARE) has been fighting for equal treatment and wages for women. The Health Project works for women's demands on the health care system. The Abortion Task Force works toward implementing the Supreme Court decision of January 1973. The Women's Graphics Collective produces feminist and political posters and cards. Posters are $1.50 each with discounts available for bulk rates; cards are $1 for 10. Posters include: "Sisterhood Is Blooming," "Cry Out," "Chicago Maternity Center," "Womankind Is Awakening," "Health Care Is for People, Not Profit," "Shy Lesbian Feminists," "Together," "Women Are Not Chicks," "Women Working," and "Women Declare War on Rape." A catalog with pictures is available. The Chicago Women's Liberation Rock Band, which is composed of an electric piano, double drums, bass, lead, acoustic electric rhythm, and vocals, performs songs about the oppression of the working woman, rebellion against the institution of marriage, and strength in the revolutionary women's movement. With the New Haven Women's Liberation Rock Band, they have made a record "Mountain Moving Day" ($3.50, bulk rates available; Rounder Records, see 111). Other groups of the CWLU are the Southside Women's Health Collective; Rape Crisis Line; Legal Clinic; Liberation School for Women; Southwest Side Project; Connecting Link, and the High School and Junior College Organizing Project. Literature, buttons, and posters are for sale. The CWLU also publishes a newsletter, *Womankind* (m. $4/yr.). *The Chicago Women's Yellow Pages* is in preparation.

185   PROFESSIONAL ORGANIZATION OF WOMEN FOR EQUAL RIGHTS (POWER). 1100 Forest St., Wilmette, Ill. 60091. (312) 726-2545. Founded September 1972. Stephanie Kanwit. 100 members.

Aims to eliminate discrimination on the basis of sex, by litigation if necessary. Currently attempting to force the Liquor Control Commission to rescind liquor licenses of institutions which discriminate on the basis of sex or race. Participating in a credit experiment under the direction of the Columbia Broadcasting System.

186   THE WOMAN'S INSTITUTE. 420 W. Melrose St., Chicago, Ill. 60657. (312) 528-8319. Founded 1973. Dues: $15; students, $5.

Has sponsored conferences and workshops on the "Psychology of Being a Woman," "Feminist Literature," and "Women and Money." Other conferences in the works are "Women and Art," "Women and Religion," "Women and the Law," "Woman's World and Man's Language," "Woman and Medicine," "Woman and Business." "Woman and Education," and "Woman and Anger." Meets weekly; coordinates rap groups. Its newsletter, *For Women Only*, contains news items, art work, writing, and photographs.

Indiana

187   WOMEN'S CENTER, INC. 414 N. Park St., Bloomington, Ind. 47401. (812) 336-8691. Founded September 1971. Lyda Hemphiel, Kasin Ford.

"A house to give a permanent home to the Women's Movement and to be responsive to the evolving needs of women in the community." Members must buy a $25 share in the corporation which is paying for the house. The center maintains back files of the Bloomington Women's Movement newsletter, *Front Page*, files on feminist issues, and a small library of feminist literature and books.

Massachusetts

BOSTON WOMEN'S COLLECTIVE (Boston, Mass.). See 1.

188 CELL 16. 2 Brewer St., Cambridge, Mass. 02138. (617) 491-0345. Founded 1968. Michele LaCroux.

Runs Korean Karate School, and publishes *No More Fun and Games; A Journal of Female Liberation* (irreg., $1.50/issue), a magazine with poems, articles, and graphics. A record, "Loner" ($3) with music written, played, and sung by Indra Allen, features feminist songs "Ten Speed Rider," "Pregnant Blues," and "Freedom Coming," and two posters "Feminist Lives" (75¢) and "Disarm Rapists—Smash Sexism" (75¢).

189 EVERYWOMAN'S CENTER. Munson Hall, Univ. of Mass., Amherst, Mass. 01002. (413) 545-0883. Founded September 1972. Pat Sackrey, Coor.

A collaborative effort of Continuing Education for Women, the Counseling Center, and the Office of Community Development and Human Relations at the University of Massachusetts. The center is open to all women, and provides a place where they can meet, get information and counseling, and work on projects. The center maintains a library of books, periodicals, and pamphlets relating to the feminist movement, career opportunities, and other issues of interest to women; sponsors Project Self, a series of noncredit workshops by, for, and about women; and puts out a newsletter.

Following is a list of publications available through Everywoman's Center; please include postage when ordering.

> *The Family as Seen from a Feminist Perspective: A Selected Bibliography* by Pat Sackrey (5¢)
> *Feminist Classics: A Ms. Bibliography* (10¢)
> *A Feminist Looks at Educational Software Materials* by Lois Hart ($1)
> *Feminist Resources for Elementary and Secondary Schools* by The Task Force on Sexism in the Schools (25¢)
> *Lesbianism: Sexual Survival in the Schools* by Kay Marion (10¢)
> *Non-Sexist Parenting* by Allison Rossett (50¢)
> *Voices of New Women: A Poetry Anthology* (75¢)
> *Who Rules Massachussets Women?* By Women's Research Center of Boston ($1)
> *Women's Film Co-op Catalog.* (donation)

A poster is also available: "Portrait of Virginia Woolfe with a Quote from *Three Guineas*" ($1)

190 FEMALE LIBERATION. Box 344, Cambridge A, Cambridge, Mass. 02139 (639 Massachusetts Ave., Cambridge, Mass.) (617) 491-1071. Founded 1968. 50 members. Dues: 25¢/m. Hours: 11 a.m.–6 p.m., weekdays and most weekday evenings.

Holds general and orientation meetings, organizes consciousness-raising groups, maintains a library and speakers bureau, and presents a weekly radio show on WBZ–FM (9 a.m., Sat.). Female Liberation publishes a bimonthly newsletter ($3/yr.), which reports conferences, meetings, and news, and contains announcements and a calendar. A magazine, *The Second Wave* (q., 75¢ issue; $3/yr.) is also available; one issue contained the following articles: "Lesbianism and Feminism: Snyonyms or Contradictions," "Natural Birth Control," "Power Failure: a Talk with Phyllis Chesler;" and "Notes of a Radical Transsexual."

NEW ENGLAND WOMEN'S RESOURCE CENTER (Boston, Mass.). See 1.

191   VALLEY WOMEN'S CENTER. Main St., Northampton, Mass. 01060. (413) 586-2025.

Acts as a base for many groups, working on consciousness-raising, film co-op, welfare counseling, personal counseling, sex stereotyping in the schools, abortion and birth control counseling, writers workshop, women against the war, and obesity. Maintains a bulletin board, speakers file, referrals to jobs and housing, drop-in area, and women's library; also publishes a newsletter.

192   WOMEN'S CENTER. 46 Pleasant St., Cambridge, Mass. 02139. (617) 354-8807. Founded January 1972. Elizabeth Bouvier, Rochelle Ziegler.

A multipurpose center which offers a variety of services; among them, birth control and abortion counseling, a rape crisis center, a lesbian women's group, and day care. Houses the Women's Center School, to educate women about "their history, bodies, etc., in a nonsexist environment and to provide and encourage ways of sharing our skills and knowledge." There are 200 students and 25 staff members. Cost is $3 per course plus one night of baby-sitting. A free brochure is available listing course descriptions, registration dates, times, and fees. The center maintains a library, and publishes a newsletter ($2/yr). A record, "Mountain Moving Day," is available at $3.50.

193   WOMEN'S RESOURCE CENTER. Appleton-Chase No. 106, Andover-Newton Theological School, Newton Centre, Mass. 02159. (617) 332-1100. Rev. Chris Blackburn.

"A place for gathering materials about the women's movement" and organizing women at the seminary. A bibliography of literature from the WRC is available.

Michigan

194   NEWS AND LETTERS WOMEN'S LIBERATION COMMITTEE. 1900 E. Jefferson St., Detroit, Mich. 48307. (313) 961-1010. Founded February 1971.

A Marxist-Humanist women's liberation group established to formulate theory for the women's liberation movement; to fight sex discrimination; to write articles on the women's movement for *News and Letters*, a Marxist-Humanist monthly newspaper; and to correspond with women throughout the world on women's liberation. The center publishes *Notes on Women's Liberation; We Speak in Many Voices*, (an anthology of articles, $1) *Rosa Luxemburg: Revolutionary Theoretician* by Lee Tracy (35¢); and *Women's Liberation as Force and Reason*.

Missouri

195 WOMEN'S LIBERATION UNION. 5138 Tracy St., Kansas City, Mo. 64110.
(816) 333-4155. Founded 1969. Priscilla Camp, Membership Coor., 1218 E.
49 Terr., Kansas City, Mo. 64110.

"A political organization which seeks to end the oppression of women and
which believes that the liberation of women will require a radical restructuring of
society." The union is a "city-wide organization composed of a variety of small
groups. . . . Some [units] operate mainly as discussion and study groups concerned
with understanding the social, economic and cultural attitudes and institutions
which oppress women. Other groups are more geared to reaching out to new
women and to developing programs in various communities (day care, the women's
school, etc.). . . . A coordinating committee, made up of two (rotating) members
from each collective (task-oriented group) or rap group, meets every two weeks and
makes decisions for the union as a whole."

Following is a list of programs and groups in the Women's Liberation Union.

Abortion, Health and Self-Help 931-7968
Day Care Collective (Operates day care at 3800 McGee, 5 days/wk. 7:30 a.m.-
    5:00 p.m. Meets Weds. evenings. 561-6168)
Gay Women's Alliance 363-5842
Rape in the Media 531-6918
Speaker's Bureau and Rap Groups 523-1389
Women's Education Project (Coordinates women's school.) 531-1410
Women-in-transition 531-1410
Women's Studies

WLU also maintains a library, and publishes a bimonthly newsletter (35¢/
issue; $2/yr.). Seven-inch reel-to-reel tapes originally heard on KCUR–FM radio,
(89.3), *A New World Coming: Voices from the Women's Liberation Movement*
radio program, are available for $1.50 rental charge plus a $10 deposit. Tapes are
15 minutes in length. Some programs have been "Learning to Be a Man," "Equal
Rights Amendment," "Recollections of the Woman Suffrage Movement," "Abortion, Rape, Sexist Language, Sexism and Advertising," "Sexism and Rock Music,"
"A Play about Abortion: 'What have You Done for Me Lately?,' " "Sexism and
Psychotherapy," and "A Lesbian-Feminist Statement."

New Jersey

196 WOMEN'S CENTER, YWCA. 395 Main St., Orange, N.J. 07052 Founded
June 20, 1972. Ruth Lee, Prog. Dir.

An action, referral, and reference center that conducts workshops in racism
and sexism, financial and legal rights, and careers. It maintains a twenty-four hour
answering service, holds consciousness-raising groups, and publishes a bimonthly
newsletter, *Focus on Women.*

197 WOMEN'S CENTER OF BERGEN COUNTY. Box 356, Ridgewood, N.J.
07450. (201) 342-8958. Founded February 1972. Zania Katz, 136 Longview Dr., Emerson, N.J. 07630. 150 members. Dues: $7.

"Feminist-oriented women desiring to help other women in major and minor crisis situations and to provide education for women as to their rights." Conducts workshops in women's legal rights, consumerism, and female sexuality, and a course on political action and education; operates a crisis intervention answering service.

New York City

198   THE FEMINISTS 120 Liberty St., New York, N.Y. 10006. (212) 344-7750. Founded 1968. Nancy Marvel, 89 City Island Ave., Bronx, N.Y. 10464.

"A group of women committed to the study of the causes underlying the persecution of women and to direct action to eradicate this persecution." Speakers are available, as well as a literature list. Buttons and posters are sold, and following is a list of selected publications.

Class Structure in the Women's Movement 15¢
Dangers in the Pro-Woman Line and Consciousness Raising 20¢
The Feminists: Organizational Principles and Structure 20¢
Five Easy Pieces: A Movie Review 15¢
The Institution of Sexual Intercourse 20¢
Man-Hating 10¢
Marriage 20¢
Notes from the Lower Classes 10¢
Radical Feminism and Love 15¢
The Rise of Man: Origins of Woman's Oppression 15¢
The Twig Benders: A Pornographic Study of Pornography 20¢
Vaginal Orgasm as a Mass Hysterical Response 10¢
Why We're against the Equal Rights Amendment 10¢

A *Complete Literature Packet* (one copy of each paper listed above) may be ordered for $1.75.

199   NEW YORK RADICAL FEMINISTS. Box 621, Old Chelsea Sta., New York, N.Y. 10011. (212) 242-5889. Founded 1969. Jean Grove, 80 Thompson St., New York, N.Y. 10012. 1200 members.

A nonstructured feminist organization striving to eradicate the "sex-class system." Sponsors conferences (previous conferences have been on rape, prostitution, and marriage), organizes consciousness-raising groups and women's forums, maintains a speakers' bureau, and holds monthly meetings. Also publishes a monthly newsletter ($3/yr.), an *Asexual Manifesto*, a *Consciousness-raising Outline*, and *Introduction to NYRF*, all available for the cost of postage.

200   REDSTOCKINGS. Box 1284, Stuyvesant Sta., New York, N.Y. 10009. Founded 1969.

A women's liberation group publishing an annual journal, *Feminist Revolution* "to serve the women's liberation movement as an organ in which theory is developed and strategies are advanced by criticizing past and present experiences." Back issues of *Woman's World*, a discontinued quarterly newspaper previously published by the group, are available for $2 for all five back issues.

201   STATEN ISLAND COMMUNITY COLLEGE WOMEN'S CENTER. 715 Ocean Terrace, Staten Island, N.Y. 10301. (212) 390-7602. Founded March 1973. Camille Gerbino, 225 Broad St., Staten Island, N.Y. 200 members.

A place for women to meet and organize, the center is supported by students, faculty, staff of Staten Island Community College and women from the community. The center offers a film series on women, a lecture series, and is formulating a feminist library.

202 THE WOMEN'S CENTER, BARNARD COLLEGE. New York, N.Y. 10027. (212) 280-2067. Founded September 1971. Jane S. Gould, Dir.

Created by the recommendation of a task force of "students, faculty, administrators, alumnae, and trustees, the Center has become both a physical and a psychological meeting ground for activities relating to women. It has initiated a wide range of programs and services, both academic and nonacademic, all designed to help women live and work with dignity, autonomy, and equality." The center "has become a national resource center and a clearinghouse of information about women's groups and feminist activities. It has collected and catalogued close to a thousand books, articles, clippings, and special issues of journals and maintains subscriptions to over thirty newsletters and periodicals, covering a broad spectrum of subject areas and women's issues. An important part of the collection is the growing number of research papers by Barnard students. . . ."

The center sponsors and cosponsors meetings, coffee hours, forums, and conferences, and has initiated a noncredit introductory course in women's studies for adult women, entitled "Explorations in Feminism." Publishing efforts include *Women's Work and Women's Studies*, an annual interdisciplinary bibliography from KNOW, Inc. (see 13), ($7.50, looseleaf $4.50); and *Help: A Resource Booklet for Women* ($1 from the Women's Center).

203 WOMEN'S CENTER, UNION THEOLOGICAL SEMINARY. 99 Claremont Ave., New York, N.Y. 10027. (212) 662-7100. Founded 1968. Sarah L. Darter.

"A center for multiple use by female staff, faculty, students and student wives, to facilitate women's research and social undertakings, and to coordinate women's concerns and activities related to UTS."

204 WOMEN'S COUNSELING PROJECT. Rm. 112, Earl Hall, Columbia University, 117 St. and Broadway, New York, N.Y. 10027. (212) 280-7477. Founded November 1971. Susan Savelle, Coor.

Crisis counseling and referral service, with telephone and walk-in facilities. Makes referrals to appropriate agencies for women needing abortions, therapy, gynecological services, legal aid, and birth control information. WCP checks all services it recommends.

205 WOMEN'S LIBERATION CENTER. 243 W. 20 St., New York, N.Y. 10011. (212) 255-9802. Founded 1970.

Housed in a former firehouse, the center offers a "public place for women to meet with each other, for women's groups to hold meetings, and a clearinghouse for services needed by women. The center is staffed weekdays after 2 p.m. and meetings go on every night. Groups meeting at the Women's Center include a Food Co-op, which sells fresh vegetables, fruit, cheese, etc., at wholesale prices; an Anti-Rape Group; Women in Transition, a group arising out of the desire of women coming out of marriage or in other crisis situations to be with each other; a White Women's Workshop on Racism; Older Women's Liberation consciousness-raising groups; self-defense classes; and the New York Radical Feminists. Abortion counsellors staff the Women's Health and Abortion Project phones four days a week. Movement literature is available for sale.

New York State

206 ITHACA WOMEN'S CENTER. 140 W. State St. Ithaca, N.Y. 14850 (607) 272-6922. Founded Summer 1970. Bunny Cramer. 300 members. No fees.

Provides services for women in a feminist context: sex discrimination counseling; abortion and birth control counseling; self-help gynecological care; per se divorce clinics; discussion groups; meeting places; a library; films; workshops; and special programs.

207 MID-HUSON WOMEN'S CENTER. 27 Franklin St., Poughkeepsie, N.Y. 12601. Founded February 1972.

A collective providing abortion and birth control referral, marriage and divorce counseling, child-care center, lending library, emergency housing and funds, consiousness-raising, and a speaker's bureau. Publishes *Women's Center Newsletter* (donation requested).

208 NEW PALTZ WOMEN'S ALLIANCE. Women's Center, Rm. 417, S. U. B., State Univ. of New York, New Paltz, N.Y. 12561. (914) 257-2237. Shelli Stein, 6 Nepale Dr., New Paltz, N.Y., 12561. 110 members.

Attempts to spread awareness of the women's movement throughout the college community. Also encompasses the Birth Control Clinic, Lesbian Liberation Committee, and Action for Women's Studies. Holds conferences, and conducts health care referrals and lesbian counseling.

209 SUFFOLK COUNTY COMMUNITY COLLEGE WOMEN'S GROUP. 533 College Rd., Suffolk County Community College, Selden, N.Y. 11784. (516) 732-1600, ext. 245. Founded September 1972. Sandra Lichenstein, Faculty Advisor.

A college group devoted to consciousness-raising and improving the status of women on campus. Operates a day care center, a rape information center, a women's center, social service referrals, and consciousness-raising groups. Participates in a women's studies program. Publishes a biweekly newsletter, *Lilith;* issues have included articles on liberation, feminity, mental health, menstruation, women in mythology, physiology, day care, and a bulletin board of local events, women's services, periodicals, etc.

WESTCHESTER WOMEN'S LIBERATION COLLECTIVE (Scarborough, N.Y.). See 51.

210 WOMEN'S CENTER OF NASSAU COUNTY. 14 W. Columbia Street., Hempstead, N.Y. 11550. (516) 292-8106. Founded September 1971. Stella Shak, 125 Green St., Valley Stream, N.Y. 11580. 500 members. Dues: $12

Offers diversified services to women, including therapy referral, abortion referral, consciousness-raising groups, birth control and sexuality workshops, speaker's bureau, and a library. Publishes *Guidelines for Consciousness-Raising; A Women's Liberation Speaker's Manual; Suggested Topics for Consciousness-Raising;* and a monthly newsletter, *The Liberated Grapevine.*

211 WOODMERE WOMEN'S CENTER. 136 Cedarhurst Ave., Cedarhurst, N.Y. (516) 569-0238. Founded April 1971. Naomi Levy.

Offers medical and legal referrals; groups for consciousness-raising (marrieds, singles, and women in transition); a rape workshop; and an emergency all-night service for troubled women.

Ohio

212 ANTIOCH WOMEN'S CENTER. Antioch College, Yellow Springs, Ohio 45387. (513) 767-7331, ext. 311.

Organizational center for all women's activities in the community. Conducts auto mechanics course, women's studies seminar, assault victims support, consciousness-raising study groups, women's health collective, and task force on women at Antioch and in Yellow Springs. The center has published *Cassandra*, a collection of prose and poetry.

213 KENT WOMEN'S PROJECT. 306 Franklin Hall, Kent State Univ., Kent, Ohio 44242. (216) 672-2653. Founded May 1972. Betty Kirschner, Dept. of Sociology.

"A multi-faceted organization which serves as a coordinating unit for the eight active women's groups on the Kent State campus." Also serves women in the community. Projects include: women's studies courses, adult education courses, referral service (therapy, legal aid, and vocational help), library, and speakers' bureau.

214 OHIO STATE UNIVERSITY. WOMEN'S SELF–GOVERNMENT ASSOCIATION. 307 Ohio Union, Columbus, Ohio 43210. (614) 422-6189.

"WSGA Women's Caucus is representative of all women on the Ohio State Campus, via representatives from living units and women's interest organizations. Its goal is to encourage women to identify, explore, develop and utilize their individual potentials. Specifically, WSGA is involved in services and programming." The association sponsors speakers (Florence Kennedy, Phyllis Chesler, and Sissy Farenthold), films, workshops and conferences, and an annual Women's Week; distributes birth control handbooks; and publishes *Women on Campus* for entering freshmen.

Oregon

215 OREGON COUNCIL FOR WOMEN'S EQUALITY. Box 8186, Portland, Oreg. 97207. (503) 666-7050 or 771-4082. Founded January 1971. Claudia Johnston, Pres., Box 06352, Portland, Oreg. 97206. 100 members. Dues: $5, individuals; $50, groups.

"An 'umbrella' organization of individuals and groups formed to coordinate, initiate and stimulate action to end discrimination against women" through "research, information clearinghouse, legislation, education." Current projects include "identifying and ending the ways in which our schools, textbooks, and mass media perpetuate the myth of feminine inferiority; lobbying on legislation; drafting necessary legislation; planning a feminist Job Bank; eliminating discriminatory employment practices; encouraging the promotion of women to positions of higher responsibility; [and] supporting women's health and welfare needs." OCWE operates via regular and special meetings, committees on employment, education, legislation, child care, health, seminars, and workshops. A newsletter is free with membership, or costs $2 per year.

Pennsylvania

216 THE ASSOCIATION FOR THE DEVELOPMENT OF OPPORTUNITY, INC. Box 10118, Pittsburgh, Pa. 15232. (412) 682-8599. Founded 1970. Eunice Friedman, Admin.

Aims "to develop programs that would make equal opportunity a reality for all persons." The staff is comprised of educators, researchers, and government and community service leaders. Projects include: Career Objectives and Self-Image: A Program for Disadvantaged Women for the Pittsburgh Board of Public Education at the Connelley Skill Learning Center; Affirmative Action Recruitment Conferences for Institutions of Higher Education; Women (The Forgotten Majority): A Mental Health Conference; the Marriage Information Service, providing information on the law as it affects married men and women; the Divorce Resource Center, providing information to those who have decided to obtain a divorce; and Career Counselling and Job Placement, covering all aspects of employment from vocational selection to career advancement.

217 PENNSYLVANIANS FOR WOMEN'S RIGHTS. 230 W. Chestnut St., Lancaster, Pa. 17603. (717) 299-5381. Founded June 1971. Nancy Whitacre. Dues: $5, individuals; $15, affiliates.

Formed to coordinate the efforts of Pennsylvania's women and men toward making state government responsive to the needs of women. Maintains committees on Education, Employment, Child Care, Problems of Older Women, and Legal Rights. Also has a speakers' bureau. Publishes a quarterly newsletter, free to members or $2.50 a year. Other publications are: *Joint Task Force on Sexism in Education Report* and *Self-Study Guide to Sexism in Schools.*

218 SLIPPERY ROCK STATE COLLEGE. ASSOCIATION FOR WOMEN'S RIGHTS. 308 J. Linwood Eisenberg Bldg., Slippery Rock, Pa. 16057. Founded 1970. Elizabeth R. Curry, Faculty Advisor.

A student-oriented, consciousness-raising service organization open to both male and female students. Projects include the successful abolition of housing hours for women and support of their faculty advisor in winning a case of sex discrimination against the state. The group plans to organize courses in manual skills: auto repair, carpentry, and plumbing; and publishes *The Hand*, a newsletter, in conjunction with the Slippery Rock Women's Liberation group.

219 WOMEN'S ACTION COALITION. 302 S. Jackson St., Media, Pa. 19063. (215) 565-2960. Founded September 1972. 43 members.

"We are women striving for the rights of all women. Our diversity of interests has led us to the coalition concept. We have become a multi-issue organization which allows each woman to participate in her areas of interest. Through our working committees, we channel our energies to the betterment of human, economic, and civil rights for women.

"Legal Committee projects have included working toward passage of the Equal Rights Amendment to the Constitution, support of candidates with a feminist viewpoint, and equal pay for equal work. We also refer discrimination cases to the ACLU and Human Relations Commission.

"Education Committee's goal is elimination of sexism in education. We are presently assisting Pennsylvanians for Women's Rights (217) in compiling a manual on the status of girls' education in Pennsylvania. Our area of responsibility is to evaluate the degree of sexism in the public schools' physical education programs." We "have also evaluated elementary school literature to define the portrayal of women and young girls as members of society. We have provided materials to the schools which will foster a better attitude toward women. We also supply speakers and films to groups interested in learning about sexism in education.

"The Services and Information Committee issues the *Feminist,* our monthly newsletter, with news about the status of women and lists of particular social actions in which individual members may participate.... We are constantly forming new consciousness-raising groups in new locations. The Services and Information Committee has provided speakers to several groups throughout the country."

220 WOMEN'S LIBERATION CENTER OF PHILADELPHIA. 4634 Chester Ave., Philadelphia, Pa. 19143. (215) 727-1717. Founded 1970. Noel Mawer.

Provides health, legal, and employment discrimination referrals; sells literature; refers women to consciousness-raising groups; maintains a speakers collective; offers meeting space for many groups: Women in Transition, Media Workshop, Self-Defense Classes, and Lesbian Hot-Line (215-729-2001). Holds discussion series for women new to the movement, and issues *Women's Survival Manual: A Feminist Handbook on Separation and Divorce* ($1.50) and *Tell-A-Woman* (newsletter, m., contribution).

Rhode Island

221 WOMEN OF BROWN UNITED. Brown Univ., Providence, R.I. 02912 Founded Fall 1969. Debbi Norden.

A campus women's coalition, working to eradicate sex discrimination and sexist attitudes at Brown University. Projects include the creation of a women's center and a day care center, speaker's programs, and consciousness-raising groups.

222 WOMEN'S LIBERATION UNION OF RHODE ISLAND. Box 2302, East Side Sta., Providence, R.I. 02906. (401) 861-5511 or 739-6075. Founded 1970. Joanne Rongo, 316 Nelson St., Providence, R.I. 02908. 615 members.

"Established to protect women's rights, to advance the interests of women and to eliminate all forms of discrimination and oppression against them." Projects include a Rape Crisis Committee, abortion law repeal actions, ratification of ERA, suit against the State of Rhode Island for job discrimination, challenge of sex-segregated want ads, and legislation to prevent discrimination in credit and housing. The union meets monthly.

223   YWCA WOMEN'S CENTER. 62 Jackson St., Providence, R.I. 02903. (401)
      861-2910. Founded 1971. Glenna Mazel, Dir. 3,000 members.

Open to women of all ages, "to provide a meeting place and programs for
women on issues pertinent to today's society." The center provides programs and
seminars on health, education, social problems, and divorce; has conducted a conference on employment; runs a day care center; and offers courses in typing, self-
defense, foreign car troubleshooting, job hunting, and women and their bodies.
The center also publishes a monthly newsletter, containing articles on legislation,
news of conferences and activities of other women's groups, and new programs for
women.

Tennessee

224   NASHVILLE WOMEN'S CENTER. 1112 19 Ave., S., Nashville, Tenn.
      37212. (615) 327-1969. Founded 1972.

Coordinates women's activities in Nashville and surrounding areas. Projects
include work on social and political reforms, education, abortion information dis-
persal, health care information, and a twenty-four-hour answering service. Also
publishes a monthly newsletter.

Texas

225   WOMEN FOR CHANGE CENTER. 2001 Bryan St., Suite 290, Dallas, Tex.
      75201. (214) 741-2391. Founded October 1971. Helen Schilling, Susie
      Deane, Co-Dirs. 500 members. Dues: $10.

An educational, communication, and research center for women to change
society's expectations of women and to provide a forum to enable women to help
themselves and others. Maintains a talent bank; a news bank, vocational, personal,
credit, and legal counseling courses, courses for newly-singled women, and courses
in basic economics and women in art. A monthly newsletter ($3.50/yr) tells of
WFC projects, meetings of other women's groups, articles on legislation, and gives
suggestions for action.

Utah

226   UNIVERSITY OF UTAH. WOMEN'S RESOURCE CENTER. 293 Union
      Building, Salt Lake City, Utah 84112. (801) 581-8030. Founded August
      1971. Shauna M. Adix, Dir.

Serves as a general advocate for women on the campus—students, faculty,
staff, and potential students. The center offers individual and group counseling services and programs, classes, conferences, workshops, and seminars especially designed to meet women's needs or to focus on women's issues. The center helps develop women's studies classes through individual departments, and there is a reentry
program for "mature women" who are entering the university for the first time or
who are returning to college. The center maintains a women's resource library of

books, periodicals, magazines, tapes, and videotapes; the library is also a regional depository for Labor Department publications on women. The Women's Resource Center helps the university administration implement its Affirmative Action program, handles grievances, serves as a general information and referral center, sponsors and administers a speakers' bureau, and puts out the bimonthly *Transition* (6/yr, $4/yr), which includes articles on women's history, news items, and women's studies. The center has also published *Utah Women in Higher Education* ($3.50), and has some video cassettes available for a small rental fee and postage.

Washington

227   RADICAL WOMEN. 3815 5 St., N.E., Seattle, Wash. 98105. (206) 632-7449. Founded 1968. 28 members. Dues: sliding fees.

"Radical Women is an organization of political radicals dedicated to exposing, resisting, and eliminating the inequities of women's existence" by "the revolutionary transformation of capitalism into a socialist society. . . ." Radical Women further believe that the oppression of women is a first-priority political, legal and economic question."

Radical Women are working for overhaul of marriage and divorce laws, the ERA, free birth control information and devices, free abortion on demand, decent free health care, free child life centers, an end to stereotyped curricula, free education at all levels, affirmative action in employment and promotion, paid pregnancy leave, an end to discrimination based on race, equal partnership in political life, guaranteed annual wage, recognition of lesbian rights, legalization of prostitution, intensified prosecution of rapes, and reform of sexist bias in the media. Since 1967, RW activities have included: "organizing for the defense of the Black Panther Party; holding forums on the history of women in the U.S.; organizing and being arrested on picketlines of women workers on strike; demonstrating for welfare rights; divorce reform; conducting classes in public speaking and in legal defense for women; participating in the struggle for black representation in the construction industry; organizing mass demonstrations for legal abortions; participating in the ongoing struggle for child care; fighting the harassment of sexual minorities; publishing new and original writing by and about women; and maintaining a growing volume of correspondence with women all over the world." Radical Women also maintains a speakers' bureau. The following position papers are available.

Chambless, Dorothy. Mejia *Race and Sex, 1972: Collision or Comradeship* 25¢
Fraser, Clara. *The Emancipation of Women* 10¢
Fraser, Clara. *Which Road towards Women's Liberation: The Movement as a Radical Vanguard or a Single-Issue Coalition?* 25¢
Fraser, Clara. *Woman as Leader: Double Jeopardy on Account of Sex* 15¢
Gipple, Cindy. *The Women's Movement and the Class Struggle* 10¢
Radical Women. *Sexual Politics* 50¢
Williams, Susan. *Lesbianism: A Socialist-Feminist Perspective* 15¢
Windoffer, Melba. *Women Who Work* 15¢

A videotape, entitled *The Shape of Radical Politics*, is also available.

Canadian National

228 CANADIAN FEDERATION OF UNIVERSITY WOMEN. 209 A, 151 Slater St., Ottawa, Ontario Can. KIP5H3. Founded 1919. R. A. Bell, Pres. 11,400 members. Dues: $4.

Aims "to promote the highest standards of education at all levels; to encourage participation in public affairs in the political, social and cultural fields; to safeguard and improve the economic, legal and professional status of Canadian women." Maintains a roster of qualified women distinguished in their fields and a Standing Committee on the Status of Women; offers various fellowships to women; and publishes *CFUW News* (three times per year), and *The Chronicle*, an annual.

229 NATIONAL ACTION COMMITTEE ON THE STATUS OF WOMEN IN CANADA. 1524 Douglas Dr., Mississauga, Ontario, Can. L5G2W8. (416) 278-2258. Founded 1966. Helen Tucker, Secy.

A federation of 50 voluntary organizations determined to see the recommendations of the Royal Comission on the Status of Women implemented. "Serves as an educational and communications link for women in Canada who are striving to improve their status and to change the traditional attitudes and habits of prejudice towards women." Works for reform of antiquated laws and the elimination of discrimination in employment, labor unions, education, the media, and family and community life. NACSW publishes conference reports, briefs to the government, and a newsletter ($3/yr).

230 THE NATIONAL COUNCIL OF WOMEN OF CANADA. 270 Maclaren St., Ottawa, Ontario, Can. K2POM3. (613) 233-4953. Founded 1893. 750,000 members.

A federation serving as a medium of communication and action functioning at international, national, provincial, and local levels. The council has acted to improve the status of women in the following areas: labor legislation for women, securing the franchise for women, easing of divorce laws, disseminating birth control information, appointment of women to government positions, and loosening of abortion laws. The council publishes *Proud Heritage*, a history of NCWC; a monthly newsletter; and an annual report.

Canadian Local

Alberta

231 ALBERTA STATUS OF WOMEN COMMITTEE. 6628 123 St., Apt. 203
Edmonton, Alberta, Can. Shirley Gifford.

British Columbia

232 VANCOUVER STATUS OF WOMEN. 2029 W. 4 Ave., Vancouver 9, B.C.,
Can. (604) 736-3746. Founded February 1971. Alice James, Pres., 1339 W.
58 Ave., Vancouver 14, B.C., Can. 850 members.

Works toward implementing the recommendations of the Royal Commission
on the Status of Women in Canada, fostering public knowledge on the status of
women in Canada, and facilitating communication between women's groups.
Operates a free "ombuds" service for women, funded by the provincial government,
and attempts to change those laws, practices, and attitudes that cause major problems for women. Develops educational material, including a guide for elementary
school teachers to help them mitigate the effects of sexist books they must use, a
counselor's kit for use in high school, and a women's studies course for high
schools. Maintains a speakers' bureau, and publishes a monthly newsletter.

Other publications available include: *Status Anyone?*, research on attitudes of
Vancouver women (50¢); *Cope Kit*, a teacher's guide to sex stereotyping in Copp-
Clark and J. M. Dent and Sons elementary readers (50¢); *Exploring Sex Roles*, a kit
for high school counselors (50¢); *An Investigation of Part Time Work for Women*
(50¢); *Day Care* (25¢); and a series of briefs to the Provincial Government on legislation (5¢-25¢).

233 VANCOUVER WOMEN'S CENTRE. 804 Richard St., Vancouver, B.C., Can.
(604) 684-0523. Founded 1969. Jane McDermot, 2232 Alder St., Vancouver, B.C., Can. Hours: 12-5 p.m., Mon.-Wed.; 12-9 p.m., Thurs.-Sat.

Publishes the *Pedestal* (1969, m., $3/yr., Canada; $3.50/yr., U.S.; $10/yr.,
institutions), and operates the Vancouver Women's Bookstore, which stocks history,
novels, practical guides, periodicals, poetry, biographies, and children's books.

Manitoba

234   MANITOBA ACTION COMMITTEE ON THE STATUS OF WOMEN. 441
Webb Pl., Winnipeg, Manitoba, Can. Founded 1971. Elizabeth Feniak, Chpn.
303 Ashland Ave., Winnipeg, Manitoba, Can. R3L1L6. Dues: $2.

The objectives are: "to promote the implementation of the recommendations
of the Status of Women Report, provincially and federally; to increase public knowledge of the rights and status of women in Canada; to facilitate communication between individuals and groups concerned about the status of women; to provide a
clearinghouse to receive and exchange information upon the action of governments,
nongovernmental enterprise, and voluntary organizations in promoting the rights of
women; to carry on basic research, by spearheading drives towards immediate action, provincially and federally." Active subcommittees work on communications,
day care, labor, political action, and sex stereotyping in books. MACSW work is
supported by individual fees, donations, and federal government grants. The committee provides information and speakers, receives and assists with complaints
about injustices to women, and holds public meetings. Two successful conferences
have been held: "Women in Employment" and "Women in Politics and Public Life:
Political Paths to Change." In addition the Labour Caucus has held a series of
meetings on "Women and the Job." The Communications Committee has set up
programs for radio and television, and edits a quarterly newsletter, *Action* ($1/yr.).

235   A WOMAN'S PLACE. 300 Victor St., Winnipeg, Manitoba, Can. (204) 786-
4581. Founded May 1973.

A women's center offering a theater troupe, women's liberation meetings,
silk screening, birth control and abortion referrals, a lesbian resource center, sexuality courses, a library, and new projects requested by the women involved. Also
publishes a monthly newsletter.

Newfoundland

236   NEWFOUNDLAND STATUS OF WOMEN COUNCIL. Box 5021, St.
John's, Newfoundland, Can. (709) 722-4533. Founded May 1972. 115
members.

Aims: "to raise the consciousness of women; to improve the status of women;
to promote the implementation of the recommendations of the Royal Commission
on the Status of Women Report; to facilitate communication between individuals
and groups concerned about the status of women. . . . NSWC is open to all women
and meets once a month at 8:00 p.m. the first Monday of each month at the
YWCA, 55 Military Rd., St. John's, Newfoundland." Study groups are working on
media, education, women and the family, women in public life, and family planning
and abortion. The council cooperates in running the Woman's Place (see 237) and
in publishing a newsletter (free to members, $5 to libraries).

237   THE WOMAN'S PLACE. 203 Water St., St. John's, Newfoundland, Can.
(mailing address: Box 5021, St. John's East, Newfoundland, Can.). (709)
722-4533. Founded May 1972.

Run by the Women's Collective with the Newfoundland Status of Women
Council (see 236). Provides a center for women to work together; an information

and referral center for women; a drop-in place; and formation of consciousness-raising groups. Offers courses for women on photography, carpentry, plumbing, automobile mechanics, women's studies, and other skills to enable women to become independent. Publications include *Women and the Law in Newfoundland* (20¢, U.S.; 14¢, Canada) and *Women's Service Handbook* (20¢, U.S.; 14¢, Canada). The Woman's Place also publishes a newsletter (10/yr.; $1/yr. to those who are not members of the Women's Collective or Newfoundland Status of Women Council).

Ontario

238 ONTARIO COMMITTEE ON THE STATUS OF WOMEN. 41 Spadina Rd., Apt. 7, Toronto, Ont., Can. Founded 1971. Lorna Marsden. 200 members. Dues: $3.

Political action group which presses for implementation of the recommendations of the Royal Commission on the Status of Women in Canada, both on provincial and federal levels. The committee works through various subcommittees. Many briefs are available on request, e.g., to Commission on Post Secondary Education in Ontario; to Toronto Board of Education; and to Air Canada. The committee also publishes a newsletter.

239 OTTAWA WOMEN'S CENTRE. 136 Lewis St., rear, Ottawa, Ont. K2POS7, Can. (613) 233-2560. Founded Summer 1972.

A place to foster women's actions and meet their needs. The following projects were initiated in 1973: medical collective, consciousness-raising groups; women's studies; notice board; theater groups, political education; fix-it workshop; day care information; career counseling; and babysitting coop. Occasional public meetings are held, and a monthly newsletter is published ($2).

240 WOMEN'S INFORMATION CENTRE. 31 Dupont St., Toronto 5, Ont., Can. (416) 929-3185. Founded June 1, 1972. Chris Lawrence, 200 Cottingham St., Toronto 5, Ont., Can.

An organizing center for women, providing a drop-in center, bookstore, library, liberation school, and a legal and medical clinic. Starts consiousness-raising groups, and sends speakers to interested groups. Also publishes a monthly newsletter, a nonsexist bibliography of children's literature, and a legal handbook, *Seizing the Reigns.*

241 WOMEN'S LIBERATION GROUP. 1309 University Ave., W., Windsor, Ont., Can. (519) 254-8800 or 252-0244. Founded July 1971. Selma McGorman, 474 Askin Blvd., Windsor, Ont., Can. (519) 256-1603.

Projects include running the Women's Place at the above address, which offers legal referrals, job discrimination referrals, and seminars and workshops on topics of concern to women (health, day care, legal status, fix-it, and careers). The group cooperates with Association for Contraceptive Counseling and Related Areas, which gives contraceptive and abortion counseling. The group established the Educated Childbirth Organization, runs a speakers' bureau, and publishes *The Windsor Woman* (6/yr.; $2/yr.; 10¢/issue), and a booklet, *Windsor Working Women* by M. A. Bellis (free).

Quebec

242 A WOMAN'S PLACE/PLACE DES FEMMES. 3764 Boulevard St.,
Laurent, Montreal 130, Que., Can. (514) 845-7146. Founded May 1973.
Cherry Van Son, 3690 Ste. Famille, Montreal 130, Que., Can.

An all purpose open facility, which provides a place for women to meet; furthers women's culture, and offers education on subjects related to women. A newspaper is planned.

243 WOMEN'S CENTRE, YWCA. 1355 Dorchester Blvd., Montreal, Que., Can.
(514) 866-9941. Founded 1971. Cerise Morris, Coor. Hours: 10 a.m.-
6 p.m., Mon.-Fri.

Offers vocational counseling; abortion counseling; birth control information; women's legal information and referral service; Montreal Women's Speakers Bureau; resource library ("a small but useful collection" of books, reprints, magazines, women's newspapers, articles, etc.); courses on Female Sexuality, Open Marriage, Developmental Drama; consciousness-raising groups; discussion groups for separated and divorced women; and a discussion and action group of single mothers. Houses Project Watchdog, a group of women concerned with the image of women on TV, and the Montreal Childbirth Education Association, a nonprofit education organization for family-centered maternity and infant care. Publishes the *Montreal Women's Yellow Pages*, a directory of services and groups for women in Montreal. Also rents the *Canadian Women TV Series*, 25 half-hour videotapes covering all aspects of women in Canadian society, produced by Montreal women for Channel 9 ($10/ tape).

Saskatchewan

244 SASKATCHEWAN ACTION COMMITTEE, STATUS OF WOMEN. 2900
Argyle St., Regina, Sask., Can. 84S2A9. (306) 584-1103. Linda Tate. 800
members.

Works for implementation of the recommendations of the Royal Commission on the Status of Women in Canada. The committee meets with women throughout the province to organize and gain support, and has sponsored two provincial conferences. Study kits on *Homemaker's Pensions* and *Matrimonial Property Rights* are available free, and the committee also publishes a newsletter.

245 SASKATOON WOMEN'S LIBERATION. 147 2 Ave., S., Saskatoon, Sask.,
Can. (306) 242-5830. Founded 1970.

Encompasses many groups: abortion law repeal committee, birth control information center, women's center, self-help clinic, University of Saskatchewan Student Union's Women's Directorate, working women's committee, and others. Publishes *Saskatoon Women's Liberation Newsletter*, (bi-m., donation) which contains articles, book reviews, poetry, and news items; an appointment calendar; a health leaflet; a *Handbook for Working Women* (free); and a health questionnaire.

Yukon

246 YUKON STATUS OF WOMEN GROUP. 10 Tutshi Rd., Whitehorse, Yukon
Territory. Joyce Hayden.

IV. Governmental and Quasi-Governmental Organizations and Agencies

International

247 UNITED NATIONS COMMISSION ON THE STATUS OF WOMEN. New York, N.Y. 10017. (212) 754-1234, ext. 1245. Founded 1946. Una Ellis. 32 members.

"A functional commission of the Economic and Social Council of the United Nations for the elimination of all forms of discrimination against women in law and in practice, and the promotion of their full integration in the development of their countries in the political, legal, economic, social and cultural fields." Projects include development and implementation of an international action program, preparation of major studies, and research in specific fields. In addition, 1975 is scheduled to be the International Women's Year. *A Newsletter on the Status of Women*, published twice a year, contains a list of the many UN publications of interest to women and articles on the international status of women (free).

U.S. Federal

248 COUNCIL OF ECONOMIC ADVISORS, ADVISORY COMMITTEE ON THE ECONOMIC ROLE OF WOMEN. Executive Office of the President, Washington, D.C. 20506. (202) 395-5042. Founded January 1973. June O'Neill, Sen. Staff Economist. 21 members.

An advisory group which meets periodically to advise the Council of Economic Advisors, initiated by the President of the U.S. "to appraise progress and problems in this crucial area" and "ensure that progress and change in this important area of human rights will be constructive." Members serve by appointment of the chairman of the C.E.A., and review major policies that influence women's economic role. Meetings of the committee are open to the public. The committee sponsors symposia (one was held on the Advancement of Women in Industry).

249 INTERSTATE ASSOCIATION OF COMMISSIONS ON THE STATUS OF WOMEN. Rm. 204, District Bldg., 14 and E St., N.W., Washington, D.C. 20016. (202) 629-5238. Founded June 1970. Joy R. Simonson, Pres. 45 members. Dues: $125, states; $25, local commissions.

A federation of official state and local government Commissions on the Status of Women, or their equivalents, designed "to improve the status of women in education, employment, civil and political rights; to disseminate information on needs, problems and achievements of women." IACSW holds annual conferences, and provides "a national clearing house for information and action." Publishes *Breakthrough*, a bimonthly four-page newsletter edited by Emily Taylor (222 Strong Hall, University of Kansas, Lawrence, Kans. 66044), which includes news of activities of member commissions and the IACSW. Cassette tapes of workshops held at conferences are also available, as are copies of resolutions.

250 UNITED STATES CITIZEN'S ADVISORY COUNCIL ON THE STATUS OF WOMEN. Dept. of Labor Bldg., Rm. 1336, Washington, D.C. 20210. Founded 1963. Hon. Jacqueline G. Gutwillig, Chpn. 20 members.

Established by President John F. Kennedy to "assure effective and continuing leadership in advancing the status of women." Specifically, the council is to "serve as a primary means for suggesting and stimulating action . . . ; review and evaluate progress of organizations in furthering the full participation of women in American life; consider the effect of new developments on methods of advancing the status of women and recommend appropriate action to the Interdepartmental Committee on the Status of Women." Annual reports are submitted to the President and are available from the council.

251 UNITED STATES COMMISSION ON CIVIL RIGHTS, WOMEN'S RIGHTS PROGRAM UNIT. 1121 Vermont Ave., N.W., Washington, D.C. 20425. (202) 254-8127. Founded October 1972. Carol B. Kummerfeld, Dir.

"The Commission on Civil Rights was established by Congress under the Civil Rights Act of 1957. On October 14, 1972, the Commission's jurisdiction was extended by Congress to cover sex as well as race discrimination. The Commission is an independent, bipartisan, fact-finding agency authorized to collect and study information concerning denials of equal protection of the laws, and to appraise the laws and policies of the Federal Government with respect to denials of equal protection of the laws because of race, ethnicity, or sex. The Commission also serves as a national Clearinghouse for civil rights and women's rights information. Because the Commission on Civil Rights is not an enforcement agency, all complaints of denials of rights . . . are referred to the appropriate Federal administrative agency for corrective action.

"The Women's Rights Program Unit, located in the Office of the Staff Director, supervises the implementation of the Commission's new jurisdiction over sex discrimination. The Unit identifies and evaluates women's rights issues, proposes Commission hearings, studies, and reports, and is involved in developing programs which investigate issues of concern to women of all races and ethnicities. The Women's Rights Program Unit also functions as a monitor of all Commission studies, to ensure that adequate attention is given to collection and analysis of data regarding the status of all women.

"Finally, the Unit organizes and maintains active liaison with national women's rights organizations as well as with private research institutions and Federal agencies concerned with women's issues.

"The Commission's current and planned program dealing with women's rights includes the following projects. Investigations for the *Federal Women's Rights Enforcement Effort* report began in September 1973. This report evaluates the Federal Government's efforts to enforce existing anti-sex discrimination laws and to end sex discrimination within the government itself. The report's focus on women's rights represents an innovation in the Commission's *Federal Civil Rights Enforcement Effort* reports, which have been published periodically since 1970.

"The Commission has recently completed a study of sex and race discrimination in mortgage finance practices. This study focuses on barriers to homeownership, as reflected in broker and lender practices, in Hartford, Connecticut. [It is] also conducting a study of minority and women-owned business participation in Federal and State Government procurement programs. A study of the image and employment of women and minorities in the television industry is also being designed, as is a project to investigate the position of women and minorities in labor unions. A project to explore the impact of Revenue Sharing on programs and policies of concern to women of all races/ethnicities and minority men is also being designed. This project will include a publication explaining both the process of distribution and expenditure of funds under Revenue Sharing and anti-discrimination compliance requirements; it will also include ideas for local action and coalition-building around the issue of Revenue Sharing.

"The Commission has eight Regional Offices, a list of which [follows]; these Offices work with fifty-one State Advisory Committees in developing and implementing programs dealing with women's rights. A number of these State Advisory

Committees are currently undertaking a study of the rights of prisoners, with special concern for the treatment of minority and women prisoners.

"The Commission has recently let a contract for a study of the legal status of women under Federal law, based on the Department of Justice computer print-out which identifies more than 800 sections of the Federal code with sex-based references. A study of the legal status of women under state laws will be undertaken in November.

"As part of the Commission's Clearinghouse function, we will be publishing a booklet describing Federal laws and regulations on sex discrimination. In addition, [an] issue of the Commission's quarterly *Civil Rights Digest* will be devoted to issues of women's rights. The Commission is also investigating the feasibility of creating an information retrieval system for information, publications, and research on women's rights and civil rights."

Following is a list of United States Commission on Civil Rights Regional Offices.

312 N. Spring St., Rm. 1730, Los Angeles, Calif. 90012. (213) 688-3437.
Ross Bldg., 1726 Champa, Denver, Colo. 80202. (303) 837-2211.
2120 L St., N.W., Rm. 510, Washington, D.C. 20425. (202) 254-6717.
Citizens Trust Bank Bldg., Rm. 362, 75 Piedmont Ave., N.E., Atlanta, Ga. 30303. (404) 526-4391.
219 S. Dearborn St., Rm. 1428, Chicago, Ill. 60604. (312) 353-7371.
Old Federal Office Bldg., 911 Walnut St., Rm. 3103, Kansas City, Mo. 64106. (816) 374-5253.
26 Federal Plaza, Rm. 1639, New York, N.Y. 10007. (212) 264-0400.
New Moore Bldg., Rm. 249, 106 Broadway, San Antonio, Tex. 78205. (512) 225-4764, 225-6821.

Write for 26-page publication catalog.

252   U.S. DEPT. OF HEALTH, EDUCATION AND WELFARE, THE FEDERAL WOMEN'S PROGRAM. Rm. 4619-N., 330 Independence Ave., S.W., Washington, D.C. 20201. (202) 962-5311. Founded May 1971. Dr. Vera Brown, Dir.

A group within HEW to develop, coordinate, and implement program activities to eliminate discrimination against women in employment opportunities. Projects for 1973 included coordination of the program in eight agencies and ten regions of HEW, upgrading of affirmative action plans, leadership in the interagency daycare group, sponsorship of the Job Informaton Center, participation in management/supervisory training, participation on Secretary's Advisory Committee on Women, publication of FWP facts in *HEW Newsletter*, and research relating to women's employment. Publications available on request include: *Positive Indicators in Employment for Women in HEW* and *A Survey of Restructured Jobs in DHEW—Opportunities for Men and for Women.*

U.S. DEPT. OF HEW, OFFICE OF CHILD DEVELOPMENT. See **406.**

253   U.S. DEPT. OF HEALTH, EDUCATION AND WELFARE, OFFICE OF SPECIAL CONCERNS, ASSISTANT SECRETARY FOR EVALUATION AND PLANNING, WOMEN'S ACTION PROGRAM. Rm. 3059 N., 330 Independence Ave., S.W., Washington, D.C. 20201. (202) 962-5106. Founded February 1971. Sharon Rose, Acting Dir.

A governmental advocacy group for women to assure that the programs of the Dept. of HEW are responsive to the needs of women in society. Federal

Women's Program (See 252) has taken over internal aspects concerning women as governmental employees. Consultations have been conducted with women in the department, affirmative action plans for women have been developed, awareness of sex discrimination has been stimulated among men and women, HEW policies and programs have been analyzed, and research projects have been designed to understand the needs of women and determine HEW's responsibility to them. Reports of the Women's Action Program are free on request.

254 U.S. DEPT. OF LABOR, EMPLOYMENT STANDARDS ADMINISTRA-
TION, OFFICE OF FEDERAL CONTRACT COMPLIANCE. Washington,
D.C. 20210. (202) 961-2063. Founded 1964. Philip J. Davis, Dir.

"Responsible under Executive Order 11246, as amended, for monitoring the Government-wide contract compliance program. This Order, which applies to Government contractors and subcontractors with contracts exceeding $10,000 and Federally-assisted construction contractors, prohibits discrimination by such employers against any employee or applicant for employment because of sex, race, color, religion or national origin. The contractor is also required to take affirmative action to assure that applicants are employed, and that employees are treated during employment without regard to their race, color, religion, sex, or national origin . . . . The principal method of enforcing the Executive Order is the compliance review which is generally conducted by the compliance agency either on its own initiative or as the result of a complaint . . . . The cornerstone of the Government's contract compliance program is Revised Order No. 4, . . . [which] spells out the requirements of affirmative action for nonconstruction Government contractors and subcontractors with 50 or more employees and a contract of $50,000 or more . . . ." Executive Order 11246, Executive Order 11375, and relevant reprints from the *Federal Register* are available on request.

255 U.S. DEPT. OF LABOR, EMPLOYMENT STANDARDS ADMINISTRA-
TION, WOMEN'S BUREAU. 14 Constitution Ave., N.W., Washington, D.C.
20210. (202) 961-2036. Founded June 5, 1920. Carmen R. Maymi, Dir.

Established by an Act of Congress, "to improve the employability of women, increase their job opportunities, and eliminate sex discrimination in employment." The Bureau serves as a national clearinghouse on the utilization of women in the labor force and their legal and economic status, and works via the national office and regional offices in Boston, New York City, Philadelphia, Atlanta, Chicago, Dallas, Kansas City, and San Francisco. The Bureau initiates conferences, cooperates with State Commissions on the Status of Women, offers technical assistance and advice on formulating proposed legislation, and is involved in policy making in the Department of Labor. Many pamphlets are available on a wide range of topics, such as: *Facts on Women Workers of Minority Races*, *Who Are the Working Mothers?*, *Help Improve Vocational Education for Women and Girls in Your Community*, *Women in Labor Unions*, and *Changing Patterns of Women's Lives*.

256 UNITED STATES EQUAL EMPLOYMENT OPPORTUNITY COMMIS-
SION. 1800 G St., N.W., Washington, D.C. 20506. (202) 343-5621.
Founded July 1965.

EEOC is concerned with discrimination by employers, public and private employment agencies, labor organizations, and joint labor-management apprenticeship programs covered by the Civil Rights Act of 1964. The commission receives and investigates charges of employment discrimination. "In addition, the Commission promotes programs of affirmative action by employers, labor organizations, and employment agencies to put the principle of equal employment opporutnity into practice." Instructions and forms are available from the Washington office or one of the 13 regional offices. Many publications are available, including *Toward Job Equality for Women*, *Title VII of the 1964 Civil Rights Act, as Amended by the EEO Act of 1972*, *Guidelines on Discrimination Because of Sex*, and *Equal Opportunity Report No.2: Job Patterns for Minorities and Women in Private Industry, 1967* (Y3.EQ2:12/2, Vols. 1 and 2, sold as a set only, $11.50). Films (loaned free of charge) include *Voice of La Raza*, 16 mm, 54 min., (job discrimination against the Spanish-speaking); and *Power vs. the People*, 16 mm, 58 min., (EEOC hearing, Houston, Tex., June 1970).

For film loan, contact Virginia Talamantes, 1800 G St., N.W., Rm. 1131, Washington, D.C. 20506. (202) 343-6037.

U.S. Local

Alabama

257 **ALABAMA WOMEN'S COMMISSION.** Samford University, Birmingham, Ala. 35209. (205) 870-2784. Founded 1971. Dean Margaret Sizemore, Chpn.

Established by the legislature to be "a continuing vehicle for the determination of effective policy and legislation in the areas which will affect Alabama's women." The commission studies the status of women in Alabama and makes "recommendations to the Governor and Legislature for constructive action in the following areas: public and private employment policies and practices; labor laws dealing with hours, wages and working conditions; legal rights and responsibilities; policies and practices with regard to education, counselling and job training; citizen volunteers; home and community." The commission is working on a "State Directory of Woman Power," and plans regional hearings on legislation of benefit to women. An annual report is submitted to the governor, but is not published.

Alaska

258 **ALASKA COMMISSION ON THE STATUS OF WOMEN.** Box 492, Petersburg, Alaska. 99833. Gertrude Reeser.

Arizona

259 **ARIZONA GOVERNOR'S COMMISSION ON THE STATUS OF WOMEN.** First National Bank, Box 20551, Phoenix, Ariz. 85036. Jane Greenwald.

Arkansas

260 **ARKANSAS GOVERNOR'S COMMISSION ON THE STATUS OF WOMEN.** Rm. 08, State Capitol, Little Rock, Ark. 72201. (501) 371-2397. Founded May 1971. Myra Rogers, Chpn., 2301 Camelot St., Fort Smith, Ark. 50 members.

Appointed by the governor, "to better the status of women in Arkansas by increasing awareness of the problems of women as a group in regard to employment, health, education, etc." The commission, via task forces, has studied and made recommendations concerning the status of women in employment, education, government, politics, legal rights, health, family and child care, and public image; the commission also maintains a talent bank. *The Status of Women in Arkansas 1973: Changing Rapidly—Improving Slowly* is available as well as the following publications which are free for single copies: *Focus on Women* (bibliography), *Possibilities for Action*, (checklist), *The Status of Women in Arkansas* (address by Diane Kincaid), *A Survey of Senior Students from Fourteen Public Schools in Arkansas*, and *Women and the Law* (questions and answers). The following are available only to institutions through special request: *Women: Their Status in State Government* prepared by the U.S. Civil Service Commission, Little Rock area; and *Women: Rights, Rules, Reasons*, final report on the 1972 conference series.

California

261   CALIFORNIA COMMISSION ON THE STATUS OF WOMEN. 1025 P St., Sacramento, Calif. 95814. (916) 445-3173. Pamela Faust, Exec. Dir. 17 members.

Created by the legislature "to study the following: (1) women's educational and employment problems, needs, and opportunities; (2) state laws in regard to the civil and political rights of women, including pensions, tax requirements, property rights, marriage and dissolution of marriage provisions, and similar matters; (3) the effect of social attitudes and pressures and economic considerations in shaping the roles to be assumed by women in the society; (4) any laws, practices, or conditions concerning or affecting women which impose special limitations or burdens upon them or upon society or which limit or tend to limit opportunities available to women."

Further the commission acts as an information center on the status of women and women's educational, employment, and other related needs; and recommends, develops, prepares, and coordinates materials, projects, or other activities. The commission gives technical and consultative advice to public or private groups or persons concerned with preventing or minimizing problems brought about by the changing roles and responsibilities of women, and developing programs to encourage and enable women to be fully contributing members of society. A prime function of the commission is to encourage women's organizations and other groups to institute local self-help activities designed to meet women's educational, employment, and other related needs.

"Conformance to the Equal Rights Amendment, the low representation of women in policy-making positions on government boards and commissions, the distorted view of women presented in the media, discrimination in employment, the condition of women in the criminal justice system, and the need for counselling and for child care were selected for the development of special projects." The commission also publishes a monthly newsletter.

262   MAYOR'S COMMITTEE ON THE STATUS OF WOMEN. 845 Monterey Blvd., San Francisco, Calif. 94127. Ilse Greer.

263   SACRAMENTO COMMUNITY COMMISSION FOR WOMEN. 1122 17 St., Sacramento, Calif. 95814. (916) 442-4741. Founded April 1969. Judith.

A. McGee, Pres., 402 Greenridge Ave., Roseville, Calif. 95678. 16,000 members. Dues: $10, organizations; $5, individuals.

Twenty-eight member organizations plus participants-at-large provide a coordinated effort in the community to develop the potential of women, at all ages, in all levels of society. The SCCW supports measures to: strengthen and assure continuation of California's Advisory Commission on the Status of Women and implement its recommendations on the community level; expand and improve opportunities for women to participate equally with men in employment, civic affairs, health, education and welfare, and all other areas vital to the well-rounded and fulfilled life; more effectively control crime in the community and improve law enforcement; bring under control problems relating to pollution of air, water, and natural resources; assure adequate protection of consumer interests; provide more adequate child care services; provide better facilities and improve opportunities for a meaningful life for the aged; and develop and expand community programs relating to the arts, working for more opportunities for women in all areas of the performing and visual and communication arts.

The SCCW maintains an active Legislative Observer Corps, which was credited by *Woman's Day* with major influences toward legislation ending sex discrimination in employment in California, and worked intensively for California approval of the ERA. The commission publishes the popular and frequently updated *Lady Do You Need Help?* (25,000 circ.) and *Lady Do You Need a Career?* plus a monthly newsletter. It produced a highly successvul TV series on *Women in the 70s* being rerun currently on Channel 6. The SCCW is currently developing a program to train volunteers to assist women in prison through counseling and information.

Colorado

264 **COLORADO COMMISSION ON THE STATUS OF WOMEN.** Colorado Women's College, 1800 Pontiac St., Denver, Colo. 80220. (303) 399-8303. Founded December 1964. Blanche T. Cowperthwaite, Chpn. 47 members. *See also* Virginia Neal Blue Resource Centers, 177.

A state agency established by the governor to improve the status of women, politically, economically, socially, and legally. The commission established the administrative headquarters of a proposed network of resource centers for Colorado women; holds fact-finding seminars throughout the state; investigated the practices of Colorado institutions of higher education in regard to women students, faculty, and staff; wrote and lobbied for a state equal rights amendment; and maintains a file on state and local appointments and has recommended qualified women to fill them. Publications are available from Virginia Neal Blue Centers, and include: *See How She Runs*, a pamphlet suggesting methods for encouraging women to run for elective office or apply for appointive positions ($1); *Interim Report on Children's Literature*, analyzing the image of women which they present ($5); and *Results of Survey on Women in Higher Education in Colorado, Fall, 1971* ($2.39).

Delaware

265 **DELAWARE GOVERNOR'S COUNCIL FOR WOMEN.** Scott Plaza, 1228 Scott St., Wilmington, Del. 19806. (302) 658-9251. Founded March 1971. Helen R. Thomas, Chpn. 36 members.

Appointed by the governor, and interested in implementing fair employment practices; improving health and child care services for women; increasing the number of women in higher governmental positions: equalizing banking, credit, and loan practices: urging Delaware schools to reorder their hiring and promotion practices; eliminating sexual stereotyping in educational materials and practices; and acting on the specific concerns of women who seek council support. The council maintains a Talent Bank of Delaware women who are trained and available for appropriate positions in the state, it also maintains a speakers' bureau. Annual reports are available on request.

District of Columbia

266 DISTRICT OF COLUMBIA COMMISSION ON THE STATUS OF WOMEN.
Rm. 204, District Bldg., 14 and E St., N.W., Washington, D.C. 20004. (202) 629-5238. Founded January 1967. Helen S. Lewis, Exec. Dir. 15–20 members.

Conducts studies; reviews progress; develops, recommends, and undertakes constructive action; and initiates and conducts programs directed toward improving the status of women in the District of Columbia. Has committees on consumer credit; female offenders; employment, vocational, guidance, and training; health; and legal status. Also has task forces on day care and rape victims. Conducts Project Women, a vocational role-model project for inner city girls, and a nationwide study of rehabilitation programs for women offenders. Write for these free publications: *Female Offenders in the District of Columbia*, 1972; *Improving the Status of Women in the Labor Force*, 1973; *Community Counseling Services on Jobs and Training for Women in the District of Columbia*, 1973; *Free Women of V.D.*, 1972; and *Residential Mortgage Lending Practices of Commercial Banks, Savings & Loan Associations and Mortgage Bankers*, 1973.

Florida

268 DADE COUNTY COMMISSION ON THE STATUS OF WOMEN. Rm. 1401, Dade County Courthouse, 73 W. Flagler St., Miami, Fla. 33130. (305) 277-5341. Founded January 1971. Muriel Solomon, Staff Asst. 27 members.

An advisory group that periodically reports to the Board of County Commissioners, and makes its findings known to the public. COSW seeks for every women a "privilege equal to her potential and responsibility" and hopes "to inspire in women desire for self-improvement and pride of being regardless of race, color or creed." At the same time, it encourages women to "recognize family environment as fundamental to the preservation of our national culture and security."

Among its first year activities, COSW supported the Equal Rights Amendment, abortion reform, the omission of male/female titles in classified ads, and urged the county to give enforcement powers to its Fair Housing and Employment Commission to revise its personnel department's maternity leave procedures, and to enact a Human Rights ordinance. COSW has also pressed for the establishment of day care centers, and requested that the county include a halfway house for women in its total plan for treating and rehabilitating alcoholics. To help determine target areas, public hearings are held periodically. Citizens also have a chance to voice suggestions or give informaton directly to the commission at any regular monthly meeting (held on the second Wednesday, 8 p.m., at the Greater Miami Coalition Building, 902 S.W. 2 Ave.). The COSW issues *Yellow Pages: A Resource Directory for the Needs of Women.*

268   FLORIDA GOVERNOR'S COMMISSION ON THE STATUS OF WOMEN. Capitol Bldg., Tallahassee, Fla. 32304. (904) 488-5152. Founded 1964, reactivated March 1973. Carol Jones, Exec. Dir. 32 members.

Advisory Commission to the governor, which works for the betterment of all women in Florida. The commission coordinates women's groups, maintains a talent bank, and studies specific areas of discrimination. The *Report on the Status of Women in Florida* was published in October 1973.

269   MAYOR'S ADVISORY COMMISSION ON THE STATUS OF WOMEN. Rm. 406, Courthouse, Jacksonville, Fla. Linda Menke.

Georgia

270   THE GEORGIA COMMISSION ON THE STATUS OF WOMEN. Georgia Dept. of Human Resources, 47 Trinity Ave., Atlanta, Ga. 30334. (404) 656-4431. Founded 1966. Jeanne Cahill, Chpn., 4141 Orchard Lake, Atlanta, Ga. 30339. 45 members.

Created by an act of the legislature, the commission is interested specifically in ratification of the ERA by Georgia in 1974, and is working with other groups toward this end; in 1972, the commission published *The Equal Rights Amendment and Georgia Law.* The commission is also involved in improving conditions at the State Prison for Women, and is studying state policies in regard to women employees.

Hawaii

271   COMMISSION ON THE STATUS OF WOMEN. Kula Sanatorium, Kula Maui, Hawaii 96790. Lois E. Andrews.

272   COMMISSION ON THE STATUS OF WOMEN, COUNTY OF HAWAII. Hilo, Hawaii 96720. Janet Fujiaka.

273   HAWAII STATE COMMISSION ON THE STATUS OF WOMEN. Box 150, Honolulu, Hawaii 96810. (808) 548-4199. Founded July 1970. Margaret Ushijima, Chpn., Box 964, Hilo, Hawaii 96720. 25 members.

Created by the legislature "to assure women full and equal coverage under the law by informing the public of women's rights, opportunities, and responsibilities, and by working toward the revision of those laws and practices which result in sex discrimination." Projects involve work on education, employment, and female offenders. The commission submits an annual report.

274   MAYOR'S COMMISSION ON THE STATUS OF WOMEN. Office of the Corporation Counsel, Honolulu, Hawaii 96813. Mary Ellen Swanton.

Idaho

275 IDAHO COMMISSION ON WOMEN'S PROGRAMS. Statehouse, Boise,
     Idaho. 83701. (208) 384-3200. Founded 1965. Marjorie Ruth Moon,
     Chpn. 35 members.

Created "to encourage and stimulate women to increase their participation in
and contributions, whether paid or unpaid, to the social, political and economic
progress of the local communities, the state and the nation." Active task forces
of the commission are Low Income Housing, Jail Conditions, Educational and
Career Choices, and Women's Wages. The 1972 *Report of the Commission* is available, which includes recommendations and task force report summaries.

Illinois

276 COMMISSION ON THE STATUS OF WOMEN. Chicago Board of Health,
     1316 W. Arthur St., Chicago, Ill. 60626. Sen. Esther Saperstein.

277 ILLINOIS DRUG ABUSE PROGRAM, OFFICE OF WOMEN'S AFFAIRS.
     Museum of Science and Industry, 5700 S. Lake Shore Dr., Chicago, Ill.
     60615. (312) 955-9800. Carolyn Gioia, Sp. Asst.

Established to assist IDAP with specific problems women were having in the
program. Committees are Child Care, Health and Medical, Consumer or Buyers,
Welfare Rights, and Job Development.

Indiana

278 COLUMBUS MAYOR'S TASK FORCE ON THE STATUS OF WOMEN.
     Mayor's Office, City Hall, Columbus, Ind. 47201. Carolyn L. Clark, Chpn.,
     Qunico Consulting Center, 2075 Lincoln Park Dr., Columbus, Ind. 47201.

A voluntary civic task force to study the status of women in the community
and to devise programs to improve the opportunities for women and the utilization
of their resources. Projects include surveys of municipal, and general employment
and of child care facilities; a bibliography of children's literature free of sexual
stereotyping; and a file of women qualified for boards and commissions.
The following publications are available: *Analysis of Male and Female Participation
in Municipal Employment in Columbus, Ind.*, Carolyn L. Clark, June 1973; and
*Results of an Employment Survey Conducted by the Employment Committee of
the Mayor's Task Force on Women*, by Lois Rose, September 1973.

279 COMMISSION ON THE STATUS OF INDIANA WOMEN. Purdue Univer-
     sity, Administration Bldg., Lafayette, Ind. 47902. Margaret G. Robb.

280 GARY COMMISSION ON THE STATUS OF WOMEN. 1200 Broadway,
     Gary, Ind. 46407. Annette Long.

281 THE MAYOR'S COMMISSION ON THE STATUS OF WOMEN. City-County Bldg., 1 Main St., Fort Wayne, Ind. 46802. Founded April 1973. Vivian Schmidt, Chpn., 2621 E. Maple Grove Ave., Fort Wayne, Ind. 46806. (219) 744-5234.

Created by Mayor Ivan A. Lebamoff "to bring women into full and equal partnership in the life of the community. Specific objectives of the Commission are: to identify and document the status of women in the areas of employment, community services, legal rights, education and religion, government and politics; to inform the community of the status of women in the above areas and of the rights of women; support legislation and public policies that promote equal status for women; provide technical assistance for organized efforts by organization, agencies, associations working toward improvement of women's status; follow up on recommendations of the Commission in cooperation with the Metropolitan Human Relations Commission." Studies are in progress to determine attitudes of women toward themselves, toward other women, and toward various issues; employment attitudes among business people; credit practices; women's role in government; and attitudes of teachers, administrators of schools, students, and the clergy relating to women's rights issues.

282 MAYOR'S TASK FORCE ON THE STATUS OF WOMEN. 112 Knox Dr., West Lafayette, Ind. Rona Ginsburg.

283 MAYOR'S TASK FORCE ON WOMEN, CITY OF INDIANAPOLIS. 2531 City-County Bldg., Indianapolis, Ind. 46204. (317) 633-6118. Founded August 1972. Mary Anne Butters, Chpn. 90 members.

"A governmental agency, assigned to assess, review and recommend means of improving the status of women." Projects include a Career and Economic Development Conference; television programs; child care promotion; development of Girls' Clubs; Big Sisters' Program; Women United Against Rape Program; servicing discrimination complaints; and job placement and counseling. The task force has published *Women in Indianapolis, A Guide to Women's Legal Rights* and task force reports; and has produced 30-minute taped radio and TV programs.

Iowa

284 IOWA STATE COMMISSION ON THE STATUS OF WOMEN. State Capitol Bldg. Des Moines; Iowa 50319. (515) 281-5952. Founded July 1, 1972. Cristine Wilson, Chpn., 3908 Maquoketa, Des Moines, Iowa 50310. 24 members.

Created by the legislature to improve the status of women in Iowa by working with Iowa legislature, state government departments, media, educational institutions, public and private employers, child care facilities, and other facilities and organizations. The commission plans to work in areas of legal and financial discrimination (insurance, inheritance tax, credit, social security, retirement plans, child care, health care, rape counseling, sex role stereotyping in education). The commission has published a booklet on state laws of special interest to women, and puts out an occasional newsletter, *IoWoman*, which includes a legislative report, news of appointments, new items of interest to women, and reports on conferences.

Kansas

285   KANSAS GOVERNOR'S COMMISSION ON THE STATUS OF WOMEN.
1101 Polk St., Topeka, Kans. 66612. Cora Hobble.

Kentucky

286   KENTUCKY COMMISSION ON WOMEN. 306 Castleview Dr., Louisville,
Ky. 40207. Mrs. Ronald Abrams.

Louisiana

287   DIVISION OF WOMEN AND CHILDREN, STATE DEPT. OF LABOR.
Box 44063 Baton Rouge, La. 70804. Anne C. Spence, Dir.

288   LOUISIANA BUREAU ON THE STATUS OF WOMEN. State Office Bldg.,
150 Riverside Mall, Baton Rouge, La. 70801. (504) 389-6136. Founded
1964. Gwen Redding, Adm. 2 members.

A state agency "to study the critical problems women face in education, employment, health, family relations, law enforcement and civil and political rights
and recommend constructive action." Studies are done on state employment,
credit for women, rape consultation, and family planning information. Following is
a list of some of the resulting research which has been published.

> *Job Patterns for Louisiana Men and Women in Private Industry*
> *Louisiana Women and Girls in Public Vocational-Technical Education Pro-
> grams—A Study of Sex Discrimination*
> *Louisiana Women in Selected Federally-Assisted Work and Training Programs,
> Fiscal Year 1971*
> *The Status of Women Workers in Louisiana, 1970*
> *Women and Poverty: The Status of Female-Headed Families in Louisiana*
> *Work Training Programs and Job Finding Assistance for Female Offenders at
> the Louisiana Correctional Institute for Women*

Maine

289   ADVISORY COUNCIL ON THE STATUS OF WOMEN. 42 Longfellow Dr.,
Cape Elizabeth, Maine 04107. Ruth Zrioka.

290   MAINE DEPT. OF MANPOWER AFFAIRS, BUREAU OF LABOR AND
INDUSTRY. Capitol Shopping Center, Western Ave., Augusta, Maine 04330.
(207) 289-3331. Madge E. Ames, Acting Dir.

The state agency responsible for the enforcement of labor laws which apply
to women.

Maryland

291 MARYLAND COMMISSION ON THE STATUS OF WOMEN. 1100 N. Eutaw St., Baltimore, Md. 21201. (301) 383-5608. Founded 1965. Elaine L. Newman, Dir. 24 members.

The commission's goals are: to encourage women to participate in the policy and decision-making levels of government; to become a center of information about women; to act as a catalyst in the initiation of activity in other groups (the Citizens Coalition for the Equal Rights Amendment was formed as a result); and to inform and assist local and regional groups. The commission issues *Women Know Your Rights, Continuing Education for Women in Maryland,* and *Educational Material on Citizenship.*

292 MONTGOMERY COUNTY COMMISSION FOR WOMEN. County Office Bldg., Rockville, Md. 20850. (301) 279-1403. Founded August 1972. Bonnie Ritter Patton, Exec. Dir.

Created by the legislature "to work to remove inequalities due to unmet needs or discrimination or prejudice on the basis of sex. Among the Commission's activities are: an Information and Referral Service for all services in the County related specifically to the needs of women; a Speakers Bureau for women and women's issues; a Talent and Job Bank for women for all areas of employment; a Women's Collection in the County's Rockville Library to contain publications for, about, and by women; a personalized, individual and informal counselling program for women in the areas of employment, housing, credit and finance, domestic relations law, public assistance, health care, transportation, child care, legal services and family financial planning; a consulting service to organizations and institutions on matters concerning women." The commission maintains committees on economics, home and community affairs, law, community relations, and educational institutions.

293 PRINCE GEORGE'S COUNTY COUNCIL ON THE STATUS OF WOMEN. Courthouse, Upper Marlboro, Md. 20870. Ellen Brandenberg.

Massachusetts

294 BOSTON COMMISSION TO IMPROVE THE STATUS OF WOMEN. City Hall, Rm. 603, Boston, Mass. 02201. (617) 722-4400. Founded October 1969. Geraldine B. Pleshaw. 12 members.

Official city commission, appointed by the mayor, to work for gains in employment for women and in child care arrangements.

295 MASSACHUSETTS DEPT. OF COMMERCE AND DEVELOPMENT, WOMEN'S BUREAU. 100 Cambridge St., Boston, Mass. 02202. (617) 727-3210 (3211). Founded 1957. Dorothy Zarick, Dir.

"Created by the legislature to conduct a program, including business workshops, to promote business opportunities and economic projects for women. To realize this purpose a program of value and worth to the established and potential business woman has been developed. Its major activities are: workshops for small businesses, workshops for homemakers desiring to convert a home-based skill or service into income, workshops for the young to make them aware of opportunities in the employment world, workshops for the older woman on how to qualify for available jobs, counselling sessions for specific business problems." The following pamphlets are available, at no charge: *A Business of Your Own. . . A Guide to Good Business Practice; Extra Money at Home, Marketing Your Handicraft; Profit in the Pantry;* and *Home Secretarial Service.*

296 MASSACHUSETTS GOVERNOR'S COMMISSION ON THE STATUS OF WOMEN. Rm. 275, State House, Boston, Mass. 02133. (617) 727-6693. Founded June 1971. Fran Henry, Dir. 40 members.

Appointed by the governor "to survey and evaluate all statutes of the Commonwealth and all governmental programs and practices, relating to the employment, health, education and welfare of women, and to advise the Governor and the General Court with respect to the adequacy thereof, recommending such changes as may be warranted . . . ," and "to investigate the need for new and expanded services that may be requested for women as wives, mothers and workers, including education, counselling, training and retraining, home services, and arrangements for the care of children whose mothers are or seek to be employed."

The Executive Committee of the commission sets policy and plans programs. Task forces work on Education, Job Opportunities, Health, and Child Care. Committees are in charge of the Talent Bank, Hearings, Legislation, and Budget. The Talent Bank maintains a roster of qualified women for positions in the government and in policy-making, technical and professional positions in the public and private sectors. All resumes are held in confidence. The commission holds hearings on women's issues, and maintains a speakers' bureau.

The commission publishes Talent Bank reports as well as several other reports. Following is a list of available publications.

Continuing Education: A Survey of Programs in Massachusetts
Girls and Women: Do You Know That?
How To Run for Ward and Town Committees
Report of the Commissioners (1972)
Report to the Governor on the Status of the Hispanic-American Woman in Massachusetts (by Argelia Maria Hermenet, 1972)
Summary of Commission and Its Work (1973-1974)

Michigan

297 MICHIGAN WOMEN'S COMMISSION. 24424 Fairmont St., Dearborn, Mich. 48124. N. Lorraine Beebe.

Minnesota

298 MINNESOTA WOMEN'S ADVISORY COMMISSION AND WOMEN'S DIVISION, DEPT. OF HUMAN RIGHTS. Capitol Square Bldg., St. Paul, Minn. 55101. (612) 296-5663. Founded 1967. Betty Howard, Dir.

Established by the legislature "to assist Minnesota women in the areas of: employment policies and practices, education and training, health and welfare, civil and political rights, home, community and family life and to assist and advise the Commissioner of Human Rights in all matters of concern to women."

The WAC operates through standing committees and task forces. Present committees include a Skills Bank to gather data on appointive offices and recommend qualified candidates for appointment by the governor and other officials; Legislation Committee; Employment Committee; and Sexual Stereotypes in Education, which "conducts surveys on sex bias in education, works with State Department of Education to eliminate such bias, provides printed information on feminist movement to schools, presents workshops on sexism in education to public schools, individuals and organizations [and] distributes material on women's movement on request." The commission "encourages formation of task forces throughout the state to work with WAC particularly in presenting conferences and providing information to outstate areas on women's issues and concerns."

"The Division on Women's Affairs performs an advocacy role for Minnesota women with particular emphasis on local, state, and federal women's rights legislation, including credit granting, sex and marital discrimination, the Equal Rights Amendment, Human Rights Act, 1964 Civil Rights Act and Executive Order 11246 as amended, and affirmative action programs, Higher Education Act, and equal pay for equal work laws." The division also makes referrals to appropriate governmental and private groups; and counsels individuals on discrimination, legal rights, employment, and education, etc.

Copies of the Minnesota Human Rights Act and brochures on the division and WAC are available on request.

Mississippi

299 MISSISSIPPI GOVERNOR'S COMMISSION ON THE STATUS OF WOMEN. Box 1633, Hattiesburg, Miss. 39401. Founded 1964. Judge Mildred W. Norris, Chpn.

Created by the legislature to "study the status of women in Mississippi and make recommendations for constructive action in the following areas: employment policies and practices; state tax laws as they affect the net earnings and other income of women; state laws dealing with such matters as hours, night work, and wages of women; legal rights of women; the family and the employed woman and expanded programs to help women as wives, mothers and workers; education; women as citizen volunteers." The commission published *Status of Women in Mississippi* in 1970, 31 pp.

Missouri

300 MISSOURI COMMISSION ON THE STATUS OF WOMEN. 210 E. Dunklin St., Jefferson City, Mo. 65101. (314) 636-5602. Founded October 1967. Alberta J. Meyer. 15 members.

Asked by the legislature to "conduct research projects and make studies as to the legal status of women and to the equality or the inequality of opportunity afforded women in government, politics, education, business, professions, sciences, arts, and social services; encourage the advancement of women in these areas; utilize the reservoir of women's talents for the best interest of our communities and state; cooperate with other agencies, public and private, in securing such objectives; and make an annual report to the governor and the general assembly . . . .

"The Commission members serve without compensation. Projects have been dependent upon contributions from interested individuals and groups. To date the activities have been primarily informational and educational, such as: issuing a quarterly newsletter; publishing a booklet on *Women and Missouri Laws*; sponsoring statewide conferences on issues of interest to women; holding discussion meetings on consumer affairs, equal pay, counseling for girls and women, and the abortion problem; conducting surveys on uniform jury service, self-employed women, and opinions on the 'women question,' furnishing speakers . . . ; and compiling a roster of able women for appointment to state boards and commissions . . . ."

Montana

301 STATUS OF WOMEN ADVISORY COUNCIL. 2130 Highland St., Helena, Mont. 59601. Natalie Connor.

Nebraska

302 MAYOR'S COMMISSION ON THE STATUS OF WOMEN. 202 Interim City Hall, 108 S. 18 St., Omaha, Nebr. 68102. (402) 341-8122, ext. 357. Founded August 26, 1972. Ricky Salisbury, Exec. Dir. 40 members.

Established to gather data on conditions of women in the following areas: education, health needs, home and family, law and legislation, city and private employment, child care, media, prisons and law enforcement, welfare, housing, and representation of women on city boards and commissions. The commission also plans programs for Public Schools of Career Education, and helps to organize Girls Clubs. The commission plans to investigate police, court, and laws concerning rape, and to survey social services provided for women and children in the community; it maintains a talent bank and a speakers' bureau. The commission publishes *Where Can You Go for Help?*, a pamphlet directory of mental health, alcoholism and drug abuse treatment facilities, *The Right to Grow*, a leaflet on employment; and an annual report.

303 NEBRASKA COMMISSION ON THE STATUS OF WOMEN. 1700 Crestline Dr., Lincoln, Nebr. 68506. Virginia L. Portsche.

Nevada

304 GOVERNOR'S COMMISSION ON THE STATUS OF WOMEN. Rm. 202, 500 Plumas St., Reno, Nev. 89502. Marjorie Da Costa.

305 RENO COMMISSION ON THE STATUS OF WOMEN. 1630 Van Ness, Reno, Nev. 89503. Mary Frazzini.

New Hampshire

306 NEW HAMPSHIRE COMMISSION ON THE STATUS OF WOMEN. Rm. 204, State House Annex, Concord, N.H. 03301. (603) 271-3685. Founded 1970. Carol Pierce, Chpn.

Established by the legislature to study and make recommendations concerning the status of women in New Hampshire; to promote more effective methods for women to develop their skills and continue their educations; and to secure recognition of women's accomplishments and contributions to the state. The commission has held state-wide hearings; conferences for women, business people, and educators; and surveys and follow-ups on affirmative action programs. Four reports are available: three of state-wide public hearings; one of discriminatory policies in state government.

New Jersey

307 N.J. DIVISION ON CIVIL RIGHTS. 1100 Raymond Blvd., Newark, N.J. 07102. (201) 648-2700. Gilbert H. Francis, Dir.

An agency of the state government which enforces New Jersey's Law Against Discrimination, prohibiting discrimination on the basis of sex (among other characteristics) in employment, public accommodations, or housing. Copies of the law are available from the division, which has branch offices in Camden, Trenton, and Paterson; information concerning application of this law and how to complain will be sent upon request. The division also publishes a newsletter, *Equal Opportunities*, which notes gains in the elimination of discrimination.

308 N.J. STATE COMMISSION ON WOMEN, DEPT. OF COMMUNITY AFFAIRS. 363 W. State St., Trenton, N.J. 08625. (609) 292-4834. Founded May 1969. Sylvia Sammartino, Chpn. 140 Ridge Rd., Rutherford, N.J. 07070. (201) 438-6134. 11 members.

A commission created by the legislature, appointed by the Governor, "to help the women of New Jersey to participate fully in the life of the State and the Nation, through equal rights in economics, social, educational and political concerns." The commission works through committees on education, legislation, penal reform and youth consultants, planning conferences and symposia, establishing information and referral centers in libraries, holding lectures and discussions on abortion and the ERA, preparing reports, and holding workshops on divorce, handicapped women, and employment rights, among other subjects. The commission also maintains a speakers' bureau, and holds public meetings. The following publications are available: a newsletter, *In Touch*; an annual report; and a brochure, *Laws of Interest to Women*.

New Mexico

309 GOVERNOR'S COMMISSION ON THE RIGHTS OF WOMEN. 1721 Ridgecrest Dr., S.E., Albuquerque, N.M. 87108. Dr. Dorothy I. Cline.

New York

310   NEW YORK COMMISSION ON HUMAN RIGHTS. 80 Lafayette St., New York, N.Y. 10013. (212) 566-5050.

Enforces City of New York Law on Human Rights; received jurisdiction over women in employment, housing, and public accommodations in 1965. The commission processes individual cases, initiates complaints against employers and landlords, and holds hearings on special issues. Publications are: *Women's Role in Contemporary Society*, the report of commission hearings on women's rights, Sept. 21–25, 1970 (Avon books, 1972); and *What Constitutes Sex Discrimination*, technical assistance package.

311   NEW YORK STATE WOMEN'S UNIT, OFFICE OF THE GOVERNOR.
Executive Chamber, State Capitol, Albany, N.Y. 12224. (518) 474-4904. Founded March 1967. Virginia Cairns, Assoc. Dir.

A special-interest agency working on specific needs of women in government, guarding legal rights, and encouraging full participation of New York State women in the governmental process. A full-time staff unit of the Governor's Office, it sponsors conferences, workshops, and seminars, and works in conjunction with other state governmental agencies. The Women's unit maintains a Roster of Women, a current compilation of New York State laws affecting women, and a speakers' bureau. It produces films, cooperates with commercial media, and selects women to receive the Governor's Achievement Award. Publications are: *Women's Unit News*, a quarterly newsletter concerning women's activities in New York State; *Women's Interests* by K. C. Hart, a report to the Governor based on recommendations of the Governor's Conference on Women; and *Organization Directory*, a listing of women's organizations throughout New York State.

North Carolina

312   MAYOR'S COMMISSION ON THE STATUS OF WOMEN. 208 S. Elm St., Greenville, N.C. 27834. Carolyn Fulghum.

313   MAYOR'S COMMISSION ON THE STATUS OF WOMEN. Drawer 89, Rockingham, N.C. 28379. Beatrice C. Allen.

314   MAYOR'S COMMISSION ON THE STATUS OF WOMEN. 1316 Statesville Blvd., Salisbury, N.C. 28144. (704) 636-1982. Founded September 1, 1970. Marlene Plyler, Chpn. 75 members.

A governmental group working to achieve "full utilization of women in appointive positions, equal education and employment opportunities." Projects include a Women's Day in North Carolina, counseling and personnel seminars, and a leadership roster. "Main thrust will be on education and a possible Center for Continuing Education."

315   MAYOR'S COMMITTEE ON STATUS OF WOMEN. Winston-Salem WXII-TV, Winston-Salem, N.C. 27101. Joyce Neeley.

316 THE MAYOR'S COMMITTEE ON THE STATUS OF WOMEN, CITY OF GREENSBORO, N.C. Founded July 1972. Katherine A. Sebo, Chpn., Guilford College, Greensboro, N.C. 27410.

Established at the request of the Greensboro City Council to report to the mayor. The committee filed a report on May 1, 1973 after making studies and recommendations "concerning education and counseling, employment, health services, welfare services, child care services, financial services, the legal system, the juvenile and criminal justice system and family relations as they affect the social and economic status of women in Greensboro." The situation inside Greensboro City Government as it affects women and the activities of the commissions on the status of women in the region and across the country were also reviewed. The establishment of a Commission on the Status of Women in Greensboro was recommended and acted upon by the City Council in May 1973. The Administrator of the Commission is Mae Douglas, Human Relations Office, City of Greensboro, Greensboro, N.C. 27410. (919) 373-2390. The report of the committee is available upon request, and a separate publication, analyzing the results of a questionnaire distributed and completed by 1400 people, is in progress.

317 NORTH CAROLINA COMMISSION ON EDUCATION AND EMPLOYMENT OF WOMEN. 1011 Benjamin Pkwy., Greensboro, N.C. 27408. Dr. Margaret A. Hunt.

North Dakota

318 NORTH DAKOTA COMMISSION ON THE STATUS OF WOMEN. Governor's Council on Human Resources, 13th flr., State Capitol Bldg., Bismark, N.Dak. 58501. (701) 224-2970. Ellie Kilander, Pres. 1338 7 St., S., Fargo, N.Dak. 58102. Founded 1963; lapsed 1964 until June 1972. 27 members.

Aims to "bring women into full partnership in the life of the state," to inform women of their rights and resources, and to perform an ombudsman function in cases of sex discrimination in employment. The commission is conducting regional hearings to assess needs of women in states, and is currently exploring involvement with the Bicentennial celebration.

Ohio

319 CINCINNATI COUNCIL ON THE STATUS OF WOMEN. 2928 Linwood Ave., Cincinnati, Ohio 45208. Dr. Edith M. Parkey.

320 CLEVELAND COUNCIL ON THE STATUS OF WOMEN. 22414 Fairlawn Court No. 4, Fairview Park, Ohio 44126. Dr. Nancy E. Dowding.

321 OHIO BUREAU OF EMPLOYMENT SERVICES, WOMEN SERVICES DIVISION. 145 S. Front St., Columbus, Ohio. 43216. (614) 469-4496. Founded September 1970. Emily L. Leedy, Dir. 11 members.

The state government unit interested in the status of women promotes programs to improve employment competencies of women and to enhance their employment opportunities, giving particular attention to education, child care, labor conditions, equality of entrance requirements, and eligibility for promotion. It has conducted studies and research to develop programs, and has gathered and disseminated information on programs and activities of federal, state, and local governments pertinent to women. The division also coordinates women's programs with other phases of the Bureau of Employment Services operation, evaluates existing and pending legislation affecting women, recommends needed or desirable changes, and maintains a file of women qualified to fill administrative and high level positions in education and government. The division publishes a monthly newsletter, *Ohio Woman*, which includes a listing of career opportunities and legislation of interest to women.

322 OHIO COMMISSION ON THE STATUS OF WOMEN, INC. 798 Craig Parkway, Newark, Ohio 43055. (614) 366-5860. Founded May 1970. Audrey Matesich, Pres. Dues: $5, individuals; $10, institutions.

A citizen's commission, incorporated as a nonprofit organization composed of individual members, organizations and city councils, committed to continuing to push for a governmental or statutory commission, ratification of the Equal Rights Amendment, and all other legislation which would end discrimination on the basis of sex. The stated purposes of the commission are: "to encourage women to full participation as citizens with equal rights in business, education, labor, politics and community affairs; to work toward removing all impediments in attitudes and laws which prevent women from developing and contributing their talents to society; to assist women in assuming initiative and accepting their responsibility to continue their education and become better qualified for their chosen vocation; to eliminate discrimination on the basis of sex in all phases of American society; to promote the dissemination of information and provide counsel on opportunities for the effective participation of women in private and public sectors; to persist in efforts to achieve a truly equal partnership with men." Available from the commission is *Guidebook for Ohio Women: Employment Discrimination*, by Catherine L. Harper.

Oklahoma

323 OKALAHOMA GOVERNOR'S COMMISSION ON THE STATUS OF WOMEN. Heavener, Okla. 74937. Maxine Looper.

Oregon

324 GOVERNOR'S COMMITTEE ON THE STATUS OF WOMEN IN OREGON. Box 38, Beaverton, Oreg. 97005. (503) 646-9101. Founded April 1967. Sharon G. Langeberg, Chpn. 22 members.

"Founded to study the legal, economic, social and political status of women in Oregon and to make recommendations to the Governor." Projects include preparation of a brochure on Oregon laws and how they effect women; upgrading the status of the domestic worker through a training program and an employment service; research on sexism in student counseling; equalization of pay and conditions of employment for male and female physical education teachers; and equalization of athletic facilities.

Pennsylvania

325 PENNSYLVANIA COMMISSION ON THE STATUS OF WOMEN. Rm. 609, Main Capitol, Harrisburg, Pa. 17120. (717) 787-8128. Founded 1972. Arline Lotman, Exec. Dir.

"Created by Executive Order of the Governor 'to be a strong advocate for the rights of women in the Commonwealth." The Commission does not have enforcement power but has been charged with the responsibility of planning and implementing programs to insure that women in Pennsylvania are equal participants in the life of the Commonwealth. CSW is currently investigating the credit policies and practices in Pennsylvania as they effect women. The Attorney's Advisory Panel, volunteer law students, and representatives of the Justice Department are cooperating with CSW in documenting the need for corrective action, both legislative and administrative, to eliminate credit discrimination based on sex and marital status. The Commission's review of State Employment application forms has led to a proposed revised Civil Service Application form which has been approved by the Civil Service Commission . . . Other CSW activities include: a proposal to establish a recruitment program for women; a proposal to develop a training program to certify in-home child-care workers for parents of children up to three; and a review of all legislation to determine what changes need to be made to bring Pennsylvania laws into consonance with the ERA. . . . "

The commission publishes *CSW News*, a monthly newsletter, and a weekly column, *The CSW Report*, which is distributed to all daily and weekly newspapers in Pennsylvania. A recent issue of *CSW News* included items on legislation, want ad discrimination, gubernatorial appointments, and insurance investigation by the Pennsylvania Insurance Department, CSW testimony before federal legislative committees, the lifting of a ban forbidding women to be licensed as boxers and wrestlers in Pennsylvania, and a listing of job openings in the state government.

Rhode Island

326 RHODE ISLAND PERMANENT ADVISORY COMMISSION ON WOMEN. 235 Promenade St., Providence, R.I. 02908. (401) 277-2734. Founded January 1970. Freda Goldman, Chpn. 24 members.

Established by the State General Assembly "to study and to submit recommendations for constructive action in the following areas related to the status of women: opportunities for education and training of women; measures to strengthen family life through programs and services which will assist women in filling their multiple roles as wives, mothers and workers; policies and practices in public and private employment opportunities for women; the status of women under the labor laws and the laws providing for social insurance; the effective participation of women as citizens and as volunteers; and the legal rights of women." Activities include participation in panel discussions, international meetings, workshops, radio and television programs, and conferences. The commission also maintains a talent bank, and has initiated studies on women offenders, employment resources, maternity leave, and academic employment policies. Publications include leaflets in English and Spanish, and the following pamphlets: *Sex and Status in Academia* (1972), *Rhode Island Women—Their Legal Status* (1973), *Before You Buy* (1973), *Divorce Law Reform* (1973), and *Rhode Island Women.*

South Carolina

327 SOUTH CAROLINA COMMISSION ON THE STATUS OF WOMEN.
2825 Millwood Ave., Columbia, S.C. 29205. Donna Culberton.

South Dakota

328 SOUTH DAKOTA COMMISSION ON THE STATUS OF WOMEN. State
House, Pierre, S. Dak. 57501. (605) 224-3165. Founded 1963. Ann McKay
Thompson, Chpn., Box 1072, Pierre, S. Dak. 57501. 12 members.

Appointed by the governor, "to make studies and conduct research into
the status of women in the state and the nation and suggest ways in which
women may reach their potential and make their full contribution as wage
earners and citizens to society and this state." Projects include state conferences,
research into education, day care, stereotyping, counseling, extensive work on
the Equal Rights Amendment. There is no funding for the projects; they are
dependent upon contributions.

Tennessee

329 TENNESSEE GOVERNOR'S COMMISSION ON THE STATUS OF
WOMEN. 921 Andrew Jackson Bldg., Nashville, Tenn. 37219. (615) 741-
1013. Founded February 1973. Mildred Buchanan. 12 members.

Established to "assure that women are afforded equal opportunities for full
participation in the life of Tennessee." Some of the duties are to conduct studies
and conferences in cooperation with state and local women's business, professional,
and civic organizations; to advise the governor and inform the state legislators on
employment policies and practices, educational needs, political and civil rights, and
domestic relations; and to recommend new and expanded services including education, counseling, training, home services, and arrangements for the care of children
during the working day. The commission is currently looking for qualified women
for responsible positions "in employment or as non-paid members of policy-
making boards and commissions"; resumes are requested. Projected are an information booklet for women of Tennessee, a survey of women in state government, a review of state laws, and conferences.

Texas

330 AUSTIN MAYOR'S COMMISSION ON THE STATUS OF WOMEN. 2700
Valley Springs Rd., Austin, Tex. 78746. Mary Ruth Beeson.

331 FORT WORTH MAYOR'S COMMISSION ON WOMEN. John Tarter and
Co., Box 11002, Fort Worth, Tex. 76109. Mrs. John Tarter.

332 HARRISON COUNTY COMMISSION ON THE STATUS OF WOMEN. 202
Adkins St., Marshall, Tex. 75670. Dr. Aggie Boyett.

333 HUNTSVILLE MAYOR'S COMMISSION ON THE STATUS OF WOMEN. McAdams Dry Goods Co., Huntsville, Tex. 77340. Mrs. J. E. Crews.

334 MAYOR'S COMMISSION ON THE STATUS OF WOMEN. 207 Beechwood La., San Antonio, Tex. 78216. Helen Jacobson.

335 SAN ANGELO COMMISSION ON THE STATUS OF WOMEN. 2102 Wilson St., San Angelo, Tex. 76901. Nellie Galindo.

Utah

336 UTAH GOVERNOR'S COMMISSION ON THE STATUS OF WOMEN. 210 State Capitol, Salt Lake City, Utah 84114. (801) 328-5231. Founded 1968. Beth Gurrister, Chpn., 160 N. 8 St., E., Brigham City, Utah 84302. (801) 723-6486. 15 members.

Designated by the legislature "to advise and confer with the governor and state agencies concerning issues of importance to women and families in Utah and to serve as a contact and coordinating group to analyze state and local programs to determine whether they adequately serve women and protect the rights of men, women and families." The commission researched and published studies on child development facilities, counseling and education needs of women, extramural sports competition for girls, and labor laws and employment opportunities affecting men, women, and families. A roster of women qualified in various fields as a potential resource was compiled. The commission has attempted to build understanding of changes affecting sex roles and to urge that institutuions and laws deal with these changes. The *Five Year Report* is available.

Vermont

337 VERMONT GOVERNOR'S COMMISSION ON THE STATUS OF WOMEN. Vermont College, Montpelier, Vt. 05602. (802) 223-2135. Founded 1964. Lenore McHeir, Chpn. 16 members.

A statewide advocacy group for women, appointed by the governor, to study and report on the social, economic, political, and educational life of women. Ratification of the Equal Rights Amendment and changing state statutes to conform to ERA are projects of the commission. An annual report is published.

Virginia

338 ALEXANDRIA MAYOR'S AD HOC COMMITTEE ON WOMEN. 204 Birch St., Alexandria, Va. 22305. (703) 750-6436. Founded January 1973. Vola Lawson. 11 members.

Appointed "to research areas of health, education, credit, employment and legal status of women, analyze, refer complaints and suggest remedies to these and related problems." The committee conducts public hearings, employment conferences, and credit discrimination studies; and recommends legislation to City Council.

339   ARLINGTON COUNTY COMMISSION ON THE STATUS OF WOMEN.
4413 N. 18 St., Arlington, Va. 22207. Ann Wright.

340   CITIZENS' COMMITTEE ON THE STATUS OF WOMEN IN VIRGINIA.
1207 Southbury Ave., Richmond, Va. 23231. Helen Gannon.

341   COMMISSION ON THE STATUS OF WOMEN. Box 5721, Richmond, Va.
23220. Mrs. Julian A. Kean.

342   FAIRFAX COUNTY COMMISSION ON WOMEN. Office of Personnel,
4100 Chain Bridge Rd., Fairfax, Va. 22030. (703) 691-2594. Founded
September 1971. Barbara Gordon, Staff. 9 members.

An official body created by the Board of Supervisors to serve women and to
study sex discrimination and sex bias in the county; to receive and process complaints of sex discrimination in the county; and to advise the Board of Supervisors
on matters relating to women and sex discrimination. The commission works for
women in many ways, including preparation of reports covering employment,
housing, credit, social services, and child care. The commission has prepared a separate report on sex bias in the county's public schools—employment, physical
education and athletics, guidance counseling, industrial arts and home economics,
textbooks, and the human relations program. A Talent Bank has been established
to bring more women into the mainstream of county government, and it is used by
the Office of Personnel for positions of employment and by the Board of Supervisors for appointive positions. The commission also advises the Board of Supervisors
on such issues as child care, affirmative action, the Equal Rights Amendment, the
fair housing ordinance, and a halfway house for girls; receives and processes complaints of sex discrimination in such areas as housing, credit, employment, education, and recreation; advises the county's Office of Personnel on improving employment opportunities for women; acts as a liaison with related groups at the local,
national and state levels; speaks on issues of concern to women at meetings and in
the news media; and recommends women to local, state, and national positions."
Complaints of sex discrimination, ideas for commission actions, and information
for education study are welcomed. Additionally, volunteers can be used on many
projects.

Washington

343   SEATTLE WOMEN'S COMMISSION. 2200 Rainier South St., Seattle, Wash.
98144. (206) 583-6830. Founded January 1971. Shirley G. Bridge, Pres.
15 members.

Staffed by the Office of Women's Rights, City of Seattle, to eliminate sex discrimination and recommend policies and legislation to implement equal opportunity for women. Projects include recruitment of minority women for city employment; recommending changes in laws concerning rape and in the Criminal Code;
child care; and a speakers' bureau. The commission has a brochure.

344   WASHINGTON STATE WOMEN'S COUNCIL. Office of the Governor,
Olympia, Wash. 98504. (206) 753-2870. Founded October 1971. Gisela E.
Taber, Exec. Dir. 15 members.

The council has three primary functions: "(1) to identify for possible coordination activities affecting women in diverse locations around the state, and to establish priorities for action; (2) to review and identify needs for legislation affecting women, and to establish a program of legislative action relating to women; [and] (3) to focus the attention of communities on the need for women to have equal privileges and responsibilities as men.

"The Council has: (1) sponsored and obtained passage of a state ERA, a community property bill equalizing management powers between spouses, Federal ERA ratification, credit provisions in state anti-discrimination law, [and a] state ERA omnibus implementation bill; (2) contributed toward public information and awareness by: conducting educationals/hearings throughout [the] state; co-sponsoring Second Annual Community Conference on Child Care, "New Federalism and Children"; sponsoring [a] state-wide legislative conference; establishing a roster of qualified women to be used in recommendations for appointments to statutory boards and commissions; writing all state newspapers containing sex-graded help-wanted ads urging they comply with law; [and] (3) affected public policy by: testifying before numerous boards and commissions on a variety of topics, including maternity benefits, assisting in establishment of state Office of Child Development; proposing changes in salary ranges to State Personnel Board; studying discriminatory life insurance policies in state agencies; [and] promoting affirmative action in state government in a variety of ways, including a Council member's serving on the Governor's Affirmative Action Evaluation and Review Committee."

West Virginia

345 GOVERNOR'S COMMISSION ON THE STATUS OF WOMEN. Harrisville, W. Va. 26362. Alma Ferguson.

Wisconsin

346 MAYOR'S COMMISSION ON THE STATUS OF WOMEN. 1005 Sturgeon Eddy Rd., Wausau, Wis. 54401. Irene Schlueter.

347 WISCONSIN'S GOVERNOR'S COMMISSION ON THE STATUS OF WOMEN. Rm. 427, Lowell Hall, 610 Langdon St., Madison, Wis. 53706. Dr. Kathryn Clarenbach.

Wyoming

348 WYOMING COMMISSION ON THE STATUS OF WOMEN. 329 Bocage Dr., Cheyenne, Wyo. 82001. (307) 632-2810. Founded 1965. Meredith E. Morrow, Chpn.

A commission created by the state legislature, and comprised of 27 members appointed by the governor, to deal with four areas concerning women: (1) legal rights and responsibilities; (2) home and community; (3) employment practices;

and (4) educational opportunities. The commission conducts seminars for women on the community college campuses, and reports biannually to the Governor and legislature. Recommendations of the commission have included improvement of child-care facilities, deletion of reference to sex in statutes concerning employment, addition of an equal rights amendment to the Wyoming constitution, and ratification of the federal ERA. Annual reports are available.

Virgin Islands

349   VIRGIN ISLANDS COMMISSION ON THE STATUS OF WOMEN. Box 189, St. Thomas, V.I. 00801. (809) 774-1281. Founded 1966. Addelita Cancryn. 11 members.

A government agency to study and improve the economic and social status of women in the Virgin Islands. The commission conducts local and national conferences, special research projects, and panel discussions, and supplies speakers for local programs and television appearances.

Canadian National

350 CANADA DEPT. OF LABOR, WOMEN'S BUREAU. 340 Laurier Ave., W. Ottawa, Ont., Can. K1AOJ2. (613) 992-0124. Founded September 1954. Sylvia Gelber, Dir.

Central government agency concerning women's special needs, aiming to foster equal opportunity for women in all areas of employment. The bureau does research on women, presents papers, and holds discussions. Publications available free from the Women's Bureau, in French and English, include annual reports from the bureau which include articles on employment, housework, careers, etc.; *Women in the Labor Force 1971: Facts and Figures*, 33 statistical tables and analytical texts on the social and economic characteristics of women in the labor force, including data on the earnings of women and men; and *International Instruments and Canadian Federal and Provincial Legislation Relating to the Status of Women in Employment*.

Canadian Local

Alberta

351 ALBERTA WOMEN'S BUREAU. Legislative Bldg., Edmonton, Alta., Can. T5K2B6 (403) 229-3970. Founded 1966. Catherine E. Arthur, Dir.

The bureau must "collect and compile information . . . on matters of particular concern to women . . . on the cultural, social, legal, public and other rights, responsibilities, interests and privileges of women in Alberta" and make such information available. The following publications are available.

Citizenship
Counseling Services in Edmonton
Facts for Mature Women Contemplating the Labor Market
The Famous Five
Interesting Statistics on Alberta Women
The Juvenile
The Landlord and the Tenant
Laws for Albertans
New Unemployment Insurance
Pioneer Women of the West
Wills and Estates for Albertans
Women in Canadian Politics
Women on Juries

Manitoba

352 MANITOBA WOMEN'S BUREAU, DEPT. OF LABOUR. Rm. 618, Norquay Bldg. York and Kennedy Sts., Winnipeg, Manitoba, Can. R3COP8. (204) 946-7179. Founded August 1972. Mary Eady, Dir.

Acts as a response center for individuals and organizations on the special problems and concerns of women; promotes the integration of women workers within the total work force; investigates areas of concern to working women; distributes information on women in the Manitoba labor force; and provides counseling and guidance for women reentering the work force.

Ontario

353 ONTARIO MINISTRY OF LABOUR, WOMEN'S BUREAU, HUMAN RIGHTS COMMISSION. 400 University Ave., Toronto, Ont., Can. M7A1T9. (416) 965-1537. Founded 1963. Elizabeth Neville, Dir.

"Has special responsibilities for prohibiting discrimination because of sex or marital status. In 1970, the Bureau was assigned the responsibility of administering the Women's Equal Employment Opportunity Act. The Act prohibited employment discrimination because of sex or marital status and provided for a guaranteed minimum standard of maternity leave. In June, 1972, this Act was incorporated into an expanded Ontario Human Rights Code. In addition to administering those sections of the Human Rights Code, the Bureau also administers the maternity leave provision of the Employment Standards Act." Any person wishing to file a complaint may do so in person, by letter or by phone in Toronto, Hamilton, Kenora, London, Ottawa, Sudbury, Thunder Bay, and Windsor.

The Women's Bureau also offers a special counseling service for women who have been out of the labor force and wish to return, and a career education program to encourage girls to raise their career expectations. Research is conducted on general working conditions, occupations, careers, and other topics of interest to women. A Resource Centre is maintained, with books, pamphlets, documents, and a bibliography on subjects relating to working women. Speakers are sent to interested groups.

The following publications are available on request.

Career Selector
14 Ways to Train for a Better Job
Guide for Employers
How to Find the Job You Want
Job Advertising Guidelines
Maternity Leave Legislation
Who Are Ontario's Working Women?
Women Returning to the Labour Force: No. 2
You're a What?

Saskatchewan

354 SASKATCHEWAN DEPARTMENT OF LABOUR, WOMEN'S BUREAU. 2350 Albert St., Regina, Sask., Can. (306) 525-3357. Founded 1965. Mary Rocan, Sup.

"A division of the Labour Standards Branch, [which] works towards the investigation, examination and evaluation of information, legislation, and assists women and employers of women in resolving some of their employment problems." The supervisor fulfills speaking engagements, and participates in seminars "designed to better inform high school students and women of their rights under existing labour legislation and acquaint them with training programs and the role played by women today in the world of work." The Women's Bureau also conducts surveys, develops training programs, and maintains liaisons with women's bureaus in other jurisdictions. Publications available from the Women's Bureau include leaflets on employment, labor legislation, and a list of recommendations of the Royal Commission on the Status of Women in Canada.

V. Special Interests

Art and Communications

(See also Nonprint Media.)

355 AIN'T I A WOMAN? PERFORMING TROUPE. Safe Return, 156 Fifth Ave., Suite 1003, New York, N.Y. 10010. (212) 242-7440. Marisa Gioffre.

Three performers, acting in a dramatic presentation of woman's struggle for equality, "to expose audiences to the rich, deep tradition of feminism." Seeks engagements and bookings throughout the United States.

APHRA. See 43.

356 ARTISTS IN RESIDENCE (AIR). 97 Wooster St., New York, N.Y. 10012. (212) 966-0799. Founded March 1972. Anne Healy. 20 members. Dues: $21/mo.

Established a gallery to show the work of women artists because of "the difficulties women artists encounter in trying to show their work," and to give women art students "the models and encouragement which a greater body of women artists' work would provide." Members' work includes performances, conceptual art, sculpture, painting, drawing and printmaking, which are displayed in scheduled exhibitions. The AIR runs Monday Programs, which are discussions conducted by AIR's members and open to the public. The Video Program, tapes of gallery artists and other women artists at work and talking in their studios, is available with the Monday Programs to schools and interested groups. Write for further information.

357 BRAINCHILD. 1004 N. 6 St., Springfield, Ill. 62702. (217) 523-8186. Founded November 1972. Sandra Martin. 15 members.

A group of women writing poetry, fiction, nonfiction, and songs; and producing films, photographs, and graphics. Also produces poetry readings and multimedia shows. Publishes an irregular anthology of poetry, *Brainchild* ($1). Issue one is a collection of original poems by 13 women read at Sangamon State University, Springfield, Ill. *Brainchild* states:

"Women have been diffident about identifying themselves as poets, as if they suspected that their own life experiences or their own styles of writing were of dubious value. . . . This anthology is part of a process in which a group of women set about to discover each other as poets without prior invitation, without indeed knowing what they would find, so isolated had they been from each other's work."

CHELSEA PICTURE STATION. See 113.

CHICAGO WOMEN'S LIBERATION ROCK BAND. See 184.

CHICAGO WOMEN'S LIBERATION UNION, WOMEN'S GRAPHICS COLLECTIVE. See 184.

358   CLEARINGHOUSE FOR FEMINIST MEDIA. Box 207, Ancaster, Ont., Can. Founded October 1971. Lorna Marsden, 41 Spadina Rd., No. 7, Toronto, Ont., Can. 200 members. Dues: $1.

"CFM is a national organization whose aim is to facilitate the access to information necessary for feminists when learning about and entering the media field. This is done by publishing an annual list of (1) women and men who are freelance or employed in the media and who consider themselves feminists, (2) those who write, record, film, etc. about topics which are of concern to feminists, and (3) feminist publications, films, organizations, etc. Three supplements are published each year which include new listings, updated listings, feature articles on the media scene in different regions of the country, and other relevant information." An individual or organization may be listed by sending (1) name, address, and telephone number; (2) a full listing of publications on feminism; (3) a description of areas in which the individual is presently working; and (4) a description of areas in which the person would like to work. (Only those who send envelopes to receive the list will have their listing repeated.)

359   CLITARTISTS 1321 A (rear) Alcatraz St., Berkeley, Calif. 94702. Founded December 1971. 10 members.

A feminist art collective and studio, founded on the premise that "art is political because the political power structure uses art to their benefit . . . We believe that the most vital artistic statements of the here and now by women are increasingly related to a redefinition of Self." Projects include seminars on women's art, past and present; slide shows of women's art; art exhibits; goddesses poster series; and a life drawing group.

360   COLLEGE ART ASSOCIATION, COMMITTEE ON THE STATUS OF WOMEN. Vassar College, Poughkeepsie, N.Y. 12601. Founded 1972. Linda Nochlin-Pommer.

A subcommittee of CAA's Board of Directors, investigating the position of women artists, art historians, and museum workers who are members of the CAA, and seeking measures to secure justice and equality for them. The committee gathers statistics, distributes information, and helps to implement ameliorating measures.

361   COMMISSION ON SEXIST ABUSE IN LANGUAGE. Dept. of English, Ball State Univ., Muncie, Ind. 47306. (317) 285-1527 Founded April 1972. Dr. William A. Sutton, Coor.

A group of representatives from colleges and universities in Indiana studying sexist language and ways to eliminate it. The commission has published *Sexual Fairness in Language* by William A. Sutton (35¢).

362   CONNECTICUT FEMINISTS IN THE ARTS, WOMEN'S INTERART COOP. 11 N. Main St., Norwalk, Conn. 06877. (203) 853-2162. Founded September 1970. Suzanne Benton, 22 Donnely Dr., Ridgefield, Conn.

Feminist artists desiring "to give exposure to the work of women artists in all media, to both influence the established culture and form a new culture; to act as a source of professional contacts and provide employment for women artists; to provide emotional (and financial) support to creative women; to engage in political action aimed at improving the condition of women generally and in the arts; to bring to light the contribution of women artists through history; to raise the consciousness of our members to the needs of women artists and our oppression, with a view to social change; through art, to bring into focus the image of women so that it reflects ourselves as we really are and can become." The group sponsors women's art festivals, workshops, and happenings. Publications are *Women* (poetry); and *Unmasking*, ed. by Valerie Sheehan (Swallow Press, 1973, $8.95).

EARTH'S DAUGHTERS. See 47.

FEMALE LIBERATION (weekly radio show). See 190.

FEMINIST ART JOURNAL. See 50.

363 FEMINIST STUDIO WORKSHOP. The Woman's Bldg., 743 S. Grandview St., Los Angeles, Calif. 90057. (213) 389-6241. Founded September 1973. Judy Chicago, Arlene Raven, Sheila de Bretteville. 32 members. Tuition: $750.

"An experimental program in female education in the arts." FSW's purpose is "to develop a new concept of art, a new kind of artist and a new art community built from the lives, feelings, and needs of women." Workshops are offered on art, performance, design methodology, printing, video, photography, autobiography, building, self-documentation, study and criticism, and art history. Members include painters, sculptors, potters, photographers, printmakers, designers, and women working in the areas of performance, video, and art history. Artists must submit a written application and samples of work. The FSW is affiliated with the International Community College and degree programs can be arranged. FSW also offers a complete summer school program. Write for further information.

MOVING OUT MAGAZINE. See 65.

364 NATIONAL ASSOCIATION OF WOMEN ARTISTS. 156 5 Ave., New York, N.Y. 10010. (212) 675-1616. Founded 1889. Beverly Boxer, Exec. Secy. 700 members. Dues: $20.

Professional organization designed to further the cultural contribution of women in the field of art by enlarging the opportunities for exposure. An annual exhibit is held at the National Academy of Design, as well as other local, national, and international exhibits. An exhibition catalog ($2) is published in May of each year.

365 NEW FEMINIST TALENT, INC. 250 W. 57 St., New York, N.Y. 10019. (212) 581-1066. Founded April 1972. Jane Field, 225 E. 116 St., New York, N.Y. 10029.

Feminist-owned and operated speakers' bureau, booking such feminists as Betty Freidan, Wilma Scott Hiede, Myrna Lamb, Bella Abzug, Ann Scott, Frances "Sissy" Farenthold, among others. The bureau also runs Cinema Femina, a referral service for feminist films, and arranges speaking engagements and one-woman film shows. Filmmakers and critics include Shirley Clarke, Martha Coolidge, Molly Haskell, and Kristina Nordstrom.

366 NEW HAVEN WOMEN'S LIBERATION ROCK BAND. 1504 Boulevard, New Haven, Conn. 06511. (203) 389-1971. Founded January 1970. Virginia Blaisdell. 6 members.
See also Chicago Women's Liberation Rock Band, 184.

A rock band (french horn, flute, trombone, sax, electric guitars, bass, drums, and vocals) creating a new kind of rock music of which women can be part and that will speak to and for women. The band performs at women's conferences, festivals, colleges, dances, etc.; recorded "Mountain Moving Day" (with Chicago Women's Liberation Rock Band) available from Rounder Records (111).

367 NEW WOMB ARTISTS. 177 Liberty St., San Francisco, Calif. (415) 285-7087. Founded 1971. Jeri Robinson. 334 Winfield St., San Francisco, Calif. 8 members.

A group of women artists, which aims to bring works of art by women to public attention by mounting women's art shows. Other projects include drawing and clay modeling classes and a crafts workshop. A portfolio of women's drawings is in preparation: *I Am Woman, I Am Artist: A portfolio of 54 Drawings and Prints by Bay Area Women Artists* ($5).

ROUNDER RECORDS. See 111.

SACRAMENTO COMMUNITY COMMISSION FOR WOMEN. See 263.

368 WESTBETH PLAYWRIGHTS' FEMINIST COLLECTIVE. 463 West St., New York, N.Y. 10014. (212) 691-0015. Founded 1970. Dolores Walker.

A collective of women playwrights, formed for the purpose of writing and producing feminist plays. Members Gwendolyn Gunn, Patricia Horan, Chryse Maile, Sally Ordway, Dolores Walker, and Susan Yankowitz have had shows produced at such theatres as Papp's Public Theatre, Cafe La Mama, Open Theatre, Caffe Cino, Eugene O'Neill Theatre Foundation, Mark Taper Forum, and the Lincoln Center. The collective helped produce *Rape-In* at the Assembly Theatre, and *Up!* at the Westbeth Cabaret; *Up!* has since been optioned for off-Broadway production. *Wicked Women* was produced at Theatre for the New City in January 1973. A new musical revue was produced at the Little Church Around the Corner. "In addition to producing plays, the Collective has an active playwrights' workshop which tours schools and colleges in the New York State area. The Collective is building a repertory of plays written by women based on self-awareness through individual consciousness-raising."

369 "WHERE WE AT" BLACK WOMEN ARTISTS. 1007 Winthrop St., Brooklyn, N.Y. 11212. (212) 744-5594. Founded Summer 1971. Kay Brown. 12 members. Dues: $15.

The group "is committed to developing creative and cultural awareness within the Black community. Members . . . have functioned in such community projects as a Mobile Art Workshop for hospitals in Ghetto areas, sponsored by the N.Y.S. Council on the Arts, and is now planning a printmaking workshop to be held on the site of Bed-Stuy Restoration Corporation in cooperation with the Museum Collaboratives and N.Y.S. Council on the Arts." The group has exhibited in several galleries and shows. An affiliate Black Women Artists group is being formed in Pittsburgh. Brochures and slides are available.

WOMAN BECOMING. See 86.

A WOMAN'S PLACE. See 235.

370 WOMANSPACE. 11007 Venice Blvd., Los Angeles, Calif. 90034. (213) 838-9668. Founded January 1973. Marge Goldwater, Judy Fiskin, Co-Dirs. 1200 members. Dues: $8/6months. Hours: 11 a.m–5 p.m, Weds–Sun.

A feminist gallery and performance center which provides exhibition space for women artists, lectures, films, and programs for and about women, and helps women to present themselves professionally. Recent events included an exhibition of drawings by women, a lecture on the position of women in the Renaissance, a series of readings by women artists, and a juried art show open to all members. Womanspace publishes *Womanspace Journal* (bi-m., free to members; $4/yr. for nonmembers). Articles in one issue included: "Sexual and Self-Image in Art—Male and Female," by Ruth Iskin; "Female Imagery," by Miriam Schapiro and Judy Chigago; "Sensory Visions of Ruth Weisberg," by Victoria Thorson; an interview with Faith Wilding by Arlene Raven; a report on the Black Mirror exhibition at Womanspace by Claudia Chapline; and a calendar of events at Womanspace.

371 WOMEN IN THE ARTS. Box 4476, Grand Central Sta., New York, N.Y. 10017. Founded April 1971. Cynthia Navaretta, 300 Riverside Dr., New York, N.Y. 10025. 500 members. Dues: $20.

An organization for all creative women, membership consists primarily of professional artists. WIA was formed to end discrimination against women in the creative professions and to encourage a closer community of women working with and for women. Action Committees implement and research projects within WIA. Projects include art shows, education actions, catalogues, demonstrations, participation in panels, conferences, and lectures. A newsletter, *WIA*, includes news items concerning women and art in the local area, and a calendar of meetings, exhibitions, and events.

372 WOMEN'S ART REGISTRY. 55 Mercer St., New York, N.Y. 10013. Mailing address: Box 539, Canal St. Sta., New York, N.Y. 10013. Founded September 1970. Sandy Gellis, Michelle Stuart. 500–800 members. Dues: $2–$10.

Maintains a slide registry, which exists as a body of information available to everyone, but aimed at museum curators, critics, dealers, and heads of departments who are becoming aware of the great number of women artists whose work has been invisible due to isolation and descrimination. The registry is open to all women artists. In addition to the original registry, there are two duplicate registries which are used by lecturers, museums, colleges, etc. To be represented in all three registries one must send up to four slides (35mm plus 2 duplicates, a total of 3 sets). Label each slide with your name at the top, title (if any), and dimensions at the bottom. Include a 3 × 5 index card with your name, address, phone number, and the categories into which the art fits: painting, sculpture, mixed media, conceptual, or other. Also send a brief biography. A $5 donation is requested.

373 THE WOMEN'S ARTS CENTER OF PHILADELPHIA. 2534 Meredith St., Philadelphia, Pa. 19130. (215) 235-6361. Ellen Lampert, 1625 Addison St., Philadelphia, Pa.

A center where women artists can meet, work, and share in their artistic endeavors. The center intends to present to the public the creative work of women in various arts, to establish and maintain an historical and contemporary collection of women's artwork, and to encourage women to make artistic contributions, all in a feminist context. Projects include art exhibitions, film shows, panel discussions, and a series of workshops.

374 WOMEN'S INSTITUTE FOR FREEDOM OF THE PRESS. 3306 Ross Pl., N.W, Washington, D.C. 20008. (202) 966-7783. Founded April 1972. Dr. Donna Allen, Dir.

Aims to ensure access to the media for all citizens, not just to those who own it. Conducts seminars on communications problems. Publishes *Media Report to Women* (irreg; free to feminists in the media) reporting on research, actions, ideas relating to feminism and women in the media, and equal access.

375 WOMEN'S INTERART CENTER. 549 W. 52 St., New York, N.Y. 10019. (212) 246-6570. Founded October 1971. Margot Lewitin Hours: 2-10 p.m., Mon.-Fri. Dues: $36 plus 24 hours of donated work at the center.

A feminist-oriented organization of women artists of all disciplines providing a common meeting ground to share artistic experiences. The center presents artistic performances to the public, art exhibits, and weekly workshops for artists. Workshops are given in painting, photography, film making, video, silkscreen, pottery, music, songwriting, and dance therapy. A theater is maintained for public productions, and an art gallery for public exhibits. Some studio space is also available. Support is given by the New York State Council on the Arts. The center publishes a monthly newsletter and a literary magazine, *Sojourner*. A film entitled *Birth Film* and three videotapes (*Another Looka*, *Priest and the Pilot*, and *Erotic Garden*) are also available.

376 WOMEN'S MEDIA EXCHANGE. R.D. 2, Box 131, New Paltz, N.Y. 12561. (914) 658-5821. Founded 1972. Shelley Farkas. 15 members.

A loose network of women artists, who work with each other to foster professional attitudes and meet common needs. The exchange arranges art exhibitions, gathers information, and runs workshops. Group members work in sculpture, crafts, painting, theater, photography, film, television, jewelry, and papier mache. The Women's Intermedia Cooperative is a subdivision concerned with buying art supplies at wholesale cost and running the workshops. *Once*, a film by Shelley Farkas (12 min., color, rental $40, $25 to feminist groups, plus shipping) is available.

WOMEN'S RADIO COLLECTIVE. See 174.

Civil Rights and Legal Services

(See also Labor Rights.)

377 AMERICAN CIVIL LIBERTIES UNION, WOMEN'S RIGHTS PROJECT.
22 E. 40 St., New York, N.Y. 10016. (212) 725-1222. Founded March
1972. Brenda Feigen Fasteau, Coor.
See also Women's Law Careers, 562.

"Undertakes precedent setting cases in a variety of areas of sex discrimination
as well as lobbying and education to end sex discrimination." As of August 1973,
the group was involved in litigation concerning (1) exclusion of women in school
athletics, citizenship, jury duty, voting, mortgages, credit, insurance, prostitution,
correctional institutions, education (admissions, life style regulations, pregnancy,
marriage, exclusion from courses), and employment (private, civil service, protective labor legislation, benefits, advertisements); (2) marriage and divorce (residence,
alimony, parental rights); (3) married women's names; (4) mandatory maternity
leave; (5) discharge for pregnancy; (6) discrimination against men in marriage laws,
employment, appearance (hair length), and parental leaves of absence; and (7)
discrimination in the military (admission requirements, benefits), private clubs,
property rights, public accommodations, abortion, contraception, sterilization,
social security, and welfare rights.

The Women's Rights Project issues memoranda on specific topics, such as
"Right of Married Women to Retain or Regain Their Birth Names," "Limitation on
Participation of Young Women in Junior Reserve Officers' Training Corps," and
"Domicile of Married Women"; and publishes *Women's Rights Project Legal
Docket: Affiliate and National Litigation Complete and in Progress* to be updated
periodically. Briefs on important sex discrimination cases are available. All publi-
cations are available for a small contribution, if possible. Also available from the
ACLU is "The Geography of Inequality," reprinted from *McCalls* magazine, an
analysis of the legal rights of women in 50 states (1971, 7pp., 20¢).

ASSOCIATION FOR THE DEVELOPMENT OF OPPORTUNITY, INC.
See **216.**

378 BELLAMY, BLANK, GOODMAN, KELLY, ROSS AND STANLEY. 36
W. 44 St., New York, N.Y. 10036. (212) 869-0020. Founded March 1,
1973.

A feminist law firm engaging in general practice of law, emphasizing the
everyday legal needs of women. Test cases of feminist litigation, particularly in
the areas of divorce and credit, are planned.

145

379   CENTER FOR A WOMAN'S OWN NAME. 261 Kimberly, Barrington, Ill. 60010. (312) 381-2113. Founded February 1973. Terri Tepper.

Compiles information for women wishing to retain their own names; can suggest local contacts, appropriate legal actions, and inexpensive attorneys. Publishes *Fact Sheet for Women Who Wish to Retain Their Own Name after Marriage* (50¢).

CHICAGO WOMEN'S LIBERATION UNION LEGAL CLINIC. See 184.

380   HUMAN RIGHTS FOR WOMEN. 1128 National Press Bldg., Washington, D.C. 20004. (202) 737-1059. Founded December 1969.

A legal and educational group designed "to advise women of their rights under the law and to assist them in gaining those rights." Advice is given by phone and letter. Literture includes a *Job Discrimination Handbook* ($1) and a newsletter (q., donation).

381   LEFCOURT KRAFT & LIBOW. 640 Broadway, New York, N.Y. 10012. (212) 677-1552. Founded February 1, 1973. Carol Lefcourt, Veronika Kraft, Carol Libow.

A general law firm, with specific interest on sex discrimination in employment and other women's issues: matrimonial law, criminal law, civil law, etc.

382   MEIKLEJOHN CIVIL LIBERTIES INSTITUTE. 1715 Francisco St., Berkeley, Calif. 94703. (415) 848-0599. Founded 1965. Ann Fagan Ginger, Esq., Pres.

A civil rights and civil liberties resource for attorneys, law students, authors, activist groups, etc. Maintains files of recent cases raising the central legal demand of the people—freedom, fair treatment, and equality. Produces many civil liberties publications; following is a list of some of interest to women.

Attorney Doris Brin Walker Discusses Angela Davis Case $1.25
Extending Women's Protective Laws to Men (friend of the court brief) $1.25
Human Rights Casefinder: Warren Court Era 1953–1969 (8,200 cases placed in 290 categories for easy reference, from Abortion to Witnesses) $25
Human Rights Organizations and Periodicals Directory $4
Women's Conference, California AFL–CIO 1973 $2.50
Women's Rights Litigation (acquisitions list) $2

383   NOW LEGAL DEFENSE AND EDUCATION FUND. 641 Lexington Ave., New York, N.Y. 10022. (212) 688-1751. Founded 1970. Nora C. Volk, Admin.
See also National Organization for Women, 163.

The tax-deductible arm of the National Organization for Women, established for the purpose of obtaining tax-deductible funds for important legal and educational projects pertaining to women. Fund monies have been allocated to public service advertising for and about women; financial support is provided to those cases in litigation that affect the majority of women; LDEF prepares "friend of the court" briefs for relevant cases. Plans include: counseling and referral centers, manual and education workshops "to familiarize women with available remedies against discriminatory practices in employment . . . to provide women with information on policy-level positions in industry, government, law, religion, education, etc., to refer women to community agencies for education and training . . . and to educate women for executing leadership roles; studies of Sex-Role Stereotypes in school textbooks and in all of the mass communications media; workshops for employers advising employers on affirmative action programs for women and providing information to alleviate sex discrimination on the part of employers; guidance materials on child care—information film and guidebook on existing child care facilities, analysis of potential functions of child care vis-à-vis the child, family, community, government and society; publication of a study of legal rights of women in specific states."

PRO SE: THE NATIONAL LAW WOMEN'S NEWSLETTER. See 74.

WASHINGTON AREA WOMEN'S CENTER. See 182.

384 WOMEN IN TRANSITION, INC. 4634 Chester Ave., Philadelphia, Pa. 19143. (215) 724-9511. Donna Lenhoff, 2408 Waverly St., Philadelphia, Pa. 19146. Hours: 10 a.m-4 p.m., Mon.-Thurs.

"A nonprofit tax-exempt corporation providing services to community women in the areas of separation and divorce." Group discussions are held for women separating or divorcing, and therapy referrals are offered. "The legal group of WIT provides legal information to help women obtain divorces, negotiate separation agreements, navigate through welfare agencies and Family Court and deal with lawyers." The organization has published *Women's Survival Manual: A Feminist Handbook on Separation and Divorce* ($3 from KNOW, Inc.; see 13). Also available are leaflets *What to Look for in a Lawyer* (5¢ from WIT), and a therapy packet.

WOMEN'S ACTION COALITION (Media, Pa.). See 219.

385 WOMEN'S AFFIRMATIVE ACTION COALITION. 101 Earl Hall, Columbia Univ., New York, N.Y. 10027. (212) 280-2174. Founded November 1971. Barbara A. Buoncristiana. 400 members.

University group monitoring policies and informing women of their legal rights. Acts as a referral service to appropriate federal, state, and city agencies in sex discrimination complaints. The coalition has published *Women's Affirmative Action Plan.*

WOMEN'S CENTRE, YWCA (Montreal, Que.) See 243.

386 WOMEN'S EQUITY ACTION LEAGUE (WEAL). 538 National Press Bldg., Washington, D.C. 20004. (202) 638-4560. Founded 1968. Arvonne Fraser, Pres. Dues: $15.

"Dedicated to improving the status of all American women through education, legislation and litigation, primarily. WEAL seeks to promote the economic progress of women, to press for full enforcement of existing antidiscrimination laws, to pass new legistlation improving women's status, to correct de facto discrimination against women and to urge that girls be prepared realistically for life." WEAL is currently working on sex discrimination in life insurance, sexism in elementary school systems, and is filing complaints against various institutions of higher learning with HEW. Local chapters work on local issues; contact headquarters for addresses.

Following is a list of available materials.

Credit Kit ($1.25, members $1)
Divorce Reform-Marriage and Family Laws Kit ($.90, members $.75)

Equal Pay Kit ($.30, members $.25)
ERA Kit ($1.25, members $1)
Higher Education Kit ($2.40, members $2)
How to Prepare a Resume ($.30, members $.25)
K-12 Education Kit: various publications concerning sexism in public schools
   ($2.40, members $2)
Percentage of Doctorates: proportion of doctorates earned by women, by
   area and field, 1960–1969 ($.30, members $.25)
Sports Kit ($2.00, members $1.50)

Buttons and pins are also available, and WEAL publishes a national newsletter and *WEAL Washington Report* (free with membership).

WOMEN'S INFORMATION CENTRE (Toronto, Can.). See **240.**

387   WOMEN'S LAW CENTER. 1414 6 Ave., New York, N.Y. (212) 838-8118.
Founded July 1972. Emily Jane Goodman.

This "registered charitable organization" is primarily a woman's informational center, serving six major functions: a library to make available to women statutes, cases, treatises, briefs, and forms used in past cases, as well as basic skills in legal research; legal consciousness-raising workshops to make women aware of their rights and obligations under the law and the legal procedures they must use; publication of pamphlets on popular categories of legal questions, i.e., keeping one's own name after marriage; training of individuals to represent themselves when possible in various legal actions; serving as a clearinghouse for women lawyers engaged in women's rights work; and a referral service for women with specific problems falling into the jurisdiction of other agencies. Women's Law Center is staffed by volunteers and supported by contributions. It publishes a *Fact Sheet on Women's Names* (50¢ and a stamped self-addressed envelope); *Women's Guide to Divorce in New York* ($3); *Monster*, feminist poems by Robin Morgan ($3); and *The Tenant Survival Book* by Emily Jane Goodman ($5).

388   WOMEN'S LEGAL CENTER. 558 Capp St., San Francisco, Calif. 94110.
(415) 285-5066. Founded June 1972. 15 members.

"A place where women with legal problems can be helped and supported by other women." Projects include a Divorce Clinic to teach women how to do their own divorces; a welfare project to provide education and publicity on women's issues in welfare; a Referral Program where women are referred to private attorneys; a Women and Law column in *The Conspiracy*, the National Lawyers Guild publication; and booklets on married women's rights to keep their own names, community property laws, and legal implications of marriage and divorce.

WOMEN'S LIBERATION UNION OF RHODE ISLAND. See **222.**

WOMEN'S RIGHTS LAW REPORTER. See **91.**

WOODMERE WOMEN'S CENTER. See **211.**

Education

General

AMERICAN ASSOCIATION OF UNIVERSITY WOMEN EDUCATIONAL FOUNDATION. See 158.

ANTIOCH WOMEN'S CENTER. See 212.

ASSOCIATION FOR THE DEVELOPMENT OF OPPORTUNITY, INC. See 216.

389 ASSOCIATION OF AMERICAN COLLEGES, PROJECT ON THE STATUS AND EDUCATION OF WOMEN. 1818 R St., N.W., Washington, D.C. 20009. (202) 387-3760. Founded Sept. 11, 1971. Dr. Bernice Sandler.

Founded to act as a clearinghouse on women in higher education, to help higher educational institutions meet responsibilities to women. Puts out many papers on various aspects of the problem including *Federal Laws and Regulations Concerning Sex Discrimination in Educational Institutions*, a list of bibliographies on women in education, summaries of governmental guidelines and policies, and a newsletter, *On Campus with Women.*

CANADIAN FEDERATION OF UNIVERSITY WOMEN. See 228.

CENTER FOR WOMEN'S STUDIES AND SERVICES. See 172.

390 DANFORTH GRADUATE FELLOWSHIPS FOR WOMEN. 222 S. Central Ave., St. Louis, Mo. 63105. (314) 862-6200. Founded 1964.

"Designed to assist able women whose academic careers have been interrupted to undertake master's or doctoral programs in preparation for teaching in secondary schools or colleges. In general terms, it is intended for women who, because of delay or postponement in graduate work, no longer qualify for conventional fellow-ship programs or whose candidacy in such programs might be given low priority. The Danforth Foundation established the Fellowships . . . with the hope of dem-onstrating that there is a reservoir of latent talent among the many college trained women in the United States who are not fully prepared to assume teaching respon-sibilities. The career of a typical candidate may have been interrupted by such factors as the raising of her family, personal illness, or the need for a paying job."

Appointment is for one year, beginning in September, and renewable annually. Stipend is a maximum of $3,000 plus tuition and fees, or $4,000 plus tuition and fees for heads of families. Applications must be in by January of the school year before the appointment is to begin, and the applicant must be neither a full-time teacher nor a full-time graduate student during that year. Applicants must have a bachelor's degree from a college or university in the United States. Write for a complete brochure.

DISTRICT OF COLUMBIA COMMISSION ON THE STATUS OF WOMEN. See 266.

EVERYWOMAN'S CENTER (Amherst, Mass.). See 189.

391   FEMINIST FORUMS. 102 E. 22 St. New York, N.Y. 10010. (212) 473-6651. Founded January 1972. Jo Hazelton, Dir.

Offers easily available formal and informal discussions with women of unusual experience and expertise in fields of concern to all people. All women and men are welcome to attend the Monday evening and Saturday morning forums. The forums are intended to help women identify and organize around their own issues. Forums offered in the spring of 1973 included Home Mechanics, Medical Care, The Woman Writer and Poet, and Women and the Law. All forums are led by women. Write for brochure, which lists fees for the various discussions.

392   MIDWEST ACADEMY. 600 W. Fullerton, Chicago, Ill. 60614. (312) 935-4100. Founded February 1973. Heather Booth, Dir.

"Formed to train activists in the skills and strategies that make an effective organization. It produces experienced and self-confident leaders and staff; people skilled in social action and organization. . . . The Midwest Academy addresses the central issue for women: they have been powerless. Women are a majority, and through conscious organization can win the rights that should be theirs. . . ." The academy includes courses, fieldwork, workshops, and consultation. Courses are available in strategy planning, building lasting organizations, and issues. Subjects of interest to particular groups will also be offered, i.e., women's history, child care, and health. There are two-week training sessions in Chicago, three-month programs following the two-week sessions, and a year-long program. A book of materials for other trainers and educational facilities is available for $100. A subscription rate is available for libraries and departments to the papers of the Academy (developing materials on organizing). Write for complete brochure and information.

NATIONAL ASSOCIATION FOR WOMEN DEANS, ADMINISTRATORS AND COUNSELORS. See 546.

NATIONAL ASSOCIATION OF COLLEGE WOMEN. See 161.

PENNSYLVANIANS FOR WOMEN'S RIGHTS. See 218.

WOMEN IN COMMUNICATIONS, INC. See 559.

393   WOMEN IN LEADERSHIP (PROJECT WIL). 730 Witherspoon Bldg., 1323 Walnut St., Philadelphia, Pa. 19107 (215) 735-6722. Founded 1970. Gail Hinand and Mary Kenyatta, Co-Dirs.

Funded by United Presbyterian Women, "an action-oriented, locally initiated project in which women bring themselves together to focus on a particular need of their community"—legal rights, quality education, tenant rights, and health care needs. Enables women to develop leadership skills. Some current projects are: Women's Team Ministry, Yale College, New Haven, Conn.; Women's Job Rights, San Francisco Bay Area, Calif.; Women's Action Training Center, Oakland, Calif.; Women for Change, Dallas, Tex.; Pro Per Collective, Berkeley, Calif.; Uoxina De Pax, San Jose, Calif.; and Main Line Cluster Housing, Radnor, Pa.

WOMEN'S CENTER SCHOOL (Cambridge, Mass.). See 192.

WOMEN'S LIBERATION UNION (Kansas City, Mo.). See 195.

OHIO STATE UNIVERSITY. WOMEN'S SELF-GOVERNMENT ASSOCIATION. See 214.

Children's Education and Welfare

(See also Publishers Section for nonsexist children's books.)

394 ACTION COUNCIL FOR COMPREHENSIVE CHILD CARE. 5889 W. Pico Blvd., Los Angeles, Calif. 90019. (213) 388-5596. Founded January 1971. Betty Willett, 1011 Rosemont Ave., Los Angeles, Calif. 90026. Dues: $2, local; $20, local and national; $5, day-care, parent or student.

Seeks "to promote the development of a network of parent/staff controlled, publicly financed, universally available child care and development services through public education, social action, and informational services to meet this need. These services must be nonracist, nonsexist, and should serve bilingual, bicultural preschool education." The ACCCC is voluntary, nondiscriminatory, and does not contemplate pecuniary gain or profit. Projects include conferences, meetings, and public speaking. The council publishes *Action for Children*, a quarterly newsletter with articles and news items on child care, and also distributes publications of the Day Care and Child Development Council of America.

AMERICAN FEDERATION OF TEACHERS, WOMEN'S RIGHTS COMMITTEE. See 521.

395 CHANGE FOR CHILDREN, A MULTIETHNIC CENTER FOR NON-SEXIST EDUCATION. 2588 Mission St., Rm. 201., San Francisco, Calif. 94110. (415) 282-3142. Founded Spring 1973. Susan Shargel.

A parent-teacher education/action project for preschool, day care, and elementary school programs in San Francisco, working toward the creation of school programs which help children develop a sense of identity according to their interests rather than their sex. The group supports children's development of cultural identity while expanding their range of choices in life. The center conducts workshops for teachers and parents, develops nonsexist educational materials, and maintains a resource center of nonsexist books and materials. An audiotape, *And That's What Little Girls Are Made Of*, which is a half-hour program describing early sex-role socialization, is available for $10. A photo series for use in the classroom, entitled "People and Their Jobs," which pictures men and women in nonstereotyped jobs, is being prepared.

396   CHILD CARE RESOURCE CENTER. 123 Mt. Auburn St., Cambridge, Mass. 02138. (617) 547-9861. Founded September 1971. Jill Herold.

A nonprofit group, which handles referrals, and provides technical assistance and materials in the area of child care to parents and community groups. The center has extensive files of material relating to child care and a list of facilities in the Boston area.

397   CHILDREN'S LIBERATION WORKSHOP. Box 207, Ancaster, Ont., Can. Founded January 1971.

Disseminates information on sex-role stereotypes in children's media. The workshop is compiling a list of nonsexist children's books emphasizing Canadian content; speaks to groups; and has produced a videotape for the Unitarian Universalist Women's Federation on sexism in children's books.

398   COGENT ASSOCIATES, PROJECT HEAR. 62 Halsted St., East Orange, N.J. 07019. (201) 746-1664. Founded 1972. Merle Breitenfeld, 411 Park St., Upper Montclair, N.J. 07043.

"HEAR (Human Educational Awareness Resource) is a 3-year project funded under the Elementary and Secondary Education Act of 1965 (Title III) to maximize the potential of all students to make career choices which are congruent with their abilities, interests and aptitudes [and without regard to sex]. The Project will develop curriculum and resource materials to inform both young men and women about the many career choices open to them, and to train elementary and high school teachers and counselors in the use of them.

"Cogent Associates . . . received the subcontract to manage the grant. HEAR has published its first two curriculum kits, one for fourth graders and one for tenth graders; and a legal rights brochure for high school girls, *A Guide to Women, the Law and Employment.*" The materials have already been in use in 14 tenth grades and 18 fourth grades in six Burlington County, New Jersey, school systems. Curriculum kits include filmstrips of working people in nonsex-typed jobs, a record, questionnaires to discover the attitudes of the student, and two stories: "The Reunion" for tenth graders, and "Dreams Sometimes Have to Wait" for fourth graders.

399   DAY CARE AND CHILD DEVELOPMENT COUNCIL OF AMERICA, INC. 1401 K St., N.W., Suite 1100, Washington, D.C. 20005. (202) 638-2316. Founded 1968   Mamie Moore, Assoc. Dir., Minority and Women's Affairs. 5000 members. Dues: $20; students, $5; agencies, $50.

"A national nonprofit, voluntary membership organization dedicated to the establishment of a system of child care for all families who need and want it, locally controlled, publicly supported, universally available." The group is engaged in public education, social action and assistance to local communities, conferences, and workshops. The council has an extensive list of publications and audiovisual aids covering such topics as organizing and programming for day care services, center facilities and equipment, child care legislation, annotated bibliographies for special interest groups, and bilingual materials. An order booklet is available upon request. The council publishes *Voice for Children*, a monthly newsletter.

Following is a list of other useful publications.

Day Care as a Child-Rearing Environment $1.75
Day Care: Resources for Decisions $4

A Family Day Care Study $2
Liberating Young Children from Sex Roles $.50
Parent Programs $1.75
Parents and Teachers Together $2.50
The Woman Question in Child Care $2
Working Mothers and the Day Nursery $4.50

400 EDUCATIONAL DAY CARE SERVICES ASSOCIATION. 11 Day St., Cambridge, Mass. 02140. Founded April 1973. George Saia, Pres.

A private group which distributes educational material concerning day care. The association presently has eight pamphlets available, all written by those engaged in actual day care operations.

Daily Programming for Infants in Day Care $1.95
Daily Programming for Three to Five-Year-Olds in Day Care $1.95
Daily Programming for Two-Year-Olds in Day Care $1.95
Day Care Administration $1.95
Day Care Supervision $1.95
Designing and Developing Environments for Day Care $2.50
Historical Perspectives on Child Care $2.50
Programming for School-Age Children in Day Care $1.95

Make checks or money orders payable to EDSCA. Any orders for more than 25 copies of an individual publication will receive a discount of 25¢ per copy. A set sells for $14.95.

401 EMMA WILLARD TASK FORCE ON EDUCATION. Box 14229, University Sta., Minneapolis, Minn. 55414. (612) 333-9076. Gerri Perreault.

An independent group of Minneapolis women with an interest in education. The group is involved in workshops, in-service training courses, and production of materials on sexism in education; it has published *Sexism in Education* ($3.50; institutions, $5). "The Task Force co-sponsored with the Minnesota Resource Center for Social Work Education a four-part series on Channel 2 (an educational TV station) on sexism in education. These tapes are available for use."

402 FEMINIST RESOURCES FOR EQUAL EDUCATION. Box 185, Saxonville Sta., Framingham, Mass. 01701. (617) 877-0601. Founded Spring 1972. Joan Chasan. 56 Agnes Dr., Framingham, Mass. 01701.

Offers educational materials for use in preschool through college, designed to break down the myth that certain jobs are only suited to one sex. Two sets of eight black and white photographs (8½ × 11) are available: "Community Helpers," photographs of women who work as police officers, pediatricians, milk carriers, mail carriers, bus drivers, etc.; and "Professional Women," women who are surgeons, judges, artists, architects, etc. ($2.50/set).

403 FORT WORTH EDUCATIONAL TASK FORCE. 2617 Hartwood Dr., Fort Worth, Tex. 76109. (817) 921-4980. Founded January 1973. Berry Bock.

The task force has produced a slide show, entitled *This Book is Rated S** *Sexist, "which is a discussion of sex-role stereotyping in children's literature, beginning with preschool picture books and continuing with novels for teenagers. The show reveals the subtle discrimination and limited role expectations for girls in much of childrens' fiction, and encourages the development of full human potential in both women and men." The show is available for a rental fee of $15. A kit includes 105 slides, carousel, cassette, and a copy of the script keyed to the slides. The running time is 18 minutes. In areas close to Fort Worth, the task force can provide a speaker or panel for group discussions following the show. Include alternate dates when writing for bookings.

404 THE NATIONAL DAY CARE ASSOCIATION. Box 62, Porter Square, Cambridge, Mass. 02140. Dues: $12, students; $15, individuals; $30, organizations.

Aims to provide basic, practical information relating to day care education. "Membership . . . will entitle you to receive a monthly *Day Care Newsletter* with articles by professionals in the field of day care on topics such as designing and developing centers, administration, supervision, curriculum for infants, curriculum for two-year-olds, curriculum for three- to five-year-olds, historical aspects of day care; provide an information resource center which enables you to address any questions on day care to our organization for reply from the research library: receive information on recent and upcoming day care publications."

405 NEW JERSEY WOMEN'S RIGHTS TASK FORCE ON EDUCATION. 549 Lenox Ave., Westfield, N.J. 07090. (201) 232-0870. Jean L. Ambrose. Founded June 1972. 50 members.

"A loose association of representatives from various women's groups and educational groups to combat sexism in education," particularly elementary and secondary schools. In 1973, a drive was concentrated on eliminating sex-segregated classes in shop and home economics. The task force publishes a bibliography of 67 books in American history for junior high schools presenting women positively (25¢); a *Women's Directory*, over 150 New Jersey women in nontraditional occupations who agreed to be resource persons for schools and colleges (50¢); and *Women, Career Education, and the World of Work* (10¢).

406 U.S. DEPT. OF HEALTH, EDUCATION AND WELFARE, OFFICE OF CHILD DEVELOPMENT. 400 6 St., S.W., Washington, D.C. 20013. Mailing address: Box 1182, Washington, D.C. 20013. (202) 755-7524. Pauline Taft.

The Office of Child Development has four major missions: (1) to operate such programs for children as Head Start and Parent and Child Centers; (2) to develop innovative programs for children and parents; (3) to serve as a point of coordination for all federal programs for children, youth, and their families; and (4) to act as an advocate for children by bringing their needs to the attention of government and the public. OCD is divided into two major bureaus: The Children's Bureau, which provides a wide range of technical assistance services for children, youth, and their families; and the Bureau of Child Development Services, which operates Head Start and other innovative programs for children and is responsible for welfare reform day care planning. The office publishes *Children*, The Children's Bureau bimonthly journal ($2/yr. Supt. of Docs., U.S. G.P.O., Washington, D.C. 20402). There is also an extensive publications list dealing with many aspects of child-rearing; write for a free copy.

VALLEY WOMEN'S CENTER (Northhampton, Mass.). See 191.

VANCOUVER STATUS OF WOMEN. See 232

407 WOMEN ON WORDS AND IMAGES. Box 2163, Princeton, N.J. 08540. Founded April 1972. 6 members.

A feminist consulting firm to eliminate sex-role stereotyping in instructional materials. The company published *Dick and Jane as Victims: Sex Stereotyping in Children's Readers*, ($1.50). The book is a study of 134 children's books from 14 major publishers. "This study has been recognized and supported by the Great Cities Organization, National Education Association, New Jersey Education Association, New York State Teachers Association, Association for Supervision and Curriculum Development, American Civil Liberties Union, Women's Bureau of the Department of Labor, reading specialists, psychologists, and school systems." A slide show based on *Dick and Jane as Victims . . .* is available for rental.

WOMEN'S ACTION COALITION (Media, Pa.) See 219.

Continuing Education

This section represents a mere sampling of groups that sponsor continuing education. Most colleges and universities operate adult education programs, and many offer fine counseling services to women (and men) who wish to continue their education. For further information, contact colleges and universities in your area, and check the local women's group listings, 158–246.

408 BROWN UNIVERSITY, HIGHER EDUCATION RESOURCE SERVICES (HERS). Providence, R.I. 02912. (401) 863-2197. Dr. Lilli S. Hornig, Exec. Dir.

"The Higher Education Resource Services (HERS), has been funded by the Ford Foundation and established at Brown University for the purpose of improving the status of women in institutions of higher education. . . . HERS simultaneously helps individual women and institutions by acting as a nation-wide clearinghouse for faculty and administrative openings. Working with women's caucuses and committees in many disciplines, HERS makes every effort to match candidate and opening, recommending highly qualified individuals who might otherwise not have come to the attention of a search committee or department chairperson. In this manner, HERS will help institutions to meet affirmative action goals, while helping women locate positions not available to them so long as traditional employment practices are followed. HERS invites individuals as well as institutional officers to send notices of positions. Candidates may register by sending a *vita* and a statement of their needs and preferences. As HERS is also frequently asked to recommend candidates for high-level advisory posts, trusteeships, etc., professional women interested in such appointments should notify HERS of their availability."

409 DISADVANTAGED WOMEN FOR A HIGHER EDUCATION, INC. 1 Incinerator Rd., Durham, N.H. 03824. (603) 862-2350. Founded April 1970. Mary E. Russell, Coor. 37 members.

A group affiliated with the University of New Hampshire to help disadvantaged women (low-income, single women with children, women with large families, and women out of school for a long time) obtain a college education. The group established a program at UNH where disadvantaged women can be accepted at the university, which helps provide financial aid, tutors, housing, and child care.

Twenty-two women are currently enrolled in the program. DWHE also provides information concerning other sources of aid, and provides legal, medical, social, and welfare referrals.

410   GEORGE WASHINGTON UNIVERSITY, CONTINUING EDUCATION FOR WOMEN CENTER. Washington, D.C. 20006. (202) 676-7036. Founded 1964. Dr. Ruth H. Osborn.

Designed to assist women to realize their personal, educational, and career goals. One of the earliest of the women's programs, it remains flexible and innovative by adapting to the needs of women in a changing society. More than 4,000 women participated in this program over a nine-year period. Courses are also open to men.

Noncredit counseling courses are a speciality. Developing New Horizons for Women is designed to help women assess and use their special abilities and acquaint them with educational, occupational, and community service opportunities. Initiated at George Washington in 1964, it has served as a model for programs in other colleges and universities. More than 3000 women, from 18 to 71, have participated in this course. Cost is $125.

Career Development for Employed Women emphasizes exploring opportunities for upward mobility in current occupations, possible new careers in related fields, and the risks and rewards of changing to an entirely different career. Each student will assess her own abilities and interests, and receive information on educational opportunities and career outlook. Tuition is $125.

Other courses include: Career Counseling for Girls (last two years of high school and first two years of college); Career Counseling for Women; Exploring Self-Awareness; Counseling and Testing; and Lifestyles: New Options for Men and Women (developed for the purpose of analyzing shifting responsibilities and changing roles of both men and women). A variety of credit courses are also available.

An audiotape of *Symposium I: Women Today and Tomorrow* (speakers: Felice Schwartz, Catharine Stimpson, Jessie Bernard, and Fan McCallum) is available for purchase.

411   RADCLIFFE INSTITUTE. 3 James St., Cambridge, Mass. 02138. (617) 495-8211. Founded 1960. Alice K. Smith, Dean.

Through fellowships, through guidance and research, and through the adult education courses offered by the Radcliffe Seminars, the institute seeks to expand the choices open to women in scholarship, the creative arts, and the professions. This institute, which was established in 1960, is an integral part of Radcliffe College and thus of Harvard University; however, it is separately financed through foundation, individual, and government grants. It is not a graduate school, but rather a community of scholars, artists, and professional women. Many of these women work at the institute while others are in greater Boston or are enrolled in part-time graduate study at colleges and universities in southern New England. Currently, the institute sponsors three fellowship programs, which provide affiliation and financial assistance to approximately 80 women each year: fellowships for research and the creative arts, fellowships in medicine, and fellowships for part-time graduate study. The institute conducts research to add to knowledge about the role of educated women in American society and to work out new and better ways of utilizing their abilities and talents.

412 UNIVERSITY OF CALIFORNIA, BERKELEY, CENTER FOR THE CONTINUING EDUCATION OF WOMEN. Women's Center, Rm. 100, Bldg. T9, University of California, Berkeley, Calif. 94720. (415) 642-4786. Beatrice Bain, Assoc. Dir.

Open to campus and community women. Services offered include: "academic advising and counselling for women students and those women who plan to begin or resume their education; career advising—new ways to use learned skills and opportunities in non-traditional job areas; discussion groups and lectures concerned with topics of special interest to women; coordination of information on educational opportunities in the Bay Area; coordination of research material." Counselors are available five days each week from 9:00 a.m. to 5:00 p.m. All services are free; call to make an appointment. The center also maintains a referral service for health care, child care, etc.

413 UNIVERSITY OF MICHIGAN, CENTER FOR CONTINUING EDUCATION OF WOMEN. 330 Thompson St., Ann Arbor, Mich. 48108. (313) 764-6555 or 0449. Patricia Wulp, Asst. Dir. Hours: 8:30 a.m.–5 p.m., Mon.-Fri. No fee.

Helps to resolve some of the practical problems for undergraduate and graduate women who are reentering school or who anticipate interruptions. "The Center provides: individual counselling toward developing educational and vocational plans; information about University procedures and policies . . .; help in locating resources in all schools and departments at the University and information about other educational resources; a clearing house for information about courses, women's caucuses and specialized services for women at the University; information about child care; annual merit scholarships for women students whose education has been interrupted; small emergency grants for women students; a library of . . . information about vocational choices, employment opportunities, history and status of women; . . . , conferences, lectures, and informal discussions."

Publications available include:

Women on Campus, proceedings of a 1970 CEW Symposium, including "Toward a New Psychology of Women," "The Case of the Woman Graduate Student," and "The University and Women—What Directions?," (1971, 65 pp., $1.50); and *A Dangerous Experiment: 100 Years of Women at the University of Michigan* (1970, 136 pp., $2.50).

UNIVERSITY OF CALIFORNIA EXTENSION, IRVINE, WOMEN'S OPPORTUNITIES CENTER. See 438.

Women's Studies

The best source of information on women's studies is the Clearinghouse on Women's Studies, Feminist Press (see entry 7). Reprinted here, with permission, is their list of colleges and universities which offer programs in women's studies, either minors, B.A.'s, or M.A.'s (as of November 1973). Following this list are several descriptions of individual women's studies programs. Most schools now offer at least a course or two in women's studies, if not an entire program, and it is suggested that you contact local institutions to see what their offerings are. See also the section Women's Organizations and Centers, entries 158-246.

414   WOMEN'S STUDIES PROGRAMS. The programs are interdisciplinary: i.e.,
they combine courses in literature, language, or culture, with work in sociology, anthropology, economics, political science, history, philosophy, psychology, biology, and related fields. Some programs offer minors, others
award the B.A., still others the M.A. Programs listed without a specific label
offer a roster of elective course. Where no chairperson is listed, either the
program is still in the process of organization or it has chosen to function
through a committee, rather than a single individual.

Alabama, Univ. of, Tuscaloosa 35486. Women's Studies, College of Arts and
Sciences.
Alverno College, 3401 S. 39 St., Milwaukee, Wisc. 53215. Research Center on
Women, Mary Austin Doherty, Co-dir.
Amherst College. See Five Colleges.
Antioch College, Yellow Springs, Ohio 45387. Women's Studies.
Arizona, Univ. of, Tucson 85721. Women's Studies.
Barnard College, New York 10027. The Women's Center, Jane Gould, Dir.
Brooklyn College, CUNY, Brooklyn, N.Y. 11210. Women's Studies, Evelyn Raskin,
(psychology), Pamella Farley (English), Coor.
Cabrillo College, Aptos, Calif. 95003. Women's Studies, Joyce Ungar, Coor.
California State College, Bakersfield 93303. Women's Studies, Jane Lester Watts,
Coor.
California State College, Hayward, 25800 Hillary Rd., Hayward 94542. Women's
Studies.
California State College, San Bernardino 92407. Women's Studies, Gloria Cowan,
Coor.
California State Univ., Chico 95926. Women's Studies, Gayle Kimball, Coor.;
Program offers a minor.
California State Univ., Fresno 93726. Women's Studies, Phyllis Irwin, Coor.;
Program offers a minor.
California State Univ., Humboldt, Arcata 95521. Women's Studies, Katherine
Marshall, Coor.
California State Univ., Long Beach 90801. Women's Studies, Deborah Rosenfelt
(English), Coor.
California State Univ., Sacramento 95819. Women's Studies Committee. Program
offers a minor.
California State Univ., San Diego, 5402 College Ave., San Diego 92115. Women's
Studies.
California State Univ., San Francisco 94132. Women's Studies Committee, Beatrice
Bain, Coor.; program offers a major with a focus on women leading to the B.A.
degree.
California State Univ., San Jose 95114. Women's Studies Committee, Fauneil J.
Rinn (political science), Chairperson. Program offers a minor.
California State Univ., Sonoma, Rohnert Park 94982. Women's Studies, J. J.
Wilson (English), Coor.
California State Univ. of Berkeley, 201 Sproul, Berkeley 94720. Campus Women's
Forum, Betty Jones, Coor.
California, Univ. of, Irvine 92664. Women's Studies Committee.
California, Univ. of, Los Angeles 90024. Women's Resource Center, Carol Adams,
Dir.
California, Univ. of, Santa Cruz 95060. Women's Studies Committee, Madeline
Hummel (Adlai E. Stevenson College), Coor.

Cambridge-Goddard Graduate School for Social Change, 5 Upland Rd., Cambridge, Mass. 02140. Feminist Studies. Program offers the M.A. degree.

City College, CUNY, New York 10031. Women's Studies, Barbara Watson (English), Coor.

Cornell Univ., Ithaca, N.Y. 14850. Women's Studies, Jennie Farlie, Dir.

Delaware, Univ. of, Newark 19711. Women's Studies Committee, Mae R. Carter (continuing education), Chairperson.

Daiblo Valley College, Pleasant Hill, Calif. 94523. Women's Studies, Marilyn Braiger, Coor.

Douglass College, New Brunswick, N.J. 08903. Women's Studies, Elaine Showalter (English). Program offers the B.A. degree.

Five Colleges (Amherst College; Hampshire College; Massachusetts, Univ. of, Amherst; Mount Holyoke College; Smith College). Women's Studies Committee, Susan Bourque (government), Smith College, Northampton, Mass. 01060; Gayle Hollander (social sciences), Hampshire College, Amherst, Mass. 01002, Co-coor.

George Washington Univ., Washington, D.C. 20006. Women's Studies Committee, Graduate School of Arts and Sciences, Ruth Osborn, Coor.; Program offers the M.A. degree.

Goddard College, Plainfield, Vt. 05667. Feminist Studies, Sally Binford, Marilyn Webb, Co-coor.; Program offers the B.A. degree. A Master's of Arts in Women's Studies may be pursued as part of Goddard's nonresident Graduate Program.

Governors State Univ., Park Forest South, Ill. 60466. Women's Studies, Sandra Whitaker, Coor.

Hampshire College, Amherst, Mass. 01002. Feminist Studies, Debbie Curtis, Coor. See also Five Colleges.

Hawaii, Univ. of, Honolulu 96822. Women's Studies, Donna Haraway (general science); Program offers the B.A. degree.

Hobart & William Smith Colleges, Geneva, N.Y. 14456. Women's Studies, Janet M. Wedel, Coor.; Program offers "individual major" in Women's Studies.

Hunter College, CUNY, New York 10021. Committee on Women's Studies, Sarah B. Pomeroy (classics), Coor.

Indiana Univ., Memorial Hall 219X, Bloomington 47401. Women's Studies, Ellen Dwyer, Dir.

Kansas, Univ. of, Lawrence 66044. Women's Studies, Janet Sharistanian (English), Coor.; Program offers a "special major" leading to the B.A. or B.G.S. degree.

Laney College, Oakland, Calif. 94606. Women's Studies Committee, Laura B. Stenson, Coor.

Los Angeles Harbor College, 1111 Figueroa Pl., Wilmington, Calif. 90744. Women's Studies, Claudia Fonda-Bonardi, Coor.; Program offers the A.A. degree.

Massachusetts, Univ. of, Amherst, 01002. Women's Studies Committee, Judy Shortsleeves (psychology), Coor.; program offers the B.A. degree. See also Five Colleges.

Massachusetts, Univ. of, Boston 02116. Women's Studies, Mary Anne Ferguson (English), Coor.

Minnesota, Univ. of, 114 Johnston Hall, Minneapolis 55455. Women's Studies, Toni H. McNaron, Coor.

Mount Holyoke College. See Five Colleges.

Mundelein College, Chicago, Ill. 60626. Women's Studies, Ann B. Matasar, Coor.

Nevada, Univ. of, Reno 89507. Women's Studies Committee, Ann Howard, Chairperson.

New Mexico, Univ. of, Albuquerque 87131. Women's Studies Collective, Gail Baker, Coor.

New Rochelle, College of, New Rochelle, N.Y. 10801. Women's Studies, Katherine Henderson, Dir.

New York, State Univ. of, Albany, 1400 Washington Ave., Albany 12222. Women's Studies, June Hahner (history), Dir.; program offers a minor.

New York, State Univ. of, Buffalo, 108 Winspear Ave., Buffalo 14214. College of Women's Studies, Liz Kennedy, Coor.

New York, State Univ. College, Old Westbury 11568. Women's Studies, Florence Howe, Coor.; program offers the B.A. degree.

Northeastern Illinois Univ., Chicago 60625. Women's Studies Committee, Donna. Iven, Chairperson.

Oregon State Univ., Corvallis 97331. Women's Studies, Jeanne Dost, Dir.

Oregon, Univ. of, Eugene 97403. Women's Studies, Joan Acker (sociology), Coor.

Pennsylvania, Univ. of, Philadelphia 19104. Women's Studies, Ann Beuf, Coor.

Pittsburgh, Univ. of, Pittsburgh, Pa. 15213. Women's Studies, Mary Louise Briscoe (English), Coor.

Portland State Univ., Portland, Ore. 97207. Women's Studies, Nancy Porter (English), Coor.

Puget Sound, Univ. of, Tacoma, Wash. 98416. Women's Studies, Chris Smith, Coor.

Queens College, CUNY, Flushing, N.Y. 11367. Women's Studies Committee, Wendy Martin (English), Coor.

Ramapo College, Mahwah, N.J. 07430. Women's Studies (School of Human Environment), Lynne Farrow, Coor.

Richmond College, CUNY, Staten Island, N.Y. 10301. Women's Studies, Bertha Harris, Coor.; program offers the B.A. degree.

Roger Williams College and University Without Walls, 24 DeBaun Ave., Suffern, N.Y. 10901. Women's Studies, Lynne Farrow, Coor.; program offers a dual B.A. from Roger Williams College (Rhode Island) and University Without Walls (Ohio).

Rutgers Univ., Newark College of Arts and Sciences, Newark, N.J. 07102. Women's Studies, Maries Collins (French), Beth Niemi (economics), Janet Siskind (anthropology), Coor.; program offers a minor.

Sangamon State Univ., Springfield, Ill. 62703. Women's Studies, Elizabeth Saries, Coor.

Sarah Lawrence College, Bronxville, N.Y. 10708. Women's History Program, Gerda Lerner, Co-dir.; program offers the M.A. degree in Women's History.

Smith College. See Five Colleges.

South Carolina, Univ. of, Columbia 29208. Women's Studies Institute, Constance Ashton Myers, Coor.; program offers a minor.

South Florida, Univ. of, Tampa 33620. Women's Studies (College of Social & Behavioral Science), Juanita H. Williams, Dir.

Southern Illinois Univ., Edwardsville 62025. Women's Studies, Sheila Ruth (philosophy), Dir.

Southern Methodist Univ., Dallas, Tex. 75275. Women's Studies, Annette Allen, Coor.

Staten Island Community College, CUNY, 715 Ocean Terrace, Staten Island 10301. Women's Studies, Terry O'Connor, Acting Coor.

Stockton State College, Pomona, N.J. 08240. Women's Studies Committee, Suzanne Levin, Coor.

Towson State College, Md. 21204. Women's Studies, Elaine R. Hedges (English), and Sara Coulter (English), Coor.

Utah, Univ. of, Salt Lake City 84112. Women's Resource Center, Shauna Adix, Dir.
Washington, Univ. of, Seattle 98105. Women's Studies, Mary Aickin, Coor.; program offers the B.A. degree.
Wayne County City College, Detroit, Mich. 48201. Women's Studies, Julie Stindt, Coor.
Weber State College, Ogden, Utah 84403. Women's Activities, Sue Stevenson, Coor.
Wesleyan Univ., Middletown, Conn. 06457. Women's Studies, Sheila Tobias, Coor.
Western Washington State College, Bellingham, Wash. 98225. Women's Studies, Meredith Cary, Coor.; Program offers a minor.
Wisconsin State Univ., Oshkosh 58901. Women's Studies Committee, Bani Mahadeva, Chairperson.
Wisconsin, Univ. of, Milwaukee 53201. Women's Studies Committee, Lila Fraser, Coor.
Wittenberg Univ., Springfield, Ohio 45501. Woman and the Human Revolution, Patricia O'Connor, Coor.

Sample women's studies programs follow.

BARNARD COLLEGE, THE WOMEN'S CENTER. See 202.

415 CALIFORNIA STATE UNIVERSITY AT LONG BEACH, WOMEN STUDIES CENTER. Special Programs, Long Beach, Calif. 90804. Founded 1972-1973. Debby Rosenfelt, Coor.

The center encourages scholarly inquiry into the nature, roles, and history of women in order to assess the validity of current cultural attitudes in this area and to extend our present knowledge, and provides the facilities necessary to enable women to face, discuss, and find solutions to the problems which impede the development of their full potential. The center seeks the entry of more women teachers, administrators, and staff into the college community, in accordance with affirmative action programs, and coordinates a program leading to a certificate, a minor, or other degree program in Women's Studies and to foster the development of courses in this area. Past course offerings have been a Senior Seminar on the Status of Women; Asian Man and Woman in America; Folklore (cross-cultural comparison of male-female concepts as expressed in folk literature); Social Psychology of Homosexuality; and Sociology of Women. Future curricula will be on Special Problems in the Education of Women; History of Women in the Western World; History of Women in the Non-Western World; and The Chicana.

416 CAMBRIDGE-GODDARD GRADUATE SCHOOL, FEMINIST STUDIES PROGRAM. (A program of Goddard College.) Upland Rd., Cambridge, Mass. 02140 (612) 492-0700. Founded June 1970.

Offers a Master's degree in Feminist Studies. Cambridge-Goddard is a one-year graduate program, offering a fully-accredited M.A. with an emphasis on programs involving social change in America. It was founded by Goddard College in collaboration with an independent research institute (the Cambridge Policy Studies Institute) and with a group of Boston area educators who supported alternative and experimental programs in graduate education. The program is a cluster of courses focusing on public, private, and political lives of women. All faculty and students are feminists. The course is a full 12 months with a tuition of $2000 (payable quarterly). Deadline for admission is June 30. Each student joins one seminar/project, which includes three to eight students who will meet about eight hours per week. Written documentation is expected. Students can choose from The American Family: History and Critique; The Lives of American Working Women (1870–1970); Socialization-Education or Let the Children in on the Revolution; Developing a Feminist Media; Women; Class and Consciousness; History of Feminism in the U. S.; and The Politics of Child Care.

The following is available from the school.

Women and Literature Bibliography. An annotated bibliography about the works of women writers and poets and relevant works of criticism. (75¢, Women and Literature, Ann Kautzman, 5 Upland Rd., Cambridge, Mass. 02140.)

Women and Psychology Bibliography. A selected annotated bibliography (40¢, Women and Psychology Bibliography, Cambridge-Goddard Graduate School, 5 Upland Rd., Cambridge, Mass. 02140.)

The Women's History Slide Show. About 600 slides with a script, portraying the lives of women at different times in history. (Rental, $10–$15 plus shipping and insurance.)

Women's Work Is Never Done. A dramatic reading on American women, four voices, about one-half hour long, useful for general audiences.

417   **CORNELL UNIVERSITY COLLEGE OF ARTS AND SCIENCES, WOMEN'S STUDIES PROGRAM.** 431 White Hall, Cornell University, Ithaca, N.Y. 14850. (607) 256-6480. Founded July 1972. Jennie Farley, Dir.

"Aims to encourage the development of teaching and research about women for women and men at Cornell and to cooperate in public service activities with the University's extension divisions." Twelve courses taught include Visual Images of the Female in the Western World, Black and White Women Since the Civil War, Psychology of Women, The Chinese Experience, and Women in Education. Special lecturers are hired especially for the program, for those courses not taught by the regular faculty. Information available includes a course list, names and addresses of 30 women's organizations in Cornell and Ithaca; list of on-going and projected research and extension projects related to Women's Studies on the campus; "Call for Course Proposals;" and "Women's Studies Library Information Sheet."

418   **GEORGE WASHINGTON UNIVERSITY, COMMITTEE ON WOMEN STUDIES.** 2130 H St., N.W., Suite 621, Washington, D.C. 20006. (202) 676-7036. Dr. Ruth H. Osborn, Coor.

Grants a Master of Arts in Special Studies with an area of concentration in Women Studies. This interdisciplinary program requires 12 semester hours in Women Studies, with 24 hours chosen from fields which are pertinent to the student's specific academic goal. The Women Studies curriculum, with or without a thesis, includes 18 semester hours in the arts and sciences (e.g., anthropology, economics, literature, philosophy, physiology, psychology, sociology, etc.) with no more than one third (12 semester hours) from any single department. Candidates must pass a written master's comprehensive examination which will be administered on a specific date each semester to those who have fulfilled all degree requirements by the end of that semester. Graduate students are expected to maintain an average of B (3.00) in all course work. There are no tool or thesis requirements.

KENT STATE WOMEN'S PROJECT, KENT STATE UNIVERSITY. See 213.

NEW PALTZ WOMEN'S ALLIANCE. See 208.

419 NORTHEASTERN ILLINOIS UNIVERSITY, WOMEN'S STUDIES INTER-
DISCIPLINARY DEGREE PROGRAM. 5500 N. St. Louis St., Chicago, Ill.
60625 (312) 583-4050, ext. 8210. Founded June 1972. Cathy Jones,
Secy.

"The Women's Studies Inter-disciplinary Degree Program combines classroom
study of the roles and socialization processes of women and men in our society
with community programs geared to respond to the day-to-day needs of women
and men. The program . . . sponsors various courses each trimester, drawing
faculty from many disciplines. Class topics include the critical analysis of the
absence of women in history and the sciences, the social psychology of women in
literature, the images of women in the arts, the legal history of the family, the role
of women in modern economic life, and the prospects for androgyny . . . The
Women's Program also operates a Women's Center . . . on the campus. . . .
Throughout the year it provides a meeting place for women's groups as well as
housing library resources for the UNI community on feminist subjects."

420 PORTLAND STATE UNIVERSITY, WOMEN'S STUDIES/UNION. P. O.
Box 751, Portland, Ore. 97202. (503) 229-4459. Peggy Norman.

"Concerned with developing an informed, scholarly intellect and an activist
consciousness about the experience of being a woman in a western society, the
culture, history, and institutions of which have been essentially defined and codi-
fied by men, often to the exclusion of interests of women. The program draws
upon a large body of neglected material in the established disciplines . . . including
feminist views of power, influence, technology, research; and encourages the open-
ended questioning of the received status of women. . . ." WS/U seeks scholarly research with emphasis on an interdisciplinary, problem-centered approach; development of new perspectives in teaching and class participation; encouragement of new
feminist writing and criticism; and coordination of activities in the Portland
community. Some courses include:

Studies in Feminist Education; Seminar in Doris Lessing; Writings of South-
ern Women; Bloomsbury Group; Psychology of Women; Social Psychology of
Homosexuality in America; Women in the American Economy; Women in
Latin America; and British Women Novelists.

421 SARAH LAWRENCE COLLEGE, WOMEN'S STUDIES PROGRAM.
Bronxville, N.Y. 10708. (914) 337-0700. Margy Heldring, Coor.

This program has three components: undergraduate courses, a Master of Arts
Program specializing in Women's History, and "a small experimental program for
women in community activities for which there are no specific academic requirements and which is not degree granting. In addition, Sarah Lawrence's Center for
Continuing Education admits students who have been out of school or college for
a period of four or more years and who wish to continue their education towards a
Bachelor of Arts degree.

"The Master of Arts Program specializing in Women's History consists of
three ten-credit components, a thesis, and a field work or teaching component. Although students' programs are individually planned, it is expected that a student
will take ten credits of graduate work in each of the following groups: Women's
History, American or European History, and a related field of study such as Literature, Anthropology, Economics, Psychology, Art History.

"A small group of women will be admitted to Sarah Lawrence for one year in an experimental program whose purpose is two-fold: to give time, space and resources for reflection and study to women who have been active in organizing or leading activities for women, and to develop a special seminar at the Center for Continuing Education where these women will work with undergraduates, graduate students and students from the Center for Continuing Education in a program combining theoretical and field work among women. There are no specific academic requirements."

Courses available in 1973–1974 are: Images of Women in American Culture; Autobiography and Biography as Literature and History; Theories of Feminism; The Family in Early America; Woman in Industrializing America; Freshman Studies in Women's History; Queens and Empresses—Women Enthroned in a Man's World; The Literature of Love in France; Women in Twentieth-Century America; Politics of Social Change; Psychology and Women; The Professional Woman's Status in America with Case Studies from Sweden, France and China; and Women Organizing Women (seminar). Publications available are bibliographies on *Women in American History*, compiled by Gerda Lerner, and *Women in European History*, compiled by Joan Kelly-Gadol ($1 each).

422   STATE UNIVERSITY OF NEW YORK AT BUFFALO, WOMEN STUDIES COLLEGE. 108 Winspear Ave., Buffalo, N.Y. 14214. (716) 831-3405. Founded May 1971. Valerie Eastman, Staff Coor.

"Each semester . . . [WSC has] offered between 20 and 30 courses with enrollments of over 500 students. Summer school programs have been offered as well during the first two years. There are five main types of courses taught in Women's Studies: introductory and outreach courses; those which develop a theoretical analysis of women's oppression; those which teach skills that are critical to women; those which analyze the institutional structures that affect our lives; and feminist approaches to traditional disciplines." Courses include: Philosophy of Human Nature; Married, Divorced or Widowed Women; Women's Automotive Course; Lesbianism; and Women in the Russian Revolution. In addition to courses, WSC is trying to develop other programs that are of value to women, such as two women's shows on WBFO-FM, the campus radio station. These are related to the Audio-Tape Workshop.

UNIVERSITY OF UTAH, WOMEN'S RESOURCE CENTER. See 226.

Employment

Consultants

(See also Civil Rights and Legal Services.)

423 ASSOCIATION OF FEMINIST CONSULTANTS. 4 Canoe Brook Dr.,
Princeton Junction, N.J. 08550. (609) 799-0378. Founded June 1972. Dr.
Jennifer MacLeod, Coor. 60 members. Dues: $25.

"Independent feminist consultants engaged in the business of providing industry, government, educational and nonprofit organizations with professional
management consulting services aimed at improving the economic and social status
of women. The purpose of the Association is to establish and maintain professional
standards, to exchange information; to promote the advantages of employing qualified experts on feminist issues when initiating or implementing programs and practices concerned with changing the role of women in society." Prospective clients
may write for a copy of the current *Directory of Members* (50¢ for postage and
handling).

424 BETSY HOGAN ASSOCIATES. 222 Rawson Rd., Brookline, Mass. 02146.
(617) 232-0066. Betsy Hogan, Pres.

Management consultants on the compliance, cultural, legal, and organizational
problems of women in employment. BHA does two things: (1) furnishes consulting
services to employers to draft and implement affirmative action plans, including
awareness seminars for managers and for female employees; and (2) publishes a
newsletter for employers, *Womanpower, A Monthly Report on Fair Employment
Practices for Women*, (m.; $37/yr.), which "provides up-to-date news on fast-
changing laws, government regulations, and developing trends as they affect the
status of women in the work-force."

425 BOYLE/KIRKMAN ASSOCIATES, INC. 230 Park Ave., New York, N.Y.
10017. (212) 689-2061. Founded September 1972. M. Barbara Boyle, Pres.

A consulting company specializing in affirmative action programs for women.
"Prepares and presents specially tailored executive summary sessions, explaining to
top management the need for—and elements of—Affirmative Action Programs for
women. Three steps—the gathering of statistics on women employees, personal
interviews with managers and women employees, and a detailed analysis of the
results—pinpoint problem areas and form the basis for the development of an action

program. Based on data gathered internally and on prior experience from external sources, B/K A assists in the development of an action plan that details overall strategy, program design and an implementation schedule. It is here that specific goals and objectives are established and programs developed to comply with all civil rights legislation. B/K A assists in developing a program to identify women with the potential to advance, to analyze their potential and set up a development plan for their future advancement. B/K A, through a series of in-house seminars, uses videotape, role playing and other advanced training techniques to stimulate participation and give managers an opportunity to bring out, discuss and understand these traditional attitudes. B/K A's development program for women is designed to help them evaluate their present and future potential. It also assists . women in investigating career opportunities, and motivates them to establish career goals and development plans."

Boyle/Kirkman's videotape, *Women: The Emerging Resource*, is available from Advanced Systems, Inc., 15 Columbus Circle, New York, N.Y. 10019. It is a complete program, with six color videotape sessions, including role playing, individual participation, group discussions and team presentations.

426   COMMUNITY LIAISON CONSULTANTS. Box 8244, Jacksonville, Fla. 32211. (904) 744-4835. Founded March 1973. Linda K. Menke.

"Provides professional consulting services to management and to individuals in their efforts to efficiently and effectively bring women into equal participation in the work world. CLC will tailor its programs to the needs of the client; however, program steps for client-selected areas generally include: survey of attitudes of executives and of workforce; report findings and recommendations; workshops and seminars; [and] aid in implementing recommendations as requested by client." Other services include: designing and conducting research related to women's issues and goals; editing and evaluating literature and media advertising to eliminate stereotypes; designing, conducting, or coordinating courses for women's groups and other civic organizations; aiding educational institutions in eliminating sexism in curriculum, extra-curricular activities, staff promotion patterns, and other affirmative action implementation; and advising on child care options for individuals and for organizations.

427   FEMINIST CONSULTATION SERVICE. 225 State Road, Princeton, N.J. 08540. (609) 921-8252. Founded May 1973. Toby Lipman, 225 State Rd., Princeton, N.J. 08540.

Consultants on motivation and management training for women in industry, etc. to encourage women to seek more power and responsibility in their jobs. Work has been in schools, prisons, companies, and within NOW. The program is basically five days, with the mornings devoted to motivation and the afternoons to hard core training.

428   JACQUELINE CEBALLOS PRODUCTIONS. 1 Lincoln Plaza, New York, N.Y. 10023. (212) 877-1894, 1895. Founded September 1973. Jacqueline Ceballos.

A public relations, promotion, and consulting firm, to promote feminists and feminism. The company is currently handling Florence Adams' book, *I Took a Hammer in My Hand*; *Year of the Woman* by Sandra Hochman, "the first major feature film conceived and created by women for mass-distribution" (a feature documentary whose cast includes Gloria Steinem, Flo Kennedy, Betty Friedan and Germaine Greer); a theater group, "Just Us"; and an advertising campaign on marriage and divorce.

429   JOHNS, NORRIS ASSOCIATES. 5720 Aylesboro Ave., Pittsburgh, Pa. 15217. (412) 422-9134. Ernest W. Norris, Jody R. Johns.

A training and personnel development firm, serving business, industrial, and educational organizations, which offers "programs, such as workshops, seminars, and conferences; consultation, on program development for in-house training, videocassette programming, affirmative action planning, and marketing and public relations; and products, including packaged multi-media programs for self- implementation . . ." In the "Developing Women" program, workshops are offered on Management Skills for Secretaries, Personal Development for Women Managers, and Life Work Planning. The firm also offers a two-day workshop in "Women in Banking and Finance" and *51%*, a color film for management about women who work.

Counseling and Training

430   ADVOCATES FOR WOMEN. 564 Market St., Rm. 218, San Francisco, Calif. 94104. (415) 989-5449. Founded February 1972. Rebecca A. Mills, Guadalupe C. Lafranchi.

An economic development center for women to open up opportunities for women in the fields of employment, business, and credit. The center holds job workshops, individual counseling sessions, and business seminars; has job listings and a skills bank; and publishes the *San Francisco Women's Business Directory* ($2.50) and *Advocates for Women Bulletin* (monthly broadside).

431   ALUMNAE ADVISORY CENTER. 541 Madison Ave., New York, N.Y. 10022. (212) 758-2153. Founded 1950. Alice Gore King, Exec. Dir. Dues: $50.

Offers assistance to college women in finding jobs, by means of counseling, seminars for job applicants, maintenance of a reference library, and many publications, such as *How Not to Write Letters of Application* (50¢), *The Job Interview* ($1), and *How to Write Your Resume* ($1). Job Fact Sheets, which contain information for job hunters, career counselors, and students on what and where the jobs are, education needed, etc., are issued every few months at 50¢ each and can be ordered individually or by subscription. Job Fact Sheets cover architecture, astronomy, banking, commercial art, insurance, law, market research, museum work, oceanography, personnel, recreation, and urban planning, to mention only a few.

ASSOCIATION FOR THE DEVELOPMENT OF OPPORTUNITY, INC. See **216.**

ATLANTA WOMEN ON THE WAY. See **436.**

BALTIMORE NEW DIRECTIONS FOR WOMEN. See **436.**

BROWN UNIVERSITY, HIGHER EDUCATION RESOURCE SERVICES (HERS). See **408.**

432   CAREER COUNSELING FOR WOMEN. 755 New York Ave., Huntington, N.Y. 11743. (516) 421-1948. Founded May 1973. Anna M. Lowenberger.

Designed to help women discover latent talents and join the mainstream of the employment market. The service is operated by two professional women with backgrounds in vocational guidance and social work, and aimed at women who are planning a career for the future, women who want to get back into the job market, and women who want to advance from a present job which they find unsatisfying.

Women are counseled in groups, to help them decide on the kind of job or career desired, and then taught how to make contacts and write resumes. An eight-week workshop course costs $150.

433   CAREER PLANNING CENTER. 1623 S. La Cienega St., Los Angeles, Calif. 90035. (213) 272-6633. Founded October 1972. Eleanor Hoskins, Exec. Dir.

A nonprofit community service sponsored by the Soroptomist Club of Beverly Hills/Century City, for women from 16 to 60 who want to know more about their job potential, their labor market, and their new career choices. Services available are vocational counseling (free), career planning seminars ($20–$1,000), resumé bank for professional women (free), rap sessions on job-seeking strategy (free), career counseling ($10/hr.), and resumé writing ($5).

434   CATALYST. 6 E. 82 St., New York, N.Y. 10026. (212) 628-2200. Founded 1962. Felice Schwartz, Pres.

"A national nonprofit organization that helps college-educated women combine career and family responsibilities, Catalyst works with employers to assimilate women at responsible levels and to promote greater flexibility in employment patterns for those who choose to work less than full-time during child-rearing years."

A woman interested in the Catalyst program receives a program description, information on resource groups in her area, a list of self-guidance publications produced by Catalyst, and a questionnaire. Using computer-processed data from completed questionnaires and other data, Catalyst publishes a *Quarterly Report*, which consists of a summary of the characteristics of women who have completed the questionnaire, a listing of women by identification number who are available for employment, so that the employer can contact qualified women, a description of local resource groups, a report on educational programs, and a current accounting of the activities of the employers with whom Catalyst is working. Catalyst publishes the *Catalyst Roster*, a computerized listing by identification number, which includes years of experience, salary range, education, and preferred location of women available for employment. The *Roster* is available to employers (free for the first use). Women are listed on the *Roster* without charge, as long as they have completed at least one year of college.

Following is a list of other Catalyst publications.

"The Career Baedeker" in *How to Go to Work When Your Husband Is Against It, Your Children Aren't Old Enough and There's Nothing You Can Do Anyhow*
The Career Opportunities Series, individual booklets on 27 fields.
The Educational Opportunities Series: General Information for the Returning Student
Booklets on business administration, counseling, environmental affairs, health services, law, library science, psychology, social work, teaching, and urban planning.
Planning for Work
Women's Life Styles: Catalyst's Position
Your Job Campaign

Below is a listing of Catalyst National Network of Local Resource Centers.

CALIFORNIA
Advocates For Women, Inc., 564 Market St., #218, San Francisco 94104. (415) 989-5449.

Monday-Friday, 9:00 a.m. to 5:00 p.m. Independent nonprofit agency. Career counseling, job referral, placement. No fees.

California State University, Long Beach Community Counseling Center, 6101 East Seventh St., 203 Adm. Annex, Long Beach 90840. (213) 498-4001. Monday-Thursday, 8:00 a.m. to 7:00 p.m. Friday: 8:00 a.m. to 5:00 p.m. Educational and career counseling, continuing education courses. Registration fee. Other fees vary.

The Claremont Colleges, Special Academic Programs and Office for Continuing Education, Harper Hall 160, Claremont 91711. (714) 626-8511. Monday-Friday, 9:00 a.m. to 5:00 p.m. College-sponsored office. Educational and career counseling, job referral, continuing education courses. Registration fee.

Foothill College, Continuing Education for Women, 12345 El Monte, Los Altos Hills 94002. (415) 948-8590 Ext. 258. Monday-Friday, 10:00 a.m. to 3:00 p.m. Official college office. Educational and career counseling, job referral, continuing education courses. No fees.

Market Place, A Management Search Agency, 1901 Avenue of the Stars, Los Angeles 90067. (213) 553-4088. Monday-Saturday, by appointment. Independent private agency. Job placement. Fees vary.

New Ways to Work, 457 Kingsley Ave., Palo Alto 94301. (415) 321-WORK. Monday-Friday, 9:30 a.m. to 2:30 p.m. Independent nonprofit agency. Career counseling, job referral, placement. No fees.

Program Advisory Service, UCLA Extension, 10995 Le Conte Ave., Rm. 215, Los Angeles 90024. (213) 825-2401 Ext. 250 or 261. Monday-Friday, 9:00 a.m. to 5:00 p.m. Monday evening, 6:00 p.m. to 9:00 p.m. College-sponsored office. Educational and career counseling, job referral information, continuing education courses. No fees.

Resource Center for Women, 1176 Emerson St., Palo Alto 94301. (415) 328-5313. Monday-Thursday, 10:00 a.m. to 3:00 p.m. Independent nonprofit agency. Educational and career counseling, adult education courses, job referral, placement. Fees vary.

UCSD Extension Counseling Services, University of California, San Diego, Box 109, La Jolla 92037. (714) 453-2000. Monday-Friday, 8:00 a.m. to 9:00 p.m. Official college office. Educational and career counseling, continuing education courses, job referral. No registration fee. Other fees vary.

The Women's Opportunities Center, UCLA Extension, Irvine, Irvine 92664. (714) 833-7128. Monday-Friday, 10:00 a.m. to 4:00 p.m. College-sponsored office. Educational and career counseling, continuing education courses. No fees.

Women's Place, Inc., 1901 Avenue of the Stars, Los Angeles 90067. (213) 553-0870. Monday-Friday, 9:30 a.m. to 2:30 p.m. Independent private. Career counseling, workshops, job referral, 5-hour day. Fees vary.

COLORADO

Colorado State University, Women's Programs, Center for Continuing Education, Ft. Collins, 80521. (303) 491-5288. Monday-Friday, 8:00 a.m. to 5:00 p.m. Official college office. Career counseling, continuing education courses. No registration fee. Other fees vary.

CONNECTICUT

Connecticut College, Career Counseling and Placement, New London 06320. (203) 442-5391 Ext. 218. Monday-Friday, 9:00 a.m. to 5:00 p.m. Official college office. Educational and career counseling, job referral, placement. No fees.

Hartford College, Counseling Center, 50 Elizabeth St., Hartford 06115. (203) 236-5838.
Monday-Friday, 8:30 a.m. to 4:30 p.m. College-sponsored office. Educational and career counseling, continuing education courses, job referral, placement. Registration fee only.

New Concept, 111 Saugatuck Ave., Westport 06880. (203) 226-5841.
Monday-Friday, 9:30 a.m. to 3:30 p.m. Independent private agency. Job referral, resume preparation, placement. No registration fee. Other fees vary.

University of Connecticut, Continuing Education for Women, U-56W, Storrs 06268. (203) 486-3441.
Monday-Friday, 8:30 a.m. to 4:30 p.m. Official college office. Educational and career counseling, continuing education courses. Fees vary.

Yale University Women's Organization, Information and Counseling Service, 215 Park St., New Haven 06520. (203) 436-8242.
Monday-Wednesday, 10:00 a.m. to 2:00 p.m. Independent nonprofit agency. Educational and career counseling, adult education courses, job referral. Registration fee. Other fees vary.

Young Women's Christian Association, 422 Summer St., Stamford 06901. (203) 348-7727.
Monday-Friday, 8:30 a.m. to 10:00 p.m. Saturday, 9:00 a.m. to 2:00 p.m. National organization. Educational and career counseling, adult education courses. Registration fee.

DELAWARE
McElroy and Doban, Inc., 2115D Concord Pike, Fairfax, Wilmington 19803. (302) 658-8647.
Monday-Friday, 8:15 a.m. to 5:00 p.m. Independent private agency. Career counseling, job referral, resume preparation, placement. No registration fee. Placement fee individually negotiated.

University of Delaware, Division of Continuing Education, Clayton Hall, Newark 19711. (302) 738-2214.

Monday-Thursday, 8:30 a.m. to 9:00 p.m. Friday, 8:30-5:00. Saturday, 9:00-noon. Official college office. Educational and career counseling, continuing education courses. No registration fee. Other fees vary.

DISTRICT OF COLUMBIA
Distaffers Research and Counseling Center, 4625a 41 Street, N.W., Washington, D.C. 20016. (202) 362-9494.
Five day, thirty hour week. Independent nonprofit agency. Educational and career counseling, job referral. No registration fee. Other fees vary.

George Washington University, Continuing Education for Women, 2029 K Street, N.W., Washington, D.C. 20006. (202) 676-7036.
Monday-Friday, 9:00 a.m. to 5:00 p.m. College sponsored. Educational and career counseling, continuing education courses, job referral. Fees vary.

Job Market, Inc., 1816 Jefferson Place, N.W., Washington, D.C. 20036. (202) 785-4155.
Monday-Friday, 9:00 a.m. to 5:30 p.m. Independent private agency. Job placement. No registration fee. Employer pays placement fee.

FLORIDA
Council for Continuing Education for Women of Central Florida, Inc., 60 West Robinson, Room 209, Orlando 32801. (305) 423-4813.
Monday-Friday, 9:00 a.m. to 12:30 p.m. Independent nonprofit agency. Educational and career counseling, adult education courses. No fees.

The Greater Miami Council for the Continuing Education of Women, Miami-Dade Community College, 141 Northeast Third Ave., Miami 33132. (305) 358-3801.
Monday-Friday, 8:30 a.m. to 5:00 p.m. College-sponsored office. Educational and career counseling, limited job referral, continuing education courses. No registration fee. Other fees vary.

ILLINOIS

Applied Potential, Box 19, Highland Park 60035. (312) 432-0620.
Monday-Friday, 9:00 a.m. to 5:00 p.m. Nonprofit educational corporation. Professional counselors. Educational, career and personal counseling. No registration fee. Other fees vary.

Harper College Community Counseling Center, Palatine 60067. (312) 359-4200.
Monday-Thursday, 8:30 a.m. to 4:30 p.m. 6:00 p.m. to 10:00 p.m. Friday, 8:30 a.m. to 4:30 p.m. College sponsored office. Educational and career counseling. No registration fee. Other fees.

Moraine Valley Community College, Adult Career Resources Center, 10900 South 88th Ave., Palos Hills 60465. (312) 974-4300.
Monday-Friday, 9:00 a.m. to 9:00 p.m. Official college office. Educational and career counseling. No registration fee.

Phillips Research Foundation, 126 North Wright, Naperville, 60540. (312) 357-3180
Monday-Friday, 9:00 a.m. to 5:00 p.m. Foundation-sponsored, independent office. Educational and career counseling, adult education courses. Registration fee. Other fees vary.

Southern Illinois University General Studies Division, Office of Continuing Education, Edwardsville 62025. (618) 692-2242.
Monday-Friday, 8:00 a.m. to 5:00 p.m. Official college office. Educational and career counseling, continuing education courses. No fees.

University of Illinois, Urbana-Champaign, Student Personnel Office for Married Students and Continuing Education for Women, 610 East John St., Champaign 61820. (217) 333-3137.
Monday-Friday, 8:00 a.m. to 5:00 p.m. Official college office. Educational and career counseling. No fees.

Women's Ink, 2051 Ogden Ave., Downers Grove 60515. (312) 969-2090
Monday-Saturday, 9:00 a.m. to 9:00 p.m. Independent private agency. Educational and career counseling, job referral and placement. No registration fee. Other fees vary.

INDIANA

Indiana University, Continuing Education for Women, Owen Hall, Bloomington 47401. (812) 337-1684.
Monday-Friday, 8:00 a.m. to 5:00 p.m. Official college office. Educational and career counseling, continuing education courses. Fees vary.

University Center for Women, Purdue University, 2101 Coliseum Blvd. East, Fort Wayne 46805. (219) 482-5121.
Monday-Friday, 8:00 a.m. to 12:00 noon. College-sponsored office. Educational and career counseling, continuing education courses, job referral. Fees vary.

IOWA

Drake University, Women's Programs, Center for Continuing Education, Des Moines 50311. (515) 271-2183.
Monday-Friday, 8:00 a.m. to 5:00 p.m. Official college office. Educational and career counseling, continuing education courses. No fee for individual counseling. Fee for group sessions.

University Counseling Service, Iowa Memorial Union, University of Iowa, Iowa City, Iowa 52242. (319) 353-4484
Monday-Friday, 8:00 a.m. to 5:00 p.m. College-sponsored office. Educational, vocational and personal counseling. Fees vary for non-students.

KANSAS

University of Kansas, Student Services, Extramural Independent Study Center, Division of Continuing Education, Lawrence, Kansas 66044. (913) 864-4792.
Monday-Friday, 8:00 a.m. to 12:00 noon, 1:00 p.m. to 5:00 p.m. College-sponsored. Educational and career counseling, continuing education (in-

dependent study, classes). No registration fee. Other fees vary.

MASSACHUSETTS

Boston Project for Careers, 83 Prospect St., West Newton 02165. (617) 969-2339.
Four days, 9:00 a.m. to 4:00 p.m. Independent nonprofit agency. Educational and career counseling, job referral, placement. Registration fee only.

Civic Center and Clearing House, Inc., 14 Beacon St., Boston 02108. (617) 227-1762.
Monday-Friday, 9:30 a.m. to 4:30 p.m. Independent nonprofit agency. Educational and career counseling, job referral. No fee for volunteer placements. $10.00 fee for consultation of the Career and Vocational Advisory Service.

Smith College, Vocational Office, Pierce Hall, Northampton 01060. (413) 584-2700.
Monday-Friday, 8:30 a.m. to 4:30 p.m. Official college office. Restricted to alumnae. Educational and career counseling, job referral and placement. No fees.

Women's Educational and Industrial Union, Career Services, 264 Boylston St., Boston 02116. (617) 536-5651.
Monday-Friday, 9:00 a.m. to 5:00 p.m. Independent nonprofit agency. Career counseling, job referral and placement. No registration fee. Placement fees vary.

Women's Opportunity Research Center, Middlesex Community College, Division of Continuing Education, Spring Rd., Bedford 01730. (617) 275-1590.
Monday-Friday, 9:00 a.m. to 2:00 p.m. College-sponsored office. Educational and career counseling, continuing education courses. Fees vary.

MICHIGAN

Michigan Technological University, Center for Continuing Education for Women, Houghton 49931. (906) 487-2270.

Monday-Friday, 8:00 a.m. to 5:00 p.m. Official college office. Educational and career counseling, continuing education courses. No registration fee. Other fees vary.

Oakland University, Continuum Center, Rochester 48063. (313) 377-3033.
Monday-Friday, 8:00 a.m. to 5:00 p.m. College-sponsored. Personal, educational and career counseling, continuing education courses. Fees vary.

Western Michigan University, Continuing Education for Women, Kalamazoo 49001. (616) 383-1860.
Monday-Friday, 8:00 a.m. to 12 noon. Official college office. Educational and career counseling, continuing education courses. Fees vary.

MINNESOTA

Minnesota Women's Center, University of Minnesota, 301 Walter Library, Minneapolis 55455. (612) 373-3850.
Monday-Friday, 7:45 a.m. to 4:30 p.m. Official college office. Educational and career counseling, continuing education courses. No fees.

MISSOURI

University of Missouri, St. Louis, Extension Division—Women's Programs, 8001 Natural Bridge Rd., St. Louis, 63121. (314) 453-5961.
Monday-Friday, 8:00 a.m. to 5:00 p.m. Official college office. Educational and career counseling, adult education courses, limited job referral. No registration fee. Other fees vary.

Washington University, Continuing Education for Women, Box 1099, St. Louis 63130. (314) 863-0100, Ext. 4261.
Monday-Friday, 9:00 a.m. to 12 noon, Official college office. Educational and career counseling, continuing education courses. Fees vary.

The Women's Resource Service, University of Missouri, Kansas City, 1020 East 63rd St. Kansas City 64110. (816) 276-1472.
Tuesday-Thursday, 10:00 a.m. to 2:00 p.m. Official college office. Educa-

tional and career counseling, job referral, continuing education courses. No fees.

NEW JERSEY
Bergen Community College, Community Counseling Service, 295 Main St., Hackensack 07601. (201) 447-1500.
Monday-Friday, 9:00 a.m. to 9:00 p.m. College-sponsored office. Educational and career counseling, adult education courses. No fees.

Douglass College, Women's Center, Gate House, New Brunswick 08903. (201) 247-1766 Ext. 1603.
Monday-Friday, 9:00 a.m. to 12 noon, 1:00 p.m. to 4:00 p.m. Educational and career counseling, continuing education courses. No fees.

Educational and Vocational Counseling Service, 97 Mountainview Rd., Millburn 07041. (201) 376-5226.
Saturday, 9:00 a.m. to 5:00 p.m. Other days by appointment. Independent private agency. Educational and career counseling. No registration fee. Counseling fee.

EVE, Newark State College, Union 07083. (201) 527-2210.
Monday-Friday, 8:30 a.m. to 4:30 p.m. College-sponsored. Educational and career counseling, job referral. No registration fee. Other fees vary.

The Professional Roster, 83 Prospect Ave., Princeton 08540. (609) 921-9561.
Monday-Friday, 10:00 a.m. to 12:30 p.m. Independent, nonprofit organization. Educational and career counseling, job referral. No fees.

NEW YORK
Barnard College, Placement and Career Planning Office, 606 West 120 St., New York 10027. (212) 280-2033.
Monday-Friday, 9:00 a.m. to 5:00 p.m. Official college office. Restricted to alumnae. Career counseling, job referral, placement. Registration fee.

Federation Employment and Guidance Service, 215 Park Ave. South, New York 10003. (212) 777-4900.

Monday-Friday, 8:30 a.m. to 4:30 p.m. Independent nonprofit agency. Educational and career counseling, adult education courses, job referral, placement. No registration fee. Other fees vary.

Hofstra University, Institute for Community Education, Hempstead 11550. (516) 560-3511.
Monday-Thursday, 9:00 a.m. to 8:30 p.m. Official college office. Educational and career counseling, continuing education courses. Fees vary.

Human Relations Work-Study Center, New School for Social Research, 66 West 12 St., New York 10011. (212) 675-2700, Ext. 348-9.
Monday-Friday, 9:00 a.m. to 5:00 p.m. Official college office. Educational counseling, continuing education courses. Fees vary.

Hunter College, Career Counseling and Placement, Room 1601, 505 Park Ave., New York 10022. (212) 360-2874.
Monday-Friday, 9:00 a.m. to 5:00 p.m. Official college office. Restricted to alumnae. Career counseling, job referral, placement. No fees.

Mercy College, Career Counseling and Placement Office, 555 Broadway, Dobbs Ferry 10522. (914) 693-4500.
Monday-Friday, 9:00 a.m. to 5:00 p.m. Official college office. Career counseling, job referral. No fees.

New Directions Division, Pace University, Bedford Rd., Pleasantville 10570. (914) 769-3200, Ext. 211 or Pace College Plaza, N.Y.C. 10038. (212) 285-3000, Ext. 3688.
Monday-Friday, 9:00 a.m. to 5:00 p.m. College-sponsored offices. Educational counseling. No fees.

Options: Career Workshops for Women (Janice LaRouche, Founder), 333 Central Park West, New York 10025. (212) MO 3-0970.
Monday-Saturday, 9:00 a.m. to 6:00 p.m. Independent private agency. Career counseling. No registration fee. Other fees vary.

Orange County Community College, Woman's Program, Office of Community Services, 115 South St., Middletown 10940. (914) 343-3311.
Monday-Friday, 9:00 a.m. to 5:00 p.m. Official college office. Educational counseling, continuing education courses. Fees vary.

Professional Skills Roster, 410 College Ave., Ithaca 14850. (607) 256-3758.
Monday-Friday, 9:30 a.m. to 12:30 p.m. Independent nonprofit agency. Job referral, limited educational and career counseling. No fees. Suggested donation.

Syracuse University/University College, Women's Center for Continuing Education, 610 East Fayette St., Syracuse 13202. (315) 476-5541.
Monday-Friday, 9:00 a.m. to 5:00 p.m. College-sponsored office. Educational and career counseling, continuing education courses. No fees.

Vassar College, Office of Career Planning, Poughkeepsie 12601. (914) 452-7000.
Monday-Friday, 8:30 a.m. to 5:00 p.m. Official college office. Restricted to alumnae. Educational and career counseling, job referral, placement. No fees.

NORTH CAROLINA

Duke University, Center for Career Development and Continuing Education, Durham 27708. (919) 684-6259.
Monday-Friday, 8:30 a.m. to 5:00 p.m. Official college office. Educational and career counseling, continuing education courses. No registration fee. Other fees vary.

Salem College, Lifespan Counseling Center for Women, Lehman Hall, Box 10548, Salem Station, Winston-Salem 27108. (919) 723-7961.
Monday-Friday, 8:30 a.m. to 4:30 p.m. College-sponsored office. Educational and career counseling, adult education courses, limited job referral. No registration fee. Other fees vary.

OHIO

Cleveland Jewish Vocational Service, 13878 Cedar Rd., University Heights 44118. (216) 321-1381.
Monday-Friday, 9:00 a.m. to 5:30 p.m. Thursday, 9:00 a.m. to 6:40 p.m. Independent nonprofit agency. Educational and career counseling, job referral, placement. No registration fee. Other fees vary.

Project EVE, Cuyahoga Community College, 2900 Community College Ave., Cleveland 44115. (216) 241-5966.
Monday-Friday, 9:00 a.m. to 5:00 p.m. Community service. College-sponsored office. Individual educational and career counseling, no fee. Group series and programs, fees vary.

University of Akron (1) Office of Student Services, Akron 44325. (216) 375-7425. Monday-Friday, 8:00 a.m. to 5:00 p.m. (2) Evening College, Akron 44325. (216) 375-7791.
Monday-Thursday, 8:00 a.m. to 9:00 p.m. Friday, 8:00 a.m. to 5:00 p.m. Saturday, 8:00 a.m. to 1:00 p.m. Educational and career counseling, adult education courses, job referral, placement. No registration fee.

OREGON

Women's Programs, Division of Continuing Education, Oregon State System of Higher Education, 1633 S.W. Park Ave., Box 1491, Portland 97207. (503) 229-4849.
Monday-Friday, 8:30 a.m. to 4:30 p.m. Official college office. Educational and career counseling, continuing education courses. No registration fee. Other fees vary.

PENNSYLVANIA

Bryn Mawr College, Office of Career Planning and Placement, Bryn Mawr 19010. (215) LA 5-1000, Ext. 397.
Monday-Friday, 9:00 a.m. to 5:00 p.m. Official college office. Educational and career counseling. Job referral and placement. No fees.

Cedar Crest College, Career Planning Office, Allentown 18104. (215) 437-4471.

Monday-Friday, 8:30 a.m. to 4:30 p.m. Official college office. Educational and career counseling, continuing education courses, job referral and placement. No fees.

Institute of Awareness, 401 South Broad St., Philadelphia 19147. (215) KI 5-4400.

Monday-Friday, 9:00 a.m. to 5:00 p.m. Independent nonprofit agency. Educational and career counseling, adult education courses, special workshops, training programs. Fees vary.

Job Advisory Service, Chatham College, Pittsburgh 15232. (412) 441-8200, Ext. 256.

Mon., Tues., Thurs., 10:00 a.m. to 2:00 p.m. Independent nonprofit office. Job referral. No fees.

Options for Women, 8419 Germantown Ave., Philadelphia 19118. (215) CH 2-4955.

Monday-Friday, 9:30 a.m. to 3:00 p.m. Independent nonprofit agency. Educational and career counseling, adult education courses, job placement. No registration fee. Other fees vary.

Robert Morris College, Department of Continuing Education, 610 Fifth Ave., Pittsburgh 15219. (412) 471-3920.

Monday-Friday, 9:00 a.m. to 5:00 p.m. Official college office. Educational counseling, continuing education courses. Fees vary.

Temple University, Career Services/Continuing Education for Women, Philadelphia 19122.

Monday-Friday, 8:30 a.m. to 4:30 p.m. College-sponsored offices. Career services—(215) 787-7981. Career counseling and job referral. No counseling fee. $10.00 per year for employment referral. Continuing Education—(215) 787-7602. Educational counseling, continuing education courses. No registration fee.

Villa Maria College, Career Counseling Center For Adult Women, 2551 West Lake Rd., Erie 16505. (814) 838-1966.

Monday-Friday, 9:00 a.m. to 4:00 p.m. Official college office. Educational and career counseling, job referral, placement, adult education courses. No fees.

TEXAS

Women for Change Center, 2001 Bryan Tower, Suite 290, Dallas 75201. (214) 741-2391.

Monday-Friday, 9:30 a.m. to 3:30 p.m. Independent nonprofit agency. Educational and career counseling, adult education courses, job referral. Fees vary.

VIRGINIA

University of Virginia, Office of Career Planning and Placement, 5 Minor Hall, Charlottesville 22903. (703) 924-3378.

Monday-Friday, 8:00 a.m. to 5:00 p.m. Official college office. Educational and career counseling, limited job referral and placement. No fees.

WASHINGTON

Individual Development Center, Inc. (I.D. CENTER), 310 15th East, Seattle 98112. (206) 329-0600.

Monday-Friday, 9:00 a.m. to 4:00 p.m. Independent private agency. Life planning, career counseling, adult education courses, job referral. No registration fee. Other fees vary.

University of Washington, Women's Guidance Center, 1209 N.E. 41st, Seattle 98195. (206) 543-2100.

Monday-Friday, 8:00 a.m. to 5:00 p.m. Official college office. Educational and career counseling, adult education courses, limited job referral. Registration fee. Other fees vary.

WISCONSIN

Part-Time Professionals, Office of Adult Education, University of Wisconsin, Green Bay 54302. (414) 465-2102.

Monday-Friday, 8:00 a.m. to 5:00 p.m. College and community sponsored.

Educational and career counseling, adult education courses, job referral, placement. Fees vary.

WYOMING

University of Wyoming, Placement Service, P.O. Box 3195, University Sta-

tion, Laramie 82071. (307) 766-2398.

Monday-Friday, 8:00 a.m. to 5:00 p.m. Official college office, restricted to students and alumnae. Educational and career counseling, job referral. No fees.

435   THE LOCKWOOD CONFERENCE. 1 Rockefeller Plaza, New York, N.Y. 10020. (212) 581-9333. Curt Lockwood. 1,000 members.

An executive search/management consulting firm, working "to get women into meaningful (at least entry level) management positions with American corporations." Three conferences have been held in New York City, and 32 women have been placed in entry-level midmanagement positions. Companies must guarantee to abide by Title 7 of the U.S. Civil Rights Act of 1964 and to offer equal pay. Women with a college degree and one year of business experience may have a resume presented on a year-round basis to companies with available positions, for a fee of $13.50. Reports are made to the applicant every 90 days.

OPPORTUNITIES FOR WOMEN (Providence, R.I.). See **436.**

RICHMOND WOMEN ON THE WAY. See **436.**

WISE-WOW. See **436.**

WASHINGTON AREA WOMEN'S CENTER. See **182.**

436   WASHINGTON OPPORTUNITIES FOR WOMEN, INC. 1111 20 St., N.W., Rm. 101, Washington, D.C. 20036. (202) 382-3872. Founded 1966. Mary D. Janney, Jane I. Fleming, Co-Dirs.

A nonprofit, tax-exempt free advisory service and information center, offering job information, career planning assistance, and training program information for Washington-area women. The center is operated by a small paid staff and trained volunteers, and works in cooperation with the U.S. Employment Service of the District of Columbia (D.C. Manpower Administration.) In 1972, WOW assisted the U.S. Labor Department in starting self-help groups in six cities:

Atlanta Women on the Way. 161 Peachtree St., Rm. 301, Atlanta, Ga. 30303. (404) 656-5918. Muriel Shishkoff, Adm. Coor. Hours: 10 a.m.-2 p.m., Mon.-Thurs.

Baltimore New Directions for Women. 1100 N. Eutah St., Baltimore, Md. 21201. (301) 383-5579. Marian Goetze, Coor. Hours: 10:15 a.m.-2 p.m., Mon.-Thurs.

Opportunities for Women. 144 Westminster St., Providence, R.I. 02902. (401) 331-3315. Angela Munro, Coor. Hours: 10 a.m.-2 p.m., Tues., Thurs.

Richmond Women on the Way. 308 E. Cary St., Richmond, Va. 23219. (804) 770-6015. Suzanne Schilling, Coor. Hours: 10 a.m.-1 p.m., Mon., Wed.

WISE-WOW. 5 N. Main St., White River Junction, Vt. 05001. (802) 295-3136. Terry Anderson, Ruth Cantor, Coors. Hours: 9 a.m.-4:30 p.m. Tues.

Wider Opportunities for Women (WOW Boston). C. F. Hurley Bldg., Government Center, Boston, Mass. 02114. (617) 727-8978. Dorothy Miller, June Levinson, Coors. Hours: 10 a.m.–2 p.m., Tues.–Thurs.

In 1970, with Labor Department funds, WOW–New Careers, a two-year paraprofessional training program for social service assistants, was inaugurated. WOW also maintains a Talent Bank of women with master's degrees available for employment, and publishes *Washington Opportunities for Women: A Guide to Part-time Work and Study* (1967, $2).

WIDER OPPORTUNITIES FOR WOMEN (WOW BOSTON). See 436.

437 **WOMEN'S JOB RIGHTS ORGANIZATION.** 620 Sutter St., Rm. 318, San Francisco, Calif. 94102. (415) 771-1092. Founded January 1972. Rae Lyn Winblad, Toni Littlestone. 50 members.

Counsels women who have sex-discrimination problems; instructs them about filing complaints; files class action suits; and conducts speaking workshops. The organization publishes *Women's Job Rights Advocate Handbook* ($2, individuals; $5, groups).

438 **WOMEN'S OPPORTUNITIES CENTER.** 468 Computer Sciences Bldg., University of California Extension, Irvine, Calif. 92664. (714) 833-7128. Founded September 1970.

A community service project of the university extension, which offers one hour of free counseling in areas of career decision, educational planning, and volunteer activities. The center is designed to assist adult women in planning for continuing education, for careers, and for high-level volunteer service. The staff includes a director, counselors, secretarial workers, research analysts, and professional consultants. Speakers are available upon request. Available publications include a brochure and a newsletter.

Labor Rights

(See also Civil Rights and Legal Services.)

AMERICAN FEDERATION OF TEACHERS, WOMEN'S RIGHTS COMMITTEE. See 521.

439 **CENTER FOR UNITED LABOR ACTION.** 167 W. 21 St., New York, N.Y. (212) 741-0633. Founded 1971. Cheryl Labash.

Dedicated to the betterment of living conditions for all working men and women of all races through organization and effective union action. The women in the group have taken action to support women's strikes by providing information and personnel for picket lines. They also testified before the EEOC in sex discrimination cases. The women at the center have published a booklet, entitled *Working Women: Our Stories and Struggles* (1973, 50¢ 72 pp.), which is updated every two years.

DIRECT ACTION FOR RIGHTS IN EMPLOYMENT (DARE). See 184.

440   NATIONAL COMMITTEE ON HOUSEHOLD EMPLOYMENT. 1625 Eye St., N.W., Suite 323, Washington, D.C. 20006. (202) 872-1056. Founded 1965. Edith B. Sloan, Exec. Dir.

A nonprofit, private body in which 23 voluntary organizations participate. NCHE is funded by the Ford Foundation, the Office of Minority Business Enterprise, and the Sachem Fund, and is the "sole national body concerned exclusively with the problems of household employees." Its goals and projects are to: "raise household wages throughout America to at least the minimum set forth by the Federal Fair Labor Standards Act; provide household workers with common working benefits, including paid vacation and holidays, sick leave and workmen's and unemployment compensation; . . . create among the workers an awareness of the value of their labor. . . . assist the development of cooperatively and privately owned household service enterprises which act as intermediaries between housewives and workers; assist the organization of household workers at a local level throughout the U.S. by the Household Technicians of America; encourage the development of training programs designed to raise the quality, status and economic value of household services; increase public awareness of the household employment problem and the efforts being made to solve it; [and] promulgate a *Code of Standards* upon which employers and employees can base their working relationship." Publications include flyers on NCHE: *Who, Why; There Must Be A Code of Standards, Improving the Status of Household Employment: A Handbook for Community Action* ($1); and *Party Aide Guide* ($1).

441   UNION WOMEN'S ALLIANCE TO GAIN EQUALITY (UNION WAGE) 2137 Oregon St., Berkeley, Calif. 94705. (415) 431-1290. Founded March 1971. Joyce Maupin, Coor. 2325 Mariposa, San Francisco, Calif. 94110. 155 members. Dues: $5.

A coalition of working women and women trade unionists organized to fight sex discrimination on the job, in unions and in society, to organize unorganized working women, and to work for legislation beneficial to all women.

"Union WAGE will fight for: (1) equal pay for equal work and equal opportunities, with jobs for all; (2) stronger efforts for affirmative action programs for better-paying jobs; (3) encouraging unionizing efforts to organize working women; (4) urging women unionists to take leadership roles and greater responsibilities; (5) raising special demands on behalf of women workers, e.g., paid maternity leaves with no loss of seniority and adequate maternity medical coverage; (6) child care facilities; employer and government supported; parent-staff controlled; (7) improvement and extension of state protective legislation to all workers; (8) interpretation of the Equal Rights Amendment to extend labor standards covering one sex to the other sex; (9) minimum wage of $3 an hour guaranteed to all workers; [and] (10) work week of 35 hours or less at 40 hours' pay with double pay for overtime." Union WAGE publishes *Union WAGE* newspaper (bi-m., $2, individuals; $5, institutions).

WASHINGTON AREA WOMEN'S CENTER. See 182.

442   WOMEN IN CITY GOVERNMENT UNITED. 225 Broadway, 22 flr., Rm. 12B, New York, N.Y. 10007. (212) 222-9084. Founded 1969. Susan Rosenfeld, Pres. 500 members.

"An organization of New York City women employees fighting to end sex discrimination in City Government. The only organization of its kind, WICGU has won major victories in the last years on a variety of discrimination-related issues, including maternity policy and pensions."

Some major accomplishments are: "revision of the City's maternity policy to allow pregnant women to work for as long as they think they're able, while at the same time, allowing women to use sick leave for maternity purposes. WICGU has filed charges against the City, its retirement system and the major city employees' union to end the system's discrimination against women employees." WICGU has also "taken surveys to pinpoint the existence of sex discrimination in several city agencies. At the same time, WICGU has pushed for the establishment of a special task force to investigate sex discrimination in city government and to draw up a comprehensive affirmative action program for women." The organization has also developed a resumé bank.

Ethnic and
Religious Groups

443 BLACK WOMEN'S ASSOCIATION. Box 193, Pittsburgh, Pa. 15230.
Founded October 1970. Jean Owens, Exec. Secy. Dues: $7.50. 50–60
members.

An "organization speaking to the issues and policies affecting our society,"
desiring to "organize, motivate and unify black women and to be of service and promote the well being of all humanity." The association is open to all black women.

444 THE BOSTON THEOLOGICAL INSTITUTE, WOMEN'S THEOLOGICAL
COALITION. 99 Brattle St., Cambridge, Mass. 02138. (617) 547-0557.
Founded 1970. 300 members.

"A program which is jointly sponsored by the eight BTI schools, and designed
to promote the cause of women in theological education. It represents the attempt
of the BTI to respond positively and creatively to valid needs at a time when the
experience of women in theological education and the church is being radically
reexamined. There are about 250 women enrolled as degree candidates in the member schools. . . . In order to meet the needs of these women, the WTC is concerned
with ways and means of reflecting the feminine experience in seminary and church
setting especially as it applies in the areas of curricular innovation and field education." The coalition sponsors symposia, conferences and lectures, a Job Placement
Service, an Orientation Program, and research relating to needs of women in theological education and recruitment programs; publishes a newsletter for women,
entitled *Sisterhood*; and keeps a file of papers written by women on women and
theology and ministry. Also available is *Women's Liberation and the Church* by
Sally Bentley Daley, ed. (Association Press, 1970).

445 CHICANA SERVICE ACTION CENTER. 435 S. Boyle Ave., Los Angeles,
Calif. 20033. (213) 268-4141. Founded June 1972. Francisca Flores,
Chpn. Hours: 9 a.m.–5 p.m., with 24-hour telephone service.

A project to serve women who need help or who want to be more active
members of the community, with special attention to problems which interfere
with women's ability to work. Offers employment counseling, referral to training
programs, and help to prepare to reenter high school or college. Maintains a resource file on federal work and education programs and on local, state, and federal
agencies. The center is sponsored by the Comision Feminil Mexicana, an organization of Mexican and Chicana women who seek equal opportunity for women in
education and employment.

COMISION FEMINIL MEXICANA. See 445.

446 EZRAT NASHIM. 306 W. 73 St., Apt. 2A, New York, N.Y. 10023. (212) 874-4906. Founded Fall 1971. Maureen McLeod. 13 members.

"The group began with the thesis that while the Jewish tradition regarding women was once far ahead of other cultures it has fallen behind in failing to come to terms with developments of the past century. . . . While many of us are very concerned about general women's liberation issues, we have all joined Ezrat Nashim because of a deep commitment to being Jewish women . . . who believe that knowledgeable change can be effected within the traditional framework." Projects involve rap groups, studying the *Talmud* and Jewish law and philosophy, organizing prayer services, preparing educational materials, and public speaking. Two publications are available: a collection of articles, *Women in Judaism* (1973, $1., 24 pp.); and a teaching guide and bibliography on women in Judaism (Spring 1974, free or donation).

447 JEWISH FEMINIST ORGANIZATION. 36 W. 37 St., New York, N.Y. 10018. (212) 564-2313. Founded April 1974.

JFO states "Jewish women of all ages, political, cultural and religious outlook and sexual preferences are all sisters. We are committed to the development of our full human potential and to the survival and enhancement of Jewish life. We seek nothing else but the full, direct and equal participation of women at all levels of Jewish life—communal, religious, educational and political." JFO intends to form local groups and facilitate communication among them; to sponsor conferences, retreats, workshops, conventions, and seminars; to act as a referral center; to publish and disseminate literature; to encourage women's studies; to monitor the media; and to maintain a speakers' bureau. A bibliography of material relevant to Judaism and feminism, by Aviva Cantor Zuckoff, is available for 50¢.

448 JOINT COMMITTEE OF ORGANIZATIONS CONCERNED WITH THE STATUS OF WOMEN IN THE CHURCH. 1600 Sunset Ave., Waukegan, Ill. 60085. Founded 1969. Bernice NcNeela. Co-Chpn.

"A committee of organizations formed for the purpose of attaining equal status for women in the [Catholic] Church." Member organizations are the Deaconess Movement; National Association of the Laity, Women's Rights Committee; National Coalition of American Nuns (451), National Organization for Women, Ecumenical Task Force on Women and Religion, Catholic Caucus; St. Joan's International Alliance, U.S. Section (453); Sisters Uniting; and Women Theologians United. "The Joint Committee has submitted to the American Bishops of the Roman Catholic Church a program of action to correct the unequal status of women in the Church. We called upon the Bishops: to proclaim that all discrimination, whether it be because of race, religion, national origin, or sex, is unjust and an offense against human dignity and must be discontinued; to establish a national office for the implementation of a program of fair and equal treatment for women in the Church." As a result, the American Bishops formed a special Bishops Committee for Women in Society and the Church. Any organization concerned with the status of women in the Catholic Church which has a Catholic constituency, is willing to work cooperatively for equal status for women in the Catholic Church, and supports the proposal presented to the American Bishops is eligible for membership.

Following is a list of writings on Women and Religion by Elizabeth Farians, Ph.D., a founder of the group.

The Coming of Woman: The Christa. 25¢
Exorcising the Sexual Demon 35¢
Human Dignity of Women in The Church (recent Papal statements) 25¢
Justice: The Hard Line 35¢
Phallic Worship: The Ultimate Idolatry 35¢
The Status of Women in the Church 30¢
The True Myth (Includes "Applesource: The Return of Lilith") 25¢
Women, Ethics and Ecology 30¢
Women in the Church NOW (Canon Law) 30¢
Women, Religion and the Law (Civil) 30¢

Another title is *Selected Bibliography on Women and Religion* (1965-1972; $1, including postage; 33 pp.; chronological order: books, news stories, and articles; fifth revised edition, 1973).

Orders should be prepaid. If separate billing is necessary, 25¢ will be charged. Make checks payable to: Elizabeth Farians, 6125 Webbland Pl., Cincinnati, Ohio 45213. If order is under $2, add 25¢ postage. Proceeds (if any) are used to further the cause of women in religion.

449 NATIONAL ASSOCIATION OF MINORITY WOMEN IN BUSINESS. Inez Kaiser & Assoc., Inc. 906 Grand St., Suite 500, Kansas City, Mo. 64106. (816) 421-3335. Founded 1973. Inez Kaiser, Pres.

"Formed for the purpose of combining efforts to further the advancement of minority women in the world of business; to share practical experience; to upgrade the image of women in the business world; to assure the implementation of the Affirmative Action laws among major corporations and city and national governmental agencies; [and] to encourage other minority women to become entrepreneurs and to address themselves to matters of related concern. The membership . . . is comprised primarily of women of all minority races who are owners of businesses as well as those who are in managerial positions. Associate members are those persons in related fields.

450 NATIONAL BLACK FEMINIST ORGANIZATION. 370 Lexington Ave., Rm. 601, New York, N.Y. 10017. (212) 685-0800. Founded May 1973. Jane Lewis, Margaret Sloan.

Established in order to address "the particular and specific needs of the larger, but almost cast aside half of the Black race in Amerikkka, the Black Woman. Black women in this country live in the phenomenon of being *both* Black and Female in a country that is *both* sexist and racist. We can't expect anyone to organize around the specific oppressions that Black women experience; not White women, because they don't experience racism; not Black men because they don't encounter sexism.

"As Black Feminists we realized the need to establish ourselves as an independent Black Feminist's organization. Our above ground presence will lend enormous credibility to the current Women's Liberation Movement. . . . We also will strengthen the current efforts of the Black Liberation struggle in this country by encouraging *all* of the talents and creativities of Black women to emerge, strong and beautiful, not to feel guilty or devisive, and assume positions of leadership and honor in the Black community. . . . We will remind the Black Liberation Movement that there can't be liberation for half a race. We must together, as a people, work to eliminate racism from without the Black community which is trying to destroy us as an entire people, but we must remember that sexism is destroying and crippling from within.

"Because of the social, political, and economic situation of the Black woman, we will work on: the Black woman's self-image, Black female unemployment, Black women prisoners, child care centers, ratification of the Equal Rights Amendment, the triple oppression of the Black Lesbian, job training programs for Black women, sex and race role stereotyping in child raising, an end to forced sterilization, the fight of the household worker, the image of the Black woman in the media, Black female addiction, supporting abortion laws and other areas of reproductive freedom, the concerns of the professional Black women, Black women and the welfare system, [and] Black women and health care."

451   NATIONAL COALITION OF AMERICAN NUNS. 1307 S. Wabash St., Chicago, Ill. 60605. (312) 922-1983 or 341-1530. Founded July 1969. Sister Ann Gillen, Exec. Dir. 1800 members.

"Roman Catholic Sisters organized to study and speak out for Gospel values and social justice. Directed toward achieving full liberation for all members of the human family, with special concern for women in the Church and in society, for minorities and those suffering from prejudice and/or injustice of any kind." Projects include street preaching, traveling workshops, Sojourner Truth Hostel for homeless girls, Third World Task Force, amicus curiae briefs for suit ending capital punishment, and testimony in support of the Equal Rights Amendment. Free publications are a study document issued in response to "Theological Reflections on the Ordination of Women," issued by U.S. Bishops Committee on Pastoral Research and Practices; "Statement in Favor of ERA" to Illinois House of Representatives, March 22, 1973, by Sister Margaret Ellen Traxler; and the newsletter of the NCAN.

452   THE NORTH AMERICAN INDIAN WOMEN'S ASSOCIATION. 3201 Shadybrook Dr., Midwest City, Okla. 73110. Founded 1970. Marie Cox, Nat. Advisor.

Nonprofit educational association, organized for the purpose of promoting among North American Indian People: betterment of home, family life, and community; improvement of health and education; inter-tribal communications; awareness of Indian culture; and fellowship among all peoples.

453   ST. JOAN'S INTERNATIONAL ALLIANCE. 435 W. 119 St., New York, N.Y. 10027. (212) 663-3555. Founded 1965, U.S.; 1911, London. Frances Lee McGillicuddy, Pres. Dues: $8, regular; $10, sustaining; $15, contributing.

An organization of Catholics, founded "to secure legal and de facto equality between women and men in all fields—state, Church and society. St. Joan's has worked with the United Nations for the advancement of women (political rights of women; equal access to education and vocational training; economic opportunities; family law; abolition of child and forced marriages; slavery and traffic in persons; elimination of discrimination against women; etc.) The U. S. Section of the alliance fought for the passage of the Equal Rights Amendment.

"The Alliance is the pioneer in working for the implementation of the Christian principle of the equality of the sexes within the Church itself. It played the leadership role in petitioning for lay (men and women) observers and women auditors at the Second Vatican Council; the revision of the nuptial liturgy; revision of those canons of the Code which adversely affect women; [and] admission of women to the deaconate and to the priesthood." The U. S. Section has presented its views at two meetings of the Liaison Committee of the U. S. Bishops Conference, and has "testified" before the Conference's Committee for Women in Society and the Church. The alliance has established an Anti-Defamation Committee to record and publicize examples of discrimination against women within the Church.

"Catholic women and men who unreservedly approve the objectives and activities of the Alliance are elgible to Full membership; like-minded women and men of other denominations are invited to join as Associate Members."

The Catholic Citizen is the official bimonthly journal of St. Joan's International Alliance (London). *St. Joan's Bulletin* is the bimonthly newsletter of the U. S. Section.

454   THIRD WORLD WOMEN'S ALLIANCE. 336 W. 20 St., New York, N.Y. 10011 and Box 3065, Berkeley, Calif. 94703. Founded 1968.

An anti-imperialist Third World women's group providing political education for third world women. The alliance publishes a newspaper, *Triple Jeopardy* ($3.50, individuals; $8, institutions; $2.50, foreign). Sample issues included the following articles: "Rising Prices Hurt Women Most," "Albanian Women Advance," "Puerto Rican Women in the Struggle," "Costa Rican Women's Statement," "Brazilian Women Used as Guinea Pigs," "Angela Davis Raps with Third World Women's Alliance," and "Chinese Women Achieve Economic Independence," among others.

455   UNITED CHURCH OF CHRIST, TASK FORCE ON WOMEN IN CHURCH AND SOCIETY. 297 Park Ave., S., New York, N.Y. 10010 (212) 475-2121. Founded 1971. Tilda Norberg, Louise Wallace, Co-Chpns. 15 members.

Working to expand "the opportunity for full participation of women in the total life of the Church and greater opportunity for all persons to realize their maximum potential." Its task is to implement the "Pronouncement on Women and Statement on Women" adopted by the Eighth and Ninth General Synods of the United Church of Christ. The task force conducted a study on the status of women within the United Church of Christ, designed consciousness-raising experiences for church members including use of film, role play, questionnaires, and group discussion; and maintains a Data Bank on UCC women seeking employment or volunteer positions within the church. Information on task force reports may be obtained from Susannah Risman at the task force office.

456   UNITED PRESBYTERIAN CHURCH, COUNCIL ON WOMEN AND THE CHURCH. 475 Riverside Dr., New York, N.Y. 10027. (212) 870-2671. Founded May 1973. Virginia Kelley Mills. 18 members.

Official council in the Presbyterian Church dealing with the status of women. to identify and work on women's issues and to ensure equal treatment of women in the church. Currently working on seminary relations, child development, Third World women, church-employed women, abortion, marriage and divorce, and language.

"WHERE WE AT" BLACK WOMEN ARTISTS. 369.

457 WOMEN TITHE FOR WOMEN. 2913 Iroquois Ave., Detroit, Mich. 48214. Mary Jo Smith, Pres.

A fund to combat sexism in the churches. "Monies contributed by women would assist in litigations against the churches in sex discrimination cases and would enable the NOW Task Force on Women and Religion to initiate other programs to improve the situation of women in religious institutions."

WOMEN'S CENTER, UNION THEOLOGICAL SEMINARY. See 203.

WOMEN'S RESOURCE CENTER, NEWTON THEOLOGICAL SCHOOL. See 193.

WOMEN'S TEAM MINISTRY. See 393.

Health, Physical, and Social Welfare Rights

Abortion, Birth Control, Health

(See also U. S. Local groups.)

458   ABORTION-BIRTH CONTROL REFERRAL SERVICE. 4224 University Way, N.E., Seattle, Wash. 98105. (206) 634-3460. Founded December 1970. Alma Arnold.

A program of the University YWCA, staffed by volunteers, to provide women with referrals to medically competent and supportive physicians.

459   ABORTION INFORMATION AND REFERRAL SERVICE OF PORT-LAND, INC. 2315 N.W. Irving St., Portland, Oreg. 97210. (503) 227-5404, 6030. Founded January 1970. Anne Bowlden, Coor.

Aids women in obtaining legal abortions with a minimum of trauma, and acts as a consumer advocate for abortion patients within the medical community. The service counsels women with problem pregnancies, sends speakers to colleges and high schools to conduct talks on abortion, and trains abortion counselors in Oregon. The service publishes *Abortion Resources Handbook* by Marge Bennett, Anne Bowlden, and Leslie Haines.

460   ABORTION RIGHTS ASSOCIATION, INC. 250 W. 57 St., Rm. 2428, New York, N.Y. 10019. (212) 541-8887. Vicki Kaplan. Exec. Dir.

"A nonprofit educational organization devoted to speeding the implementation of the Supreme Court decisions which make abortion legal in the U.S.," by acquainting the medical and social service communities with information regarding rights and responsibilities of all concerned and by supplying information and counseling guidelines. Outreach programs are in progress in labor unions and youth organizations. Pamphlets include: *Abortion: A Women's Right* (also in Spanish); *Abortion: Guidelines for the Clergyman, Counselor, Health Educator, Nurse, Social Worker; Abortion: A Physician's Rights and Responsibilities;* and *Listing of Selected N.Y.S. Abortion Clinics* (25¢ each, 10 for $1.80, reduced price for quantity orders).

461   ACCESS CENTER FOR HUMAN REPRODUCTIVE HEALTH. 1226 E. Michigan Ave., Lansing, Mich. 48912. (517) 485-3271. Founded May 1973.

Offers pregnancy testing with pelvic exam, problem pregnancy counseling, birth control information, contraceptives, vasectomy, and pregnancy termination. Open for appointments for all services Monday through Saturday, the Access Center performs abortions up to the twelfth week, using the vacuum aspirator technique under local anesthesia which complies with guidelines recommended by the Michigan Department of Public Health. The center hopes to enable patients to get low cost, high quality care and to teach the patients something about their bodies at the same time; it plans to begin second trimester pregnancy terminations and out-patient female sterilization.

462 ARCADIA CLINIC. 4224 University Way, N.E., Seattle, Wash. 98105. (206) 634-2090. Founded March 1972.

Feminist family planning clinic to enable women to be responsible for their own health care and to share information and skills. Maintains paramedic training for gynecological assistants.

463 ASSOCIATION FOR THE STUDY OF ABORTION, INC. 120 W. 57 St., New York, N.Y. 10021. (212) 245-2360. Founded 1964. Jimmye Kimmey, Exec. Dir. 25,000 members.

An educational, nonprofit organization to accumulate and disseminate information about abortion. Emphasizes public and professional implementation of the U.S. Supreme Court decision Jan. 22, 1973 prohibiting restriction of abortion during the first trimester. The association publishes a newsletter (irreg.), bibliographies, and reprints, and produces a film, *Unfinished Story.* . . .

464 BIRTH CONTROL INFORMATION CENTER. 45 Eagle St., North Addams. Mass. 01247. (413) 663-8846. Founded February 1971. Virginia White.

A feminist group, which does birth control and abortion counseling, talks to community groups, and distributes feminist literature.

465 CANADIAN WOMEN'S COALITION TO REPEAL THE ABORTION LAWS. Box 5673, Sta. A, Toronto, Ont., Can. (416) 863-9773. Founded March 1972. Gwen Taylor.

A feminist group organized to fight for the repeal of Canada's abortion laws, freely available contraceptive information and devices for all, the right to choose voluntary sterilization, and an end to forced sterilization. Works through demonstrations, public meetings, conferences, etc. The coalition held a Tribunal on Abortion in November 1973, at which women testified about their experiences of having been denied control of their bodies.

CHICAGO WOMEN'S LIBERATION UNION HEALTH PROJECT. See 184.

CHICAGO WOMEN'S LIBERATION UNION RAPE CRISIS LINE. See 184.

466 THE COMMITTEE FOR ABORTION INFORMATION AND REFERRAL (CAIR). 426 Fir Ave., Absecon, N.J. 08201. (609) 345-2249. Cindy Shur.

Provides free information on and referrals to area and out-of-state abortion clinics and hospitals to women requesting aid. Most of the group members are social workers who alternate throughout the month accepting calls during the evening hours on their own home phones. An individual requesting abortion information can call CAIR's answering service, donated by the Metropolitan Ministry, and the caller will be given the name and number of the woman who is "on call" that particular day. CAIR's main goal is to provide quality abortion care at a minimum cost. The abortion clinics and hospitals have been carefully screened, and feedback is requested from referrals. CAIR is also involved in trying to liberalize South Jersey's attitude and abortion laws. CAIR is constantly in contact with area doctors, hospitals, and social service agencies, and also provides public speakers to interested groups.

467   CONCERN FOR HEALTH OPTIONS: INFORMATION, CARE AND EDUCATION (CHOICE). 2027 Chestnut St., Philadelphia, Pa. 19103. (215) 567-2904. Founded Spring 1971. Winnie Schoefer, Dir.

A free problem pregnancy counseling service, affiliated with the Clergy Consultation Service. "CHOICE offers a pregnant woman counseling and information on *all* options available to her—adoption, pre-natal care, foster care, single parenthood and abortion. Besides providing individual counseling and referral, CHOICE has developed a health advocacy role to expand and improve abortion resources in the city. [The] basic concern is women—that they be able to have control over their lives and bodies, and when pregnancy is problematic, be able to choose the best possible personal solution. The role of the CHOICE counselor is one of support and information—a facilitator of the woman's decision."

468   EASTERN WOMEN'S CENTER. 14 E. 60 St., New York, N.Y. 10022. (212) 832-0033. Founded June 1971. Ilene Cooper.

A New York State licensed, multiservice, out-patient health faculty concerned with women's reproductive and gynecologic care. Services offered are free pregnancy testing, counseling, abortion, gyn/contraceptive clinic, and community education program. Two pamphlets are free: *Abortion. . . . Every Woman's Right* and *Eastern Women's Center.*

469   FEMINIST SEXUALITY PROJECT. NOW, 19 E. 47 St., New York, N.Y. 10003. (212) 874-7985. Shere Hite.

Designed to investigate female sexuality, "to create a fund of information which will strengthen and enrich our lives." A lengthy questionnaire was distributed, 2,000 of which were returned. Selected replies were compiled into a book, *Sexual Honesty by Women for Women*, edited by Shere Hite, (New York: Warner Paperback Library, 294 pp., $1.50). "The ultimate intention of this research is to formulate a critique of our current cultural definitions of sex, based on what we have said." This book will be published in 1975. The project is not affiliated with NOW; however, as a member, the author was permitted to use NOW's name and address as a heading for the questionnaire, to alert the reader about the project's viewpoint.

470   FEMINIST THERAPY REFERRAL COLLECTIVE. 749 W. End Ave., New York, N.Y. 10025, Apt. 1W. (212) 787-4600. Founded May 1971. Linnie Frank. 5 members.

Provides free referrals for women to psychotherapists screened by the collective. There are about 90 therapists on the list, practicing various types of therapy, at a wide range of fees. Therapists are chosen for referral if they consider therapy a reciprocal process between equals. The collective also runs rap groups for therapists on feminist issues and workshops on therapy for interested women, and publishes a newsletter.

471 FEMINIST WOMEN'S HEALTH CENTER SELF-HELP CLINIC. 746 S. Crenshaw, Los Angeles, Calif. 90005. (213) 936-7219. Carol Downer, Shelly Farber, Francie Hornstein.
See also New Moon Communications, 481.

A women's health group to educate women about health care and put their health back into their own hands. Projects include clinics for self-help, abortion, menopause, and gynecological help; as well as pregnancy screening and referrals to physicians. Speakers are sent to interested groups. A literature packet and speculum is available for $2. Videotapes and films on abortion and tubal ligation are also available. Co-publishes the *Monthly Extract*, Stamford, Conn. 06905 with New Moon Communications (see 481).

472 FREMONT WOMEN'S CLINIC. 6817 Greenwood Ave., N., Seattle, Wash. 98103 (206) 782-5788. Founded Summer 1972.

A free feminist medical clinic for women and children, designed to "demystify gynecology and provide excellent, sensitive, free and accessible health care" and to teach women self-help techniques.

473 HEALTH POLICY ADVISORY CENTER (HEALTH PAC). 17 Murray St., New York, N.Y. 10007. (212) 267-8890. Founded 1968. Nancy Jervis.

A nonprofit, private research and education organization to expose the inequities of the health system and monitor new developments in health reform. Provides speakers, and organizes conferences and workshops, aiming to create a new health system of high quality care paid for by taxation, based on preventative care, and governed by health workers and consumers. Publishes *Health PAC Bulletin* ($7, individuals; $5, students; $15, institutions.) Articles in the *Health PAC Bulletin* concern women and health care. The organization also distributes other publications of interest to women. Write for list.

474 ILLINOIS CITIZENS FOR THE MEDICAL CONTROL OF ABORTION. 100 E. Ohio St., Chicago, Ill. 60611. (312) 644-0972. Founded 1966. Helen Smith, Exec. Dir., 6839 N. Kilpatrick St., Lincolnwood, Ill. 60696. 5000 members. Dues: $7.50. $3, students.

A statewide organization originally established to legalize abortion, but now counteracting the threat to the 1973 Supreme Court decision. The group lobbies Congresspersons and state legislators, sends speakers to interested groups, and publishes a newsletter.

475 IOWANS FOR MEDICAL CONTROL OF ABORTION. Box 232, West Des Moines, Iowa 50265. (515) 277-0886. Founded December 1969. Barbara Madden, 5900 N. Waterbury Rd., Des Moines, Iowa 50312. 3000 members.

A statewide group, now interested in supporting the Supreme Court decision and monitoring the situation in Iowa. Publishes a newsletter.

ITHACA WOMEN'S CENTER. See **206.**

476 LEHIGH VALLEY ABORTION RIGHTS ASSN. Box 252, Bethlehem, Pa. 18015. (215) 435-2502. Founded May 1971. Carole Shafer, 121 S. Mulberry St., Easton, Pa. 18042. 75 members. Dues: $3.

Established to make information about abortions and birth control available to women of all ages. Maintains a 24-hour answering service for referral for low-cost medically sound abortions. Also runs a speaker's bureau.

477   MASSACHUSETTS ORGANIZATION TO REPEAL ABORTION LAWS,
      INC. Box 238, Boston, Mass. 02134. (617) 969-7660. Founded 1969.
      Lynda G. Christian, Pres., 23 Fredana Rd., Waban, Mass. 02168. 600 members.
      Dues: $10; $5, students.

A political action group to insure that the Supreme Court decision on abortion is implemented. The organization is currently encouraging political pressure on Congress to overturn any action toward a Constitutional amendment which would overrule the Supreme Court decision.

478   MICHIGAN CITIZENS FOR MEDICAL CONTROL OF ABORTION. 201
      E. Liberty St., Ann Arbor, Mich. 48108. (313) 761-2398. Jean King.

Aims to assure the women of Michigan the right to safe and reasonable means of controlling their fertility. Alerts women's groups to the current political situation, with particular reference to abortion and other fertility-control matters; interested in preventing a constitutional amendment rescinding the Supreme Court decision of January 1973.

479   MINNESOTA ORGANIZATION FOR REPEAL OF ABORTION LAWS.
      5205 Duncraig Rd., Minneapolis, Minn. 55436. (612) 929-0941. Founded
      1966. Betty Benjamin. 1,050 members. Dues $6.

Working toward implementation of the U.S. Supreme Court decision on abortion and the promotion of family life education and sex education to prevent unwanted pregnancy. The organization sends public speakers to interested groups, testifies at state legislative hearings, and conducts research on abortion. The following free literature is available: *The Supreme Court Decisions, Churches That Have Taken Official Positions in Favor of Making Abortion an Individual Decision, Amniocentesis,* and *Physical and Mental Health Aspects of Abortion.*

MONTREAL HEALTH PRESS, INC. See 19.

480   NATIONAL ASSOCIATION FOR REPEAL OF ABORTION LAWS. 250
      W. 57 St., New York, N.Y. 10019. (212) 265-5125. Founded 1968.
      Roxanne Olivo, Exec. Dir. 900 members.

A coalition of 75 local and state organizations dedicated to the right of all women to obtain abortions. Aims to implement the Supreme Court decision on abortion in all states; make abortions available at low cost to the poor; and oppose any restrictive Constitutional amendments. With the American Civil Liberties Union, NARAL is suing public hospitals in ten states that refuse to perform abortions. The association publishes: *Do You Want to Return to the Horrors of Back-Alley Abortion?* (25¢); *Abortion: Questions and Answers* (10¢); *50 Physicians Evaluate Legal Abortion in New York* (10¢); and a newsletter (25¢). Also available is a debater's kit (4 pieces, 25¢) and black-and-white photos and slides. Write for list.

481   NEW MOON COMMUNICATIONS. Box 3488, Ridgeway Sta., Stamford,
      Conn. 06905. (202) 348-8529. Founded December 1972. Lolly Hirsch.
      See also Feminist Women's Health Center Self-Help Clinic, 471.

A gynecological self-help group which lectures and publishes a newsletter, *The Monthly Extract; An Irregular Periodical* ($3.50/6 issues). One issue included excerpts from the autobiography of Margaret Sanger, book reviews on books concerning birth control, listings of research papers and books on gynecological subjects, and letters from women concerning self-help. Other publications are *The*

Witch's Os ($2), a description of the history of gynecology in relation to the self-help movement, and *Proceedings of the First International Childbirth Conference* ($2).

NEW PALTZ WOMEN'S ALLIANCE. See 208.

OTTAWA WOMEN'S CENTRE MEDICAL COLLECTIVE. See 239.

482 PLANNED PARENTHOOD FEDERATION OF AMERICA, INC. 810 7 Ave., New York, N.Y. 10019. (212) 541-7800.

A nonprofit agency offering service and information on birth control, abortion, pregnancy detection, voluntary sterilization, infertility and adoption, and venereal disease. Some local Planned Parenthood groups operate clinics, which offer general health checks, pregnancy detection, and abortion. Speakers, literature, and films are often available from local groups, relating to basic education in human sexuality and family planning. Consult local telephone directories for the nearest PP group.

483 PORTLAND WOMEN'S HEALTH CLINIC. 3537 S.E. Hawthorne Blvd., Portland, Oreg. 97214. Founded February 1971.

A free clinic run by and for women to encourage women to learn about their own bodies so that they can take care of and control them. Services available include pregnancy counseling, pap smears, blood pressures, free doctor referrals, and individual counseling on pregnancy, abortion, and adoption. "The clinic has been teaching a course, 'The Biology of Women,' in several high schools in the city, as well as at Portland State University and Rocky Butte Prison. There is also a program of community education at the clinic on alternative Tuesday nights open to interested women." Volunteers at the clinic include nurses, medical students, and lab technicians.

484 PREGNANCY CONSULTATION SERVICE. 14 N. College St., Oxford, Ohio. 45056. (513) 523-3818. Founded 1968. Mary-Ellen Miller, 621 S. College St., Oxford, Ohio 45056. (513) 523-6216.

Counsels women with problem pregnancies, and makes referrals to abortion clinics, homes for unwed mothers, adoption agencies, and agencies and doctors which can provide birth control at a reasonable cost. The service is free. PCS also provides speakers on problem pregnancy and contraception, and works with Planned Parenthood and Together, Inc. (a crisis center hot-line) to provide discussions, films, etc. on venereal disease, contraception, and sexuality. PCS may also be reached via the Together Hot-line, 24 hours a day: (513) 532-4146.

485 RHODE ISLAND COALITION TO REPEAL THE ABORTION LAWS. 21 Oriole Ave., Providence, R.I. 02906. (401) 751-7648. Founded 1970. Alice Quinn.

"Recognizing the basic human right of a woman to limit her own reproduction," RICRAL "is dedicated to the repeal of all laws that would compel any woman to bear a child against her will." The organization is presently working to get hospitals and clinics to broaden services and fighting attempts to overturn the Supreme Court decision by Constitutional amendment.

486 RICHMOND COLLEGE WOMEN'S SELF HELP COLLECTIVE. 130 Stuyvesant Pl., Staten Island, N.Y. 10301. (212) 448-8433. Founded July 1973. Georgine Gorra, 82 Brook St., Staten Island, N.Y. (212) 720-8510.

A women's medical group, offering gynecological services, abortion referral and counseling, birth control information, etc. for free. The collective serves the women of Richmond College and the surrounding community.

487   SAN FRANCISCO WOMEN'S HEALTH CENTER. 3789 24 St., San Francisco, Calif. 94114. (415) 282-6999. Founded January 1971. P. Hinman, 177 Liberty St., San Francisco, Calif. 94110. Hours: 4–8 p.m., Mon.; 1:30–4 p.m., Tues., Fri.

A group of women interested in learning more about their bodies and how they function and in finding ways to get better health care for themselves and all women. The center offers courses in self-help; and conducts research projects concerning women and health. The following leaflets are available: *The Basic Self Exam, Pregnancy Testing, Trichomonas Vaginitis, Herpes Genitalis,* and *Diaphragm Fitting.*

488   TEXAS CITIZENS FOR ABORTION EDUCATION. Box 8241, Dallas, Tex. 75204. Dues: $1, students; $5, individuals; $10, families.

Founded to make safe, legal abortion available to all women who choose to have one. Publishes an occasional newsletter, suggesting action to take to influence legislators, etc.

489   VANCOUVER WOMEN'S HEALTH COLLECTIVE. 146 E. 18 St., Vancouver 9, B.C., Can. (604) 873-3984. Founded Fall 1971.

A women's health education group, which aims to share information between women regarding health needs; to involve laywomen in treating women and counseling concerning prevention and health maintenance; and to develop health resources for women who oppose the traditional, male-dominated, authoritarian medical model. A women's self-help clinic, operated by women paramedics and a woman physician, does v.d. detection, birth control, pregnancy tests, pelvic and breast examinations, and nutrition and sexuality problem counseling. Self-educational health groups meet, and a phone line and reference library is maintained. *A Vancouver Women's Health Book* (50¢) contains articles on health care, childbirth, and nutrition; and a directory of doctors, free clinics, etc.

490   VERMONT WOMEN'S HEALTH CENTER. Box 29, Burlington, Vt.; Exit 16, Rte. 89, Colchester, Vt. 05401. (802) 655-1600. Sue Adams, Sue Wisehart. 50 members.

A small, private, nonprofit corporation, operating as a collective, which specializes in education and services relevant to the health of women, with special emphasis on family planning, contraception, pregnancy detection, termination of pregnancy by vacuum aspiration or Early Uterine Evacuation, and venereal disease. The center offers yearly gynecological examinations, pregnancy detection and counseling, menopause counseling, breast and cervical cancer examination, discussion groups, books, movies, speakers, and Lamaze classes. A 24-hour emergency telephone line is available, and fees may be adjusted to the ability to pay.

WASHINGTON AREA WOMEN'S CENTER. See 182.

WOMEN'S CENTER (Cambridge, Mass.). See 192.

WOMEN'S COUNSELING PROJECT. See 204.

491 WOMEN'S COUNSELLING SERVICE. 3764 St. Laurent, Montreal, Que., Can. (514) 845-7145. Founded November 1971.

A birth control and abortion counseling and referral service. The group also provides speakers to interested groups.

492 WOMEN'S HEALTH CARE EDUCATION COUNCIL, INC. 555 Central Ave., Scarsdale, N.Y. 10583. (914) 725-1292, 725-1534. Founded July 1970. Susan E. Browne.

Offers abortion counseling, birth control, and birth control counseling and referrals; conducts workshops on birth control, pregnancy, and abortion.

493 WOMEN'S HEALTH CLINIC. 1556 Wisconsin Ave., N.W., Washington, D.C. 20007. (202) 965-5476. Founded June 1973. Alice Aldrich, 1916 N. Wayne St., Arlington, Va. 22201.

A self-help health care group which "combines health care with feminist politics." Women are taught to do pelvic examinations, and discussions are conducted on women and health, "a blend of factual information and consciousness-raising about women, their bodies, attitudes and the health system." The clinic operates on a paramedical basis under the supervision of a woman doctor. A 15-minute film has been produced on pelvic examinations. Write for further information.

494 WOMEN'S HEALTH FORUM AND HEALTHRIGHT, INC. 156 5 Ave., Rm. 1228, New York, N.Y. 10010. (212) 691-1140. Founded June 1973. Pamela Booth, Diana Parness, Jan Heininger.

"Designed to educate and support women in their struggle for quality health care." Objectives of the group concern promotion of research, education of women about their reproductive and sexual anatomy, the establishment of model projects for health and sex education courses to be used in high schools, universities, workplaces, etc., encouragement of the entry of women into health careers, and the education of consumers about health facilities. WHF intends to act as a clearinghouse for the exchange of information in this area. The group maintains a speakers' bureau and a literature center.

The following health education courses are offered by WHF: Know Your Body, Teen-Age Sex Education, Older Women and Menopause, Women and Psychology, Women and Drugs, and Sexuality Workshops. The following pamphlets are 15¢ each; 25 or more, 10¢: *The Gynecological Checkup, Infections of the Vagina, Vacuum Aspiration Abortion, Saline Abortion,* and *Venereal Disease.*

The following leaflets are 10¢ for single copies; 5¢ each in bulk of 25: *What Women Should Know about the Pill,* and *Women and Health Care.*

WOMEN'S LIBERATION CENTER (New York, N.Y.). See **205.**

WOMEN'S LIBERATION GROUP (Windsor, Ont.). See **241.**

WOMEN'S LIBERATION UNION (Kansas City, Mo.). See **195.**

495 WOMEN'S NATIONAL ABORTION ACTION COALITION. 150 Fifth Ave., Rm. 737, New York, N.Y. 10011. (212) 691-3495. Founded July 1971. Evelyn Kirsch, Susan Lamont.

A nationwide coalition of individual women and women's organizations whose goal is to repeal all abortion laws, repeal restrictive contraception laws, and end forced sterilization, via legislative and judicial actions, peaceful mass demonstrations, and educational programs. There are WONAAC chapters in many cities and on college campuses; locations are obtainable on request. WONAAC is supported by contributions. *WONAAC Newsletter* is published monthly ($3/yr., 15¢/ issue).

WOODMERE WOMEN'S CENTER. See 211.

496   WORCESTER PREGNANCY COUNSELING SERVICE, INC. 529 Park Ave., Worcester, Mass. 01603. (617) 791-7201. Founded February 1972. Becky Sakakeeny, Coor. Hours: 5–9 p.m., Mon., Tues., Thurs.; 1–4 p.m., Sat.

"A voluntary, non-profit organization providing counseling by women for women with problem pregnancies." The group offers information on health and social services, clinic and hospital resources, maternity homes, adoption, prenatal care, abortion facilities in Massachusetts or New York State, birth control, and pregnancy testing. There is a 24-hour phone service.

497   YALE LAW WOMEN'S ASSOCIATION, WOMEN V. CONNECTICUT. Box 89, Yale Law School, New Haven, Conn. 06520. (203) 436-0364. Founded August 1969. Judy Robison. 200 members.

A collective of women working on issues related to women's health, particularly the availability of abortion. The group operates a mobile women's health unit, and monitors abortion facilities.

498   ZERO POPULATION GROWTH. 4080 Fabian Way, Palo Alto, Calif. 94303. Founded December 1968. 20,000 members. Dues: $15, individuals; $8, students; $20, families.

A nonprofit, volunteer organization devoted to establishing the population of the United States by urging that couples limit their families to two children. To promote these goals, ZPG works through political action and education, lobbying on the local and national levels, to make contraception easily available to everyone, to eliminate income tax provisions that encourage large families, and to change attitudes which foster continued population growth. More than 400 chapters decide their own strategies.

Membership includes the monthly *National Reporter*, ZPG's newsletter. Other publications available through ZPG include *The Population Bomb* by P. Ehrlich (95¢; 10 or more, 85¢); *Who Shall Live?* A report on abortion prepared by the American Friends Service Committee ($1.95; 10 or more, $1.35); *Population and the American Future* by the U.S. Population Commission ($1.50; 10 or more, $1.35); *The Case for Small Families* by E. J. Lieberman (5¢; 10 to 499, 4¢; 500 or more, 3.5¢); and *Population Bibliography* (5¢; 10 to 499, 4¢; 500 or more, 3.5¢). Buttons, posters, bumper stickers, and 10- to 30-second radio tapes are also available.

Prison Groups

DISTRICT OF COLUMBIA COMMISSION ON THE STATUS OF WOMEN. See 266.

SACRAMENTO COMMUNITY COMMISSION FOR WOMEN. See 263.

499 WOMEN'S PRISON ASSOCIATION AND HOME. 110 2 Ave., New York, N.Y. 10003. (212) 674-1163. Founded 1844. Michele Smollar, Exec. Dir.

A nonprofit, publicly supported organization to rehabilitate women prisoners by providing counseling, housing, and help in securing employment. In 1972, with the Ford Foundation, the WPA studied the situation of women in the correctional system in New York and the United States. Also initiated in 1972 was Court Diversion, a community program enabling women convicts to live outside of prison under the aegis of the WPA instead of going to prison. WPA also conducts a Work Release Program and a Children of Offenders Program.

500 WOMEN'S PRISON PROJECT. 3189 16 St., San Francisco, Calif. 94103. (415) 863-1604. Founded October 1971. Betty Wood.

A prison support group, which provides transportation for friends and family members of prisoners in the California Institution for Women; conveys information about community alternatives; and holds general meetings inside the prison to exchange information on health care issues, drugs, child care, and personal problems. The group also maintains a speakers' bureau, and publishes a newsletter, *Connections*.

Self-Defense and Anti-Rape

CELL 16. See 188.

CHICAGO WOMEN'S LIBERATION UNION HEALTH PROJECT. See 184.

CHICAGO WOMEN'S LIBERATION UNION RAPE CRISIS LINE. See 184.

DISTRICT OF COLUMBIA COMMISSION ON THE STATUS OF WOMEN. See 266.

INDIANAPOLIS MAYOR'S TASK FORCE ON WOMEN, CITY OF INDIANAPOLIS. See 283.

501 LOS ANGELES COMMISSION ON ASSAULTS AGAINST WOMEN. 218 S. Venice Blvd., Venice, Calif. 90291. (213) 653-6333. Founded June 1973. Lauri Gindoff, 27A Fleet St., Marina Del Rey, Calif. 90291.

Established "to stop rape and to stop the humiliation which victims meet at the hands of police, hospitals, courts and society." The commission operates a 24-hour rape crisis telephone line and a rap group for victims; works with police, hospitals, and the court system to work to change laws; and plans to institute self-defense classes and to compile lists of sympathetic doctors, lawyers, and mental health professionals. A pamphlet is available for $1.

502 RAPE CRISIS CENTER. Box 2971, University City, Mo. 63130. (314) 727-2727. Founded March 1973. 35 members.

A volunteer organization organized by and for women which operates an emergency telephone "hotline" from 6 p.m. to 7 a.m. every night to offer aid to rape victims: transportation to hospitals, health and legal information, counseling, self-defense, and educational workshops. The center maintains a speakers' bureau, participates in conferences, and publishes a newsletter.

SUFFOLK COUNTY COMMUNITY COLLEGE WOMEN'S GROUP RAPE INFORMATION CENTER. See 209.

WASHINGTON AREA WOMEN'S CENTER. See 182.

503 WOMEN'S ANTI-RAPE GROUP. 243 W. 20 St., New York, N.Y. 10011. (212) 255-9802.

An activist group combating rape, of which, according to the group, there were 3,000 reported in New York City in 1972. The group meets every Thursday night at 6:30, and urges women to "report rape to the police, to refuse to answer questions concerning chastity, and to refuse to accept the blame for rape." The organization protests, "by letter, by phone and by public demonstration, mistreatment of women by police, hospitals, courts and public opinion."

WOMEN'S CENTER RAPE CRISIS CENTER (Cambridge, Mass.). See 192.

WOMEN'S LIBERATION CENTER (New York, N.Y.). See 205.

WOMEN'S LIBERATION CENTER OF PHILADELPHIA. See 220.

WOMEN'S LIBERATION UNION OF RHODE ISLAND. See 222.

504 THE WOMEN'S MARTIAL ARTS UNION (WMAU). Box 1463, New York, N.Y. 10027. Founded October 1972.

New York feminists involved in the martial arts (karate, judo, aikido, and other fighting systems). The organization will promote communications among women in the martial arts throughout the country, and hopes to aid others in finding ways to fight the sexism found in most martial arts schools. Current projects include developing a speakers and demonstration service, and compiling a file on the various martial arts schools in New York and their attitudes towards women. Future projects will include: developing a system of self-defense for women based on their own needs and physiologies that would combine elements of the different martial arts; setting up self-defense and martial arts classes that will be more relevant to women's needs; and establishing a women's martial arts center where classes could be held as well as space provided for women to work out for general physical fitness purposes (at N.Y. Women's Liberation Bldg., 243 W. 20 St., New York, N.Y.). WMAU has available an article explaining some of the basic aspects of the martial arts and self-defense courses for those who know little about the subject. The article also provides information on how to choose a good school—what to look for in price, equipment, instruction, etc. (25¢).

WOODMERE WOMEN'S CENTER. See 211.

Lesbian Interests

AIN'T I A WOMAN. See 40.

AMAZON QUARTERLY. See 42.

505 ATLANTA LESBIAN FEMINIST ALLIANCE. 1190 Mansfield Ave., N.E., Atlanta, Ga. 30307. (404) 524-3192. Founded July 1972. Lorraine Fontana, Corinne Smith.

A women's social, educational, and political organization working toward the ending of legal, social, religious, and other descrimination against lesbians as women and as gay people. The alliance maintains a women's center, a feminist and gay library, and a speakers' bureau; produces a radio show; offers counseling, educational programs, discussion groups, and aid for women involved in legal battles.

506 DAUGHTERS OF BILITIS. Chapters: 1005 Market St., No. 402, San Francisco, Calif. 94103. (415) 861-8689; Rm. 323, 419 Boylston St., Boston, Mass. 02116. (617) 262-1592; Box 62, Fanwood, N.J. 07023. (201) 674-1111; Box 162, Ada, Okla. 74820; Box 5944, Dallas, Tex. 75222. (214) 824-0770. Founded 1955 (San Francisco).

"A nationwide network of Lesbian/Feminist organizations . . . striving to create and maintain a multifaceted program which includes educational, social service, civil rights and women's liberation activities." DOB is also a "home for the Lesbian, where she can relax with others like herself, socialize, and feel comfortable and at ease in a congenial atmosphere . . . . DOB's stand on Lesbianism is that it is not sin, sickness or criminal, but a completely normal and valid alternate lifestyle on a par with any other." The organization is also interested in encouraging responsible research dealing with homosexuality, and changing the penal code, to remove prejudice against lesbianism. The DOB groups offer meetings, counseling, referral services, consciousness-raising, speakers' bureaus, and social get-togethers. "Membership in DOB is open to any female 18 years or over, regardless of race, creed, color, national origin, marital status or sexual orientation." Publications are: *Focus: A Journal for Gay Women* (see 54); *Lazette* (N.J. DOB, newsletter, m., $2.50/yr.); and *Sisters: A Magazine by and for Gay Women* (see 75).

507 EVE OF DETROIT. 18700 Woodward St., Detroit, Mich. 48203. (313) 892-7161. Founded May 1973.

A lesbian-feminist group to help lesbians grow together as women, to raise dual lesbian-feminist consciousness. The organization plans to open a lesbian-feminist resource center and coffeehouse, to establish craft workshops, and to publish a newspaper. The group holds rap sessions on Tuesday nights, and sells T-shirts with "Eve" written on them ($3.50 each).

508   GAY COMMUNITY SERVICES CENTER. 1614 Wilshire Blvd., Los Angeles, Calif. 90017. (213) 482-3062. Founded October 1971. Ken Bartley, Adm. Dir.

"A professional and paraprofessional social service agency established within and operated under the laws and regulations of the State of California governing all nonprofit corporations. The Center, which is in its first year of operation, was founded by local gay men and women to meet the needs of their own community. Virtually all the services of the Center are provided free to the gay community." The center runs on donations. The following services are available: a 24-hour gay hotline; counseling; food and shelter programs; a job clinic, with employment counseling and placement services; legal counseling and referral; medical referral; senior citizens program; a youth program; a thrift shop and recycling center; a gynecological clinic; social activities; and prisoners, parole, and probation program. The center also sponsors a one-hour radio program on KPFK-FM, dealing with topics of interest to gay women and men.

GAY LIBERATOR. See 55.

GAY SUNSHINE. See 56.

THE LADDER. See 59.

LAVENDER WOMAN. See 14.

509   LESBIAN RESOURCE CENTER. 4224 University Way, N.E., Seattle, Wash. 98105. (206) 632-4747. Founded Summer 1971. Marlene Russ, Tudi Haasl. Hours: 11 a.m.–8 p.m.

Part of the university YWCA program, it is totally staffed by volunteers and coordinated by the YWCA staff. A Survival file, small library, a speakers' bureau, small rap groups, counseling (parental or otherwise), and information on homophile organizations in the Seattle area are available over the phone or in person.

LESBIAN TIDE. See 60.

NEW PALTZ WOMEN'S ALLIANCE. See 208.

SAPPHO '71. See 29.

SOJOURNER TRUTH PRESS. See 31.

VIOLET PRESS. See 36.

WOMEN'S CENTER (Cambridge, Mass.). See 192.

WOMEN'S LIBERATION CENTER OF PHILADELPHIA LESBIAN HOT LINE. See 220.

WOMEN'S LIBERATION UNION (Kansas City, Mo.). See 195.

Political Action

510 THE FEMINIST PARTY. 311 W. 24 St., New York, N.Y. 10011. (212) 242-2046. Founded November 1971. Irene Davall, Nat. Coor. 110 chapters.

Goals are "economic and political guerrilla warfare." Has held conventions and demonstrations to dramatize and combat sexism, racism, and imperialism in politics, schools, prisons, employment, and the media. A column by Irene Davall, entitled "The Liberated Woman," is available bimonthly for local newspapers through the Yorktowner, 1766 Front St., Yorktown Heights, N.Y.

511 NATIONAL WOMAN'S PARTY. 144 Constitution Ave., N.E., Washington, D.C. 20002. (202) 546-1210. Founded 1913. Elizabeth Chittick, Nat. Chpn. Dues: $5-$100.

Founded by Alice Paul, NWP was the originator of the first equal rights amendment to the Constitution in 1923, and has been working for its passage continuously. The NWP has also been active in ensuring attention is given to the rights of women by international organizations, notably the United Nations and the Inter-American Commission of Women. The NWP is presently sponsoring a bill in Congress to establish their headquarters, the Sewall-Belmont House, as a National Historic site, which will include many items of historical interest to women. The NWP maintains a speakers' bureau and the Florence Bayard Hilles Library, which houses "the most comprehensive" collection of books on the Equal Rights Amendment, including many items which are unique. The library is not now open to the public. Publications of the NWP are an irregular bulletin, free to members, and a pamphlet, *Answers to Questions on the Equal Rights Amendment.*

512 NATIONAL WOMEN'S POLITICAL CAUCUS. 1302 18 St., Washington, D.C. 20036. (703) 785-2911. Founded July 1971. 50,000 members.

"A multi-partisan organization founded to awaken, organize, and assert the vast political power that women, 52 percent of the population, represent." The caucus plans to do this by building state and local caucus organizations, educating women about the depths of discrimination which affect them, raising women's issues at all levels of government and in campaigns, and electing and monitoring appointments of large numbers of women to public office. The organization has established caucuses in 48 states, and worked with state and local leadership, providing organizing techniques and speakers. The NWPC was active in ensuring reasonable representation for women as delegates to both National Party Conventions, and keeps track of and supports women running for office and those male candidates who take strong stands on women's issues. The caucus is working strongly for the ratification of the ERA and other pieces of legislation of interest to women.

A list of state contacts follows (asterisk indicates members of National Steering Committee).

ALASKA
*Jan Erickson, 2261 Wheystone St., Vienna, Va 22180
Jane Rice, Box 71, Naknek 99633

ALABAMA
*P. S. McDaniel, 5106 Cater Dr., Montgomery 36108. (205) 288-0012

ARIZONA
*Janet Andress, 1717 E. Turquoise Ave., Phoenix 85016. (602) 944-8871
Karen Lamb, 2139 N. Columbus, Tuscon 85712. (602) 944-8871

ARKANSAS
*Judith Rogers, Box 5285, N. Little Rock 72201. (501) 374-9892 or 374-1027
Pat Youngdahl, 7108 Rockwood Rd., Little Rock 72201. (501) 663-8284

CALIFORNIA
*Alicia Escalante (At large), 5602 Monterey Rd., Los Angeles 90042
Barbara Zerbe Macnab, 1717 Berkeley Way, Berkeley 94103. (415) 845-4256

COLORADO
*Mary Scharf (At large), 2909 Forest St., Denver 80207
*Cynthia Small, 1571 S. Clayton, Denver 80210. (303) 287-3311 (H) or 777-2865 (O)

CONNECTICUT
Donna Brunstad, R.D. #1, W. Redding 06875
*Lee Novick, 62 Edgewood Way, New Haven 06515. (203) 389-4911

DELAWARE
Eleanor Doban, Box 3978, Greenville 19807
*Janet Niland, 812 Kenyon La., Newark 19711. (302) 368-3714 H

DISTRICT OF COLUMBIA
*Penny Addiss, 2700 Conn. Ave., N.W., Washington, D.C. 20008. (202) 387-8172
Donna Allen, 3306 Ross Pl., N.W., Washington, D.C. 20008. (202) 966-7783
Robin Beckett, Senate Interior Comm., 3204 New Senate Bldg., Washington, D.C. 20510. (202) 225-2657
Joyce Errecart, 1131 Longworth Bldg., Washington, D.C. 20515. (202) 225-4115

FLORIDA
Dorothy DaValt, 1305 E. Fisher St., Pensacola 32503. (904) 432-0864, 222-6526, or 224-1161
*Monna Lighte, 1429 N. Venetian Way, Miami 33139. (305) 379-4855 or 379-4475

GEORGIA
*Mary Bankester, 18 Peachtree Ave., N.E., Apt. G4, Atlanta 30305. (404) 261-0976 (H) or 897-4001 (O)
*Betty Harmon (At large), 52 Wakefield Dr., N.E., Atlanta 30309. (404) 351-3382

HAWAII
Glenn Brooks, 1675 Hoolulu Rd., Wahiawa 96786. (808) 621-5941

IDAHO
Ann Martinez, 518 S. 6 St., Pocatello 83201. (208) 233-4380
Mary Swanson, 295 E. Anderson, Idaho Falls 83401. (208) 522-6191
Lana Vance, Box 8533, Boise 83707

INDIANA
Jane DuComb, 16329 State Rd. 23, Granger 46530. (291) 272-8188

IOWA
*Roxanne Conlin, 1623 S.W. Evans, Des Moines 50315. (515) 285-0962 or 281-5353

ILLINOIS
Susan Bellow, 1765 E. 55 St., Chicago 60615. (312) 324-6868

KANSAS
*Kay Camin, Dept. Economics, Wichita State Univ., Wichita 67208. (316) 682-5352 or 689-3223

Annabelle Haupt, 1006 Amidon, Wichita 67203. (316) 264-4197

KENTUCKY
*Pam Elam, 307 Euclid Ave., Apt. #8, Lexington 41016. (606) 254-7409

LOUISIANA
Karline Tierney, 1025 E. Lakeview Dr., Baton Rouge 70810. (504) 766-3361

*Carolyn Tucker, 3528 Virgil Blvd., New Orleans 70122. (504) 288-8218 or 529-4444

MAINE
Barbara McGough, 18 Buck La., Cumberland, Foreside 04110. (207) 781-5610

MARYLAND
*Sigrid Deeds, 5042 Hesperus Dr., Columbia 21044. (301) 997-3250 (O) or 730-8992 (H)

MASSACHUSETTS
*Gerladine Pleshaw, 128 Shore Ave., Quincy 02169. (617) 472-2826 or 723-4400

*Marge Schiller (At-large), 49 Rockwood Rd., Hingham 02043

MICHIGAN
*Lavon Bleissner (At-large), 404 E. Michigan Ave., Lansing 48933. (517) 371-1498 or 332-0848

Dorothy Haener, 8000 E. Jefferson, Detroit 48214. (517) 373-2421

Susan McPhee, 223 Delta, E. Lansing 48823. (517) 351-4208 (H) or 332-0848 (O)

MINNESOTA
*Mary Ziegenhagen, 158 Birnamwood Dr., Burnsville 55337. (612) 890-6847

MISSISSIPPI
Tina Benagh, Box 4470, Miss. State Univ. 39762. (601) 323-8592 (H) or 325-3826 (O)

MISSOURI
*Mary Lou Bussaburger, 1914 Princeton, Columbia 65201. (314) 445-4147

Ora Lee Malone (At-large), 4605 Shirley Pl., St. Louis 63115

*Doris Quinn, 3302 N. Osage, Independence 64050. (816) 254-1910 or 796-3900 Ext. 523

MONTANA
*Geraldine Travis, 5413 6th Ave. S., Great Falls 59401. (406) 453-9673

NEBRASKA
Ann Crowley, 4014 Burt, Omaha 68131. (402) 556-6890

Sr. Mary Gabriel, Good Shepherd, 1106 N. 36th, Omaha 68131

Jeanne O'Hara, 3344 Dudley, Lincoln 68503. (402) 466-2452

NEVADA
*Barbara Bennett, 123 Carnation, Reno 89502

NEW HAMPSHIRE
*Sylvia Chaplain, 7 Wendover Way, Bedford 03102. (603) 625-5335

NEW JERSEY
*Judy Murphy, 366 Ogden Ave., Teaneck 07666. (201) 837-4555

NEW MEXICO
*Hannah Best, 4304 Rio Grande Blvd. N.W., Albuquerque 87107. (505) 344-1816

Mary Walters, 4108 Delmar N.E., Albuquerque 87110. (505) 344-5920

NEW YORK
*Ferne Steckler, 35 Wood Lane S., Woodmere 11598. (516) 295-1255

NORTH CAROLINA
*Pat Locke, Box 4363, Charlotte
28204. (704) 334-0740

NORTH DAKOTA
*Cheryl Watkins, 1012 S. 9th St.,
Fargo 58102. (701) 235-0714 (H)
or 232-3351 (O)

OHIO
*Jo Marino, 910 Ludlow Ave.,
Cincinnati 45220. (513) 541-0400

OKLAHOMA
*Donna Meyer, 3406 Venice Blvd. N.,
Oklahoma City 73112. (405) 943-
8284

OREGON
Jeanne Dost, 7620 N.W. Mountain View
Dr., Corvallis 97330. (503) 745-5416
(H) or 754-1335 (O)

*Margaret Patoine, 2552 Alder, Eugene
97405

PENNSYLVANIA
*Kay Camp, 200 Hughes Rd., King of
Prussia 19406. (215) 687-2546

RHODE ISLAND
*Susan McCalmont, 49 Rochambeau
Ave., Providence 02906

SOUTH CAROLINA
Barbara Snyder, P.O. Box 11688,
Columbia 29211. (803) 779-5231
(O), 252-9634, or 782-8676

SOUTH DAKOTA
*Roylene Schwab, Rt. 3, Box 129,
Aberdeen 57401. (605) 225-6711

TENNESSEE
*Kitty Smith, 829 Kirkwood La.,
Nashville 37204.

TEXAS
*Jane Hickie, 6921 Thorncliffe, Austin
78731. (512) 345-2730

UTAH
Brenda Hancock, 1116 E. 4th St., Salt
Lake City 84102. (801) 359-5860

VERMONT
*Caryl Stewart, Box 187, Shelburne
05482. (802) 864-9807

VIRGINIA
*Flora Crater, 4310 Barbour Rd.,
Falls Church 22043. (703) 573-8716.

WASHINGTON
*Marilyn Sloan, 4547 Fourth Ave.
N.E., Seattle 98105. (206) ME 2-5002

WISCONSIN
*Kathryn Morrison, 885 Stonebridge
Apts., Platteville 53818. (608) 342-
1576

WYOMING
*Maco Miller, 111 14th W., Casper
82601. (307) 234-2317

Special Interest Caucus Contacts:

BLACK
Joan Cashin, 416 Owens Dr. S.E.,
Huntsville, Ala. 35801. (205)
536-6975 (O) or 536-3240 (H)

Gwen Kyles, 2215 S. Parkway E.,
Memphis, Tenn. 38114. (901) 323-
0565

CHICANA
Lupe Anguiano, Box 7306, San
Antonio, Tex. 78207. (512) 224-
7526

NATIVE AMERICAN
Shirley Hill Witt, Colorado State Bldg.,
Colorado Springs, Colo. 80903

PUERTO RICAN
Carole DeSenne, 516 Fairfax Ave.,
Norfolk, Va. 23507

Carmen L. Perez, 253 W. 72 St.,
New York, N.Y. 10023 (212) 724-
8184 (H) or 661-4147 (O)

*Marisara Pont, 206 Pres. Bamirel,
Puerto Rico 00918. (809) 723-0090
Ext. 242 or 766-5605

RADICAL WOMEN
Sue Silber, 726 Linwood Ave., Buffalo,
N.Y. 14209. (716) 884-0629

SEXUAL PRIVACY
Elaine Noble, 70 Daniel St., Franklin, Mass. 02038. (617) 528-4492

UNION WOMEN
Maxine Lee, Communications Workers of America, 3033 Fannin St., Houston, Tex. 77004

NEWFOUNDLAND STATUS OF WOMEN COUNCIL. See 236.

ONTARIO COMMITTEE ON THE STATUS OF WOMEN. See 238.

RADICAL WOMEN (Seattle, Wash.). See 227.

SASKATCHEWAN ACTION COMMITTEE. See 244.

513 SIREN ANARCHO-FEMINISTS. 713 W. Armitage St., Chicago, Ill. 60614. Founded June 1970. Arlene Meyers.

"We believe that a Women's Revolutionary Movement must not mimic but destroy all vestiges of the male-dominated power structure, up to and including the apex of that power structure, the State itself—with its whole ancient and dismal apparatus of jails, armies and armed robbery (taxation); with all of its murder; with all of its grotesque and repressive legislative and military attempts, internal and external, to interfere with people's private lives and freely-chosen cooperative ventures. We are all socialists .... Anarchism ... is the affirmation of human freedom and dignity expressed in a negative, cautionary term signifying that no person should rule or dominate another person by force or threat of force. Anarchism indicates what people should not do to one another. Socialism, on the other hand, means all the groovy things people can do and build together, once they are able to combine efforts and resources on the basis of common interest, rationality and creativity." The group publishes *Siren Feminists Newsletter* ($2/yr.; $5, institutions).

VANCOUVER STATUS OF WOMEN. See 232.

514 WOMEN'S LOBBY. 1345 G St., S.W., Washington, D.C. 20003. (202) 547-0082. Founded August 1972. Carol Burris, Pres. 30 Washington lobbyists; 40 state organizations.

Registered professional lobbyists to promote full legal equality for women through legislation. Major goals are child care, pension reform, health care, minimum wage for domestics, women's education act, welfare reform, and credit legislation. The group publishes *Women's Lobby Quarterly* ($10 contribution).

Professions

515 AD HOC COMMITTEE ON THE STATUS OF WOMEN IN JOURNALISM EDUCATION. University of Nebraska School of Journalism, Lincoln, Nebr. 68508. (402) 472-3045. Wilma Crumley, Chpn.

A group of educators in journalism concerned with the status of women in the profession.

516 AMERICAN ASSOCIATION FOR THE ADVANCEMENT OF SCIENCE, OFFICE OF OPPORTUNITIES IN SCIENCE. 1776 Massachusetts Ave., N.W., Washington, D.C. 20036. (202) 467-4496. Founded January 1973. Janet W. Brown, Dir.

"To enhance the status and increase the numbers of women and minority scientists in all the sciences and engineering." Also aims to sharpen public recognition of accomplishments of women and minority scientists. The group formulates rosters of women and scientists, and offers counseling in career opportunities.

517 AMERICAN ASSOCIATION FOR THE ADVANCEMENT OF SCIENCE, WOMEN'S CAUCUS. University of Georgia, Athens, Ga. 30601. (404) 542-1334. Founded December 1971. Virginia Walbot, Dept. of Biochemistry. 150 members.

Aims to make the AAAS recognize the problems of women through the creation of an Office of Opportunities in Science (516). The caucus meets informally to suggest programs to the Office and the Council of the AAAS.

518 AMERICAN ASSOCIATION OF IMMUNOLOGISTS, COMMITTEE ON THE STATUS OF WOMEN. Institute of Technology, 77 Massachusetts Ave., Cambridge, Mass. 02139. (617) 253-1000. Lisa Steiner, Biology Dept.

Investigates the role of women in immunology.

519 AMERICAN ASSOCIATION OF UNIVERSITY PROFESSORS, COMMITTEE W. 1 Dupont Circle, Washington, D.C. 20003. (202) 466-8050. Founded 1918, reactivated 1970. Margaret L. Rumbarger, Assoc. Secy.

Aims to help secure the rights of academic women by education on local campuses and on state and national levels, and to encourage institutions to eliminate discrimination and undertake programs of internal reform. The committee has worked on policies regarding child-bearing and child-rearing leave, part-time appointments, and antinepotism; and serves as a clearinghouse for information on women in academe. Over 200 local committees are in existence.

520   AMERICAN ECONOMICS ASSOCIATION, COMMITTEE ON THE STATUS OF WOMEN IN THE ECONOMICS PROFESSION. 131 Kent St., Brookline, Mass. 02146. (617) 731-1722. Founded 1971. H. B. Munzer, Exec. Secy.

Established to "investigate conformity" to the following principles adopted by the AEA: (1) women shall be encouraged to study economics; (2) no department of economics shall discriminate against women students with respect to admission or financial aid; (3) no employer shall discriminate against women economists; (4) salaries, fringe benefits, facilities, and resources for research shall be the same for women and for men; (5) there shall be no distinction between men and women as to what constitutes full employment; and (6) employment may not be denied to any qualified economist on the grounds of family relationship to another employee. With accumulated data on the supply of women economists maintained in a roster, the committee has attempted to respond to the demand for women economists, and has worked out programs for affirmative action. The first annual report appeared in the *American Economic Review* (May 1973), and the committee publishes a newsletter, which includes job openings.

521   AMERICAN FEDERATION OF TEACHERS, WOMEN'S RIGHTS COMMITTEE. 1012 14 St., N.W., Washington, D.C. 20005. (202) 737-6141. Marjorie Stern, Chpn., 520 Summit St., E., Seattle, Wash. 98102.

Formed to implement policy resolutions of the AFT, dealing with women in unions, the ERA, sexism in teaching materials, parental leave, continuing education for women, women's rights, counseling of women, and day care.

The following publications are available from this committee.

Kaye, Nancy and Stern, Marjorie. *A Guide to Improving Maternity Leave . . . Contract Clauses.*
Lulkin, Sheli. *Fight for ERA Reaches Crucial Stage.*
Mulrooney, Virginia. *Women in Higher Education.*
Schmid, Anne McEvoy. *Let Brother Bake the Cake.*
Stern, Marjorie. *California's Children's Centers.*
Stern, Marjorie. *How to Get Started in Women's Rights.*
Stern, Marjorie. *Setting Goals for Local Women's Rights Committees Using AFT Policy as a Guide.*
Stern, Marjorie. *Teacher Unions and Women's Rights.*
Stern, Marjorie. *Who Were They? Some American Feminists Who Came Before Us.*
Women in Education: Changing Sexist Practices in the Classroom (a 74-page resource manual, $1).
Women's Rights Policy Resolution (single sopy, 10¢).

Also available from the Women's Rights Committee are copies of articles dealing with topics such as: sexist practices in the classroom, day care facts, and legislation affecting discrimination against women.

522   AMERICAN HISTORICAL ASSOCIATION, ROSTER OF WOMEN HISTORIANS. 400 A St., S.E., Washington, D.C. 20003. (202) 544-2422. Founded 1971. Eleanor F. Straub, Asst. Exec. Secy. 2,000 members.

To inform institutions about the existence of women in various fields of history for employment purposes as well as for statistics and as a body of information for HEW. The roster has been computerized by the University of Maryland in order to provide speedy and efficient service to employers. Institutions seeking candidates submit the job description and requirements to the roster, which will promptly forward curriculum vitae on qualified women to the employing institution. Departments using the roster are charged a fee of $12. The roster also includes listings of women with administrative experience and interest in working in this area.

523   AMERICAN INSTITUTE OF PLANNERS/AMERICAN SOCIETY OF PLANNING OFFICIALS, WOMEN'S RIGHTS COMMITTEE. 1313 E. 60 St., Chicago, Ill. 60637. (312) 324-3400. Founded 1970. Karen Hapgood. 12 members.

"To establish equal opportunity for women within the planning profession, and in planning agencies, firms, etc." Projects include an ASPO-HUD-sponsored workshop in Planning for Women, a women's planning roster, and policies and guidelines for equal treatment of women planners. Also in process is a research paper on women as clients in planning. Various research papers on women in planning can be obtained from Ms. Hapgood.

524   AMERICAN LIBRARY ASSOCIATION, SOCIAL RESPONSIBILITIES ROUND TABLE, TASK FORCE ON WOMEN. 50 E. Huron St., Chicago, Ill. 60611. (312) 944-6780. Founded June 1970. Lynne Rhoads, Coor., 4004 Whitman Ave., N., Seattle, Wash. 98103. 150 members.

Works for equal opportunity in library education, hiring, retention, fringe benefits and promotion, and the elimination of sexism in children's literature. Operates a job roster and a talent bank. The task force has published *Women in Librarianship*, a bibliography of literature published since 1920 on the status of women in librarianship, and a newsletter (irreg., $1 donation).

525   THE AMERICAN MEDICAL WOMEN'S ASSOCIATION, INC. 1740 Broadway, New York, N.Y. 10019. (212) 586-8683. Founded 1915.

A service organization whose purposes are: "to further the art and science of medicine; to promote interests common to women physicians and the public; to aid and encourage premedical, medical and post-graduate medical students; to foster medical relief projects; and to cooperate with other organizations having comparable interests." A prime goal is the recruitment of qualified, capable young women for the medical profession. The association publishes the *Journal of the American Medical Women's Association*; *Medicine . . . A Woman's Career*; *Medicine Can Be for You*; and *Career Choices for Women in Medicine*. There is also a 30-minute roundtable discussion of women in medicine suitable for school libraries (cassettes) or educational radio (reel-to-reel tape).

526   AMERICAN PHILOLOGICAL ASSOCIATION (CLASSICAL STUDIES), COMMITTEE ON WOMEN. Wellesley College, Wellesley, Mass. 02181. (617) 235-0320. Prof. Mary R. Lefkowitz, Chpn., Depts. of Greek and Latin.

Investigates discrimination against women and minority groups in the profession, ensures equal opportunity, and provides information on women's studies. The committee conducted a survey on the status of Women in Classics (Summer 1973), and published it in *Transactions & Proceedings of the American Philological Association* (No. 104, 1974).

527 AMERICAN PHILOLOGICAL ASSOCIATION, WOMEN'S CAUCUS.
Hunter College, 695 Park Ave., New York, N.Y. 10021. (212) 360-2406.
Founded December 1972. Prof. Sarah B. Pomeroy, Chpn., Dept. of Classics.

Established to improve the status of women in the Classics profession. Projects include the compilation of a roster of female classical scholars and the encouragement of women into high positions in the APA hierarchy and in various organizations related to the field of Classics. The caucus publishes a *Caucus Newsletter*.

528 AMERICAN PHYSICAL SOCIETY, COMMITTEE ON WOMEN IN
PHYSICS. 335 E. 45 St., New York, N.Y. 10017. (212) 685-2014. Founded
April 1971. Dr. Esther M. Conwell, Xerox, Xerox Sq., W-114, Rochester,
N.Y. 14644. 7 members.

Created "to study the situation of women physicists and to make recommendations based on this study." The committee surveyed the position of women physicists in colleges, government and national laboratories, industry, and universities, and published a report, *Women in Physics*. The committee also maintains a roster of women physicists, available to organizations and physics administrators, containing an alphabetical listing of names, with addresses and other information; classification of entries by degree and type of employer; and classification of entries by degree and field of specialization ($5 prepaid, $6 billed).

529 AMERICAN PSYCHOLOGICAL ASSOCIATION, AD HOC COMMITTEE
ON WOMEN IN PSYCHOLOGY. 1200 17 St., N.W., Washington, D.C.
20036. (202) 833-7594. Founded 1973. Dr. Brenda Gurel.

A professional association, which aims to further the goals of women in psychology, and is investigating sexism in graduate training. The association has special publications available. Write for further information.

530 AMERICAN SOCIETY FOR MICROBIOLOGY, COMMITTEE ON THE
STATUS OF WOMEN MICROBIOLOGISTS. George Washington University
Medical Center, 2300 I St., N.W., Washington, D.C. 20037. (202) 331-6535.
Founded April 1970. Dr. Mary Louise Robbins, Chpn., Dept. of
Microbiology.

Investigates the present situation regarding the status of women members, makes recommendations, and actively works with institutions and departments to ensure full and equal opportunity for educational, career, and personal development for all microbiologists. The committee publishes articles (available on request) resulting from membership surveys; conducts seminars; and maintains a roster of qualified women microbiologists.

531 AMERICAN SOCIETY FOR PUBLIC ADMINISTRATION, STANDING
COMMITTEE ON WOMEN IN PUBLIC ADMINISTRATION. 1225 Connecticut Ave., N.W., Washington, D.C. 20036. (202) 785-3255. Founded
December 1972. Dona Wolf, Prog. Devel. Dir. 35 members.

Established to promote equal employment and educational opportunities for women in the public service. The committee maintains a national network of liaisons from local chapters of the ASPA, encourages affirmative action programs, and serves as an exchange for information regarding programs for women in government.

**532   AMERICAN SOCIETY OF BIOLOGICAL CHEMISTS, COMMITTEE ON
THE STATUS OF WOMEN.** 9650 Rockville Pike, Bethesda, Md. 20014.
(301) 530-7145. Founded April 1972. Dr. Loretta Leive.

"Devoted to obtaining complete equality for female members of the professional constituency, all female biochemists with doctoral degrees. Presently establishing a computerized registry of female and minority group biochemists, supporting relevant legislation and prodding department chairmen and administrators to
achieve greater rights for women."

**533   AMERICAN STATISTICAL ASSOCIATION, CAUCUS FOR WOMEN
IN STATISTICS.** 165 West End Ave., New York, N.Y. 10023. (212) 787-
4319. Founded August 1969. Regina Lowenstein. 90 members.

"Professional statisticians interested in employment, education, and development of statisticians who are women." The caucus sponsors a session of papers at
the annual meeting of the ASA, and publishes a quarterly newsletter which features
job listings and reports on sexism in the literature.

534   AMERICAN STUDIES ASSOCIATION, COMMITTEE ON WOMEN. Box 1,
Logan Hall, Univ. of Pa., Philadelphia, Pa. 19104. Founded Fall 1972.
Joanna Schneider Zangrando, Nat. Coor., 501 Mineola Ave., Akron, Ohio
44320. (216) 836-5878.

Aims to study and help meet needs of women in the American Studies Association; to improve the status and participation of women in the ASA; to inform
women of affirmative action legislation; to act as a grievance committee; and to
gather information on women's studies. The Committee on Women is compiling a
roster of women in American Studies and a listing of periodical articles on women
in the annual *American Quarterly*. Information on the committee is published in
the *American Quarterly* under the heading "Women's Committee" in the American
Calendar section. A pamphlet is available containing resolutions on women approved by the ASA Council in April 1972. KNOW, Inc. (See 13) has published two
volumes which contain the results of surveys on the status of women in the ASA.

**535   ASSOCIATION FOR ASIAN STUDIES, COMMITTEE ON THE STATUS
OF WOMEN.** 1 Lane Hall, University of Michigan, Ann Arbor, Mich. 48104.
Founded 1971. Joyce K. Kallgren, Chpn., Center for Chinese Studies, Uni-
versity of California, Berkeley, Calif. 94720. 9 members.

Aims to increase participation of women in the organization and to develop a
directory of women in Asian studies.

536   ASSOCIATION FOR WOMEN IN MATHEMATICS. Dept. of Mathematics,
American University, Washington, D.C. 20016. (202) 686-2393. Founded
January 1971. Mary Gray. 700 members.

"To promote the study of mathematics by women and to assist women mathematicians in their careers." The association supplies guidance material for young
women, distributes information concerning jobs, conducts discussions and meetings, and publishes a monthly newsletter ($2/yr.).

537   ASSOCIATION FOR WOMEN IN PSYCHOLOGY. 7012 Western Ave.,
Chevy Chase, Md. 20015. (301) 654-5401. Founded September 1969.
Dorothy Camara. 700 members. Dues: $10; $3, students.

A nonprofit scientific and educational organization dedicated to the following: ending the role psychology has had in perpetuating myths about "the nature" of women and men; unbiased research on sex differences; research on alternative sex-roles, child-rearing practices, and life-styles; education within the psychology profession and the public to the psychological, social, political, and economic problems of women; and achieving equality of opportunity within the psychology profession. The association maintains a job placement service and feminist therapist roster. Although the association is composed primarily of female psychologists, it is open to all. The organization publishes a bimonthly newsletter (free to members; $15/yr. to institutions).

538 ASSOCIATION OF AMERICAN LAW SCHOOLS, COMMITTEE ON WOMEN IN LEGAL EDUCATION. University of Connecticut School of Law, West Hartford, Conn. 06117. Founded 1969. Prof. Shirley R. Bysiewicz. 25 members.

Established to encourage and assist women toward full participation with men in legal education. The committee conducts surveys on the status of women in legal education, and held a Symposium on Law School Curriculum and the Legal Rights of Women, in October 1972. The committee is preparing a roster of women lawyers interested or engaged in law school teaching or administration. Reports are regularly included in *AALS Newsletter*. For papers and videotapes relating to the October 1972 symposium, write to Sandra Mitchell Caron, 536 E. 87 St., New York, N.Y. An article on the surveys appears in *Journal of Legal Education* (vol. 25, 1973, p. 5).

539 ASSOCIATION OF WOMEN IN SCIENCE. 1818 R St., N.W., Washington, D.C. 20009. (202) 483-5814. Founded April 1971. Dr. Estelle Ramey, Pres., Georgetown University Medical School, Physiology and Biophysics, Washington, D.C. 1500 members. Dues: $18; $5, students; $25, institutions.

"A professional association set up to promote equal opportunities for women to enter the professions and to achieve their career goals." The association, which is open to women professionals and graduate students in the sciences or social sciences, has developed a computerized registry; participated in law suits on behalf of professional women; and works on affirmative action regarding advancement of professional women in colleges and universities and the elimination of sexism in textbooks. A newsletter, published quarterly, is free to members.

540 CENTER FOR WOMEN IN MEDICINE. The Medical College of Pennsylvania, 3300 Henry Ave., Philadelphia, Pa. 19129. (215) 849-0400. Founded July 1973. Nina B. Woodside.

"Designed to interest and recruit women into the field of medicine and deal with the special problems of women in the medical profession. . . . It is anticipated that model programs for recruitment and training will be developed and that the office will help to establish such programs in other locales." The library has a collection of materials on women, with focus on women in medicine, and books written by women M.D.'s.

541 COMMITTEE ON THE STATUS OF WOMEN IN JOURNALISM. College of Journalism and Communication, University of Florida, 234 Stadium St., Gainesville, Fla. 32601. (904) 392-6558. Ramona R. Rush, Chpn. 7 members.

Studies ways to help female students in journalism prepare for careers.

**542   COORDINATING COMMITTEE ON WOMEN IN THE HISTORICAL PRO-
FESSION.** Richmond College, CUNY, Staten Island, N.Y. 10301. (212)
448-8433. Founded 1969. Prof. S. Cooper, Nat. Co-Chpn. 600 members.
Dues: $5.

A caucus on the status of women historians and a clearinghouse for women's
history studies. The committee aims to improve the status of women historians
and women graduate students and to restore women's place in history. A quarterly
newsletter is published.

543   FEDERALLY EMPLOYED WOMEN. 621 National Press Bldg., Washington,
D.C. 20004. (202) 638-4404. Founded 1968. Priscilla B. Ransohoff, Pres.
Dues: $10.

Works to ensure the enforcement of Executive Order 11375 prohibiting discrimination on the basis of sex by Federal contractors and to end sex discrimination in all areas of government employment. Membership is open to all employees
of the Federal government; associate membership is open to those who are not.
FEW publishes a newsletter, *FEW's News and Views* (bi-m., $4/yr. or free with
membership), a pamphlet entitled *A Few Facts About FEW* (free), and two booklets, *Agency Accountability Studies* ($4), and *ABCs of Your Job; A Handbook of
Personnel Management Matters* ($2).

544   FEDERATION OF ORGANIZATIONS FOR PROFESSIONAL WOMEN.
1818 R St., N.W., Washington, D.C. 20009. (202) 483-5814. Founded
November 1972. Pamela Jacklin, Assoc. Dir.

A coordinating body of 25 groups aimed at achieving equality for women in
education and careers, a clearinghouse which collects and disseminates relevant
information, and a resource and referral agency for inquiries relating to the status
of women. A Registry Committee, Legislative Committee, Careers Committee,
and Research Committee conduct various projects. Among the available federation
reports are: *Optimal National Policy on the Status of Women* (Legislative Committee Seminar, $2), *Survey of Rosters and Registries for Women* (Registry Committee
Study, $2), and *Expanding Career Options for Women* (Careers Committee Confer-
ence, $2).

**545   MODERN LANGUAGE ASSOCIATION OF AMERICA, COMMISSION
ON WOMEN.** 62 5 Ave., New York, N.Y. 10011. (212) 691-3200. Founded
1969. Elaine Reuben, Co-Chpn.

Working to improve employment opportunities for academic women, the
commission has sought to alter ideas of women as they appear in academic courses
and in scholarship in the modern languages. Studies have been conducted on the
status of women studying and teaching in the modern languages and on guidelines
for the improvement of the employment of academic women and progress toward
affirmative action in departments granting the Ph.D. in languages. The commission
published, with the Women's Caucus for the Modern Languages, *Academic Women,
Sex Discrimination, and the Law: An Action Handbook*, which describes modes of
redress available to women who have experienced discrimination; and *Female Studies* II, III, IV, and VI (Know, Inc., and the Feminist Press, entries 13 and 7). A collection of papers, sponsored by the commission for presentation at the annual MLA
meeting, has been reprinted as *A Case for Equity* by the National Council of
Teachers of English.

546 NATIONAL ASSOCIATION FOR WOMEN DEANS, ADMINISTRATORS AND COUNSELORS. 1028 Connecticut Ave., N.W., Suite 922, Washington, D.C. 20036. (202) 659-9930. Founded 1916. Joan M. McCall, Exec. Dir. 2,400 members. Dues: $27; $7.50, students.

"The basic purpose of [the NAWDAC] is to provide information, assistance, and support for all women educators as they serve students at all levels of education through performance of student/pupil personnel related functions, such as: guidance, counseling, advising, administration, research, or teaching in an educational institution or agency."

The organization offers the Kathryn Sisson Phillips Fellowship award annually for graduate study in student personnel, counseling and related fields; a placement service for candidates and employers; a roster/talent bank for members available for referral to top-level administrative positions and appointment to governmental advisory committees; and the Ruth Strang Research Award given annually for outstanding research by a woman. The association supports the Equal Rights Amendment; participated in writing the "Joint Statement on Women in Higher Education;" developed a monograph by the Committee on Concerns of Women to offer action plans for implementation of the Joint Statement; and developed affirmative action plans for K-12, based on NAWDAC "Statement on Primary and Secondary Education for Girls and Their Mentors." The association publishes the *Journal of NAWDAC* (q., $7.50). Individual issues ($2 each) on women have been published: *The Women's Movement*, Winter 1973; *Programming for the Education of Women*, Winter 1972; *Femininity, Feminism and Educational Change*, Fall 1972; *Women's Roles, Labels and Stereotypes*, Spring 1971; and *Problems and Opportunities Challenging Women Today*, Fall 1970.

547 NATIONAL ASSOCIATION OF BANK-WOMEN, INC. 111 E. Wacker Dr., Chicago, Ill. 60601. (312) 644-6610. Phyllis Haeger, Exec. Dir. 11, 277 members. Dues: $25; $10, retired members.

A nonprofit professional association of women bank officers in the United States. "More than 120 NABW Groups are organized throughout the United States to serve the banking community and further the careers of women in banking." The association conducts management seminars, regional conferences, and an annual convention; and makes career information available. The group also publishes *NABW Journal* (bi-m.) and pamphlets: *Career for Women in Banking*, and *Money and the Mature Citizen*, available on request (charges made for additional copies).

548 NATIONAL ASSOCIATION OF WOMEN LAWYERS. American Bar Center, 1155 E. 60 St., Chicago, Ill. 60637. (312) 493-0533 ext. 508. Founded 1899. Helen Miney Porter, Pres., 3825 N. Alta Vista Terrace, Chicago, Ill. 60613. 2,000 members.

Professional group, which aims to promote the welfare and interests of women lawyers, maintain the integrity of the legal profession, and enact legislation for the common good. The group has been working for ratification of the ERA, passage of women's rights legislation, and increasing numbers of women in the judiciary and in higher offices of the Bar Associations. The association publishes the *President's Newsletter* (to members) and *Women Lawyers Journal* ($4 yr.).

549 NATIONAL COUNCIL ON FAMILY RELATIONS, TASK FORCE ON WOMEN'S RIGHTS AND RESPONSIBILITIES. 1426 Merritt Dr., El Cajon, Calif. 92020. (714) 447-1641. Founded 1971. Rose Somerville.

A group of professionals in the family field (educators, counselors, researchers, home economists, sociologists, psychologists, and doctors) to encourage more courses and research about women and to combat sexism in the parent organization, in the mass media, and relevant institutions. The task force participates in radio and television talks, and consults on films and conferences. Individual members are encouraged to write from a feminist viewpoint.

550 POPULATION ASSOCIATION OF AMERICA, WOMEN'S CAUCUS. Dept. of Sociology, Brown University, Providence, R.I. 02912. Nancy E. Williamson, Coor. 150 members.

The caucus publishes a newsletter, which provides members with information of interest to them as women demographers, and includes reports on the study of discrimination being done by the association, fellowships available, and job openings. The caucus helped to revise a career pamphlet on demography to include women demographers.

551 REGISTRY OF WOMEN IN SCIENCE AND ENGINEERING. Rush Medical College, 1753 W. Congress Pkwy., Chicago, Ill. 60612. Founded 1972. Dr. Julia T. Apter, M.D., Ph. D.

"The Biophysical Society, The Institute of Electrical and Electronics Engineers, and the Association of Women in Science have cooperated to prepare a registry of over 5,000 women engineers, scientists, medical and paramedical specialists. The women are categorized by area of expertise with degree and present position. . . . This registry or portions of it are available at cost to Equal Employment Opportunities officers at academic, industrial and governmental organizations." The list costs approximately $50, and approximately $200 for the list with vitae.

552 SETON HALL UNIVERSITY SCHOOL OF LAW, WOMEN'S LAW FORUM. 1095 Raymond Blvd., Newark, N.J. 07102. (201) 642-8500. Founded September 1972. Dianna Armenakis. 40 members.

"To study and attempt to alleviate problems of women in the legal professions and in the law as it relates to women." The Women's Law Forum is involved in college recruitment of interested students by women who are law students now; collection of pertinent legislation and articles on legal problems of women; and administration of seminars and debates held throughout the school year to raise topics of interest relevant to women and the law.

553 SOCIETY FOR CELL BIOLOGY, WOMEN IN CELL BIOLOGY. Mary Clutter, Osborn Laboratories, Yale University, New Haven, Conn. 06520. (404) 542-1334. Founded November 1971. Virginia Walbot, Dept. of Biochemistry, Univ. of Georgia, Athens, Ga. 30601. 200 members.

Informal caucus, which distributes information concerning job openings; publishes a monthly newsletter ($5/yr.), with articles on women, Society events, and a listing of jobs.

554 SOCIETY FOR WOMEN IN PHILOSOPHY. Dept. of Philosophy, Western Illinois University, Macomb, Ill. 61455. Hannah Hardgrave.

Philosophy professors and graduate students interested in obtaining professional equity for women in philosophy. The society maintains a list of women who are seeking employment in philosophy, and the list is sent to all employing departments who request it. The group holds frequent meetings at which papers and panel discussions are presented. There are current attempts to publish a *Directory of Women Philosophers* and the Society now publishes a nationally distributed newsletter. The group is organized by region. The Illinois address is for the Midwestern region; for the Eastern region contact Susan Larson, Barnard College, New York, N.Y. 10027; and for the Pacific region, contact Gay Justin, Dept. of Philosophy, California State University, Sacramento, Calif.

555 SOCIETY OF AMERICAN ARCHIVISTS, COMMITTEE ON THE STATUS OF WOMEN IN THE ARCHIVAL PROFESSION. Nat. Archives and Records, Washington, D.C. 20408. Mabel E. Deutrich, General Services Admin.

An ad hoc group established "to determine as many facts as possible on the situation of women in our profession." A survey is being conducted within the SAA; results are to be tabulated.

556 SOCIETY OF WOMEN ENGINEERS. 345 E. 47 St., New York, N.Y. 10017. (212) 752-6800, ext. 551. Founded 1952. Winifree D. White, Exec Secy. 1,200 members.

Graduate women engineers in a nonprofit, educational, service organization dedicated to making known the need for women engineers and encouraging young women to consider an engineering education. The society informs the public of the achievements of women engineers and the opportunities opened to them; assists women engineers who are reentering the work force; and serves as an information center on women in engineering. Student sections have been chartered on 33 campuses, and the Men's Auxiliary Society of Women's Engineers was established in 1967.

The Society conducts surveys among women engineers and students, publishes the surveys and other items relating to career opportunities, and publishes a newsletter (5/yr.).

Following is a list of some other free publications.

Lillian Moller Gilbreth Scholarship Brochure
A Profile of the Woman Engineer
SWE Achievement Award (a brochure with pictures)
SWE Report on Women Undergraduate Students in Engineering (biennial Survey 1959-1971)
Wanted: Women Engineers and More Chance for Them
What You Should Know about Women Engineers
Women in Engineering
Women in Engineering Revisited

557 SOCIOLOGISTS FOR WOMEN IN SOCIETY. Dept. of Sociology, Univ. of Illinois, Urbana,. Ill. 61801. (217) 352-5744. Founded April 1970. Joan Huber, Pres., 1,500 members. Dues: $3, students; $10, full professors.

Women's professional caucus in sociology, "dedicated to maximizing the effectiveness of and professional opportunities for women in sociology, to exploring the contributions which sociology can, does and should make to the investigation and humanization of current sex roles." The group is enquiring into sex discrimination in academia, and publishes a quarterly newsletter. An annual, *Bibliography of Research on Sex Roles*, is available from Carol Weisman, Sociology Dept., University of Maryland, College Park, Md. or Lucy Sells, 1181 Euclid St., Berkeley, Calif. ($2, faculty; $1, graduate students).

558   STEWARDESSES FOR WOMEN'S RIGHTS. 30 Rockefeller Plaza, Suite 52, New York, N.Y. 10020. (212) 586-7804. Founded 1972. Nan Frost Welmers, Nat. Coor. 400 members. Dues: $15.

A new organization of concerned women in the airline industry. Immediate goals are to secure opportunity for professional advancement, ensure the recognition of legal rights, establish working conditions favorable to health and safety, and secure accurate representation in the media. The group has "filed class action suits with the EEOC and other agencies to protect stewardesses against employee discrimination; obtained reinstatement for stewardesses refused employment after having children; initiated research on the psychological effect of jet lag on the body chemistry of flight attendants; established national headquarters in New York City with centralized information on affirmative action, media discrimination and legal rights." Other projects are legal counseling for members, a health referral service, a library and lounge at SFWR headquarters, and a newsletter, published ten times a year for members.

559   WOMEN IN COMMUNICATIONS, INC. (founded as Theta Sigma Phi). 8305–A Shoal Creek Blvd., Austin, Tex. 78758. (512) 452-0119. Founded 1909. Maxine Elam, Exec. Dir. 7,000 members. Dues: $20.

Aims "to work for a free and responsible press, to unite women engaged in all fields of communications, to recognize distinguished achievements of women journalists, to maintain high professional standards, [and] to encourage members to greater individual effort." This professional organization is working to end job discrimination practices, to raise the self-image of women both on a professional and on a personal basis, to extend professional recognition and membership to women of racial minorities, and to combat attempts to undermine the First Amendment. The organization operates a Job Information Service; offers scholarship grants to talented journalists; sponsors publicity clinics, writer's workshops, and public relations campaigns to provide instruction in journalistic techniques; maintains a National Resource Center, including professional papers and "how to" manuals; and runs College Career Conferences. Women in Communications publishes *Matrix* (q., $4/yr.), the official news magazine of WICI; a monthly *Newsletter* ($4/yr.), with job information; and a pamphlet, *Careers Unlimited: A Forecast of Opportunities in Journalism and Communications* (50¢).

560   WOMEN'S CAUCUS FOR POLITICAL SCIENCE. Mount Vernon College, 2100 Foxhall Rd., N.W., Washington, D.C. 20007. Founded 1969. Dr. Marie B. Rosenberg. 725 members.

"Seeks to improve professional opportunities for women political scientists wherever they may work; to advance their professional status and to encourage scholarly research. In promoting these objectives, the WCPS acts to influence the policies and practices of the American Political Science Association, the regional political science associations, educational institutions, professional publications, and other actual and potential beneficiaries of our intellectual labor." The caucus presses the APSA to insist on open recruitment by employers using its personnel service for all levels of job openings, and requests the association to act more effectively in referring specific cases of sex discrimination to appropriate agencies.

The caucus also "recommends to universities and colleges that they make more flexible use of part-time faculty appointments with commensurate tenure and promotion scales and eliminate antinepotism rules." The caucus supports ratification of the Equal Rights Amendment and effective implementation of existing laws and "presses universities and colleges to conduct accurate analyses of the employment and utilization of women on their campuses and to pursue vigorously affirmative action." Regional caucuses are autonomous. All members receive the quarterly newsletter.

561 WOMEN'S LAW ASSOCIATION, HARVARD LAW SCHOOL. Austin Hall, Harvard Law School, Cambridge, Mass. 02138. (617) 495-3195. Founded 1969. Sydelle Pettas, 15 Glengarry, Winchester, Mass. 01890. 150 members.

Women law students, professors, and teaching fellows "interested in helping women within the law school and in assisting or referring others with legal concerns touching women's rights issues." At Harvard, the association has been particularly interested in admission and placement procedures vis-a-vis women. Task forces are conducted on recruitment and admissions, research, and clinical education. Speakers are available.

562 WOMEN'S LAW CAREERS, UNIVERSITY OF LOUISVILLE. Louisville, Ky. 40208. (502) 635-5885. Fall 1971 Emmy Hixson, 1215 S. 3 St., No. 203, Louisville, Ky. 40203. 50 members.

An organization of women law students and attorneys in Louisville, which aims to encourage feminism in the legal profession. The group conducted a seminar on sex discrimination, research on Kentucky law for women, and activities within the law school; and worked with the Kentucky Civil Liberties Union on *A Woman's Rights Handbook on Kentucky Law*.

563 WOMEN'S NATIONAL BOOK ASSOCIATION. 222 Valley Rd., Montclair, N.J. 07042. (201) 746-5166. Founded 1917. Anne J. Richter, Nat. Treas. 800 members.

Composed of women who are editors, authors, booksellers, librarians, literary agents, book manufacturers, etc., "to serve the world of books and provide a meeting place for bookwomen." The WNBA presents the Constance Lindsay Skinner award annually to a bookwoman for "outstanding contribution to the world of books;" sponsors dinners and book fairs; and published a fiftieth anniversary book, *Women in the World of Words*.

Miscellaneous

564 MOMMA: THE ORGANIZATION FOR SINGLE MOTHERS. Box 567,
Venice, Calif. 90291. (213) 821-2464. Founded March 1972. Karol Hope.

"A nonprofit self-help organization for single mothers, i.e., divorced, wid-owed, never-been-married mothers." The organization offers workshops on "how to change jobs to careers; going back to school while keeping the family together; parent education; nonauthoritarian problem solving; technical maintenance of our homes; basic plumbing, wiring, construction; car buying; maintenance; group insurance investigation; welfare . . . ; [and] men, us and our children." The group has accumulated a growing resource file, including: jobs offered/wanted, baby-sitters, welfare information, problem pregnancy alternatives, housing available and wanted, and medical and legal aid. There are hot lines for therapists, attorneys, and emergency housing. The group also maintains a speakers' bureau. Courses for single parents on communicating and problem-solving (PRE classes) are available throughout the Los Angeles area. The organization publishes *MOMMA: The Newspaper/Magazine for Single Mothers*, nationally distributed to fill the practical and emotional needs of single mothers across the nation. ($2.50/6 issues; $5/12 issues; $8 and $15, institutions.) Some issues included articles on children's books, "supermom," juvenile courts, aggression in women, welfare, work in skilled trades, and articles on single parents.

565 THE NATIONAL ORGANIZATION FOR NON-PARENTS. Box 10495.
Baltimore, Md. 21209. (301) 358-7387. Founded January 1972. Ellen
Peck, 2231 Rogene Dr., Baltimore, Md. 21209. 1500 members. Dues:
$10.

An educational, nonprofit, tax-deductible group to eliminate the social and economic discrimination against those who choose to remain childless, and to eliminate "pronatalist" influences. Projects include examination of pronatalism in textbooks, the armed forces and in Ob-Gyn education; media monitoring; and high school and college programs. The organization publishes a newsletter six times a year.

566 VEGETARIAN-FEMINISTS. 616 6 St., Brooklyn, N.Y. 11215. (212) 788-1362. Founded Spring 1973. C. Salamone.

"Feminists who believe that the basic premise of feminism is the termination of oppression of all living beings by the male power structure, and that this *includes* all species outside of our kind." The group gives talks to interested parties. Literature kits are available for $1.

567 WIDOWS CONSULTATION CENTER. 136 E. 57 St., New York, N.Y. 10022. (212) 688-8850. Founded September 1969. Diana C. Horowitz, Exec. Dir.

"A nonprofit, nonsectarian agency providing widows, on an individual or group basis, with information, counseling, and advisory services on varied problems confronting them. The Center's professional staff consists of mature, highly qualified social workers experienced in helping widows with their emotional and practical difficulties. Financial guidance is available on an individual basis from a recognized and highly regarded consultant. Discussion groups on problems of widowhood are conducted by qualified group leaders." Appointments are made by telephone 9:30 to 5:30, Monday through Friday. The fee is $12.50, but special fees are possible.

Geographic Index

United States

ALABAMA

Birmingham: Alabama Women's Commission, 257
Dadeville: Alexander City NOW, 163
Huntsville
  Huntsville NOW, 163
  National Women's Political Caucus, Black, 512
Montgomery
  Montgomery NOW, 163
  National Women's Political Caucus, Alabama, 512
Tuscaloosa: Alabama, Univ. of, Tuscaloosa, Women's Studies, College of Arts and Sciences, 414

ALASKA

Anchorage Women's Liberation Movement Group, 168
Fairbanks, Alaska NOW, 163
Naknek: National Women's Political Caucus, Alaska, 512
Petersburg: Alaska Commission on the Status of Women, 258

ARIZONA

Phoenix
  Arizona Governor's Commission on the Status of Women, 259
  National Women's Political Caucus, Arizona 512
  Phoenix NOW, 163
Tempe: Women's Center, 169

Arizona, Univ. of, Women's Studies, 414
National Women's Political Caucus, Arizona, 512
State of Arizona NOW, 163
Tucson Arizona NOW, 163

ARKANSAS

Little Rock
  Arkansas Governor's Commission on the Status of Women, 260
  Little Rock NOW, 163
  National Women's Political Caucus, Arkansas, 512
North Little Rock: National Women's Political Caucus, Arkansas, 512

CALIFORNIA

Aptos: Cabrillo College, Women's Studies, 414
Arcata: California State Univ., Humboldt, Women's Studies, 414
Bakersfield
  Bakersfield NOW, 163
  California State College, Women's Studies, 414
Berkeley
  Berkeley NOW, 163
  Berkeley Women's Affirmative Action Union, 170
  Berkeley Women's Center, 171
  Women's History Research Center, Inc., 156

California State Univ., Campus Women's Forum, 414
Clitartists, 359
Meiklejohn Civil Liberties Institute, 382
National Women's Political Caucus, California, 512
Third World Women's Alliance, 454
Union Women's Alliance to Gain Equality (WAGE), 441
Univ. of California, Berkeley Center for the Continuing Education of Women, 412
Blythe California NOW, 163
Boulder Creek: Santa Cruz County NOW, 163
Burlingame: San Mateo County NOW, 163
Canoga Park: San Fernando Valley, Calif. NOW, 163
Chico
California State Univ., Women's Studies, 414
Chico Women's Center, 173
Claremont
The Claremont Colleges Special Academic Programs and Office for Continuing Education, 434
Pomona Valley, Calif. NOW, 163
Women's Track & Field World, 93
Corona California NOW, 163
Corona Del Mar: Orange County NOW, 163
Davis NOW, 163
El Cajon: National Council on Family Relations, Task Force on Women's Rights and Responsibilities, 549
Escondido: North San Diego County NOW, 163
Fairfax: Sappho '71, 29
Fairfield: Solano NOW, 163
Fresno
California State Univ., Women's Studies, 414
Fresno NOW, 163
Glen Ellen: Sonoma County, California NOW, 163
Goleta: Santa Barbara County NOW,163
Hayward: California State College, Women's Studies, 414
Hermosa, Calif. NOW, 163
Hollywood: Matrix: For She of the New Aeon, 18
Hydesville: Humboldt County NOW, 163

Imperial, Calif. NOW, 163
Irvine
California, Univ. of, Irvine, Women's Studies Committee, 414
Women's Opportunities Center, 438
The Women's Opportunities Center, University of California Extension, Irvine, 434
Isla Vista
Isla Vista Women's Center, 174
Our Catalogue Company, 25
La Habra: La Puente, Calif. NOW, 163
La Jolla: UCSD Extension Counseling Services, University of California, San Diego, 434
Lafayette: Contra Costa County NOW, 163
Laguna Beach
Laguna Beach NOW, 163
Nanny Goat Productions, 20
Lomita: 51%: A Paper of Joyful Noise for the Majority Sex, 53
Long Beach
California State Univ., Long Beach Community Counseling Center, 434
California State Univ., Women's Studies, 414
California State Univ. at Long Beach, Women Studies Center, 415
Long Beach NOW, 163
The Sportswoman Magazine, 79
Los Altos Hills: Foothill College, 434
Los Angeles
Action Council for Comprehensive Child Care, 394
Amani, 126
Anarygos Film Library, 96
Ann Forfreedom, 10
California NOW, 163
California, Univ. of, Los Angeles: Women's Resource Center, 414
Career Planning Center, 433
Chicana Service Action Center, 445
Churchill Films, 97
Feminist Studio Workshop, 363
Feminist Women's Health Center Self-Help Clinics, 471
Gay Community Services Center, 508
Hollywood, Calif. NOW, 163
Lesbian Tide, 60
Los Angeles NOW, 163
Market Place, A Management Search Agency, 434
National Women's Political Caucus, California, 512

Joyce Nielsen, Feminist Jewelry, 137
Pacifica Program Service/Pacifica
  Tape Library, 108
Program Advisory Service, UCLA
  Extension, 434
San Gabriel Valley NOW, 163
Sisterhood Bookstore, 124
Wollstonecraft, Inc., 38
Womanspace, 370
Women's Heritage Series, Inc., 142
Women's News Service, 117
Women's Place, Inc., 434
Women's Resource Center at Univ. of
  California, Los Angeles, 176
Menlo Park
  California NOW, 163
  Los Gatos NOW, 163
  Menlo Park NOW, 163
Merced, Calif. NOW, 163
Modesto: Stanislaus County NOW, 163
Monterey NOW, 163
Moorpark: Conejo Valley NOW, 163
Norwalk NOW, 163
Novato: Marin County NOW, 163
Oakland
  Amazon Quarterly, 42
  Laney College, Women's Studies, 414
  Mama's Press, 17
Oceanside: North San Diego County
  NOW, 163
Orange County NOW, 163
Pacific Grove: Monterey NOW, 163
Pacific Palisades, Calif. NOW, 163
Palo Alto
  New Ways to Work, 434
  Palo Alto NOW, 163
  Resource Center for Women, 434
  Zero Population Growth, 498
Palos Verdes Estates: Palos Verdes
  Peninsula NOW, 163
Pleasant Hill: Diablo Valley College,
  Women's Studies, 414
Redding NOW, 163
Reseda: Creative Film Society, 98
Ridgecrest NOW, 163
Riverside: Riverside-San Bernardino,
  Calif. NOW, 163
Rolling Hills: Palos Verdes Peninsula
  NOW, 163
Sacramento
  California Commission on the Status
    of Women, 261
  California State Univ., Women's
    Studies, 414

Sacramento Community Commission
  for Women, 263
Sacramento NOW, 163
Sacramento (new) NOW, 163
Skirting the Capitol: A Newsletter
  about Legislation and Women, 76
San Bernardino: California State
  College, Women's Studies, 414
San Diego
  California State Univ., Women's
    Studies Committee, 414
  Center for Women's Studies and
    Services, 172
  San Diego NOW, 163
San Francisco
  Advocates for Women, 430
  Advocates for Women, Inc., 434
  California State Univ., Women's
    Studies Committee, 414
  Change: A Working Women's News-
    paper, 46
  Change for Children, A Multiethnic
    Center for Nonsexist Education, 395
  China Books and Periodicals, 119
  Daughters of Bilitis, 506
  Gay Sunshine, a Journal of Gay
    Liberation, 56
  Joyful World Press, 12
  Mayor's Committee on the Status of
    Women, 262
  Mother Lode, 64
  New Womb Artists, 367
  San Francisco NOW, 163
  San Francisco Women's Health
    Center, 487
  Sisters, 75
  United Front Press, 35
  Women's Job Rights Organization, 437
  Women's Legal Center, 388
  Women's Prison Project, 500
San Jose
  California State Univ., Women's
    Studies Committee, 414
  San Jose NOW, 163
San Lorenzo: Shameless Hussy Press, 30
San Mateo: Womensports, 94
San Pedro: Harbor-South Bay, Calif.
  NOW, 163
San Rafael
  Larin Women's News Journal, 63
  Marin County Chapter NOW, 163
Santa Ana: Orange County NOW, 163
Santa Barbara
  Feminist Writer's Workshop, 8
  Rainbow Institute, 28

Santa Clara: South Bay NOW, 163
Santa Cruz: California, Univ. of, Santa
    Cruz, Women's Studies Committee,
    414
Santa Maria NOW, 163
Santa Rosa: Alica Foster's Patchwork
    Fashions and Crafts, 133
Sherman Oaks: Allend'or Productions,
    95
Sonoma: California State Univ.,
    Women's Studies, 414
Soquel: Santa Cruz County NOW, 163
Stanford: New Seed Press, 23
Stockton: San Joaquin NOW, 163
Venice
    Everywoman, 48
    Feminist History Research Project, 149
    Los Angeles Commission on Assaults
        against Women, 501
    MOMA: The Organization for Single
        Mothers, 564
    Westside Women's Center, 175
Ventura, Calif. NOW, 163
Visalia NOW, 163
Walnut Creek: Contra Costa County
    NOW, 163
Whittier: Southeast Los Angeles NOW,
    163
Wilmington: Los Angeles Harbor
    College, Women's Studies, 414

COLORADO

Boulder
    Boulder, Colo. NOW, 163
    Women's Liberation Coalition, 178
Colorado Springs
    El Paso County NOW, 163
    National Women's Political Caucus,
        Native American, 512
Denver
    Colorado Commission on the Status
        of Women, 264
    Denver NOW, 163
    National Women's Political Caucus,
        Colorado 512
    Virginia Neal Blue Resource Centers
        for Colorado Women, 177
    The Women's Voice Bookstore, 125
Durango NOW, 163
Fort Collins
    Colorado NOW, 163
    Colorado State Univ., Women's
        Programs, 434
Ft. Collins, Colo. NOW, 163

Grand Junction
    Grand Junction NOW, 163
    Mesa NOW, 163
Greeley NOW, 163
Gunnison NOW, 163
Lakewood: Metropolitan Denver NOW,
    163
Longmont NOW, 163
Pueblo NOW, 163

CONNECTICUT

Bridgeport: Greater Bridgeport,
    Connecticut NOW, 163
Coventry: Northeastern Connecticut
    NOW, 163
Fairfield
    Fairfield NOW, 163
    Western Connecticut NOW, 163
Greenwich, Connecticut NOW, 163
Hamden: New Haven, Connecticut
    NOW, 163
Hartford
    Hartford College Counseling Center,
        434
    Women's Liberation Center of Greater
        Hartford, 181
Ivoryton: Essex County, Connecticut
    NOW, 163
Middletown
    Alert, the Connecticut Legislative
        Review for Women, 41
    Wesleyan Univ., Women's Studies,
        414
New Haven
    National Women's Political Caucus,
        Connecticut, 512
    New Haven Women's Liberation, 179
    New Haven Women's Liberation Rock
        Band, 366
    Society for Cell Biology, Women in
        Cell Biology, 553
    Yale Law Women's Association,
        Women v. Connecticut, 497
    Yale Univ. Women's Organization
        Information and Counseling Ser-
        vice, 434
New London
    American Woman's Collection,
        Connecticut College Library, 146
    Connecticut College Career
        Counseling and Placement, 434
Norwalk
    Connecticut Feminists in the Arts,
        Women's Interart, 362

Women's Liberation Center, 180
Norwich: Connecticut NOW, 163
Quaker Hill: Southeastern Connecticut
NOW, 163
Stamford
New Moon Communications, 481
Stamford, Connecticut NOW, 163
Young Women's Christian Associa-
tion, 434
Storrs: Univ. of Connecticut Continuing
Education for Women, 434
Stratford, Connecticut NOW, 163
Weathersfield: Central Connecticut
NOW, 163
West Hartford: Association of American
Law Schools, Committee on Women
in Legal Education, 538
West Redding: National Women's
Political Caucus, Connecticut, 512
Westport
New Concept, 434
Westport NOW, 163

DELAWARE

Dover: Kent County NOW, 163
Greenville: National Women's Political
Caucus, Delaware, 512
Newark
Delaware, Univ. of, Women's Studies
Committee, 414
National Women's Political Caucus,
Delaware, 512
Newark, Delaware NOW, 163
Univ. of Delaware, Division of Con-
tinuing Education, 434
Wilmington
Delaware Governor's Council for
Women, 265
Delaware NOW, 163
McElroy & Doban, Inc., 434

DISTRICT OF COLUMBIA

American Association of University
Professors, Committee, 519
American Association of University
Women, 158
American Federation of Teachers,
Women's Rights Committee, 521
American Historical Association's
Roster of Women Historians, 522
American Psychological Association,
Ad Hoc Committee on Women in
Psychology, 529
American Society for Microbiology,
Committee on the Status of Women
Microbiologists, 530
American Society for Public Administra-
tion, Standing Committee on
Women in Public Administration,
531
Association for Women in Mathematics,
536
Association of American Colleges Pro-
ject on the Status and Education of
Women, 389
Association of Women in Science, 539
Center for Women Policy Studies, 145
Council on Economic Advisors, Ad-
visory Committee on the Economic
Role of Women, 248
Q. M. Dabney & Co., Inc., 120
Day Care and Child Development
Council of America, Inc., 399
Distaffers Research & Counseling
Center, 434
District of Columbia Commission on
the Status of Women, 266
Federally Employed Women, 543
Federation of Organizations for Pro-
fessional Women, 544
First Things First—Books for Women—A
Fe-Mail Order House and Mobile
Unit, 122
George Washington Univ., Committee
on Women Studies, 414, 418
George Washington Univ., Continuing
Education for Women Center, 410,
434
Human Rights for Women, 380
Interstate Association of Commissions
on the Status of Women, 249
Job Market, Inc., 434
League of Women Voters of the United
States, 159
Library of Congress, 151
Marija Matich Hughes, 11
National Association for Women Deans,
Administrators and Counselors, 546
National Association of College Women,
161
National Committee on Household
Employment, 440
National Federation of Business and
Professional Women's Clubs, Inc.,
162
National Welfare Rights Organization,
164

National Women's Party, 511
National Women's Political Caucus,
    512
National Women's Political Caucus,
    Capitol Hill, 512
National Women's Political Caucus,
    District of Columbia, 512
Off Our Backs: A Women's News
    Journal, 70
Office of Opportunities in Science, 516
Radio Free Women of Washington D.C.,
    110
Society of American Archivists, Com-
    mittee on the Status of Women in
    the Archival Profession, 555
Today Publications and News Service,
    33
U.S. Dept. of Health, Education, and
    Welfare, The Federal Women's
    Program, 252
U.S. Dept. of Health, Education, and
    Welfare, Office of Child Develop-
    ment, 406
U.S. Dept. of Health, Education, and
    Welfare, Office of Special Concerns,
    Assistant Secretary for Evaluation
    and Planning, Women's Action
    Program, 253
U.S. Dept. of Labor, Employment
    Standards Administration, Office
    of Federal Contract Compliance,
    254
U.S. Dept. of Labor, Employment
    Standards Administration, Women's
    Bureau, 255
United States Citizen's Advisory
    Council on the Status of Women,
    250
United States Commission on Civil
    Rights, Women's Rights Program
    Unit, 251
United States Equal Employment
    Opportunity Commission, 256
Washington Area Women's Center, 182
Washington Opportunities for Women,
    Inc., 436
Women's Caucus for Political Science,
    560
Women's Equity Action League
    (WEAL), 386
Women's Health Clinic, 493
Women's Institute for Freedom of the
    Press, 374
Women's Lobby, 514

FLORIDA
Boca Raton: South Palm Beach NOW,
    163
Coconut Grove: Dade County NOW,
    163
Deland NOW, 163
Ft. Lauderdale: Florida NOW, 163
Fort Myers NOW, 163
Gainesville
    Committee on the Status of Women
        in Journalism, 541
    Gainesville NOW, 163
Indialantic By-the-Sea: Those Uppity
    Women, 139
Jacksonville
    Community Liaison Consultants, 426
    Jacksonville NOW, 163
    Mayor's Advisory Commission on the
        Status of Women, 269
Lake Worth: North Palm Beach County
    NOW, 163
Lakeland: Polk County NOW, 163
Maitland: Orlando NOW, 163
Miami
    Dade County Commission on the
        Status of Women, 267
    The Greater Miami Council for the
        Continuing Education of Women,
        434
    National Women's Political Caucus,
        Florida, 512
    South Dade County NOW, 163
Orlando: Council for Continuing Educa-
    tion for Women of Central Florida,
    Inc., 434
Ormond Beach: Daytona-Ormond
    Beach NOW, 163
Pensacola
    National Women's Political Caucus,
        Florida, 512
    Pensacola, Fla. NOW, 163
Plantation: Broward County, Fla. NOW,
    163
Rockledge: Brevard County NOW, 163
St. Augustine: St. Johns County NOW,
    163
St. Petersburg, Fla. NOW, 163
Sarasota NOW, 163
Tallahassee
    Florida Governor's Commission on
        the Status of Women, 268
    Praxis Press, 27
    Tallahassee NOW, 163

Tampa
  South Florida, Univ. of, Women's
    Studies, 414
  Tampa, Fla. NOW, 163
  US Magazine, 83

GEORGIA

Albany NOW, 163
Athens
  American Association for the
    Advancement of Science, Women's
    Caucus, 517
  Athens NOW, 163
Atlanta
  Atlanta Lesbian Feminist Alliance,
    505
  Atlanta NOW, 163
  The Georgia Commission on the
    Status of Women, 270
  Georgia NOW, 163
  National Women's Political Caucus,
    Georgia, 512
  Sojourner Truth Press, 31
  South Metro. Atlanta NOW, 163
  Women's Information Center, 183
Augusta: CSRA NOW, 163
Columbus NOW, 163
Doralville: Dekalb County NOW, 163
Lithia Springs: Douglas County NOW,
  163
Macon NOW, 163
Rome NOW, 163
St. Simon's Island NOW, 163
Savannah NOW, 163
Wadley: South Central Georgia NOW,
  163

HAWAII

Hilo
  Commission on the Status of
    Women, County of Hawaii, 272
  Hilo, Hawaii NOW, 163
Honolulu
  Hawaii State Commission on the
    Status of Women, 273
  Hawaii, Univ. of, Women's Studies,
    414
  Honolulu NOW, 163
  Mayor's Commission on the Status
    of Women, 274
Kula Maui: Commission on the Status
  of Women, 271
Wahiawa: National Women's Political
  Caucus, Hawaii, 512

IDAHO

Boise
  Idaho Commission on Women's
    Programs, 275
  National Women's Political Caucus,
    Idaho, 512
Idaho Falls
  Idaho Falls NOW, 163
  National Women's Political Caucus,
    Idaho, 512
Pocatello: National Women's Political
  Caucus, Idaho, 512

ILLINOIS

Aurora NOW, 163
Barrington
  Center for a Woman's Own Name, 379
  North Suburban Chicago NOW, 163
Carbondale: Southern Ill. NOW, 163
Champaign
  Champaign NOW, 163
  Greater Champaign NOW, 163
  Univ. of Illinois, Urbana-Champaign
    434
Chicago
  American Institute of Planners/
    American Society of Planning
    Officials, Women's Rights Com-
    mittee, 523
  American Library Association, Social
    Responsibilities Round Table, Task
    Force on Women, 524
  Chicago NOW, 163
  Chicago Women's Liberation Union,
    184
  Commission on the Status of Women,
    276
  Illinois Citizens for the Medical
    Control of Abortion, 474
  Illinois Drug Abuse Program, 277
  Lavender Woman, 14
  Midwest Academy, 392
  Mundelein College, Women's Studies,
    414
  National Association of Bank-Women,
    Inc., 547
  National Association of Women
    Lawyers, 548
  National Coalition of American
    Nuns, 451
  National Organization for Women, 163
  National Women's Political Caucus,
    Illinois, 512

Northeastern Illinois Univ., Women's
  Studies Committee, 414
Northeastern Illinois Univ., Women's
  Studies Inter-disciplinary Degree
  Program, 419
Registry of Women in Science and
  Engineering, 551
Siren Anarch Feminists, 513
The Spokeswoman, 78
The Woman's Institute, 186
Decatur, Ill. NOW, 163
Downers Grove: Women's Ink, 434
Edwardsville
  Edwardsville NOW, 163
  Southern Illinois Univ., General
    Studies Division, 434
  Southern Illinois Univ., Women's
    Studies, 414
Elgin: Fox Valley–Elgin, Ill. NOW, 163
Glen Ellyn: Du Page County NOW, 163
Highland Park: Applied Potential, 434
Macomb: Society for Women in
  Philosophy, 554
McHenry Ill. NOW, 163
Naperville: Phillips Research Founda-
  tion, 434
Orland Park: Southwest Cook County
  NOW, 163
Palatine: Harper College Community
  Counseling Center, 434
Palos Hills: Moraine Valley Community
  College, Adult Career Resource
  Center, 434
Park Forest South: Governors State
  Univ., Women's Studies, 414
Rock Island
  Illinois NOW, 163
  Quad Cities, Ill. NOW, 163
Rockford, Ill. NOW, 163
Springfield
  Brainchild, 357
  Sangamon State Univ., Women's
    Studies, 414
  Springfield, Ill. NOW, 163
Urbana: Sociologists for Women in
  Society, 557
Waukegan: Joint Committee of
  Organizations Concerned with the
  Status of Women in the Church, 448
Wilmette: Professional Organization of
  Women for Equal Rights
  (POWER), 185
Zion: Lake County NOW, 163

INDIANA

Anderson NOW, 163
Bloomington
  Bloomington, Ind. NOW, 163
  Indiana NOW, 163
  Indiana Univ., Continuing Education
    for Women, 434
  Indiana Univ., Memorial Hall 219X,
    Women's Studies, 414
  Women's Center, Inc., 187
Briston: Elkhart, Ind. NOW, 163
Butler: Ford Associates, Inc., 9
Columbus Mayor's Task Force on the
  Status of Women, 278
Fort Wayne
  The Mayor's Commission on the
    Status of Women, 281
  University Center for Women, Purdue
    Univ., 434
Franklin, Ind. NOW, 163
Gary Commission on the Status of
  Women, 280
Granger: National Women's Political
  Caucus, Indiana, 512
Hammond: Lake County NOW, 163
Indianapolis
  Indianapolis, Ind. NOW, 163
  Mayor's Task Force on Women, City
    of Indianapolis, 283
Lafayette: Commission on the Status
  of Indiana Women, 279
Muncie
  Commission on Sexist Abuse in
    Language, 361
  Muncie NOW, 163
Newburgh: Tri-State NOW, 163
South Bend NOW, 163
Terre Haute NOW, 163
Valparaiso NOW, 163
West Lafayette
  Mayor's Task Force on the Status of
    Women, 282
  Tippecanoe County NOW, 163

IOWA

Ames, Iowa NOW, 163
Cedar Falls: Univ. of Northern Iowa
  NOW, 163
Cedar Rapids NOW, 163
Clinton, Iowa NOW, 163
Des Moines
  Des Moines NOW, 163

Drake University, Women's
Program, 434
Iowa NOW, 163
Iowa State Commission on the Status
of Women, 284
Iowans for Medical Control of Abortion, 475
National Women's Political Caucus,
Iowa, 512
Dubuque, Iowa NOW, 163
Iowa City
Ain't I a Woman, 40
University Counseling Service, Iowa
Memorial Union, Univ. of Iowa,
434
Marion: Cedar Rapids Women's Caucus
163
Mount Pleasant, Iowa NOW, 163
Pocahontas, Iowa NOW, 163

KANSAS

Lawrence
Kansas NOW, 163
Kansas, Univ. of, Women's Studies,
414
Lawrence NOW, 163
Univ. of Kansas, Student Services,
Extramural Independent Study
Center, 434
Manhattan NOW, 163
Ottawa NOW, 163
Topeka
Kansas Governor's Commission on
the Status of Women, 285
Topeka NOW, 163
Wichita
National Women's Political Caucus,
Kansas, 512
Wichita, Kans. NOW, 163

KENTUCKY

Bowling Green NOW, 163
Lexington: National Women's Political
Caucus, Kentucky, 512
Louisville
Kentucky Commission on Women,
286
Kentucky NOW, 163
Louisville NOW, 163
Women's Law Careers, Univ. of Louisville, 562

LOUISIANA

Baton Rouge
Baton Rouge, La. NOW, 163
Louisiana Bureau on the Status of
Women, 288
Louisiana NOW, 163
National Women's Political Caucus,
Louisiana, 512
State Dept. of Labor, Division of
Women and Children, 287
Hammond NOW, 163
Monroe: Monroe-Ouachita Parish,
La. NOW, 163
New Orleans
National Women's Political Caucus,
Louisiana, 512
New Orleans NOW, 163
Shreveport: Shreveport-Bossier, La.
NOW, 163

MAINE

Augusta: Maine Dept. of Manpower
Affairs, Bureau of Labor and
Industry, 290
Bangor: Heart of Maine NOW, 163
Cape Elizabeth: Advisory Council on
the Status of Women, 289
Foreside: National Women's Political
Caucus, Maine, 512
Franklin: National Women's Political
Caucus, Sexual Privacy, 512
Saco: Kennebunk, Maine NOW, 163
South Portland
South Maine NOW, 163
State of Maine NOW, 163

MARYLAND

Annapolis: Anne Arundel NOW, 163
Baltimore
Baltimore City NOW, 163
Baltimore County NOW, 163
Maryland Commission on the Status
of Women, 291
The National Organization for Non-
Parents, 565
Women: A Journal of Liberation, 87
Bethesda
American Society of Biological
Chemists, Committee on the Status
of Women, 532
Elizabeth Cady Stanton Publishing
Co., 6

Chevy Chase: Association for Women
in Psychology, 537
Clinton: South Prince George's County
NOW, 163
Columbia
Howard County NOW, 163
National Women's Political Caucus,
Maryland, 512
Edgewater: Maryland NOW, 163
Gaithersburg: Montgomery County
NOW, 163
Garrett Park: National Capitol Area
NOW, 163
Greenbelt: Northern Prince George's
NOW, 163
Hagerstown
Frederick County NOW, 163
Hagerstown NOW, 163
Rockville
Montgomery County Commission for
Women, 292
Montgomery County NOW, 163
Towson: Towson State College,
Women's Studies, 414
Upper Marlboro: Prince George's
County Council on the Status of
Women, 293
Westminster: Carroll County NOW, 163

MASSACHUSETTS
Amherst
Everywoman's Center, 189
Five Colleges, Women's Studies
Committee, 414
Arlington: Lanlyre Liggera, 15
Bedford: Women's Opportunity Re-
search Center, Middlesex
Community College, 434
Boston
Boston Commission to Improve the
Status of Women, 294
Boston Women's Collective, Inc., 1
Civic Center and Clearing House, Inc.,
434
Daughters of Bilitis, 506
Eastern Mass. NOW, 163
Focus: A Journal for Gay Women, 54
Massachusetts Dept. of Commerce and
Development, Women's Bureau, 295
Massachusetts Governor's Commission
on the Status of Women, 296
Massachusetts Organization to Repeal
Abortion Laws, Inc., 477
Massachusetts, Univ. of, Women's
Studies, 414

Pro Se: The National Law Women's
Newsletter, 74
Women's Educational & Industrial
Union Career Services, 434
Zion Research Library, 157
Brookline
American Economics Association,
Committee on the Status of Women
in the Economics Profession, 520
Betsy Hogan Associates, 428
Cambridge
American Association of Immunolo-
gists, Committee on the Status of
Women, 518
The Boston Theological Institute,
Women's Theological Coalition,
444
Cambridge-Goddard Graduate School,
Feminist Studies Program, 416
Cambridge-Goddard Graduate School
for Social Change, Feminists
Studies, 414
Cell 16, 188
Child Care Resource Center, 396
Educational Day Care Services
Association, 400
Female Liberation, 190
The National Day Care Association,
404
Nine to Five: Newsletter for Boston
Area Office Workers, 69
Radcliffe Institute, 411
The Arthur and Elizabeth Schlesinger
Library on the History of Women in
America, Radcliffe College, 153
Women's Center, 192
Women's Coalition for the Third
Century, 166
Women's Law Association, Harvard
Law School, 561
Framingham
Feminist Resources For Equal Educa-
tion, 402
South Middlesex, Mass. NOW, 163
Haverhill: Univ. of Mass. NOW, 163
Hingham
National Women's Political Caucus,
Massachusetts, 512
Plymouth NOW, 163
Lexington NOW, 163
Nahant: North Shore, Mass. NOW, 163
Newton Centre
Newton, Mass. NOW, 163
Women's Resource Center, 193

North Addams: Birth Control Information Center, 464
Northampton
Smith College, Vocational Office, 434
The Sophia Smith Collection, Smith College, 154
Valley Women's Center, 191
Women's Film Coop., 114
Quincy
Massachusetts NOW, 163
National Women's Political Caucus, Massachusetts, 512
Sharon: Norfolk NOW, 163
Somerville
Boston Women's Health Book Collective, 2
New England Free Press, 21
Rounder Records, 111
Wellesley: American Philological Association (Classical Studies), Committee on Women, 526
West Newton: Boston Project for Careers, 434
Williamstown: Pittsfield NOW, 163
Worcester
Worcester NOW, 163
Worcester Pregnancy Counseling Service, Inc., 496

MICHIGAN
Ann Arbor
Ann Arbor NOW, 163
Association for Asian Studies, Committee on the Status of Women, 535
Her-self, Community Women's Newspaper, 58
Michigan Citizens for Medical Control of Abortion, 478
Michigan Historical Collection, Bentley Historical Library, 144
Univ. of Michigan, Center for Continuing Education of Women, 413
Big Rapids NOW, 163
Birmingham: Oakland County NOW, 163
Comstock: Kalamazoo NOW, 163
Dearborn
Michigan NOW, 163
Michigan Women's Commission, 297
Detroit
Detroit NOW, 163
Eve of Detroit, 507
The Fifth Estate, 52
Gay Liberator, 55
Moving Out Magazine, 65

National Women's Political Caucus, Michigan, 512
News and Letters Women's Liberation Committee, 194
Wayne County City College, Women's Studies, 414
Women Tithe For Women, 457
East Lansing: National Women's Political Caucus, Michigan, 512
Flint, Mich. NOW, 163
Grand Rapids: Western Michigan NOW, 163
Hancock: Houghton, Mich. NOW, 163
Houghton: Michigan Technological Univ. Center for Continuing Education for Women, 434
Kalamazoo: Western Michigan Univ., Continuing Education for Women, 434
Kewadin: Traverse City NOW, 163
Lansing
Access Center for Human Reproductive Health, 461
Lansing NOW, 163
National Women's Political Caucus, Michigan, 512
Livonia: Schoolcraft NOW, 163
Midland NOW, 163
Mount Clemens: Macomb County NOW, 163
Muskegon: Muskegon-Ottawa, Mich. NOW, 163
Port Huron, Mich. NOW, 163
Rochester: Oakland Univ., Continuum Center, 434
St. Joseph: Benton Harbor-St. Joe NOW, 163
Taylor NOW, 163

MINNESOTA
Autsin: Southern Minnesota NOW, 163
Burnsville: National Women's Political Caucus, Minnesota, 512
Little Falls NOW, 163
Minneapolis
Amazon Bookstore, 118
Emma Willard Task Force on Education, 401
Gold Flower: A Twin Cities Newspaper for Women, 57
Minnesota, Univ. of, Women's Studies, 414
Minnesota Organization for Repeal of Abortion Laws, 479

Minnesota Women's Center, Univ. of
Minnesota, 434
Minnetonka: Twin Cities, Minn. NOW,
163
Rochester NOW, 163
St. Paul
Minnesota NOW, 163
Minnesota Women's Advisory Com-
mission and Women's Division,
Dept. of Human Rights, 298
St. Paul, Minn. NOW, 163
Stillwater: St. Croix Valley NOW, 163
Wayzata NOW, 163

MISSISSIPPI

Hattiesburg
Mississippi Governor's Commission on
the Status of Women, 299
U.S.M. Hattiesburg NOW, 163
Jackson
Jackson NOW, 163
Mississippi NOW, 163
Meridian NOW, 163
Pascakoula, Miss. NOW, 163
State College: National Women's
Political Caucus, Mississippi, 512

MISSOURI

Cape Girardeau NOW, 163
Chillicothe NOW, 163
Clayton: St. Louis NOW, 163
Columbia
Columbia NOW, 163
National Women's Political Caucus,
Missouri, 512
Independence: National Women's
Political Caucus, Missouri, 512
Jefferson City
Jefferson City NOW, 163
Missouri Commission on the Status of
Women, 300
Kansas City
Greater Kansas City NOW, 163
National Association of Minority
Women in Business, 449
Women's Liberation Union, 195
The Women's Resource Service, Univ.
of Missouri, Kansas City, 434
Kirksville NOW, 163
St. Charles NOW, 163
St. Louis
Danforth Graduate Fellowships for
Women, 390

Missouri NOW, 163
National Women's Political Caucus,
Missouri, 512
St. Louis NOW, 163
Univ. of Missouri, St. Louis Extension
Division—Women's Program, 434
Washington Univ. Continuing Educa-
tion for Women, 434
University City: Rape Crisis Center, 502

MONTANA

Butte NOW, 163
Great Falls
Great Falls NOW, 163
National Women's Political Caucus,
Montana, 512
State of Utah NOW, 163
Helena: Montana Status of Women Ad-
visory Council, 301
Missoula, Mont. NOW, 163

NEBRASKA

Grand Island, Nebr. NOW, 163
Kearney, Nebr. NOW, 163
Lincoln
Ad Hoc Committee on the Status of
Women in Journalism Education,
515
Lincoln NOW, 163
National Women's Political Caucus,
Nebraska, 512
Nebraska Commission on the Status
of Women, 303
Nebraska NOW, 163
Omaha
Mayor's Commission on the Status of
Women, 302
National Women's Political Caucus,
Nebraska, 512
Omaha NOW, 163

NEVADA

Las Vegas
Southern Nevada NOW, 163
State of Nevada NOW, 163
Reno
The Ladder, 59
National Women's Political Caucus,
Nevada, 512
Nevada Governor's Commission on
the Status of Women, 304

Nevada, Univ. of, Women's Studies Committee, 414
Reno Commission on the Status of Women, 305

NEW HAMPSHIRE

Bedford: National Women's Political Caucus, New Hampshire, 512
Concord: New Hampshire Commission on the Status of Women, 306
Durham: Disadvantaged Women for a Higher Education, Inc., 409
Franconia: Barbara B. Cooper Handweaving and Jewelry, 130
Hanover NOW, 163
Merrimack N.H. NOW, 163
Portsmouth: The Whole Woman Catalog, 37

NEW JERSEY

Absecon: The Committee for Abortion Information and Referral, 466
Boonton: Morristown NOW, 163
Brick Town: Ocean County NOW, 163
Clifton: Passaic County Chapter NOW, 163
Dover: New Directions for Women in N.J., 67
Edison
    Edison NOW, 163
    Middlesex County NOW, 163
Fanwood: Daughters of Bilitis, 506
Franklin Lakes: New Day Films, 105
Hackensack: Bergen Community College, Community Counseling Service, 434
Ho Ho Kus: Northern New Jersey NOW, 163
Iselin: Middlesex County NOW, 163
Mahwah: Ramapo College, Women's Studies, 414
Martinsville: Somerset County NOW, 163
Millburn: Educational & Vocational Counseling Service, 434
Montclair
    Essex County NOW, 163
    N.J. Women's Information and Referral Service, 152
    New Jersey NOW, 163
    Women's National Book Association, 563

Mullica Hill: South Jersey NOW, 163
Murray Hill: Summit Area NOW, 163
Newark
    N.J. Division on Civil Rights, 307
    Rutgers Univ., Newark College of Arts and Sciences, Women's Studies, 414
    Seton Hall Univ. School of Law, Women's Law Forum, 552
    Women's Rights Law Reporter, 91
New Brunswick
    Center for the American Women and Politics, Eagleton Institute, 148
    Douglass College Women's Center, 434
    Douglass College, Women's Studies, 414
New Monmouth: Monmouth County NOW, 163
Orange
    Cogent Associates Project HEAR, 398
    Women's Center, 196
Pennington: Central New Jersey NOW, 163
Princeton
    Central New Jersey NOW, 163
    Feminist Consultation Service, 427
    The Professional Roster, 434
    Women on Words and Images, 407
Princeton Junction: Association of Feminist Consultants, 423
Pomona: Stockton State College, Women's Studies Committee, 414
Ridgewood: Women's Center of Bergen County, 197
Rockaway: Lakeland Area, N.J. NOW, 163
Springfield: Union County NOW, 163
Teaneck: National Women's Political Caucus, New Jersey, 512
Tenafly: Northern New Jersey NOW, 163
Trenton: N.J. State Commission on Women, Dept. of Community Affairs, 308
Union: Eve, Newark State College, 434
Washington: Times Change Press, 32
Wayne: Passaic County NOW, 163
West Orange: Ferne Williams, 140
Westfield
    New Jersey Women's Rights Task Force on Education, 405
    Westfield N.J. NOW, 163

NEW MEXICO

Albuquerque
  Albuquerque NOW, 163
  National Women's Political Caucus,
    New Mexico, 512
  New Mexico Governor's Commission
    on the Rights of Women, 309
  New Mexico, Univ. of, Women's Stud-
    ies Committee, 414
Deming NOW, 163
Los Alamos NOW, 163
Portales: Roosevelt County NOW, 163
Sante Fe NOW, 163

NEW YORK STATE

Albany
  New York State Women's Unit, Office
    of the Governor, 311
  New York, State Univ. of, Women's
    Studies, 414
  Speakout, A Feminist Journal, 77
Albion: Orleans NOW, 163
Attica: Batavia NOW, 163
Auburn NOW, 163
Babylon: South Shore, N.Y. NOW, 163
Bayport: So. Suffolk NOW, 163
Binghamton Area, N.Y. NOW, 163
Bronxville
  Sarah Lawrence College, Women's His-
    tory Program, 414
  Sarah Lawrence College, Women's
    Studies Program, 421
Buffalo
  Buffalo, N.Y. NOW, 163
  Earth's Daughters, 47
  National Women's Political Caucus,
    Radical Women, 512
  New York, State Univ. of, College of
    Women's Studies, 414
  State University of New York at Buf-
    falo, Women Studies College, 422
Burnt Hills: Schenectady NOW, 163
Clinton
  Kirkland College NOW, 163
  Utica NOW, 163
Commack: Western Suffolk Co. NOW,
  163
Dobbs Ferry: Mercy College Career
  Counseling and Placement Office,
  434
Elmira NOW, 163
Endicott: Binghamton Area, N.Y. NOW,
  163
Fredonia: Dunkirk-Fredonia NOW, 163

Geneseo, N.Y. NOW, 163
Geneva: Hobart & William Smith Col-
  leges, Women's Studies, 414
Great Neck: Long Island NOW, 163
Greenville: C. W. Post College NOW,
  163
Hamilton, N.Y. NOW, 163
Hempstead
  Hofstra Univ. Institute for Commu-
    nity Education, 434
  Women's Center of Nassau County,
    210
Huntington: Career Counseling for
  Women, 432
Ithaca
  Cornell Univ., College of Arts and
    Sciences, Women's Studies Program,
    417
  Cornell Univ., Women's Studies, 414
  Ithaca NOW, 163
  Ithaca Women's Center, 206
  Professional Skills Roster, 434
Jamestown NOW, 163
Middletown: Orange County Commu-
  nity College Woman's Program, 434
Mt. Vernon: Lower Westchester NOW,
  163
  Macmillan Audio Brandon, 102
Muncie: Rockland County NOW, 163
New Paltz
  New Paltz NOW, 163
  New Paltz Women's Alliance, 208
  Women's Media Exchange, 376
New Rochelle
  New Rochelle, College of, Women's
    Studies, 414
  Soul Survivor, 138
North Salem: NOWestchester, 163
Oakdale, N.Y. NOW, 163
Old Westbury
  The Feminist Press, 7
  New York, State Univ. College,
    Women's Studies, 414
Otisville: Middletown, N.Y. NOW, 163
Piermont: Underwater Women of the
  20th Century Renaissance, 34
Plattsburgh NOW, 163
Pleasantville: New Directions Division,
  Pace University, 434
Potsdam NOW, 163
Poughkeepsie
  College Art Association Committee
    on the Status of Women, 360
  Mid-Hudson Women's Center, 207

Vassar College, Office of Career Planning, 434
Remsen, N.Y. NOW, 163
Rochester
American Physical Society, Committee on Women in Physics, 528
Genesee Valley, N.Y. NOW, 163
Rush: Women Studies Abstracts, 89
Saratoga Springs: Skidmore College, N.Y. NOW, 163
Setauket: Suffolk County NOW, 163
Scarborough: The Feminist Bulletin, 51
Scarsdale: Women's Health Care Education Council, Inc., 492
Selden: Suffolk County Community College Women's Group, 209
Suffern
Aurora, 44
Roger Williams College and University Without Walls, Women's Studies, 414
Syracuse
Central New York NOW, 163
New York NOW, 163
Syracuse NOW, 163
Syracuse University/University College Women's Center for Continuing Education, 434
Troy: Albany NOW, 163
Utica: Alfred, N.Y. NOW, 163
Wappinger Falls NOW, 163
Watertown: Jefferson County NOW, 163
Woodmere: National Women's Political Caucus, New York, 512
Yorktown Heights: Westchester County NOW, 163
Youngstown: Niagara Falls, N.Y. NOW, 163

NEW YORK CITY

Abortion Rights Association, Inc., 460
Ain't I a Woman? Performing Troupe, 355
Alumnae Advisory Center, 431
American Civil Liberties Union, Women's Rights Project, 377
The American Medical Women's Association, Inc., 525
American Philological Association, Women's Caucus, 527
American Statistical Association, Caucus for Women in Statistics, 533
Aphra, 43

Artists in Residence (AIR), 356
Association for the Study of Abortion, Inc., 463
Barnard College Placement and Career Planning Office, 434
Barnard College, The Women's Center, 414
Beahive Enterprises, 128
Bellamy, Blank, Goodman, Kelly, Ross and Stanley, 378
Boyle/Kirkman Associates, Inc., 424
Bronx NOW, 163
Brooklyn College, CUNY, Women's Studies, 414
Brooklyn NOW, 163
Catalyst, 434
Center for United Labor Action, 439
China Books and Periodicals, 119
City College, CUNY, Women's Studies, 414
Coordinating Committee on Women in the Historical Profession, 542
Council on Economic Priorities, 147
Eastern Women's Center, 468
The Equation Collective Inc., 131
The Executive Woman, 49
Ezrat Nashim, 446
Federation Employment & Guidance Service, 434
Feminist Art Journal, 50
Feminist Book Mart, 121
Feminist Forums, 391
The Feminist Party, 510
Feminist Sexuality Project, 469
Feminist Therapy Referral Collective, 470
The Feminists, 198
Greyfalcon House, 134
Health Policy Advisory Center (Health PAC), 473
Herstory Films, 99
Human Relations Work-Study Center, New School for Social Research, 434
Hunter College Career Counseling and Placement, 434
Hunter College, CUNY, Committee on Women's Studies, 414
Impact Films, 100
Information Center on the Mature Woman, 150
Jacqueline Ceballos Productions, 425
Jewish Feminist Organization, 447
Labyris Books, 123
Lefcourt Kraft & Libow, 381

Liberation Enterprises, 135
Liberation News Service, 116
The Lockwood Conference, 435
Lucinda Cisler, 4
The Lucy Stone League, Inc., 160
Majority Report, 62
McGraw-Hill Contemporary Films, 101
Media Plus, Inc., 103
Modern Language Association of America, Commission on Women, 545
Ms., 66
National Association for Repeal of Abortion Laws, 480
National Association of Women Artists, 364
National Black Feminist Organization, 450
National Film Board of Canada, 104
National Women's Political Caucus, Puerto Rican, 512
New Feminist Talent, Inc., 365
New Line Cinema, 106
The New Woman's Survival Catalog: A Woman-made Book, 24
New York Commission on Human Rights, 310
New York, N.Y. NOW, 163
New York Radical Feminists, 199
Newsreal, 107
NOW Legal Defense and Education Fund, 383
Options: Career Workshops for Women, 434
Pathfinder Press, Inc., 26
Planned Parenthood Federation of America, Inc., 482
Prime Time: For the Liberation of Women in the Prime of Life, 73
Queens College, CUNY, Women's Studies Committee, 414
Queens NOW, 163
Radio Free People, 109
Redstockings, 200
Richmond College, CUNY, Women's Studies, 414
Richmond College Women's Self Help Collective, 486
St. Joan's International Alliance, 453
Society of Women Engineers, 556
Staten Island Community College, CUNY, Women's Studies, 414
Staten Island Community College Women's Center, 201

Staten Island NOW, 163
Stewardesses for Women's Rights, 558
Task Force on Women in Church and Society, United Church of Christ, 455
Third World Women's Alliance, 454
13th Moon, 81
United Nations Commission on the Status of Women, 247
United Presbyterian Church Council on Women and the Church, 456
Up from Under: A New Magazine By, For and About Women, 82
Vegetarian-Feminists, 566
Violet Press, 36
West Bronx, N.Y. NOW, 163
Westbeth Playwrights' Feminist Collective, 368
"Where We At" Black Women Artists, 369
Widows Consultation Center, 567
Women Enterprises, Inc., 141
Women in City Government United, 442
Women in the Arts, 371
Women Make Movies, Inc., 113
Women's Action Alliance, 165
Women's Affirmative Action Coalition, 385
Women's Anti-Rape Group, 503
Women's Art Registry, 372
The Women's Center, Barnard College, N.Y., 202
Women's Center, Union Theological Seminary, 203
Women's Counseling Project, 204
Women's Health Forum and Health-right, Inc., 494
Women's Interart Center, 375
Women's Law Center, 387
Women's Liberation Center, 205
The Women's Martial Arts Union (WMAU), 504
Women's National Abortion Action Coalition, 495
Women's Prison Association and Home, 499
Women's Studies: An Interdisciplinary Journal, 92
Woodmere Women's Center, 211
Young Women's Christian Association of the U.S.A., 167
Zizi Press, 39

NORTH CAROLINA

Asheville: Buncombe Co., N.C. NOW, 163
Chapel Hill
  Chapel Hill-Durham NOW, 163
  Lollipop Power, Inc., 16
Charlotte
  Charlotte NOW, 163
  National Women's Political Caucus, North Carolina, 512
  North Carolina NOW, 163
Clemmons: Winston-Salem NOW, 163
Durham
  Durham NOW, 163
  Duke Univ. Center for Career Development and Continuing Education, 434
Fayetteville NOW, 163
Goldsboro NOW, 163
Greensboro
  Greensboro NOW, 163
  Walter Clinton Jackson Library, University of North Carolina at Greensboro, 155
  The Mayor's Committee on the Status of Women, City of Greensboro, N.C., 316
  North Carolina Commission on Education and Employment of Women, 317
Greenville
  Greenville NOW, 163
  Mayor's Commission on the Status of Women, 312
Havelock NOW, 163
Jacksonville NOW, 163
Raleigh NOW, 163
Rockingham: Mayor's Commission on the Status of Women, 313
Salisbury: Mayor's Commission on the Status of Women, 314
Statesville NOW, 163
Wilmington, N.C. NOW, 163
Winston-Salem
  Mayor's Committee on the Status of Women, 315
  Salem College Lifespan Counseling Center for Women, 434

NORTH DAKOTA

Bismark: North Dakota Commission on the Status of Women, 318

Dickinson NOW, 163
Fargo
  Fargo, N.D.-Moorhead, NOW, 163
  National Women's Political Caucus, North Dakota, 512
Grand Forks
  Grand Forks, N.D. NOW, 163
  State of North Dakota NOW, 163

OHIO

Akron
  University of Akron, 434
  Akron NOW, 163
Avon Lake, Ohio NOW, 163
Cincinnati
  Cincinnati Council on the Status of Women, 319
  Cincinnati NOW, 163
  National Women's Political Caucus, Ohio, 512
Cleveland
  Cleveland NOW, 163
  Project Eve, Cuyahoga Community College, 434
Columbus
  Columbus, Ohio NOW, 163
  Ohio Bureau of Employment Services, Women Services Division, 321
  Ohio NOW, 163
  Women's Self-Government Association, 214
Danville: Knox County NOW, 163
Delaware, Ohio NOW, 163
Fairborn, Ohio NOW, 163
Fairview Park: Cleveland Council on the Status of Women, 320
Gambier: Knox County NOW, 163
Girard: Youngstown NOW, 163
Huron: Erie County, Ohio NOW, 163
Kent
  Kent NOW, 163
  Kent Women's Project, 213
Mansfield, Ohio NOW, 163
Newark: Ohio Commission on the Status of Women, Inc., 322
Oxford: Pregnancy Consultation Service, 484
Richmond: Steubenville NOW, 163
Shaker Heights: Cleveland, Ohio NOW, 163
Springfield: Wittenberg Univ., Women and the Human Revolution, 414

Toledo: Greater Toledo Area NOW, 163
Trotwood: Dayton NOW, 163
University Heights: Cleveland Jewish
    Vocational Service, 434
Wooster, Ohio NOW, 163
Yellow Springs
    Antioch College, Women's Studies,
    414
    Antioch Women's Center, 212

OKLAHOMA

Ada: Daughters of Bilitis, 506
Heavener: Oklahoma Governor's Com-
    mission on the Status of Women,
    323
Macomb: Shawnee NOW, 163
Midwest City: The North American
    Indian Women's Association, 452
Norman, Okla. NOW, 163
Oklahoma City
    National Women's Political Caucus,
    Oklahoma, 512
    Oklahoma City NOW, 163
    Oklahoma NOW, 163
Tulsa NOW, 163

OREGON

Beaverton: Governor's Committee on
    the Status of Women in Oregon, 324
Corvallis
    National Women's Political Caucus,
    Oregon, 512
    Oregon State Univ., Women's Studies,
    414
Eugene
    Lane County NOW, 163
    National Women's Political Caucus,
    Oregon, 512
    Oregon, Univ. of, Women's Studies,
    414
    Women's Press, 90
Klamath Falls NOW, 163
Portland
    Abortion Information and Referral
    Service of Portland, Inc., 459
    Oregon Council for Women's Equal-
    ity, 215
    Portland NOW, 163
    Portland State Univ., Women's Stud-
    ies, 414
    Portland State Univ., Women's Stud-
    ies Union, 420

Portland Women's Health Clinic, 483
Women's Programs, Division of Con-
    tinuing Education, 434
Roseburg, Oreg. NOW, 163
Salem: Willamette Valley NOW, 163
Troutdale: Portland NOW, 163

PENNSYLVANIA

Allentown
    Cedar Crest College Career Planning
    Office, 434
    Lehigh Valley, Pa. NOW, 163
Altoona, Pa. NOW, 163
Bellefonte: Centre County NOW, 163
Bethlehem: Lehigh Valley Abortion
    Rights Assn., 476
Bryn Mawr College Office of Career
    Planning and Placement, 434
Easton: Lafayette College NOW, 163
Erie
    Erie, Pa. NOW, 163
    Villa Maria College Career Counseling
    Center for Adult Women, 434
Harrisburg: Pennsylvania Commission
    on the Status of Women, 325
Hershey NOW, 163
Industry: Beaver County, Pa. NOW, 163
Jeannette: Greater Greensburg, Pa.
    NOW, 163
Johnstown, Pa. NOW, 163
King of Prussia: National Women's Po-
    litical Caucus, Pennsylvania, 512
Lancaster: Pennsylvanians for Women's
    Rights, 218
Media: Women's Action Coalition, 219
McKeesport NOW, 163
New Cumberland: Harrisburg, Pa. NOW,
    163
Penndel: Northeast-Lower Bucks Co.
    NOW, 163
Philadelphia
    American Studies Association, Com-
    mittee on Women, 534
    Center for Women in Medicine, 540
    Concern for Health Options: Informa-
    tion, Care, and Education
    (CHOICE), 467
    Institute of Awareness, 434
    Options for Women, 434
    Pennsylvania, Univ. of, Women's
    Studies, 414
    Philadelphia, Pa. NOW, 163

Temple Univ. Career Services/Continuing Education for Women, 434
Women in Leadership (Project WIL), 393
Women in Transition, Inc., 384
The Women's Art Center of Philadelphia, 373
Women's Liberation Center of Philadelphia, 220
Pittsburgh
The Association for the Development of Opportunity, Inc., 216
Black Women's Association, 443
East Hills NOW, 163
Job Advisory Service, Chatham College, 434
Johns, Norris Associates, 429
Know, Inc., 13
Oakland, Pa. NOW, 163
Ohio Valley North Hills NOW, 163
Pennsylvania NOW, 163
Pittsburgh NOW, 163
Pittsburgh, Univ. of, Women's Studies, 414
Robert Morris College, Dept. of Continuing Education, 434
South Hills NOW, 163
Pottstown NOW, 163
Slippery Rock
Association for Women's Rights, 217
Swarthmore NOW, 163
Swiftwater: Pocono, Pa. NOW, 163
University Park, Pa. NOW, 163
Washington: Washington County, Pa. NOW, 163
Wilkinsburg: Woman Becoming, 86
Womelsdorf: Berks County, Pa. NOW, 163

RHODE ISLAND

Barrington: Rhode Island NOW, 163
Providence
Brown Univ. Higher Education Resource Services (HERS), 408
National Women's Political Caucus, Rhode Island, 512
Population Association of America, Women's Caucus, 550
Rhode Island Coalition to Repeal the Abortion Laws, 485
Rhode Island Permanent Advisory Commission on Women, 326
Women of Brown United, 221

Women's Liberation Union of Rhode Island, 222
YWCA Women's Center, 223
Warwick: Rhode Island NOW, 163

SOUTH CAROLINA

Aiken: Aiken County NOW, 163
Charleston, S.C. NOW, 163
Clemson: Piedmont NOW, 163
Columbia
Columbia, S.C. NOW, 163
National Women's Political Caucus, South Carolina, 512
South Carolina Commission on the Status of Women, 327
South Carolina, Univ. of, Women's Studies Institute, 414
Greenville, S.C. NOW, 163
Hilton Head, S.C. NOW, 163
Spartanburg
Spartanburg, S.C. NOW, 163
State of South Carolina NOW, 163

SOUTH DAKOTA

Aberdeen: National Women's Political Caucus, North Dakota, 512
Brookings NOW, 163
Madison NOW, 163
Pierre
South Dakota Commission on the Status of Women, 328
South Dakota NOW, 163
Sioux Falls NOW, 163
Vermillion NOW, 163

TENNESSEE

Arlington NOW, 163
Chattanooga NOW, 163
Cookeville NOW, 163
Huntingdon NOW, 163
Johnson City NOW, 163
Knoxville, Tenn. NOW, 163
Martin: UTM NOW, 163
Memphis
Memphis NOW, 163
National Women's Political Caucus, Black, 512
Nashville
Nashville, Tenn. NOW, 163
Nashville's Women Center, 224
National Women's Political Caucus, Tennessee, 512

Tennessee Governor's Commission on the Status of Women, 329
Tennessee NOW, 163
Oak Ridge, Tenn. NOW, 163

TEXAS
Austin
Austin Mayor's Commission on the Status of Women, 330
Austin NOW, 163
National Women's Political Caucus, Texas, 512
The Texas Woman, 80
Women in Communications, Inc. (founded as Theta Sigma Phi), 559
Dallas
Dallas County NOW, 163
Daughters of Bilitis, 506
Southern Methodist Univ., Women's Studies, 414
Texas Citizens for Abortion Education, 488
Women for Change Center, 225, 434
Del Rio: Val Verde County NOW, 163
Denton NOW, 163
Edinburg: Hidalgo Co., NOW, 163
Fort Worth
Fort Worth Educational Task Force, 403
Fort Worth Mayor's Commission on Women, 331
Fort Worth, Tex. NOW, 163
The Liberator, 61
Nana Workshop, 136
Houston
Bay Area, Tex. NOW, 163
Houston, Tex. NOW, 163
National Women's Political Caucus, Union Women, 512
Huntsville
Huntsville Mayor's Commission on the Status of Women, 333
Huntsville, Tex. NOW, 163
Marshall: Harrison County Commission on the Status of Women, 332
San Angelo Commission on the Status of Women, 335
San Antonio
Mayor's Commission on the Status of Women, 334
National Women's Political Caucus, Chicana, 512
San Antonio NOW, 163

Texarkana NOW, 163
Waco NOW, 163

UTAH
Ogden: Weber State College, Women's Activities, 414
Provo NOW, 163
Salt Lake City
National Women's Political Caucus, Utah, 512
Salt Lake City NOW, 163
State of Utah NOW, 163
Utah Governor's Commission on the Status of Women, 336
Utah, Univ. of, Women's Resource Center, 414
Women's Resource Center, Univ. of Utah, 226

VERMONT
Bennington: Bennington College NOW, 163
Burlington: Vermont Women's Health Center, 490
Montpelier: Vermont Governor's Commission on the Status of Women, 337
Plainfield
Daughters, Inc., 5
Goddard College, Feminist Studies, 414
Shelburne
National Women's Political Caucus, Vermont, 512
Vermont NOW, 163
South Londonderry NOW, 163

VIRGINIA
Alexandria Mayor's Ad Hoc Committee on Women, 338
Arlington
Arlington County Commission on the Status of Women, 339
Athena Associates, Inc., 127
Roanoke NOW, 163
Charlottesville
Charlottesville, Va. NOW, 163
University of Virginia Office of Career Planning and Placement, 434
Christianberg: Blacksburg NOW, 163
Danville, Va. NOW, 163
Fairfax County Commission on Women, 342

Falls Church
  National Women's Political Caucus,
    Virginia, 512
  The Woman Activist, 85
Harrisonburg, Va. NOW, 163
Herndon: State of Virginia, 163
Lynchburg, Va. NOW, 163
Martinsville, Va. NOW, 163
McLean: Northern Virginia NOW, 163
Newport News
  Newport News NOW, 163
  Peninsula NOW, 163
Petersburg, Va. NOW, 163
Richmond
  Citizen's Committee on the Status of
    Women in Virginia, 340
  Commission on the Status of Women,
    341
  Richmond NOW, 163
Vienna: National Women's Political
  Caucus, Virginia, 512
Virginia Beach
  Tidewater, Va. NOW, 163
  Virginia Beach, Va. NOW, 163
Williamsburg, Va. NOW, 163
Wise, Va. NOW, 163

WASHINGTON

Bellingham
  Bellingham-Whatcom NOW, 163
  Western Washington State College,
    Women's Studies, 414
Bothell: Washington NOW, 163
Bremerton: Kitsap County NOW, 163
Federal Way-Auburn NOW, 163
Gig Harbor: Tacoma NOW, 163
Kent: Highline NOW, 163
Longview NOW, 163
Monroe: Snohomish County NOW, 163
Mountlake Terrace: Snohomish County
  NOW, 163
Olympia
  Olympia NOW, 163
  Washington State Women's Council
    344
Pullman–Moscow, ID NOW, 163
Renton
  Bellevue-Eastside NOW, 163
  Renton NOW, 163
Richland: Tri City NOW, 163
Seattle
  Abortion-Birth Control Referral Ser-
    vice, 458

Arcadia Clinic, 462
ERA Enterprises, 132
Fremont Women's Clinic, 472
Individual Development Center, Inc.,
  434
Lesbian Resource Center, 509
National Women's Political Caucus,
  Washington, 512
Pandora, 72
Radical Women, 227
Seattle-King County NOW, 163
Seattle Women's Commission, 343
Second Moon Music, 112
Univ. of Washington, Women's Guid-
  ance Center, 434
Washington, Univ. of, Women's Stud-
  ies, 414
Spokane NOW, 163
Tacoma: Puget Sound, Univ. of,
  Women's Studies, 414
Vancouver NOW, 163
Yakima NOW, 163

WEST VIRGINIA

Charleston NOW, 163
Harrisville: West Virginia Governor's
  Commission on the Status of
  Women, 345
Morgantown: Mor-Fair NOW, 163

WISCONSIN

Appleton: Fox Cities NOW, 163
Beaver Dam NOW, 163
Beloit: Rock County NOW, 163
Eau Claire
  Eau Claire NOW, 163
  Wisconsin NOW, 163
Green Bay
  Green Bay NOW, 163
  Part-time Professionals Office of
    Adult Education, Univ. of Wiscon-
    sin, 434
Janesville: Rock County NOW, 163
Kenosha NOW, 163
La Crosse NOW, 163
Madison
  Madison NOW, 163
  Whole Woman Newspaper, 84
  Wisconsin Governor's Commission on
    the Status of Women, 347
Marshfield Area, Wis. NOW, 163

Milwaukee
  Alverno College, Research Center on
    Women, 143, 414
  Alverno College Women's Research
    Center, 163
  Milwaukee NOW, 163
  Wisconsin, Univ. of, Women's Studies
    Committee, 414
Oostburg: Sheboygan County NOW,
  163
Oshkosh
  Winnebago NOW, 163
  Wisconsin State Univ., Women's Stud-
    ies Committee, 414
Platteville: National Women's Political
  Caucus, Wisconsin, 512
Ripon NOW, 163
Stevens Point: Central Wisconsin NOW,
  163
Sturgeon Bay NOW, 163
Two Rivers-Manitowoc NOW, 163
Waukesha NOW, 163
Wausau: Mayor's Commission on the
  Status of Women, 346
Winneconne: Women In Struggle, 88

WYOMING

Casper
  Casper NOW, 163
  National Women's Political Caucus,
    Wyoming, 512
Cheyenne
  Cheyenne NOW, 163
  Wyoming Commission on the Status
    of Women, 348
Laramie
  Laramie NOW, 163
  University of Wyoming NOW, 163
  University of Wyoming Placement
    Service, 434

PUERTO RICO

Condado, P.R. NOW, 163
National Women's Political Caucus,
  Puerto Rico, 512

VIRGIN ISLANDS

St. Thomas: Virgin Islands Commission
  on the Status of Women, 349

Canada

ALBERTA

Edmonton
  Alberta Status of Women Committee,
    231
  Alberta Women's Bureau, 351

BRITISH COLUMBIA

Vancouver
  Vancouver NOW, 163
  Vancouver Status of Women, 232
  Vancouver Women's Centre, 233
  Vancouver Women's Health Collective,
    489

MANITOBA

Winnipeg
  Manitoba Action Committee on the
    Status of Women, 234
  Manitoba Women's Bureau, Dept. of
    Labor, 352
  A Women's Place, 235

NEWFOUNDLAND

St. John's
  Newfoundland Status of Women
    Council, 236
  The Woman's Place, 237

ONTARIO

Ancaster
  Children's Liberation Workshop, 397
  Clearinghouse for Feminist Media, 358
Mississauga: National Action Committee
  on the Status of Women in Canada,
  229
Ottawa
  Canada Dept. of Labor—Women's
    Bureau, 350
  Canadian Federation of University
    Women, 228
  Collage and Road Crafts, 129
  The National Council of Women of
    Canada, 230
  National Film Board of Canada, 104
  Ottawa Women's Centre, 239
Toronto
  Canadian Women's Coalition to Re-
    peal the Abortion Laws, 465
  Canadian Women's Education Press, 3

The New Feminists, 68
New Hogtown Press, 22
Ontario Committee on the Status of Women, 238
Ontario Ministry of Labor, Women's Bureau, Human Rights Commission, 353
Women's Information Centre, 240
Women's Involvement Program, 115
Waterloo: Canadian Newsletter of Research on Women, 45
Windsor: Women's Liberation Group, 241

QUEBEC

Montreal
Montreal Health Press, Inc., 19
National Film Board of Canada, 104
Our Generation, 71
A Woman's Place/Place Des Femmes, 242

Women's Centre, YMCA, 243
Women's Counseling Service, 291

SASKATCHEWAN

Regina
Saskatchewan Action Committee, Status of Women, 244
Saskatchewan Dept. of Labor, Women's Bureau, 354
Saskatoon Women's Liberation, 245

YUKON TERRITORY

Whitehorse: Yukon Status of Women Group, 246

Other Countries

Paris, France: Paris NOW, 163
Taipei NOW, 163

Media Title Index

(Titles are grouped under these categories: Books and Print Media; Children's Books; Films; General Products; Mixed Media; Posters; Records and Audiotapes; Videotapes.)

Books and Print Media (pamphlets, leaflets, brochures, flyers, etc.)

ABCs of Your Job: A Handbook of Personnel Management Matters, 544

Abortion: A Physician's Rights and Responsibilities, 461

Abortion: A Woman's Right, 26, 461

Abortion Eve, 20

Abortion . . . Every Woman's Right, 469

Abortion: Guidelines for the Clergyman, Counselor, Health Educator, Nurse, Social Worker, 461

Abortion: Questions and Answers, 481

Abortion Resources Handbook, 460

Academic Women, Sex Discrimination, and the Law: An Action Handbook, 545

Agency Accountability Studies, 544

Alice Paul, 142

American Economic Review, 521

American Women: Their Use and Abuse, 21

Amniocentesis, 480

Analysis of Male and Female Participation in Municipal Employment, 278

Annual Reports, 151

Answers to Questions on the Equal Rights Amendment, 512

Approaching Simone, 7

Are Women Equal under the Law?, 163

Asexual Manifesto, 199

Attorney Doris Brin Walker Discusses Angela Davis Case, 382

Basic Self Exam, The, 488

Before You Buy, 326

Bibliographies on Women, Indexed by Topic, 156

Bibliography of Research on Sex Roles, 557

Birth Control Handbook, The, 19, 21

Black Panther Sisters Talk about Women's Liberation, 21

Books by Women (and some Men) Relevant to Women's Liberation, 21

Brainchild, 357

Bread and Roses, 35

Burn This and Memorize Yourself: Poems for Women, 32, 71

Business of Your Own . . . a guide to good business practice, A, 295

California's Children's Centers, 522

Career Baedeker in How to Go to Work When Your Husband Is Against It, Your Children Aren't Old Enough and There's Nothing You Can Do Anyhow, The, 434

Career Choices for Women in Medicine, 526

Career for Women in Banking, 547

Career Opportunities Series, The, 434

Careers Unlimited: A Forecast of Opportunities in Journalism and Communications, 559

Case for Equity, A, 545

Case for Small Families, The, 499

Cassandra, 214

Catalog of the Sophia Smith Collection, 154

Catalog, The, 156
Catalyst Roster, 434
Changing Patterns of Women's Lives, 255
Chicago Women's Yellow Pages, The, 184
Chicanos Speak Out, 26
Child's Right to Equal Reading, 7
Chinese Women Liberated, 119
Chronicle, The, 228
Churches That Have Taken Official Positions in Favor of Making Abortion an Individual Decision, 480
Citizenship, 351
Class Structure in the Women's Movement, 198
Coalition, 227
Collected Stories, 7
College English, 545
Coming of Woman, The: The Christa, 449
Community Counseling Services on Jobs and/or Training for Women in the District of Columbia, 266
Community Workshops on Children's Books, 7
Complaints and Disorders, 7
Complete Literature Packet, 198
Conference on Women Theologians, 143
Conscious-raising Outline, 199
Consciousness Razors, 7
Conspiracy, The, 388
Constance de Markievicz, 7
Consumerism and Women, 22
Continuing Education; A Survey of Programs in Massachusetts, 296
Cook and the Carpenter, The, 5
Cope Kit, 232
Counseling Services in Edmonton, 351
Credit Kit, 386
Daily Programming for Infants in Day Care, 400
Daily Programming for Three to Five-Year-Olds in Day Care, 400
Daily Programming for Two-Year Olds in Day Care, 400
Dangerous Experiment: 100 Years of Women at the University of Michigan, The, 413
Dangers in the Pro-Woman Line and Consciousness Raising, 198
Daughter of Earth, 7
Daughter of Han, A, 119

Day Care, 232
Day Care Administration, 400
Day Care as a Child-Rearing Environment, 399
Day Care Book, The, 3, 71
Day Care: Resources for Decisions, 399
Day Care Supervision, 400
Day Care, Who Cares?: Government and Day Care Plans, 21
Designing and Developing Environments for Day Care, 400
Dick and Jane as Victims: Sex Stereotyping in Children's Readers, 163, 407
Directory of Feminist Services, 163
Directory of Films by and/or about Women, 156
Directory of Members, 423
Directory of Women Attorneys in the United States, 9
Directory of Women Philosophers, 554
Directory of Women's Periodicals, 156
Divorce Law Reform, 326
Divorce Reform-Marriage and Family Laws Kit, 386
Divorce Trial in Canada, A, 35
Divorce Trial in China, A, 21, 71
Do It Now, 163
Do You Want to Return to the Horrors of Back-Alley Abortion?, 481
Double Cross, The, 449
Double Jeopardy: To Be Black and Female, 35
Dual Profession Family: Research Summary, The, 162
ERA Kit, 386
ERA: What It Means to Men and Women, The, 159
Early Development of the Family, The, 21
Early Feminist Movement in the U.S., The, 21
Early Losses, 5
Eastern Woman's Center, 469
Education of Women, The, 142
Educational Opportunities Series, The, 434
Elizabeth Barrett Browning, 7
Elizabeth Cady Stanton, 7, 142
Emancipation of Women, The, 227
Equal Opportunity Report No. 2: Job Patterns for Minorities and Women in Private Industry, 1967, 256

Equal Rights Amendment and Georgia Law, The, 270
Exclusion of Women from Canadian Medical Schools, The, 22
Exorcising the Sexual Demon, 449
Expanding Career Options for Women—Careers Committee Conference, 544
Exploring Human Space, 167
Exploring Sex Roles, 232
Extending Women's Protective Laws to Men, 382
Extra Money at Home, 295
Fact Sheet for Women Who Wish to Retain Their Own Name after Marriage, 379
Fact Sheet on Women's Names, 387
Facts for Mature Women Contemplating the Labor Market, 351
Facts on Woman Workers of Minority Races, 255
Families, 21
Family as Seen from a Feminist Perspective, The: A Selected Bibliography, 189
Family Day Care Study, A, 399
Famous Five, The, 351
Federal Laws and Regulations Concerning Sex Discrimination in Educational Institutions, 389
Feeding Ourselves, 17
Female Artists Past and Present, 156
Female Liberation as the Basis for Social Revolution, 21, 71
Female Offenders in the District of Columbia, 266
Female Studies, 7, 545
Female Studies I-V, 13
Feminine Figures, 167
Femininity, Feminism and Educational Change, 546
Feminism and Socialism, 26
Feminism and the Marxist Movement, 26
Feminist Classica: A Ms. Bibliography, 189
Feminist Looks at Educational Software Materials, A, 189
Feminist Resources for Elementary and Secondary Schools, 189
Feminist Resources for Schools and Colleges, 7
Feminist Revolution, 200
Feminists, The: Organizational Principles and Structure, 198

Ferment of Freedom, 167
Few Facts About Few, A, 544
50 Physicians Evaluate Legal Abortion in New York, 481
Fight for ERA Reaches Crucial Stage, 522
First Five Years—1966-1971, The, 163
Five Easy Pieces: A movie review, 198
Five Year Report, The, 336
Focus on Women, 260
Free Space: A Perspective on the Small Group in Women's Liberation, 32,71
Free Women of V.D., 266
Fucked-Up in America, 71
General Information for the Returning Student, 434
Generations of Denial: 75 Short Biographies of Women in History, 32, 71
Girl Sleuth, The: A Feminist Guide to Nancy Drew and Her Sisters, 7
Girls and Women: Do You Know That?, 296
Gold Flower's Story: Women's Liberation in Revolutionary China, 21
Graphic Notebook on Feminism, A, 32, 71
Guide to Archives and Manuscripts in the United States, 151
Guide to Current Female Studies, 7
Guide to Curricular Materials, A, 7
Guide to Improving Maternity Leave . . . Contract Clauses, A, 522
Guide to Women, the Law and Employment, A, 398
Guidelines for Consciousness-Raising, 207
Guidelines on Discrimination Because of Sex, 256
Gynecological Checkup, The, 495
Hand, The, 218
Handbook for Working Women, A, 245
Handbook of Manuscripts, 151
Help: A Resource Booklet for Women, 202
Help Improve Vocational Education for Women and Girls in Your Community, 255
Herpes Genitalis and Diaphragm Fitting, 488
Hidden History of the Female, The/A History of the Rise of Women's Consciousness in Canada and Quebec, 22

High School Feminist Studies, 7

Higher Education Kit, 386

Historical Perspectives on Child Care, 400

Home Secretarial Service, 295

Homemaker's Pensions, 244

How Not to Write Letters of Application, 431

How the Russian Revolution Failed Women, 21

How to Get Started in Women's Rights, 522

How To Run for Ward and Town Committees, 296

How to Write Your Resumé, 431

How We (Finally) Got the Stockton Record to Desegragate Its Help Wanted Ads, 163

Human Dignity of Woman in the Church, 449

Human Rights Casefinder: Warren Court Era 1953-1969, 382

Human Rights Organizations and Periodicals Directory, 1973, 382

I Am Woman, I Am Artist: A portfolio of 54 drawings and prints by Bay Area women artists, 367

I Don't Want to Change My Lifestyle—I Want to Change My Life, 21

I Took a Hammer in My Hand, 425

I'm Running Away from Home but I'm Not Allowed to Cross the Street, 13

Immersion, 30

Improving the Status of Household Employment: A Handbook for Community Action, 441

Improving the Status of Women in the Labor Force, 266

In Defense of the Women's Movement, 26

In Touch, 307

Infections of the Vagina, 495

Institution of Sexual Intercourse, The, 198

Interesting Statistics on Alberta Women, 351

Interim Report on Children's Literature, 264

International Bibliography of Women Writers, 172

International Instruments and Canadian Federal and Provincial Legislation Relating to the Status of Women in Employment, 350

Introduction to N.Y.R.F., 199

Investigation of Part Time Work for Women, An, 232

Is Biology Woman's Destiny?, 26

Job Discrimination Handbook, 380

Job Interview, The, 431

Job Patterns for Louisiana Men and Women in Private Industry, 288

Joint Task Force on Sexism in Education Report, 217

Journal of Legal Education, 539

Journal of NAWDAC, 546

Journal of the American Medical Women's Association, 526

Jumping the Track: High School Student, 21

Justice: The Hard Line, 449

Juvenile, The, 351

K-12 Education Kit, 386

Kaethe Kollwitz, 7

Kate Millett's Sexual Politics–A Marxist Appreciation, 26

Landlord and the Tenant, The, 351

Laws for Albertans, 351

Lesbianism: A Socialist-Feminist Perspective, 227

Lesbianism: Sexual Survival in the Schools, 189

Lesbians and the Health Care System, 36

Let Brother Bake the Cake, 522

Let Them Be Said, 17

Letters to Women, 30

Liberating Young Children from Sex Roles, 399

Liberation of Women: Sexual Repression and the Family, 21

Life and Times of My Mother and Me, The, 7

Life in the Iron Mills, 7

Lillian Moller Gilbreth Scholarship Brochure, 556

List of Manuscript Collections in the Library of Congress July 1931 to July 1938, 151

Listing of Selected N.Y.S. Abortion Clinics, 461

Little Prick, The, 39

Lonely Girl in the Big City, The, 21

Looking at Women, 36

Louisiana Women and Girls in Public Vocational-Technical Education Programs—a Study of Sex Discrimination, 288

Louisiana Women in Selected Federally-Assisted Work and Training Programs, Fiscal Year 1971, 288
Lucy Stone, 142
Ms. ERY, 38
Man-Hating, 198
Marketing your Handcraft, 295
Marriage, 198
Marxism: A Syllabus Design for a Women's Course, 21
Marxism and Feminism, 3
Matrimonial Property Rights, 244
Matrix: For She of the New Aeon, 18
Medicine . . . A Women's Career, 526
Medicine Can Be for You, 526
Midwest Conference on Women's Studies, 143
Mod Donna and Scyklonz, 26
Money and the Mature Citizen, 547
Monster, 387
Monster Coloring Book, 17
Montreal Woman's Yellow Pages, 242
Mother Was Not a Person, 71
Moynihan, Poverty Programs, and Women—A Female Viewpoint, 163
Myth of the Vaginal Orgasm, The, 21, 71
Myth of Women's Inferiority: Women's Role in Prehistoric Societal Development, The, 21
NOW Feminist Products Catalog, 163
NOW Newsletter Directory, 156
National Business Woman, 162
National Union Catalog of Manuscript Collections, 151
Nerves, 5
New Jersey Teenagers and Contraception, 163
New Unemployment Insurance, 351
New Woman's Survival Catalog, The: A Woman-made Book, 24
New Women in New China, 119
1972 Report of the Commission, The, 275
Non-Sexist Parenting, 189
Nonsexist Curricular Material for Elementary Schools, 7
Notes from the Lower Classes, 198
Notes on Women's Liberation; We Speak in Many Voices, 194
On Day Care, 21
On the Job Oppression of Working Women: A Collection of Articles; Secretary, Housewife, Switchboard Operator, Nurse, Cocktail Waitress, 21
On the Verge, 38
Opportunities Part Time: A Guide to Work and Further Training for Women, 177
Oppression of Women in the Hard Drug Culture, The, 172
Optimal National Policy on the Status of Women, 544
Organization Directory, 311
Origin of the Family, The, 22
Our Bodies, Our Selves, 2
Our Struggle Against Levi-Strauss, 21
PM 3: The Women's Movement, Where It's At, 27
Parent Programs, 399
Parents and Teachers Together, 399
Party Aide Guide, 441
Personae Non Gratae, 30
Phallic Worship: The Ultimate Idolatry, 449
Physical and Mental Health Aspects of Abortion, 480
Picture Catalog, The, 154
Pioneer Women of the West, 351
Pioneers of Women's Liberation, 26
Planning Our Work, 434
Political Economy of Male Chauvinism, The, 21
Political Economy of Women, The, 71
Political Economy of Women's Liberation, The, 21, 22, 35, 71
Political Women: Careers of Women State Legislators, The, 148
Politics of Housework, The, 21
Poor Black Women, 21
Population and the American Future, 499
Population Bibliography, 499
Population Bomb, The, 499
Positive Indicators in Employment for Women in HEW, 252
Possibilities for Action, 260
Pregnancy Testing, 488
Preliminary Bibliography of Resources for Women's History at the Michigan Historical Collections, 144
Probable Cause for Alarm, 163
Problems and Opportunities Challenging Women Today, 546
Problems of Women's Liberation, 26
Proceedings of the First International Childbirth Conference, 482

Profile of the Woman Engineer, A, 556
Profit in the Pantry, 295
Programming for School-Age Children in Day Care, 400
Programming for the Education of Women, 546
Proud Heritage, 230
Psychology Constructs the Female, 71
Psychology Constructs the Female: or, The Fantasy Life of the Male Psychologist, 21
Race and Sex, 1972: Collision or Comradeship, 227
Racism and Sexism, 167
Radical Feminism and Love, 198
Rainbow Snake, 172
Rape, 38
Red Detachment of Women, 119
Report of the Commissioners, 1972, 296
Report on the Status of Women in Florida, The, 267
Report to the Governor on the Status of the Hispanic-American Woman in Massachusetts, 296
Residential Mortgage Lending Practices of Commercial Banks, Savings & Loan Associations and Mortgage Bankers, 266
Results of an Employment Survey Conducted by the Employment Committee of the Mayor's Task Force on Women, 278
Results of Survey on Women in Higher Education in Colorado, Fall, 1971, 264
Rhode Island Women, 326
Rhode Island Women—Their Legal Status, 326
Right to Grow, The, 303
Rise of Man: Origins of Woman's Oppression, The, 198
Rosa Luxemburg: Revolutionary, Theoretician, 194
Rubyfruit Jungle, 5
SWE Achievement Award, 556
SWE Report on Women Undergraduate Students in Engineering, 556
Saline Abortion, 495
San Francisco Women's Business Directory, 430
Sappho '71, 29
See How She Runs, 264
Seizing the Reigns, 240

Selected Bibliography on Women and Religion, 449
Self-Study Guide to Sexism in Schools, 217
Setting Goals for Local Women's Rights Committees Using AFT Policy as a Guide, 522
Sex and Status in Academia, 326
Sex Bias in the Public Schools, 163
Sex Discrimination in Employment: What to Know about It, What to Do about It, 163
Sex Discrimination in the Academic World: Research Summary, 162
Sex Roles and Female Oppression, 21, 71
Sexism in Education, 401
Sexual Barrier, The, 11
Sexual Fairness in Language, 361
Sexual Honesty by Women For Women, 470
Sexual Politics, 227
Sexual Repression and the Family, 22
Shameless Hussy Review, 30
Shortchanged, 147
Sister, Can You Spare a Dime, 163
Sisterhood is Powerful, 26
Sisters in Struggle 1848-1920, 26
Sleeping Beauty, 31
Some Pictures from My Life: A Diary, 32
Sports Kit, 386
Status Anyone, 232
Status of Women in Arkansas, The, 260
Status of Women in Mississippi, 299
Status of Women in the Church, The, 449
Status of Women Workers in Louisiana, 1970, The, 288
Struggling into Existence: the Feminism of Sarah and Angelina Grimke, 21
Suggested Topics for Consciousness-Raising, 207
Summary of Commission and Its Work, 296
Supreme Court Decisions, The, 480
Survey of Restructured Jobs in DHEW—Opportunities for Men and for Women, 252
Survey of Rosters and Registries for Women, 544
Survey of Senior Students from Fourteen Public Schools in Arkansas, A, 260

Survey of Statewide Women's Legislation 73, 296

Synopsis of Women in World History, 156

Task Force Guidelines and Information, 296

Teacher Unions and Women's Rights, 522

Tenant Survival Book, The, 387

They Almost Seized the Time, Women and Socialism, 35

Thunder from the Earth, 14

Title VII of the 1964 Civil Rights Act, as Amended by the EEO Act of 1972, 256

Tits & Clits, 20

To Oedipus, From Mother, 34

Toward a Female Liberation Movement, 71

Toward Job Equality for Women, 256

Towards a Female Liberation Movement, 21

Traffic in Women and Other Essays, The, 71

Traffic in Women and Other Essays on Feminism, The, 32

Trans. & Proc. of American Philological Association, 526

Treasure, The, 5

Trichomonas Vaginitis, 588

True Myth, The, 449

True Story, 17

Twig Benders, The: A Pornographic Study of Pornography, 198

Uncertain, Coy and Hard to Please: The Myth of Femininity, 21

Unmasking, 362

Utah Women in Higher Education, 226

VD Handbook, 19

WTFW Yearbook, 93

Wanted: Women Engineers and More Chance for Them, 556

Washington Opportunities for Women: A Guide to Part-time Work and Study, 437

We Are All Lesbians, 36

We May Not Have Much, but There's a Lot of Us, 35

Welfare Is a Woman's Issue, 164

Welfare: The Big Lie, 21

What Constitutes Sex Discrimination, 310

What Is the Revolutionary Potential of Women's Liberation?, 21

What to Look for in a Lawyer, 384

What Women Should Know about the Pill, 495

What You Should Know about Women Engineers, 556

Where Can You Go for Help?, 302, 303

Which Road towards Women's Liberation: The Movement as a Radical Vanguard or a Single-Issue Coalition, 227

Who Are the Working Mothers?, 255

Who Rules Massachusetts Women?, 189

Who Shall Live?, 499

Who Were They? Some American Feminists Who Came before Us, 522

Who, Why and There Must Be a Code of Standards, 441

Who's Who and Where in Women's Studies, 7

Whole Woman Catalog, The, 37

Why We're Against the Equal Rights Amendment, 198

Wills and Estates for Albertans, 351

Windsor Working Women, 241

Witch's Os, The, 482

Witches, Midwives and Nurses, 7

Witches, Midwives and Nurses, A History of Women Healers, 21, 71

Woman and Her Mind: The Assaults of Daily Life: Female Schizophrenia, Consumerism, a Marxist Analysis, 21

Woman as Leader: Double Jeopardy on Account of Sex, 227

Woman from Welfare Rights, The, 164

Woman Identified Woman, and a Letter From Mary, 21

Woman in the Church NOW (canon law), 449

Woman Is a Sometime Thing, A, 22

Woman Is My Name, 15

Woman's Collection, The; A bibliography, 155

Woman's Lobby of Legislation in 1973, 296

Womansbook, The, 38

Women, 362

Women: A Bibliography, 4

Women and Health Care, 495

Women and Literature Bibliography, 416

Women and Missouri Laws, 300

Women and Poverty: The Status of Female-Headed Families in Louisiana, 288

Women and Psychology Bibliography, 416

Women and Socialism: Women in the Liberation Struggle—an Overview; Ma Bell Has Fleas— and a Lot of Angry Workers, 21

Women and the Cuban Revolution, 26

Women and the Law, 260

Women and the Law: A collection of Reading Lists, 13

Women and the Law in Newfoundland, 237

Women and Welfare, 21

Women at Work in Nova Scotia, 22

Women, Career Education, and the World of Work, 405

Women, Ethics and Ecology, 449

Women Executives: Annotated Bibliography, 162

Women: Rights, Rules, Reasons, 260

Women: The Longest Revolution, 21, 35, 71

Women: Their Status in State Government, 260

Women in Canadian Politics, 351

Women in Education: Changing Sexist Practices in the Classroom, 522

Women in Engineering, 556

Women in Engineering Revisited, 556

Women in Evolution, 22

Women in Higher Education, 522

Women in Labor Unions, 255

Women in Librarianship, 525

Women in Physics, 529

Women in Public Life in Wisconsin, 143

Women in the Labor Force 1971: Facts and Figures, 350

Women in the World of Words, 563

Women of the Convicted Class, 172

Women of the Telephone Company, 21

Women on Campus, 212, 413

Women on Juries, 351

Women Out of History: A Herstory Anthology, 10

Women Question in Child Care, The, 399

Women, Religion and the Law, 449

Women Rights Project Legal Docket: Affiliate and National Litigation Complete and in Progress, 377

Women State Legislators: Report from a Conference, 148

Women Under the Law, 38

Women Unite!, 3

Women Who Work, 227

Women Workers: Some Basic Statistics, 21

Women Workers: The Forgotten Third of the Working Class, 21

Women's Affirmative Action Plan, 385

Women's Collection, The: A Bibliography, 155

Women's Conference, California AFL-CIO 1973, 382

Women's Directory, A, 405

Women's Film Co-op Catalog, 189

Women's Guide to Divorce in New York, 387

Women's Heritage Calendar and Almanac, 142

Women's Interests, 311

Women's Job Rights Advocate Handbook, 438

Women's Legal Handbook Series on Job and Sex Discrimination, 9

Women's Liberation and the Church, 445

Women's Liberation as Force and Reason, 194

Women's Liberation—How and Why, 21

Women's Liberation Speaker's Manual, A, 207

Women's Life Styles: Catalyst's Position, 434

Women's Movement and the Class Struggle, The, 227

Women's Movement, The, 546

Women's Movement, Where It's At, The, 27

Women's Organizations and Leaders, 33

Women's Rights Almanac, 6

Woman's Rights Handbook on Kentucky Law, A, 562

Women's Rights Litigation, 382

Women's Rights Policy Resolution, 522

Women's Role in Contemporary Society, 310

Women's Roles, Labels and Stereotypes, 546

Women's Service Handbook, 237

Women's Songbook, 156

Women's Studies Courses, Indexed by Topic, 156

Women's Survival Manual: A Feminist Handbook on Separation and Divorce, 218, 384

Women's Work, 71
Women's Work: A Collection of Articles by Working Women, 22
Women's Work and Women's Studies, 202
Women's Yellow Pages, The, 1
Work Trianing Programs and Job Finding Assistance for Female Offenders at the Louisiana Correctional Institute for Women, 288
Working in Hospitals, 71
Working Mothers and the Day Nursery, 399
Working Women: Our Stories and Struggles, 440
Yellow Pages: A Resource Directory for the Needs of Women, 268
Yellow Walpaper, The, 7
Your Job Campaign, 434
Vacuum Aspiration Abortion, 495
Vaginal Orgasm as a Mass Hysterical Response, 198
Vancouver Women's Health Book, A, 488
Venereal Disease, 495
Voices of New Women: A Poetry Anthology, 189

Children's Books

ABC Workbook, The, 7
Amelia Earhart Storypack #1, 7
And So They Helped Each Other Out, 23
Carlotta and the Scientist, 16
Challenge to Become a Doctor: the Story of Elizabeth Blackwell, 7
Children and Their Families, 23
Coleen the Question Girl, 7
Did You Ever?, 16
Dragon and the Doctor, The, 7
Exactly Like Me, 16
Firegirl, 7
Grownups Cry Too, 16
I'm Like Me, 7
Jo, Flo and Yolanda, 16
Joshua's Day, 16
Little Doctor, The, 119
Magic Hat, The, 16
Martin's Father, 16
My Mother the Mail Carrier, 7

Nothing but a Dog, 7
Penelope and the Earth, 12
Penelope and the Mussels, 12
Penelope Goes to the Farmer's Market, 12
Sheep Book, The, 16
Some Things You Just Can'd Do by Yourself, 23
Stories from Liu Hu-lan's Childhood, 119
Surprise for Everyone, 8

Films

Abortion, 114
Anything You Want to Be, 105
Aretha Franklin, Soul Singer, 101
Bed and Sofa, 102
Behind the Veil, 100
Best of the New York Festival of Women's, Films, The 106
Betty Tells Her Story, 105
Birth Film, 375
Black Woman, 100
Breakfast Dance, 114
Campaign, 97
Ceiling, The, 100
Charlie Company, 98
Childcare: People's Liberation, 107
Circles, 98
Cleo from 5 to 7, 101
Color Rhapsodie, 98
Country Doctor, The, 102
Cycles, 98
Day of Plane Hunting, 107
Do Blonds Have More Fun, 114
Do You Take This Woman?, 99
Doll, A, 101
Domestic Tranquility, 113
Donna and Gail: A Study in Friendship, 101
Enigma, 98
Fear, 113
Fear Women, 101
For Better or Worse, 113
Freedom from Pregnancy, 95
Gertrude Stein: When This You See, Remember Me, 101
Girl, You Need a Change of Mind, 113
Girls (Flickorna), The, 106
Goodbye in the Mirror, 100

Growing Up Female, 100, 105, 107
Happy Mother's Day, 114
Harriet Tubman and the Underground
   Railroad, 101
Helen Keller and Her Teacher, 101
Herstory, 107
Home Movie, 114
I Am Somebody, 101
It Happens to Us, 105
It's a Miracle, 113
Jane Addams, 101
Jeannette Rankin Brigade, 107
Joyce at 34, 105
Just Looking, 113
Katie Kelly, 113
Laurette, 101
Lavender, 14
Make Out, 107, 114
Margaret Sanger, 101
Mariana, 101
Matter of Life, A, 104
Mrs. Case, 104
My Country Occupied, 107
Nun, The, 102
Once, 376
Other Women, Other Work, 97
Painter's Journal, A, 98
Paranoia Blues, 113
Patricia Harris, 101
Phoebe: Story of a Premarital
   Pregnancy, 101
Phyllis and Terry, 98
Planned Families, 95
Polka Graph, 98
Power vs. the People, 256
Pumpkin Eater, The, 102
Rama, 98
Roberta Flack, 100
Roll Over, 99
Salt of the Earth, 102
Schmeerguntz, 102
Sex Stereotyping in Children's Books,
   143
She and He, 102
She's Beautiful When She's Angry, 107
Shirley Chisholm, 101
Sisters, 114
Something Different, 100
Sometimes I Wonder Who I Am, 105,
   114
Spook Sport, 98
Sweet Bananas, 113
Sylvia, Fran and Joy, 97
Testing, Testing, How Do You Do?, 113
Three Lives, 100

Three Women Stories: Caroline,
   Fabienne, Françoise, 104
Trials of Alice Crimmins, The, 113
Unfinished Story. . . , 464
Unwanted Pregnancy, 95
Voice of La Raza, 256
Window Water, 102
Windy Day, 114
Woman, 102
Woman's Film, The, 107
Woman's Place?, 158
Women Get the Vote, The, 101
Women in Viet Nam, 114
Women of Telecommunications Station
   #6, 107
Women on the March: The Struggle for
   Equal Rights, 101, 104
Women Talking, 100
Women Up in Arms, 101
Women Who Have Had an Abortion,
   100
Women Win Voting Rights, 96
Women's Film, 114
Women's Happy Time Commune, The,
   113
Women's Images in Advertising, 114
Woo Who? May Wilson, 105
Year of the Woman, 425
You Don't Have to Buy War, Mrs.
   Smith, 100

General Products

Brassy, The, 142
Confrontation, 142
NOW Feminist Products Catalog, 163
Power of Personhood, 142
Red Detachment of Women, 119
She Is Risen, 136
She'll Provide, 136
Trust in God, 136
Woman & Man, 142
Women Belong in the House—and in the
   Senate, 136

Mixed Media (slides, multimedia kits, microfilms)

Beginnings of a Long and REAL
   Revolution, The, 163

Dick and Jane as Victims, 407
Herstory, 156
Herstory 1 Update, 156
Herstory 2, 156
Sex Education—Let's Get Going, 167
Silenced Majority, The: A Women's
    Liberation Multimedia Kit, 103
To Be Free, 173
Women's History Slide Show, The, 416

Posters

Chicago Maternity Center, 184
Cry Out, 184
Fuck Housework, 12
God Created Women, 134
Health Care Is for People, Not Profit,
    184
Love Poem, 30
On Target, 142
Portrait of Virginia Woolfe, 189
Pregnant Man, 21
Shy Lesbian Feminists, 184
Sisterhood Is Blooming, 184
Together, 184
Union House, 30
Vow, The, 30
Woman Who Dared, The, 142
Womankind Is Awakening, 184
Womanpower, 142
Woman's Poem, A, 12
Women Are Not Chicks, 184
Women Declare War on Rape, 184
Women Working, 184

Records and Audiotapes

Abortion, 195
Abortion: Beyond Legalization, 108
Adrienne Rich Reading Her Poems, 108
Affair of Gabrielle Russier, The, 108
All Issues Are Women's Issues, 108
American Women in History, 108
And That's What Little Girls Are Made
    of, 395
Aunt Mally Jackson, 111
Bard at Large, 108
Beverly Grant: Chain Reaction, 109
Changing Lives of Women Around the
    Globe, The, 108
Cock Rock, 109

Contemporary Lesbian, The: Beyond
    Stereotypes, 108
Courageous Sisters, 108
Diane di Prima Reads, 109
Diane di Prima: The Revolutionary
    Letters, 109
Do Women Dare?, 108
Dream Power, 108
Education and the Weaker Sex, 108
Equal Rights Amendment, 195
Evening with Anais Nin, An, 108
Feminist Art Movement, 108
Feminist Forum: Selling Women Short,
    108
Feminist Forum: The Equal Rights
    Amendment, 108
Feminist Forum: Women's National
    Abortion Action Coalition, 108
Free Our Sisters, Free Ourselves, 109
Germaine Greer Meets the National
    Press Club, 108
Gettin' on Woman, 109
Growing Up Female in the 50's, 108
Here She Is!: The Making of Miss
    America, 108
I Wish I Knew How It Would Feel to Be
    Free, 109
I'm a Woman, 109
I'm Female, I'm Proud, 109
International Women, 162
Interview with Anais Nin, An, 108
Interview with Angela Davis, 109
Interview with Juliette Mitchell, An,
    108
Kathleen Cleaver on Black Panther
    Politics & the Feminist Movement,
    108
Lady Doesn't Take Karate, A, 108
Lawrence Strike, The, 108
Laying Down the Tower, 109
Learning to Be a Man, 195
Lesbian-Feminist Statement, A, 195
Lesbian Record, A, 36
Lesbians, The, 108
Liberation Now, 103
Loner, 188
Marge Piercy: Poems, 109
Me Jane, You Tarzan, 108
Menstrual Blood, 108
Mothers and Daughters, 108
Mountain Moving Day, 111, 184, 366
My Body Is Mine to Control, 109
New World Coming, A: Voices from
    the Women's Liberation Movement,
    195

Off We Go, 108
On Sylvia Plath, 108
Play about Abortion, A: What Have You Done for Me Lately, 195
Plight of Women in Broadcasting, The, 108
Poems for Uppity Women, 108
Pro-Life: The Movement in California Against Abortion, 108
Promise Her Anything, 108
Psychology of Abortion & Birth Control, 108
Psychology of Inferiority, The, 108
Rape, 195
Rapping with the Feminists, 103
Reaction to "Three Women," 108
Recollections of the Woman Suffrage Movement, 195
Red Detachment of Women, 119
Robin Morgan Reads Her Poems, 108
Ruthie Gorton: Last Days of Rome, 109
Ruthie Gorton: This Bird Is Learning How to Fly, 109
Sappho Was a Right on Woman, 108
Sexism and Advertising, 195
Sexism and Psychotherapy, 195
Sexism and Rock Music, 195
Sexist Language, 195
Sexual Liberation and Women's Liberation, 108
She Also Ran . . . , 108
Sherry Finkhine on Abortion, 108
Shirley Chisholm at Mills College: Women in Politics—Why Not?, 108
Socialization: The Pink Blanket Routine, 108
Symposium I: Women Today and Tomorrow, 410
This Ad Insults Women, 103
This Tape Is about Abortion, 109
Three Women, 108
To Set Free, 112
Training Woman to Know Her Place, 108
True Story, 108
Up Against the Mattress: Down in the Valley, 109
White Haired Girl, The, 119

Womankind: Everyone Was Brave, 108
Womankind: Radical Feminists, 108
Woman's Abortion Coalition, 108
Woman's Cry, A, 108
Women and Education, 103
Women as Health Consumers, 108
Women in Art, 108
Women in Media, 108
Women in Prison, 109
Women in the Arts: In the Beginning, 108
Women in the Universities, 108
Women, Jobs and the Law, 103
Women Is Losers, 108
Women of the Press: Harriet Van Horne, 108
Women's Center Feminist Theatre, 108
Women's Liberation and the Arts, 108
Women's Liberation in Mexico, 108
Women's School, The: Woman's Liberation and Black Civil Rights, 108
Women's Work is Never Done, 416
You'll Be Hearing More from Me, 112

Videotapes

Abortion, 115
Anatomy and Birth Control, 115
Another Generation, 115
Another Lookal, 375
Canadian Women T.V. Series, 242
Erotic Garden, 375
Free Mum, Free Dad, Free Daycare, 115
History I, 115
History II, 115
Priest and the Pilot, 375
Rape, Justice and Karate, 115
Rita MacNeil, 115
Sex Stereotyping in Children's Books, 143
Shape of Radical Politics, The, 227
Socialization, 115
Women at Work, 115
Women in Indianapolis, A Guide to Women's Legal Rights, 283
Women Is the 70's, 262
Women: The Emerging Resource, 424

Name Index of Groups Listed

Abortion-Birth Control Referral Service, 458

Abortion Information and Referral Service of Portland, 459

Abortion Rights Association, 460

Access Center for Human Reproductive Health, 461

Action Council for Comprehensive Child Care, 394

Ad Hoc Committee on the Status of Women in Journalism Education, 515

Advisory Committee on the Economic Role of Women. *See* Council of Economic Affairs

Advocates for Women, 431

Ain't I a Woman?, 40

Ain't I a Woman? Performing Troupe, 355

Alabama Women's Commission, 257

Alaska Commission on the Status of Women, 258

Alberta Status of Women Committee, 231

Alberta Women's Bureau, 351

Alert, 41

Alexandria Mayor's Ad Hoc Commission on Women, 338

Alica Foster's Patchwork Fashions and Crafts, 133

Allend'or Productions, 95

Alumnae Advisory Center, 431

Alverno College, Research Center on Women, 143

Amani, 126

Amazon Bookstore, 118

Amazon Quarterly, 42

American Association for the Advancement of Science, Office of Opportunities in Science, 516

American Association for the Advancement of Science, Women's Caucus, 517

American Association of Immunologists, Committee on the Status of Women, 518

American Association of University Professors, Committee W, 519

American Association of University Women, 158

American Civil Liberties Union, Women's Rights Project, 377

American Economics Association, Committee on the Status of Women in the Economics Profession, 520

American Federation of Teachers, Women's Rights Committee, 521

American Historical Association, Roster of Women Historians, 522

American Institute of Planners/American Society of Planning Officials, Women's Rights Committee, 523

American Library Association, Task Force on Women, 524

American Medical Women's Association, 525

American Philological Association, Committee on Women, 526

American Philological Association, Women's Caucus, 527

American Physical Society, Committee on Women in Physics, 528

American Psychological Association, Ad

hoc Committee on Women in Psychology, 529
American Society for Microbiology, Committee on the Status of Women Microbiologists, 530
American Society for Public Administration, Standing Committee on Women in Public Administration, 531
American Society of Biological Chemists, Committee on the Status of Women, 532
American Statistical Association, Caucus for Women in Statistics, 533
American Studies Association, Committee on Women, 534
Anarygos Film Library, 96
Anchorage Women's Liberation Movement Group, 168
Andover-Newton Theological School, Women's Resource Center. *See* Women's Resource Center, Andover-Newton Theological School
Antioch Women's Center, 212
aphra, 43
Arcadia Clinic, 462
Arizona Governor's Commission on the Status of Women, 259
Arkansas Governor's Commission on the Status of Women, 260
Arlington County Commission on the Status of Women, 339
Arthur and Elizabeth Schlesinger Library. *See* Radcliffe College, The Arthur & Elizabeth Schlesinger Library on the History of Women
Artists in Residence, 356
Association for Asian Studies, Committee on the Status of Women, 535
Association for the Development of Opportunity, 216
Association for the Study of Abortion, 463
Association for Women in Mathematics, 536
Association for Women in Psychology, 537
Association for Women's Rights, 217
Association of American Colleges, Project on the Status and Education of Women, 389
Association of American Law Schools, Committee on Women in Legal Education, 538

Association of Feminist Consultants, 423
Association of Women in Science, 539
Athena Associates, 127
Atlanta Lesbian Feminist Alliance, 505
Atlanta Women on the Way. *See* Washington Opportunities for Women
Aurora, 44
Austin Mayor's Commission on the Status of Women, 330
Baltimore New Directions for Women. *See* Washington Opportunities for Women
Beahive Enterprises, 128
Bellamy, Blank, Goodman, Kelly, Ross & Stanley, 378
Bentley Historical Library, 144
Berkeley Women's Affirmative Action Union, 170
Berkeley Women's Center, 171
Betsy Hogan Associates, 425
Birth Control Information Center, 464
Black Women's Association, 443
Boston Commission to Improve the Status of Women, 294
Boston Theological Institute, Women's Theological Coalition, 444
Boston Women's Collective, Inc., 1
Boston Women's Health Book Collective, 2
Boyle/Kirkman Associates, 426
Brainchild, 357
Brown University, Women of Brown United. *See* Women of Brown United
Business and Professional Women's Foundation. *See* National Federation of Business & Professional Women's Clubs
California Commission on the Status of Women, 261
California State University at Long Beach Women Studies Center, 415
Cambridge-Goddard Graduate School, Feminist Studies Program, 416
Canada Dept. of Labor, Women's Bureau, 350
Canadian Federation of University Women, 228
Canadian Newsletter of Research on Women, 45
Canadian Women's Coalition to Repeal the Abortion Laws,
Canadian Women's Education Press, 3

Career Counseling for Women, 432
Career Planning Center, 433
Catalyst, 434
Ceballos Productions. *See* Jacqueline Ceballos Productions
Cell 16, 188
Center for the American Women and Politics. *See* Eagleton Institute, Center for the American Woman and Politics
Center for United Labor Action, 439
Center for a Woman's Own Name, 379
Center for Women in Medicine, Medical College of Pennsylvania, 540
Center for Women Policy Studies, 145
Center for Women's Studies and Services, 172
Change: A Working Women's Newspaper, 46
Change for Children, 395
Chicago Women's Liberation Rock Band. *See* Chicago Women's Liberation Union
Chicago Women's Liberation Union, 184
Chicana Service Action Center, 445
Chico Women's Center, 173
Child Care Resource Center, 396
Children's Liberation Workshop, 397
China Books and Periodicals, 119
Churchill Films, 97
Cincinnati Council on the Status of Women, 319
Cisler, Lucinda, 4
Citizens' Committee on the Status of Women in Virginia, 340
Clearinghouse for Feminist Media, 358
Clearinghouse on Women's Studies. *See* Feminist Press
Cleveland Council on the Status of Women, 320
Clitartists, 359
Cogent Associates. Project HEAR, 398
Collage and Road Crafts, 129
College Art Association, Committee on the Status of Women, 360
Colorado Commission on the Status of Women, 264
Columbia University. Women's Affirmative Action Coalition. *See* Women's Affirmative Action Coalition
Columbus Mayor's Task Force on the Status of Women, 278
Comision Feminil Mexicana. *See* Chicana Service Action Center

Commission on Sexist Abuse in Language, 361
Committee for Abortion Information and Referral (CAIR), 466
Committee on the Status of Women in Journalism, 541
Community Liaison Consultants, 427
Concern for Health Options: Information, Care, and Education (CHOICE), 467
Connecticut College Library, American Woman's Collection, 146
Connecticut Feminists in the Arts, 362
Cooper Handweaving and Jewelry, 130
Coordinating Committee on Women in the Historical Profession, 542
Cornell University, College of Arts and Sciences. Women's Studies Program, 417
Council of Economic Advisors, Advisory Committee on the Economic Role of Women, 248
Council on Economic Priorities, 147
Creative Film Society, 98
Dabney, Q. M., 120
Dade County Commission on the Status of Women, 267
Danforth Graduate Fellowships for Women, 390
Daughters, Inc., 5
Daughters of Bilitis, 506
Day Care and Child Development Council of America, 399
Delaware Governor's Council for Women, 265
Disadvantaged Women for a Higher Education, 409
District of Columbia Commission on the Status of Women, 266
Eagleton Institute, Center for the American Woman and Politics, 148
Earth's Daughters, 47
Eastern Women's Center, 468
Educational Day Care Services Association, 400
Elizabeth Cady Stanton Publishing Co., 6
Emma Willard Task Force on Education, 401
Equation Collective, 131
ERA Enterprises, 132
Eve of Detroit, 507
Everywoman, 48
Everywoman's Center, 189

Executive Woman 49

Ezrat Nashim, 446

Fairfax County Commission on Women, 342

Federally Employed Women, 543

Federation of Organizations for Professional Women, 544

Female Liberation, 190

Feminist Art Journal, 50

Feminist Book Mart, 121

Feminist Bulletin, 51

Feminist Consultation Service, 428

Feminist Forums, 391

Feminist History Research Project, 149

Feminist Party, 510

Feminist Press, 7

Feminist Resources for Equal Education, 402

Feminist Sexuality Project, 469

Feminist Studio Workshop, 363

Feminist Therapy Referral Collective, 470

Feminist Women's Health Center Self-Help Clinic, 471

Feminist Writer's Workshop, 8

The Feminists, 198

The Fifth Estate, 52

Fifty-one Percent: A Paper of Joyful Noise for the Majority Sex, 53

First Things First Books for Women, 122

Florida Governor's Commission on the Status of Women, 268

Focus, 54

Ford Associates, 9

Forfreedom, Ann, 10

Fort Wayne Mayor's Commission on the Status of Women, 281

Fort Worth Educational Task Force, 403

Fort Worth Mayor's Commission on Women, 331

Foster's Patchwork Fashions and Crafts. *See* Alica Foster's Patchwork Fashions and Crafts

Fremont Women's Clinic, 472

Gary Commission on the Status of Women, 280

Gay Community Services Center, 508

Gay Liberation Book Service. See *Gay Sunshine*

Gay Liberator, 55

Gay Sunshine: A Journal of Gay Liberation, 56

George Washington University, Committee on Women Studies, 418

George Washington University, Continuing Education for Women Center, 410

Georgia Commission on the Status of Women, 270

Gold Flower, 57

Greensboro Mayor's Commission on the Status of Women, 316

Greenville Mayor's Commission on the Status of Women, 312

Greyfalcon House, 134

Harrison County Commission on the Status of Women, 332

Hawaii State Commission on the Status of Women, 273

Hawaii County Commission on the Status of Women, 272

Health PAC, 473

Her-Self, 58

Herstory Films, 99

Higher Education Resource Service (HERS), 408

Hogan Associates. *See* Betsy Hogan Associates

Honolulu Mayor's Commission on the Status of Women, 274

Hughes, Marija Matich, 11

Human Rights for Women, 380

Huntsville Mayor's Commission on the Status of Women, 333

Idaho Commission on Women's Programs, 275

Illinois Citizens for the Medical Control of Abortion, 474

Illinois Commission on the Status of Women, 276

Illinois Drug Abuse Program, Office of Women's Affairs, 277

Impact Films, 100

Indiana Commission on the Status of Indiana Women, 279

Indianapolis Mayor's Task Force on Women, 283

Information Center on the Mature Woman, 150

Interstate Association of Commissions on the Status of Women, 249

Iowa State Commission on the Status of Women, 284

Iowans for Medical Control of Abortion, 475

Isla Vista Women's Center, 174

Ithaca Women's Center, 206

Jacksonville Mayor's Advisory Commission on the Status of Women, 269

Jacqueline Ceballos Productions, 429
Jewish Feminist Organization, 447
Johns, Norris Associates, 430
Joint Committee of Organizations Concerned with the Status of Women in the Church, 448
Joyful World Press, 12
Kansas Governor's Commission on the Status of Women, 285
Kent Women's Project, Kent State University, 213
Kentucky Commission on Women, 286
KNOW, Inc., 13
Kula Maui, Hawaii, Commission on the Status of Women, 271
Labyris Books, 123
The Ladder, 59
Lavendar Woman, 14
League of Women Voters, 159
Lefcourt, Kraft & Libow, 381
Lehigh Valley Abortion Rights Association, 476
Lesbian Resource Center, 509
Lesbian Tide, 60
Liberation Enterprises, 135
Liberation News Service, 116
The Liberator, 61
Library of Congress, 151
Liggera, Lanlyra, 15
Lockwood Conference, 435
Lollipop Power, Inc., 16
Los Angeles Commission on Assaults Against Women, 501
Louisiana Bureau on the Status of Women, 288
Louisiana Division of Women and Children, 287
Lucy Stone League, Inc., 160
McGraw Hill Contemporary Films, 101
Macmillan Audio Brandon, 102
Maine Advisory Council on the Status of Women, 289
Maine Dept. of Manpower Affairs, Bureau of Labor and Industry, 290
Majority Report, 62
Mama's Press, 17
Mána Workshop, 136
Manitoba Action Committee on the Status of Women, 234
Manitoba Women's Bureau, Dept. of Labour, 352
Marin Women's News Journal, 63
Maryland Commission on the Status of Women, 291

Massachusetts Dept. of Commerce and Development, Women's Bureau, 295
Massachusetts Governor's Commission on the Status of Women, 296
Massachusetts Organization to Repeal Abortion Laws, 477
Matrix, 18
Media Plus, 103
Meiklejohn Civil Liberties Institute, 382
Michigan Citizens for Medical Control of Abortion, 478
Michigan Historical Collections. *See* Bentley Historical Library
Michigan Women's Commission, 297
Mid-Hudson Women's Center, 207
Midwest Academy, 392
Minnesota Organization for Repeal of Abortion Laws, 479
Minnesota Women's Advisory Commission and Women's Division, 298
Mississippi Governor's Commission on the Status of Women, 299
Missouri Commission on the Status of Women, 300
Modern Language Association, Commission on Women, 545
MOMMA: The Organization for Single Mothers, 564
Montana Status of Women Advisory Council, 301
Montgomery County Commission for Women, 292
Montreal Health Press, 19
Mother Lode, 64
Moving Out Magazine, 65
Ms., 66
Nanny Goat Productions, 20
Nashville Women's Center, 224
National Action Committee on the Status of Women in Canada, 229
National Association for Repeal of Abortion Laws, 480
National Association for Women Deans, Administrators, and Counselors, 546
National Association of Bank Women, 547
National Association of College Women, 161
National Association of Minority Women in Business, 449
National Association of Women Artists, 364
National Association of Women Lawyers, 548

National Black Feminist Organization, 450

National Coalition of American Nuns, 451

National Committee on Household Employment, 440

National Council of Women of Canada, 230

National Council on Family Relations, Task Force on Women's Rights and Responsibilities, 549

National Day Care Association, 404

National Federation of Business and Professional Women's Clubs, 162

National Film Board of Canada, 104

National Organization for Non-Parents, 565

National Organization for Women, 163

NOW Legal Defense and Education Fund, 383

National Welfare Rights Organization, 164

National Woman's Party, 511

National Women's Political Caucus, 512

Nebraska Commission on the Status of Women, 303

Nevada Governor's Commission on the Status of Women, 304

New Day Films, 105

New Directions for Women in New Jersey, 67

New England Free Press, 21

New Feminist, 68

New Feminist Talent, 365

New Hampshire Commission on the Status of Women, 306

New Haven Women's Liberation, 179

New Haven Women's Liberation Rock Band, 366

New Hogtown Press, 22

New Jersey Division on Civil Rights, 307

New Jersey State Commission on Women, 308

New Jersey Women's Information and Referral Service, 152

New Jersey Women's Rights Task Force on Education, 405

New Line Cinema, 106

New Mexico Governor's Commission on the Rights of Women, 309

New Moon Communications, 481

New Paltz Women's Alliance, 208

New Seed Press, 23

New Woman's Survival Catalog, 24

New Womb Artists, 367

New York Commission on Human Rights, 310

New York Radical Feminists, 199

New York State Women's Unit, 311

Newfoundland Status of Women Council, 236

News and Letters Women's Liberation Committee, 194

Newsreel, 107

Nielsen Feminist Jewelry, 137

Nine to Five: Newsletter for Boston Area Office Workers, 69

The North American Indian Women's Association, 452

North Carolina Commission on Education and Employment of Women, 317

North Dakota Commission on the Status of Women, 318

Northeastern Illinois University Women's Studies Inter-disciplinary Degree Program, 419

Off Our Backs, 70

Ohio Bureau of Employment Services, Women Services Division, 321

Ohio Commission on the Status of Women, Inc., 322

Ohio State University, Women's Self-Government Assn., 214

Oklahoma Governor's Commission on the Status of Women, 323

Omaha Mayor's Commission on the Status of Women, 302

Ontario Committee on the Status of Women, 238

Ontario Ministry of Labour, Women's Bureau, 353

Opportunities for Women. *See* Washington Opportunities for Women, 436

Oregon Council for Women's Equality, 215

Oregon Governor's Commission on the Status of Women in Oregon, 324

Ottawa Women's Centre, 239

Our Catalog Company, 25

Our Generation, 71

Pacifica Program Service/Pacifica Tape Library, 108

Pandora, 72

Pathfinder Press, Inc., 26

Pennsylvania Commission on the Status of Women, 325

Pennsylvanians for Women's Rights, 217

Planned Parenthood Federation of America, 482

Population Association of America, Women's Caucus, 550

Portland State University, Women Studies/Union, 420

Portland Women's Health Clinic, 483

Praxis Press, 27

Pregnancy Consultation Service, 484

Presses de la Santé de Montréal. *See* Montreal Health Press

Prime Time, 73

Prince George's County Council on the Status of Women, 293

Professional Organization of Women for Equal Rights, 185

Project HEAR. *See* Cogent Associates

Pro Se, 74

Radcliffe College, The Arthur and Elizabeth Schlesinger Library on the History of Women, 153

Radcliffe Institute, 411

Radical Women, 227

Radio Free People, 109

Radio Free Women of Washington, D.C., 110

Rainbow Institute, 28

Rape Crisis Center, Missouri, 502

Redstockings, 200

Registry of Women in Science and Engineering, 551

Reno Commission on the Status of Women, 305

Rhode Island Coalition to Repeal the Abortion Laws, 485

Rhode Island Permanent Advisory Commission on Women, 326

Richmond College Women's Self-Help Collective, 486

Richmond Women on the Way. *See* Washington Opportunities for Women

Rockingham Mayor's Commission on the Status of Women, 313

Rounder Records, 111

Sacramento Community Commission for Women, 263

Saint Joan's International Alliance, 453

Salisbury Mayor's Commission on the Status of Women, 314

San Angelo Commission on the Status of Women, 335

San Antonio Mayor's Commission on the Status of Women, 334

San Francisco Mayor's Committee on the Status of Women, 262

San Francisco Women's Health Center, 487

Sappho '71, 29

Sarah Lawrence College, Women's Studies Program, 421

Saskatchewan Action Committee, Status of Women, 244

Saskatchewan Dept. of Labour. Women's Bureau, 354

Saskatoon Women's Liberation, 245

Schlesinger Library on the History of Women in America. *See* Radcliffe College

Seattle Women's Commission, 343

Second Moon Music, 112

Seton Hall University School of Law, Women's Law Forum, 552

Shameless Hussy Press, 30

Siren Anarcho Feminists, 513

Sisterhood Bookstore, 124

Sisters, 75

Skirting the Capitol, 76

Slippery Rock State College, Association for Women's Rights, 218

Smith College, Sophia Smith Collection, 154

Society for Cell Biology, Women in Cell Biology, 553

Society for Women in Philosophy, 554

Society of American Archivists, Committee on the Status of Women in the Archival Profession, 555

Society of Women Engineers, 556

Sociologists for Women in Society, 557

Sojourner Truth Press, 31

Sophia Smith Collection. *See* Smith College, Sophia Smith Collection

Soul Survivor, 138

South Carolina Commission on the Status of Women, 327

South Dakota Commission on the Status of Women, 328

Speakout, A Feminist Journal, 77

Spokeswoman, 78

Sportswoman Magazine, 79

State University of New York at Buffalo, Women Studies College, 422

Staten Island Community College Women's Center, 201

Stewardesses for Women's Rights, 558

Suffolk County Community College Women's Group, 209

Tennessee Governor's Commission on the Status of Women, 329

The Texas Woman, 80

Texas Citizens for Abortion Education, 488

Third World Women's Alliance, 454

13th Moon, 81

Those Uppity Women, 139

Times Change Press, 32

Today Publishers and News Service, 33

Underwater Women of the 20th Century Renaissance, 34

Union Theological Seminary, Women's Center. *See* Women's Center. Union Theological Seminary

Union WAGE, 441

United Church of Christ, Task Force on Women in Church and Society, 455

United Front Press, 35

United Nations Commission on the Status of Women, 247

United Presbyterian Church, Council on Women and the Church, 456

United States Citizen's Advisory Council on the Status of Women, 250

United States Commission on Civil Rights, Women's Rights Program Unit, 251

United States Dept. of Health, Education and Welfare, Federal Women's Program, 252

United States Dept. of Health, Education and Welfare, Office of Child Development, 406

United States Dept. of Health, Education and Welfare, Women's Action Program, 253

United States Dept. of Labor. Employment Standards Administration, Office of Federal Contract Compliance, 254

United States Dept. of Labor. Employment Standards Administration, Women's Bureau, 255

United States Equal Employment Opportunity Commission, 256

University of California at Los Angeles, Women's Resource Center. *See* Women's Resource Center at University of California

University of California, Berkeley. Center for Continuing Education of Women, 412

University of California, Irvine. Women's Opportunities Center. *See* Women's Opportunities Center

University of Massachusetts, Everywoman's Center, 188

University of Michigan, Center for Continuing Education of Women, 413

University of North Carolina, Jackson Library, 155

University of Utah. Women's Resource Center, 226

Up from Under, 82

US Magazine, 83

Utah Governor's Commission on the Status of Women, 336

Valley Women's Center, 191

Vancouver Status of Women, 232

Vancouver Women's Centre, 233

Vancouver Women's Health Collective, 489

Vegetarian Feminists, 566

Vermont Governor's Commission on the Status of Women, 337

Vermont Women's Health Center, 490

Violet Press, 36

Virgin Islands Commission on the Status of Women, 349

Virginia Commission on the Status of Women, 341

Virginia Neal Blue Resource Centers for Colorado Women, 177

Walter Clinton Jackson Library. *See* University of North Carolina, Jackson Library

Washington Area Women's Center, 182

Washington Opportunities for Women, 436

Washington State Women's Council, 344

Wausau Mayor's Commission on the Status of Women, 346

West Lafayette Mayor's Task Force on the Status of Women, 282

West Virginia Governor's Commission on the Status of Women, 345

Westbeth Playwrights Feminist Collective, 368

Westside Women's Center, 175

"Where We At" Black Women Artists, 369

The Whole Woman Catalog, 37

Whole Woman Newspaper, 84

Wider Opportunities for Women. *See* Washington Opportunities for Women

WISE-WOW. *See* Washington Opportunities for Women
Widows Consultation Center, 567
Williams, Ferne, 140
Winston-Salem Mayor's Committee on the Status of Women, 315
Wisconsin Governor's Commission on the Status of Women, 347
Wollstonecraft, Inc., 38
The Woman Activist, 85
Woman Becoming, 86
The Woman's Institute, 186
A Woman's Place, Winnipeg, 235
The Woman's Place, St. John's, 237
A Woman's Place/Place des Femmes, Montreal, 242
The Woman's Voice Bookstore, 125
Womanspace, 370
Women: A Journal of Liberation, 87
Women Enterprises, 141
Women for Change Center, 225
Women in Cell Biology. *See* Society for Cell Biology, 553
Women in City Government United, 442
Women in Communications, 559
Women in Leadership, 393
Women in Struggle, 88
Women in the Arts, 371
Women in Transition, 384
Women Make Movies, 113
Women of Brown United, Brown University, 221
Women on Words and Images, 407
Women Studies Abstracts, 89
Women Tithe for Women, 457
Women v. Connecticut. *See* Yale Law Women's Association
Women's Action Alliance, 165
Women's Action Coalition, 219
Women's Affirmative Action Coalition, Columbia Univ., 385
Women's Anti-Rape Group, 503
Women's Art Registry, 372
Women's Arts Center of Philadelphia, 373
Women's Caucus for Political Science, 560
Women's Center, Tempe, Ariz., 169
Women's Center, Inc., Bloomington, Ind., 187
Women's Center, Cambridge, Mass., 192
Women's Center, Orange, N.J., 196
Women's Center of Bergen County, N.J., 197

The Women's Center, Barnard College, N.Y., 202
Women's Center, Union Theological Center, N.Y., 203
Women's Center of Nassau County, N.Y., 210
Women's Centre, Y.W.C.A., Montreal, Quebec, 243
Women's Coalition for the Third Century, 166
Women's Counseling Project, 204
Women's Counseling Service, 491
Women's Equity Action League, 386
Women's Film Co-op, 114
Women's Graphics Collective. *See* Chicago Women's Liberation Union
Women's Health Care Education Council, 492
Women's Health Clinic, 493
Women's Health Forum and Healthright, 494
Women's Heritage Series, 142
Women's History Research Center, Inc., 156
Women's Information and Referral Service, N.J., 152
Women's Information Center, Atlanta YWCA, 183
Women's Information Centre, Toronto, Ont., 240
Women's Institute for Freedom of the Press, 374
Women's Interart Center, 375
Women's Involvement Programme, 115
Women's Job Rights Organization, 437
Women's Law Association, 561
Women's Law Careers, 562
Women's Law Center, 387
Women's Legal Center, 388
Women's Liberation Center of Greater Hartford, Conn., 181
Women's Liberation Center, South Norwalk, Conn., 180
Women's Liberation Center, New York, N.Y., 205
Women's Liberation Center of Philadelphia, Pa., 220
Women's Liberation Coalition, Univ. of Colorado, 178
Women's Liberation Group, Windsor, Ont., 241
Women's Liberation Union, Kansas City, Mo., 195

Women's Liberation Union of Rhode Island, 222
Women's Lobby, 514
Women's Martial Arts Union, 504
Women's Media Exchange, 376
Women's National Abortion Action Coalition, 495
Women's National Book Association, 563
Women's News Service, 117
Women's Opportunities Center, Univ. of California, Irvine, 438
Women's Press, 90
Women's Prison Association and Home, 499
Women's Prison Project, 500
Women's Resource Center, Andover-Newton Theological School, 193
Women's Resource Center at University of California, L.A., 176
Women's Resource Center, University of Utah. *See* University of Utah. Women's Resource Center
Women's Rights Law Reporter, 91
Women's Studies: An Interdisciplinary Journal, 92
Women's Studies Programs, 414
Women's Track and Field World, 93
Womensports, 94
Woodmere Women's Center, 211
Worcester Pregnancy Counseling Service, 496
Wyoming Commission on the Status of Women, 348
Yale Law Women's Association, 497
Young Women's Christian Association of the U.S.A., 167
YWCA Women's Center, Providence, R.I., 223
Yukon Status of Women Group, 246
Zero Population Growth, 498
Zion Research Library, 157
Zizi Press, 39

Subject Index

(Entry numbers preceded by state or province abbreviations designate local listings.)

Abortion. *See* Birth control and
   abortion
Academic administrators, 546
Acting companies. *See* Theatrical
   companies
Affirmative action consultants and training, 253, 256, 383, 424-426, CO
   177; MD 292; PA 216
See also Consultants
Airline cabin personnel, 558
Alcoholism, CA 172; FL 267
American studies, women in, 534
Archivists, 555
Arts and literature, CA 263
   collectives, CA 359, 367; IL 184, 357;
     NY 368
   directories, 358, 372
   exhibitions, CA 359, 367, 370; CT
     362; NY 356, 364, 371, 375-376;
     PA 373
   periodicals, 30, 42-43, 47, 50, 65, 81,
     86, 364, 370-371, 375
   professional associations, 360, 364,
     371
   publishers, 29
   speakers' bureaus, 365
   supplies co-op, NY 376
   workshops, CA 8, 359, 363, 370; CT
     362; MA 114, 191; NY 113, 139,
     368-369, 375-376; PA 220, 373;
     Que. 243
Asian studies, women in, 535
Athletics, discrimination in, 219, 324,
   336, 377
See also Nonsexist education
Athletics periodicals, 79, 93-94
Bicentennial year, 166, 318

Biochemists, 532
Birth control and abortion, 163, 320,
   377, 460, 463, 465, 480, 485, 495;
   FL 267; IA 475; IL 184, 474; MA
   477; MI 478; MN 479; MO 195; PA
   476; RI 222; TX 488; WA 227
   services, CA 175, 471; CT 181; DC
     182; MA 191, 464; MI 461; NJ 466;
     NY 204-208, 210, 468, 486, 492;
     OR 459; TN 224; WA 458, 462;
     Man. 235; Ont. 241; Que. 243, 491;
     Sask. 245
   speakers bureaus, IL 474; MN 479;
     NJ 466; OR 459; PA 476; Que. 491
   See also Counseling, Information and
     referral agencies
Birth name, right to, 377, 379, 387
Bookwomen, 563
Businesswomen, 162, 251, 295, 449,
   547
   periodicals, 49
   talent banks, 162
Catholic women, 448, 451, 453
Cell biologists, 553
Child care and development, 3, 163,
   383, 394, 399-400, 404, 406, 450,
   514, 521; AR 260; CA 261-262,
   395; DC 266; DE 265; FL 267; IA
   284; IL 277; IN 278, 283; MA 294,
   296, 396; NC 316; NE 302; OH 321;
   PA 218, 325; SD 328; TN 329; UT
   336; VA 342; WA 227, 343-344; WY
   348; Man. 234; Ont. 241; Que. 242
   research centers & collections, 404
Child care services, DC 182; MA 192,
   396; MO 195; NY 207, 209; RI 221,
   223; Ont. 239

Children's media, 143, 215, 219, 234, 278, 383, 397, 403, 407
  distributors, CA 119, 124; CO 125; DC 122; IL 119; NY 119; 121, 123; B.C. 233
  publishers, 3, 7-8, 12, 16-17, 23, 28, 39
  See also Nonsexist education
Civil rights, 163, 229-230, 232, 249, 251, 377, 379-380, 382-383, 386-387, 521; AL 257; AK 168; CA 170, 261; DC 182, 266; IL 184-185; MO 300; NJ 196-197; NY 385, 387; OR 215; PA 218-219; RI 222, 326; TN 224, 329; VA 338; VT 337; WY 348; V.I. 349; Alb. 351; B.C. 232; Man. 234; Ont. 241
  clearinghouses, 251, 255, 387
  enforcement agencies, 254, 256; IN 283; MI 290; NJ 307; NY 310; VA 342; Ont. 353
  periodicals, 85, 91, CA 76; CT 41
  publishers, 6, 9, 11
  research centers and collections, 377, 382, 387
Classicists, 526-527
College and university centers, CA 173, 176, 438; CO 177-178; IN 281; MA 189, 193; NY 201-204, 208-209, 385; OH 212-214; PA 217; RI 221; UT 226; Sask. 245
College women, 161
  talent banks, 158, 434-435
  See also Professional women and special classes of women, e.g., Biochemists, Businesswomen
Communications, women in, 374
Consultants, 423-429, 435; CA 261; MA 295
  professional association, 423
  See also Affirmative action consultants and training
Consumer groups, CA 176, 262; IL 277; NJ 197
Counseling, CA 172, 175-176; CT 179, 181; DC 182; MA 189; MD 292; NY 204, 206; TX 225; UT 226
  academic, CA 412, 445; MI 413
  career, 398, 434-435; AL 257; CA 172, 412, 430, 433, 437-438; CO 177; DC 266, 436; GA 436; IL 277; IN 283; MA 296, 436; MD 436; MI 413; NJ 196; NY 431-432; PA 216;

RI 436; TX 225; VA 436; VT 436; Ont. 234, 241; Que. 243
  See also information and referral agencies
Day care. *See* Child care and development
Demographers, 550
Disadvantaged women, NH 409; NJ 308; PA 216
Discrimination in credit, housing, retirement benefits, salary, etc. *See* Economic rights
Divorce. *See* Marriage, separation, divorce
Domestic workers. *See* Household workers
Drug abuse, 450; CA 172; IL 277
Economic rights, 163, 248, 251, 377, 386, 514; CA 261; DC 182, 266; DE 265; IA 284; ID 275; IL 185; IN 281; LA 928; MS 299; NC 316; NE 302; NJ 196; OR 324; PA 325; RI 222; VA 338, 342; VT 337; WA 344
Economists, 520
Education, 163, 228-229, 249, 377, 389-390, 392-394, 398-407, 450, 514; AL 257; AR 260; CA 261; CO 264; DC 266; HI 271; ID 275; MA 296; MS 299; NC 314, 316; NE 302; NH 306; NJ 308; OH 321; PA 218; RI 326; SD 328; TN 224, 329; UT 336; VA 338; VT 337; WA 227; WY 348; Nfld. 236; Ont. 238
  continuing, 165, 409-413; CO 177; OH 213; PA 216
  feminist, 392; DC 182, IL 186; MA 189, 192; MO 195; NJ 196-197; NY 199, 201, 210, 391; OH 214; RI 223; UT 226; Ont. 239-241; Que. 242-243
  manual skills, CA 174; DC 182; OH 212; PA 217; RI 223; Nfld. 237; Ont. 239, 241
  See also Nonsexist education
Employment rights, 163, 165, 229, 249, 255, 350, 377, 383; AL 257; AR 260; CA 261-262; DC 182, 266; DE 265; FL 267; GA 270; HI 271; IN 278, 281; MA 294; MN 298; MS 299; NC 316; ND 318; NE 302; NJ 308; OH 321; OR 215; PA 218-219; RI 222, 326; TN 329; UT 336; VA 338, 342; WY 348

academic, 360, 386, 519, 526, 539, 546, 560; RI 326
research centers and collections, 147, 255
See also Civil rights
Engineers. *See* Scientists and engineers
Equal Rights Amendment, 9, 159, 162, 163, 511–512, 521, 546, 548, 560; CA 261, 263; CT 41; FL 268; GA 270; IL 451; MD 291; MN 298; NJ 308; NY 450, 453; OH 322; PA 219; RI 222; SD 328; VA 342; VT 337; WA 227, 344; WY 348
Family and community relations, 229, 383; AL 257; AR 260; CO 177; DC 182; FL 267; MS 299; NE 302; RI 326; TN 329; UT 336; VA 342; WY 348; Nfld. 236
Family planning, 482, 498; LA 288; WA 462; Nfld. 236
See also Birth control and abortion
Feminist services, 163
First amendment protection, 374, 559
Government, women in. *See* Politics and government, women in
Government employees, 251–252, 543; FL 270; LA 288; NH 306; NY 311, 442; PA 325; WA 344
Health care, 450, 473, 481–482, 494; AR 260; CA 263, 487; DC 266; DE 265; IA 284; IL 184, 277; MA 296; NC 316; NE 302; OR 215; VA 338; WA 227; B.C. 489; Ont. 241
publishers, 2, 19–20
services, CA 173–174, 471; CT 481, 497; DC 182, 493; IL 184; MO 195; NY 206, 468, 486; OH 212; TN 224; VT 490; WA 462, 472; B.C. 489; Ont. 240; Sask. 245
Historians, 522, 542
Household workers, 440, 450, 514; OR 324
See also Working women
Information and referral agencies, 165, 167; AZ 169; CA 171–172, 175–176; CO 177; CT 179, 181; GA 183; MA 191; MD 292; NJ 152, 196, 308; NY 204–205, 207–209, 211; OH 213; PA 220; UT 226; Nfld. 237; Ont. 241
International Women's Year 1975, 247
Jewish women, 446–447
Journalists, 515, 541, 559

Law education, 538, 552, 561–562
periodicals, 74
Lawyers, 548, 552, 561–562
Leadership training, 392–393, 427, 429
Legal counsel, feminist, 378, 381
directories, 9, 163
Legal counseling and referral, 383; CA 388; IL 184; NY 385, 387; PA 384; Ont. 240; Que. 243
See also Information and referral agencies
Legal defense funds, 383; DC 182
Lesbian feminists, 450, 506; CA 508; CT 181; GA 505; IL 184; MA 192; MI 507; MO 195; NY 208; PA 220; WA 509; Man. 235
periodicals, 40, 42, 54, 55–56, 59–60, 75
publishers, 14, 29, 31, 36
speakers bureaus, 506; GA 505; WA 509
Librarians, 524
Literature. *See* Arts and literature
Lobbyists, 514
Maiden name. *See* Birth name, right to
Marriage, separation, divorce, 163, 230, 377, 384; CA 175, 261, 388; CT 179; MO 195; NJ 308; NY 205–207, 211, 567; PA 216, 220; TX 225; WA 227, 344; Que. 243
See also Legal counseling and referral
Maternity and paternity leave, 163, 377, 519, 521; FL 267; RI 326; WA 227, 344
Mathematicians, 536
Mature women. *See* Older women
Medicine, women in, 525, 540, 551
Men's liberation, 163; PA 217
Microbiologists, 530
Minority women, 443, 445, 449–450, 452, 454
artists, 369
businesswomen, 450
Modern languages, women in, 545
Movement clearinghouses, 37, 165, 202, 229–230, 249; CA 173, 261; CO 177; MD 291; B.C. 232; Man. 234; Nfld. 236
Movement directories, 24–25, 33
Nonparents, 565
Nonsexist education, 386, 395, 401, 405, 521, 546; DE 265; IA 284; MN 298; PA 219; VA 342; B.C. 232

curriculum materials, 7, 395, 398, 402
  speakers bureaus, PA 219
  See also Children's media, Education
Older women, 150; CA 262; CO 177;
  NY 205; PA 218
  education, 158, 390; CA 438; NH
  409; NY 202; UT 226
  employment and employment counseling, MA 295; MAN 352; Ont. 353
  periodicals, 73
  publishers, 34
  speakers bureaus, 150
Performing arts. *See* Arts and literature;
  Playwrights; Rock bands; and Theat-
  rical companies
Philosophers, 554
Physicists, 528
Planners, 523
Playwrights, 368
Political scientists, 560
Politics and government, women in,
  159, 230, 512, 531; AR 260; CA
  261-262; CO 264; IN 278, 281; MD
  291; NY 311; TN 329; WA 227;
  Nfld. 236
  research centers and collections, 148
Prison groups, 251, 266, 377, 450, 499;
  CA 172, 262, 500; DC 266; GA 270;
  HI 271; ID 275; NE 302; NJ 308;
  RI 326
Problem pregnancy counseling, MA 496;
  MI 461; NY 496; OH 484; OR 483;
  PA 467
  See also Counseling and Information
  & referral centers
Problem pregnancy speakers bureaus,
  OH 484
Professional women, 162, 228, 450,
  544, 549
  talent banks, 162-163, 228, 408, 433,
  436, 519
Protestant women, 193, 203, 281, 393,
  444, 455-456
Psychologists, 529, 537
Psychotherapy referral, 537; NY 204,
  210, 470
  See also Information & referral
  agencies
Rape. *See* Self defense and anti-rape
Referral agencies. *See* Information and
  referral agencies
Religion and women, 163, 193, 203,
  281, 444, 446-448, 451, 453, 455-
  457
  research centers and collections, 157

Research centers and collections, 143,
  145-151, 153, 160, 162, 202, 512;
  MI 144; NJ 152; UT 226
  See also as subdivision under Child
  care and development, Civil rights,
  Employment rights, Politics and
  government, women in, Religion
  and women
Research in progress, periodicals, 45
Revenue sharing compliance requirements, 251
Rock bands, 184, 366
Scholarships, 158, 160-162, 172, 228,
  390, 411, 413, 546, 550, 559
Scientists and engineers, 516-517, 539,
  551, 556
Self defense and anti-rape, AK 168; CA
  174, 501; CT 181; DC 182, 266; IA
  284; IL 184; IN 283; LA 288; MA
  188, 192; MO 502; NE 302; NY
  205, 209, 211, 503, 504; OH 212;
  PA 220; RI 222-223; WA 227, 343
  speakers bureau, MO 502
Self-employment, MA 295; MO 300
Self image—Media image, 163, 215, 229,
  251, 281, 383, 450; AR 260; CA
  261; MO 195; NE 302; SD 328; WA
  227; Que 243
Separation and divorce. *See* Marriage,
  separation, divorce
Sexism in language, 361, 407
Sexism in student counseling, 324, 398
  See also Nonsexist education
Sexuality, 469; NJ 197; NY 210; Man.
  235; Que. 243
Single parents, 564; Que. 243
Social scientists, 539
Sociologists, 557
Speakers bureaus, 143, 365, 511-512;
  AK 168; CA 438; DE 265; MA 190-
  191, 296; MD 292; MO 195, 300;
  NE 302; NJ 308; NY 198-199, 207
  210, 311; OH 213; OR 459; PA
  218-220; UT 226; WA 227, 343;
  V.I. 349; B.C. 232; Man 234; Ont.
  240-241, 353; Que. 243; Sask. 354
  See also as subdivision under Arts and
  literature, Birth control and abor-
  tion, Health care, Lesbian feminists,
  Nonsexist education, Older women,
  Problem pregnancy, Self defense and
  anti-rape
Statisticians, 533
Stewardesses. *See* Airline cabin personnel

Talent banks, AR 260; CA 430; CO 264; DE 264; FL 267; IN 278, 282; MA 296; MD 292; MN 298; MO 300; NC 314; NE 302; NY 311, 442; OH 321; OR 215; RI 326; TN 329; TX 225; UT 336; VA 342; WA 344
  See also as subdivision under Business-women, College women, Professional women

Teenage women, 167; AK 168; IL 184; IN 283; NE 302; NJ 308; VA 342
  career choice, DC 266, ID 275; MA 295; Ont. 353; Sask. 354

Theatrical companies, 235, 355, 428

Union groups, 229, 251, 439, 441, 521

Vegetarians, NY 566

Volunteerism, 163; AL 257; CA 438; MS 299; RI 326

Welfare rights, 164–165, 450, 514; CA 388; IL 277; MA 191; NC 316; NE 302

Widows. *See* Marriage, separation, divorce, Older women, Single parents

Women in transition. *See* Marriage, separation, divorce

Women's studies, 414–422, 534; CO 178; MO 195; NY 208–209; OH 212–213; UT 226; B.C. 232
  abstracts and bibliographies, 10, 89
  clearinghouses, 7, 542
  periodicals, 92

Working women. *See also* Employment rights

Working women, Man. 352; Nfld. 234; Ont. 353; Sask. 245, 354
  periodicals, 69, 82
  publishers, 22, 35, 46

DATE   DUE